JUN 2 2 2009
kept 3/16

INSIDERS' GUIDE® TO

HUDSON RIVER VALLEY

FIRST EDITION

SHEILA BUFF

INSIDERS' GUIDE®

GUILFORD, CONNECTICUT
AN IMPRINT OF THE GLOBE PEQUOT PRESS

The prices and rates in this guidebook were confirmed at press time. We recommend, however, that you call establishments before traveling to obtain current information.

To buy books in quantity for corporate use or incentives, call **(800) 962–0973** or e-mail **premiums@GlobePequot.com**.

INSIDERS' GUIDE®

Project manager: Ellen Urban
Interior design: Sheryl Kober
Maps: XNR Productions, Inc. © Morris Book Publishing, LLC
Layout: Maggie Peterson

ISBN 978-0-7627-4438-1

Printed in the United States of America
10 9 8 7 6 5 4 3 2 1

CONTENTS

DIRECTORY OF MAPS

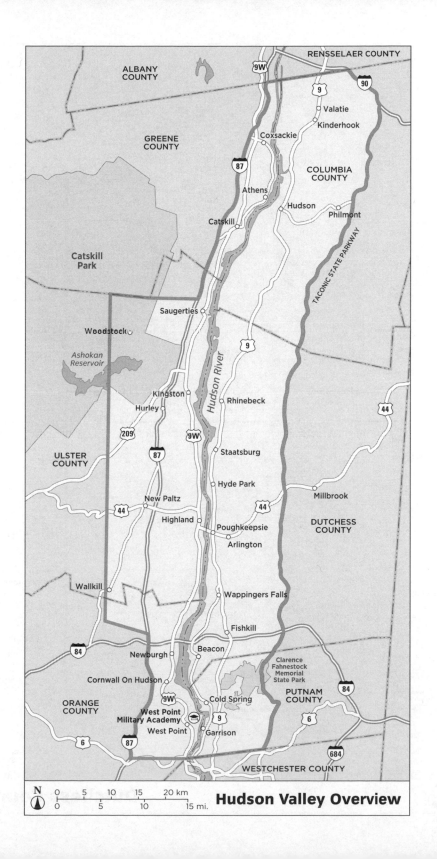

Hudson Valley Overview

RENSSELAER COUNTY

ALBANY COUNTY

GREENE COUNTY

COLUMBIA COUNTY

Valatie
Kinderhook
Coxsackie
Athens
Hudson
Philmont
Catskill

Catskill Park

Saugerties
Woodstock
Ashokan Reservoir
Kingston
Rhinebeck
Hurley
Staatsburg
Hyde Park
ULSTER COUNTY
New Paltz
Millbrook
Highland
Poughkeepsie
DUTCHESS COUNTY
Arlington
Wallkill
Wappingers Falls
Fishkill
Newburgh
Beacon
Clarence Fahnestock Memorial State Park
Cornwall On Hudson
Cold Spring
ORANGE COUNTY
PUTNAM COUNTY
West Point Military Academy
West Point
Garrison
WESTCHESTER COUNTY

Hudson River

TACONIC STATE PARKWAY

9W · 9 · 90 · 87 · 44 · 209 · 84 · 6 · 684

N

| 0 | 5 | 10 | 15 | 20 km |
| 0 | 5 | 10 | 15 mi. |

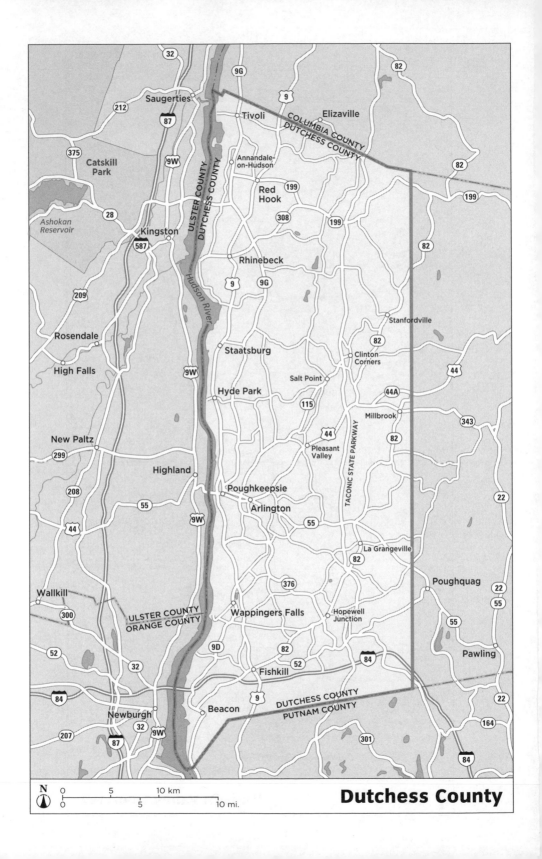

Dutchess County

N

0   5   10 km
0   5   10 mi.

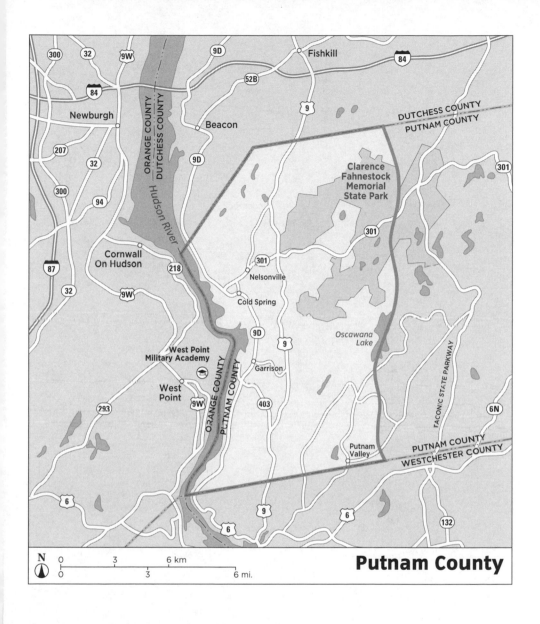

Putnam County

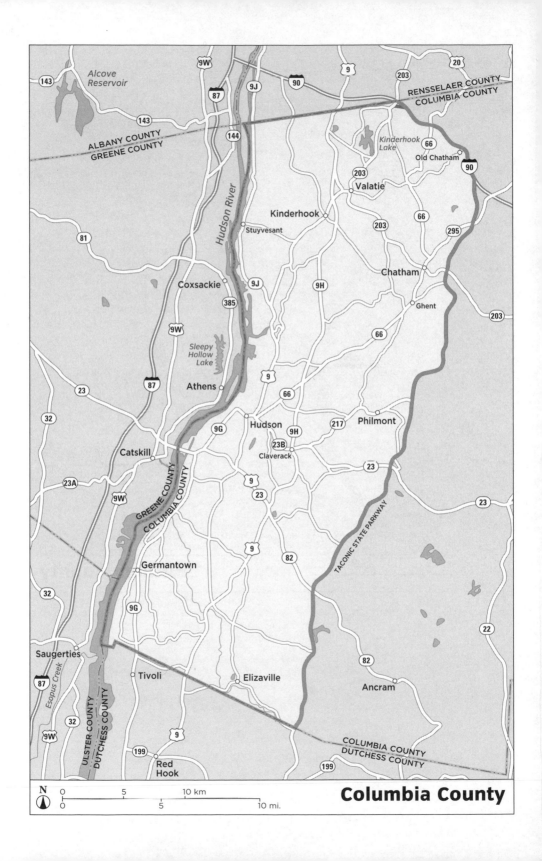

Columbia County

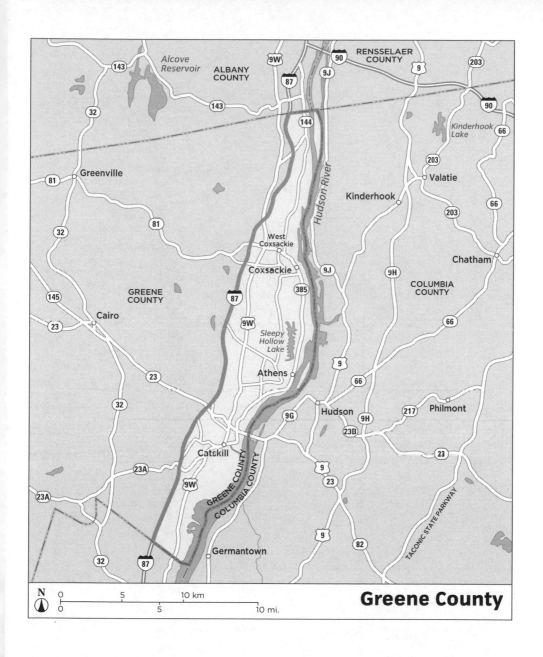

Greene County

N

0   5   10 km
0   5   10 mi.

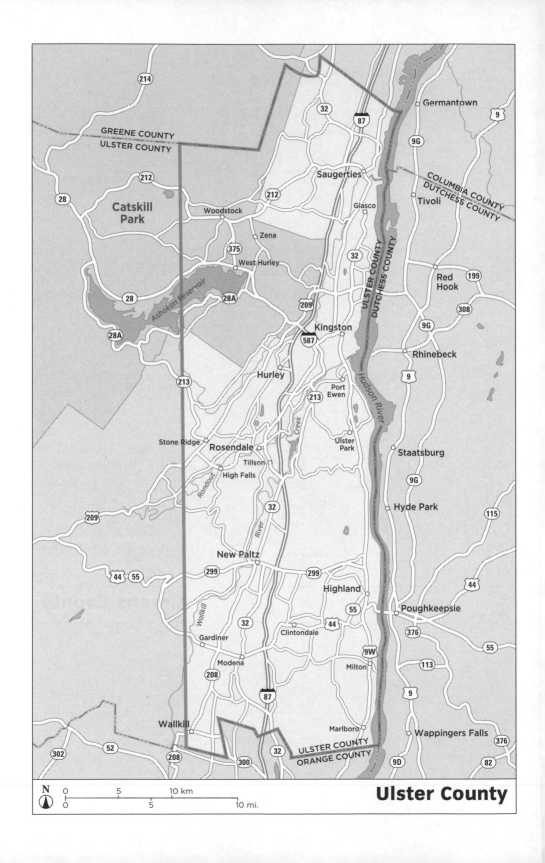

Ulster County

N

0   5   10 km

0   5   10 mi.

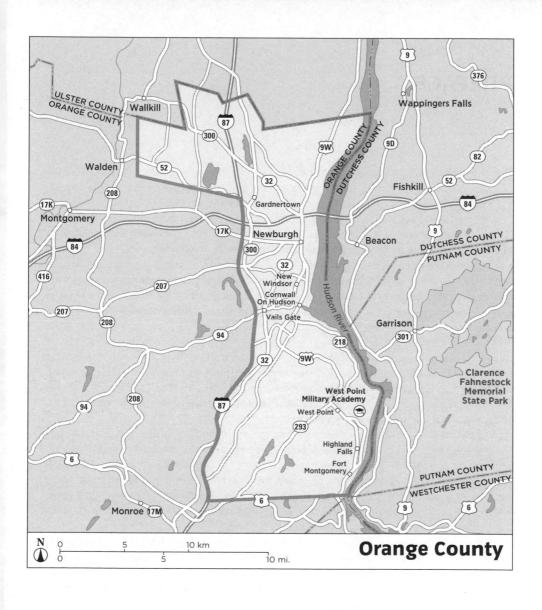

ULSTER COUNTY
ORANGE COUNTY

Wallkill

9

376

Wappingers Falls

87

300

9W

9D

82

52

Walden

52

32

Fishkill

52

208

Gardnertown

84

17K

17K

Montgomery

17K

Newburgh

9

Beacon

DUTCHESS COUNTY
PUTNAM COUNTY

84

300

416

32

207

New
Windsor

Cornwall
On Hudson

207

Vails Gate

Garrison

208

94

301

218

Hudson River

ORANGE COUNTY
DUTCHESS COUNTY

Clarence
Fahnestock
Memorial
State Park

32

9W

94

208

87

West Point
Military Academy

West Point

293

6

Highland
Falls

Fort
Montgomery

PUTNAM COUNTY
WESTCHESTER COUNTY

94

6

Monroe 17M

6

9

6

N

0   5   10 km

0   5   10 mi.

Orange County

PREFACE

The mid–Hudson River Valley has been my home for more than twenty years. In all that time, the beauty and vitality of the region have never ceased to impress me. And even after more than twenty years of exploring the area, there are always new things to see, do, and especially in recent years, eat.

Although the region has faced issues of overdevelopment and creeping sprawl, it has retained its unique character, a mixture of sophistication and country charm. Here in the mid–Hudson Valley, an outstanding restaurant or interesting new art gallery might be on the revitalized waterfront of a large city, or it might be in a small town at the end of a scenic country road. The vibrant mix of small towns and cities, high-tech industry and agriculture, antiques shops and cutting-edge galleries, makes the mid–Hudson Valley endlessly interesting. The region boasts a lively arts scene, an outstanding array of great restaurants, shopping that goes way beyond big-box stores, a rich and well-preserved history, and scenery that is unsurpassed.

In 1609, when Henry Hudson sailed up the broad tidal river that led north from New York bay, he saw a landscape that was spectacularly beautiful and richly productive. The heavily wooded region was home to Native Americans who drew on the teeming river for fish; hunted deer; cultivated corn, beans, and tobacco; and developed a sophisticated culture based on woodland products. Hudson said of the country he saw that autumn, "The land is the finest for cultivation that I ever in my life set foot upon, and it also abounds in trees of every description."

Hudson was seeking the fabled Northwest Passage, and when the river near present-day Albany became too narrow and shallow to sail any further, he turned back in disappointment. Others soon returned, however, seeking not the water route to the riches of Cathay but commerce and land. The river that came to bear Henry Hudson's name was the route that opened up and tied together the settlements and farms that quickly came to line its banks. Starting in the early 19th century, the scenic beauty that Hudson admired attracted artists such as Thomas Cole and Frederic Church, who took the Hudson River and its environs as their theme. By breaking free of the European classical tradition, they created a new, distinctly American style known as the Hudson River School. The landscapes they admired and painted can still be seen today, much as they appeared then. These artists brought an appreciation of the visual arts to the region that persists strongly to this day. The influx of talented artists in recent years, the continued vitality of the artistic community in Woodstock, and the opening of the Dia:Beacon museum in 2003 are all part of a long tradition.

Four hundred years and more after Henry Hudson's voyage, the mid–Hudson River Valley region still has both the awesome natural beauty he saw and the economic strength he predicted. This very large region—it includes parts of six counties and stretches for about 90 miles up and down the Hudson—offers amazing diversity. Once-faded cities such as Hudson, Kingston, Poughkeepsie, Newburgh, and Beacon have attracted new growth by improving their historic waterfront areas and encouraging the arts. Today the many galleries and performing arts venues in the area are a major draw for locals and visitors alike. In rural areas, both government action and local land trusts have placed thousands of acres into conservation, preserving family farms, maintaining the open landscape, and creating new parks and preserves for all to enjoy. The long effort of dedicated conservationists in the region has made the Hudson River itself cleaner and more accessible than it has been in many decades.

The history of the Hudson River Valley is in many ways the history of America, from the earliest explorations and settlements in North America to the present day. This long history is remarkably well preserved—historic sites in the region range from early colonial settlements to numerous Revolutionary War sites to Springwood, the home of Franklin Delano Roosevelt. Walking in the footsteps of the people, famous and obscure, who settled the region and helped it grow, brings history alive.

Insiders' Guide to the Hudson River Valley is designed to help you discover this accessible and endlessly interesting region. And wherever your explorations in the Hudson River Valley take you, you'll find something that a book can't really capture: a friendly, small-town atmosphere that makes visitors feel genuinely welcome.

ACKNOWLEDGMENTS

Many friends, friends of friends, and even distant acquaintances have contributed to this book by sharing their favorite places in the mid-Hudson Valley with me or joining me for explorations of the area. They are too many to name, but I hope they all know how much their help is appreciated. Any mistakes, poor choices, or omissions in this book are despite them. Roving editor David Emblidge got me started on this project; Amy Lyons, my editor at Globe Pequot, saw it through to the end. My prose was improved by the editorial skills of Amy Paradysz. As always, love and support from Joe and Dina made the difference.

ABOUT THE AUTHOR

Sheila Buff has been a resident of the small town of Milan, in the mid–Hudson Valley, since 1987. A contributor to *About Town,* a quarterly guide to the region, she is also the author of many other books, *including Best Hikes with Children in the Hudson Valley and Catskills, Traditional Country Skills* (Lyons Press), and *The Complete Idiot's Guide to Birdwatching.*

HOW TO USE THIS BOOK

The mid–Hudson River Valley region is large—it covers six counties, and the portion of the Hudson River that runs through it is about 90 miles long. That makes for a long book, because the region is packed with attractions that appeal to just about anyone from the casual tourist to longtime residents.

Insiders' Guide to the Hudson River Valley begins with a short area overview and then moves on to a chapter about getting here and getting around. These two chapters give readers the lay of the land and a good idea of what's where.

American history truly comes alive in the Hudson Valley. The short history of the region that follows is just an appetizer to the two later chapters that are devoted just to the many fascinating historic sites on both sides of the river. These places date from the earliest days of European settlement to well into the 20th century. They illuminate the past in a way no book, photo, or even DVD can. When visiting a place like Huguenot Street in New Paltz—the oldest street in America—it's just possible to imagine yourself as a colonist in the 1670s. The many Revolutionary War sites, the FDR Home, and other fascinating places transform dry textbook history into something vivid and three-dimensional.

Because the mid–Hudson Valley is only a tank of gas away from the New York City metro region, it's a very popular area for weekend getaways year-round. Two chapters of this book cover accommodations on both sides of the river. The focus is on the many charming small inns and bed-and-breakfast operations in the region. Even though there are also a number of good hotels and motels up and down the valley, visitors to the region should be aware that there's still something of a shortage of accommodations, especially during the summertime peak tourism period. Reserve well in advance whenever possible.

The mid-Hudson region has become foodie heaven in recent years. There are so many fine restaurants in the area that two entire chapters, one for each side of the river, are devoted just to eating out. In addition, an entire chapter is devoted to farms, farm markets, and wineries.

Much of the mid-Hudson is still fairly rural, but there's enough going on here at night to fill an entire chapter. The nightlife in the region is surprisingly lively, with some great venues for live music and comedy. The cultural nightlife—concerts, theater, dance, and more—is also very active in the region. The chapter on the performing arts and film covers the many venues for live performances. Going to the movies in the region can be a lot of fun. Many independent theaters that preserve the old movie palace architecture are still in operation in small towns—and you can have your choice of three drive-in movies.

The visual arts have become a signature of the mid–Hudson Valley. The opening of the astonishing Dia:Beacon museum of modern art in 2003 gave a boost to an already active arts scene. Today museums, sculpture gardens, galleries, and studios are all over the region. The Art Along the Hudson program features the cities of Beacon, Newburgh, Poughkeepsie, and Kingston, with special events and programs rotating among them from Saturday to Saturday. There's plenty of visual art in other areas as well—Hudson, Cold Spring, Rhinebeck, and Woodstock are particularly notable, but galleries have sprung up everywhere.

An area as historic and long-settled as the Hudson Valley is full of old stuff, and antiquing is a popular activity. Hudson and Cold Spring, at opposite ends of the valley, are major antiques centers, but there are many clusters of antiques shops in between, such as those in Hyde Park, Rhinebeck, and

Kingston. The well-known Rhinebeck Antiques Fair is a major draw three times a year in May, July, and October.

Shopping in the region goes way beyond antiques, however, to the point that this book has two entire chapters (east and west sides of the river) devoted to the many interesting shops and boutiques in the region. Not included here are chain stores—every shop discussed in this book is individual and unique.

Dozens of annual events in the Hudson Valley draw thousands of tourists and residents every year. They range from county fairs (the Dutchess County Fair at Rhinebeck in late August is the best known) to car shows to horse shows to craft shows to the Mid-Hudson Balloon Festival. Hardly a month goes by without at least one major fun event in the region.

The mid-Hudson is fortunate to have many parks and preserves that offer great opportunities for outdoor fun. The chapter on parks and outdoor recreation lists many places to enjoy hiking, biking, swimming, kayaking, rock climbing, and more, usually for free or at nominal cost. The area also has so many beautiful and challenging golf courses that it took a whole chapter to cover them. Spectator sports, including the Hudson Valley's very own minor-league baseball team, the Renegades, are covered in a separate chapter as well.

There are only so many historic sites a kid can tolerate in one weekend. Fortunately for parents, there are many kid-oriented activities in the region. The kidstuff chapter explores the many places for kids to have fun (and maybe even learn something). Nature programs abound at the region's parks and preserves, and there's a children's museum in Poughkeepsie. Music and theater performances for kids, art programs, places to see and touch animals, and fun places like water parks and bowling alleys are all included in this chapter.

Insiders' Guide to the Hudson River Valley wraps up with some chapters full of practical information, including local media, hospitals, and higher education in the region.

In a book of this length covering such a wide area, not every restaurant, B&B, boutique, gallery, and attraction could be included. Choices were made on the basis of uniqueness, quality, and longevity—subjective criteria, to be sure. Some deserving places have doubtless been left out, and errors of judgment and fact have doubtless occurred. Also, the area is so dynamic that new places are constantly opening and old places are constantly closing or changing. We'd like to know if we've made any mistakes or omissions, if you disagree with any descriptions, and if someplace new has opened and is worthy of inclusion in future editions. You may e-mail us at editorial@Globe.Pequot.com or write to us at:

The Globe Pequot Press
Reader Response/Editorial Department
P.O. Box 480
Guilford, CT 06437-0480

AREA OVERVIEW

The region covered by this book includes six counties, three on each side of the Hudson River. From north to south on the west side of the river, the mid–Hudson River Valley region includes Greene, Ulster, and Orange Counties; on the east side from north to south, the counties are Columbia, Dutchess, and Putnam. Within each county, only the portion that is within the watershed of the Hudson River is included. Since the boundaries of a watershed aren't particularly obvious to anyone who isn't a geologist, for all practical purposes, the area covered by this book is bounded to the west by the New York State Thruway and to the east by the Taconic State Parkway. The region has so many things to do and places to see that some worthwhile locales outside that very approximate definition are also included.

The Albany/Saratoga area, often called the Capital District, lies to the north of the mid–Hudson region. The densely populated suburbs of New York City in Westchester and Rockland Counties define the start of the lower Hudson Valley. On the west side of the Hudson, the Catskill Mountains and the Catskill Forest Preserve and other rugged areas cover much of Greene, Ulster, and Orange Counties. Most of the Catskills region is strictly excluded from this book—otherwise the book would be easily twice its length—and the emphasis is on places that are on or near the Hudson. (One notable exception: Woodstock, which is in the Catskills, is included—it's too well known and too much fun to leave out.) On the east side of the river, the eastern half of Columbia County is geographically more closely tied to the Berkshires region of Massachusetts than to the Hudson. For purposes of this book the line isn't sharply drawn, but the focus is on the western side of the county. The eastern one-third or so of Dutchess County lies in the Harlem River valley, not the Hudson Valley, and is mostly not included here (with some exceptions for particularly interesting places). Most of Putnam County within the Hudson River watershed is rugged parkland or preserves; open space aside, only the river towns of Cold Spring and Garrison are included.

COLUMBIA COUNTY

Originally part of Albany County back when Albany, now the capital city of New York, was a tiny fur-trading outpost, what is now Columbia County was split off in 1772 and divided into districts. The formal county structure that continues to this day was established in 1786. Columbia County today has a population of only about 65,000 people spread across 18 townships. The lovely rolling hills of Columbia still shelter a number of working farms and orchards. With a population density of just under 100 per square mile, the region is very rural.

Chatham

The township of Chatham covers some 53 square miles, making it the largest township in Columbia County, but the total population is only about 4,000 people. Somewhat confusingly, a number of charming hamlets within the overall township all have some variation of Chatham in their name—there's East Chatham, Old Chatham, North Chatham, and the village of Chatham. The delightful, old-fashioned village of Chatham, which still has its own independent movie theater, is where most of the restaurants and shops in the area are located.

Hudson

The antiques capital of the Hudson Valley, the city of Hudson is also the seat of Columbia County. The roots of Hudson go deep into American history. Henry Hudson probably visited the area that is now the city, and Dutch colonists were in the area soon after. The area remained a quiet Dutch settlement called Claverack Landing until after Independence, when it underwent an abrupt change. A group of Yankee whalers from Nantucket convinced themselves that the British would retaliate against them for the loss of the colonies. They decided to move, lock, stock, and whale-oil barrel, away from their vulnerable island to a more protected place. In 1783, they chose Claverack Landing for its convenient riverside location. The whalers very systematically laid out a town grid that is pretty much still in existence—Warren Street, the main street in Hudson, was laid out at that time. They moved in quickly, in some cases dismantling their frame houses on Nantucket and reassembling them in the new location. In 1785, Claverack Landing was chartered as the city of Hudson. It was the third chartered city in New York, but the first in the country to receive a charter after Independence, making Hudson the first chartered city in United States. Whaling quickly turned Hudson into a prosperous port, with docks, warehouses, nautical supply manufacturers, and a variety of other industries. During this boom period, many elegant homes and commercial buildings went up in the Federal and Greek Revival styles.

By the late 1840s, however, whale oil was being replaced by kerosene, and ships were being replaced by railroads. Hudson went into a decline, but the shrewd Yankee merchants of the city soon turned to new industries, such as textile manufacturing. The city prospered again, and construction of mansions, mills, and storefronts resumed. From 1850 into the 1900s, buildings went up in every popular architectural style of the day, from Gothic Revival to Second Empire to Queen Anne to Stick Style. Starting around 1900, Hudson went into another long period of slow decline. Aside from the cement industry and a notorious red-light district (closed down in 1950), the economy of the city didn't have much going for it, and the many superb examples of period architecture were mostly just neglected.

In the 1980s, Hudson was rediscovered by antiques dealers, artists, and people looking for weekend homes. The city started a major renaissance as the old buildings began to be bought up and restored to their original splendor. Walking the streets here is like looking through an encyclopedia of American vernacular architecture. Hudson is also a great place for antiquing, shopping, and eating at the many outstanding restaurants, and there's a very lively arts scene, with plenty of galleries and cultural events.

Kinderhook

The oldest town in Columbia County, Kinderhook was visited by Henry Hudson on his historic voyage in 1609 and became a Dutch settlement soon after. The town prospered, and by the time of the Revolution had become an important commercial and manufacturing center. The new railroads of the 1840s bypassed Kinderhook, however, and the town turned into and remained a quiet place surrounded by farms. Kinderhook was the home of Martin Van Buren, the eighth president of the United States, and his home, Lindenwald, is still there and open to the public. The town has a number of interesting historic homes, also open to the public, and a well-kept historic district definitely worth visiting.

DUTCHESS COUNTY

Dutchess County was among the first 12 counties of New York established in 1683. The territory included what is now Putnam County. Putnam was separated in 1812, reducing the size of Dutchess County to about 825 square miles. The name Dutchess was given as a compliment to the Duchess of York, the second wife of King James II. When the county was founded, her title was spelled with a "t" in it. It wasn't until 1755, long after the county was named, that the standard spelling changed.

In the early settlement period, most colonists were Dutch. A major influx of German settlers fleeing religious turmoil in their homeland came from about 1715 to about 1730. At the same time, many New England farmers moved into the area in search of better land and easier access to markets. By Independence, the county had a fairly cosmopolitan population—a characteristic that continues strongly to the present day.

Dutchess grew steadily in the years after the Revolution. Agriculture remained a major part of the economy, but after the Erie Canal opened in 1824, river ports such as Poughkeepsie and Beacon became major shipping and manufacturing centers. When the railroads arrived beginning in the 1840s, the region became much more closely connected to New York City, only a couple of hours away by train. The area soon attracted wealthy New Yorkers, who built themselves magnificent country homes overlooking the Hudson. Franklin Delano Roosevelt grew up at his family mansion in Hyde Park. Many of these old homes are now historic sites open to the public—one reason tourism is now about 10 percent of the county's economy. Dutchess is full of history, and it's also full of wineries, farms, horse farms, great shopping, art galleries, antiques stores, cultural events, wonderful restaurants (the Culinary Institute of America is in Hyde Park), and charming villages, such as Rhinebeck and Millbrook.

The population of Dutchess County is now about 295,000. Much of the northern part of the county remains rural and agricultural. In the southern portion, suburbanization, overdevelopment, and industry, such as IBM's major facility in Fishkill, have taken away some of the rural charm, but a surprising amount still remains along the back roads.

Beacon

During the Revolutionary War, American troops lit signal fires at the top of a tall peak near the river settlements of Fishkill Landing and Matteawan. After the war, the peak was named Mt. Beacon. It became a major tourist attraction in 1902, when an inclined railway was built to carry passengers to the top quickly. By 1913, the two old villages had grown together. They combined and incorporated as the City of Beacon. The area is rich in history—it contains numerous historic homes and sites, including the Madam Brett House, built in 1709 and the oldest existing house in Dutchess County.

Beacon was once a major river port and manufacturing center. Hat making, brick manufacturing, textile production, shipbuilding, and tourism made the town prosper. In 1928, Nabisco built a huge printing plant here to make boxes and wrappings. Manufacturing gradually moved away, however, and by the 1970s the town was badly faded. Empty storefronts and abandoned factories, however, turn out to be very attractive to artists looking for large, well-lit, cheap studio space. A steady trickle of artists moved in over the years. The trickle turned to a flood after Dia:Beacon, the largest modern art museum in North America, opened in the old Nabisco factory in 2005. Beacon is easy to reach from Manhattan—it's only an hour away on the MetroNorth trains, making it accessible for both commuting and day trips. The Beacon rebirth can be seen everywhere—on the newly accessible waterfront, at Dia:Beacon, and on Main Street, now full of shops, galleries, and restaurants.

Hyde Park

Famous as the home of Franklin Delano Roosevelt, Hyde Park preserves several historic sites. Foremost is Springwood, the FDR home. The mansion and grounds were left to the nation after Roosevelt died and have been open to the public ever since. Up the road from the relatively modest FDR home is the ostentatious Vanderbilt Mansion—visiting both sites in one day is a study in contrasts. Val-Kill, the very modest home of Eleanor Roosevelt from 1945 until her death in 1962, is nearby. Also in Hyde Park is the Culinary Institute of America, a destination for foodies from around the world. The town has some good antiquing, but aside from the historic sites, much of the town has, unfortunately, been allowed to become a giant strip mall. Little of the original old village remains.

Millbrook

Millbrook is a village in the town of Washington, one of the more rural parts of Dutchess County. This is estate country, full of rolling hills, impeccably restored old farmhouses, and horse barns—it's the home of the Millbrook Hunt. It's also home to Millbrook Vineyards and Winery, the flagship winery for the mid–Hudson Valley. Millbrook is a quiet little place, with a number of good restaurants and shops, including the outstanding Merritt Book Store.

Poughkeepsie

"The Queen City of the Hudson," Poughkeepsie is the Dutchess County seat. The unusual name derives from the Indian name for the area, meaning "the reed-covered lodge by the little-water place." The first European settlement in the area dates back to around 1659. By the time of the Revolutionary War, Poughkeepsie had become the second capital of New York State (after Kingston was burned in 1777). It was in Poughkeepsie that New York State ratified the Constitution in 1788. By the early 1800s, Poughkeepsie was a major shipping and industrial center, producing hats, paper, and beer from the breweries owned by Matthew Vassar, a major benefactor to the city and founder of Vassar College.

The city soon also became the center of county government and commerce and developed a lively cultural life. The Bardavon 1869 Opera House has been in continual operation ever since it opened. Like many other industrial cities, from the 1950s onward Poughkeepsie steadily lost jobs and population; by the early 1990s, it was far from being the Queen City. Also like many other cities in the region, something of a rebirth then began. Housing renovations began, waterfront access was improved, the MetroNorth station was upgraded, the stores along Main Street were slowly revived, restaurants opened, and a lively cultural life returned to the city as artists were drawn to the inexpensive studio and gallery space. Today Poughkeepsie is steadily returning to its former glory—the city is an exciting place to visit.

Rhinebeck

A major destination in the mid–Hudson Valley, the historic village of Rhinebeck dates back to 1686, when it was founded by four Dutchmen who bought 2,200 acres from the local Sepasco Indians. By the 1700s it was already a well-established small village, and in 1766 the Beekman Arms was built as a local tavern. The Beek, as it's known to the locals, is still there—it's the oldest inn in America. George Washington really did sleep here. By the early 1800s Rhinebeck had broad, leafy streets lined with gracious homes; as the railroads arrived, Astors, Vanderbilts, Livingstons, and others of their social set built mansions along the riverfront. Most of these grand estates are gone or converted to other uses, but some remain in private hands—and two, Wilderstein and Montgomery Place in nearby Red Hook, are open to the public. The village remained a residential and agricultural place for decades, enlivened every August by the Dutchess County Fair but sleepy most of the time. After IBM, a major employer in the area, downsized in the 1970s, sleepy and residential wasn't working for Rhinebeck anymore. The town looked at its long history, its large collection of well-kept historic homes and sites, a four-corner business district that had a lot of turn-of-the-century charm, and the many cultural events at nearby Bard College, and decided tourism was the way to go. Cultural events at Bard draw many to the area, as do popular events at the Dutchess County Fairgrounds such as antiques shows, car shows, and craft shows. Today Rhinebeck is a lively, charming place, full of great shops and excellent restaurants.

GREENE COUNTY

Greene County was founded in 1800 and named in honor of the Revolutionary War general Nathanael Greene. Most of the county is in the Catskill Mountains, including a large portion within the boundaries of the Catskill Park. Greene County remains very rural—approximately 50,000 people scattered across some 660 square miles. Several small riverfront towns tie the county to the Hudson, but today the region looks mostly westward and depends heavily on tourism in the Catskills.

Athens

Walking through Athens is like stepping into a time tunnel—more than 300 buildings in the village are listed on state and national historic registers. Athens is a very small place, with a population of under 2,000. The busiest intersection in town doesn't have a stoplight. So much of the village looks exactly as it did 75 years ago or more that the 2004 film *War of the Worlds*, set in the 1930s, was filmed here. Athens has a nice waterfront area with docking space for boats and some good restaurants.

Catskill

Located at the mouth of the historic Catskill Creek, the town of Catskill is the seat of Greene County. It was founded in 1806 and quickly became an industrial center based on water power and easy boat transport on the Hudson. Catskill became famous as the home of the painter Thomas Cole, the founder of the Hudson River School, a style of painting that focused on the grandeur of the landscape. Cole and his family lived at Cedar Grove from 1836 until his death in 1848. Today the home is a historic site open to the public.

Like many other manufacturing towns, however, Catskill gradually lost its mills and found little to replace them. The town became something of a time capsule, full of faded but gracious homes. Recently the walkable downtown area has become a lot more lively. A number of new art galleries, shops, and restaurants have opened, and access to the waterfront has been improved.

ORANGE COUNTY

The first settlers of Orange County were Dutch, and they named their county for William III of Orange (1650–1702). As Prince of Orange, William was Stadtholder of the Dutch Republic; in the Glorious Revolution of 1689, he became King of England, ruling with his wife Mary, daughter of the deposed King James II. He was, needless to say, a hero to the Dutch. Orange County is one of the 12 original counties established in 1683. Most of the county is geographically oriented toward the Wallkill River, the Shawangunk Mountains, and the rugged Hudson Highlands. The portion that is oriented toward the mid–Hudson River Valley is small but richly historic—the United States Military Academy is here at West Point, and the historic city of Newburgh is nearby. Stewart Airport, a rapidly growing regional air hub, is outside of Newburgh. Orange County covers some 839 square miles and has a population of about 350,000—it's densely populated compared to the other counties of the mid-Hudson region.

Cornwall on Hudson

A charming village crammed in between massive Storm King Mountain and the Hudson River, Cornwall on Hudson has some nice restaurants and interesting shops. The Hudson Highlands Nature Museum, a great place to take the kids, is here, as is Black Rock Forest. The village is also conveniently close to the famed Storm King Art Center.

Newburgh

Newburgh's first settlers arrived in the early 1700s and quickly took advantage of the area's location on the Hudson to become a major port. George Washington spent the last months of the Revolutionary War at Hasbrouck House, the oldest house in Newburgh. It was from here that he issued the order formally ending the war on April 19, 1783. Hasbrouck House is preserved as a historic monument open to the public. By 1810, Newburgh was incorporated as a city. Shipbuilding, shipping, manufacturing, and commerce made the city wealthy, and civic-minded residents made it beautiful. They built churches, mansions, and handsome commercial buildings. They hired native son Andrew Jackson Downing to build a number of Gothic Revival homes (still visible); after his death they hired Frederick Law Olmstead and Calvert Vaux to design the lovely 35-acre Downing Park in the heart of the city. As railroads eclipsed ships, Newburgh gradually lost a lot of its industry. By the 1960s, the city was a ghost of its former vibrant self. In an incredibly ill-considered move, the city tore down block after block of waterfront structures, hoping in vain to attract new industry. Instead, Newburgh ended up with blocks of rubble-strewn vacant lots, a destroyed downtown, and thousands of displaced residents who left the city for good. After nearby Stewart Air Force base was closed in 1969, even more people left. The city became a deserted and sometimes dangerous place. Cheap real estate eventually attracts renewal, however, and in the 1990s developers began to build in Newburgh. Improvements to the waterfront have led to a lively bar and restaurant scene, and the area is now attracting restaurants, shops, artists, galleries, and home renovators. The conversion of the old air base to Stewart International Airport has also done a lot to revitalize the city.

PUTNAM COUNTY

Putnam County was separated from Dutchess County in 1812. It's a small place, only 246 square miles, but with a population of nearly 100,000. Putnam is also a wealthy place—the median family income is over $82,000, the highest in the state. Most of the county is outside the Hudson Valley watershed. Many residents of the county commute to Westchester and New York City, making most of Putnam an outer suburb of the metro area.

Cold Spring

The village of Cold Spring was supposedly given its name by George Washington himself. Despite this historic association, Cold Spring remained obscure until the War of 1812 started, when President James Madison ordered the creation of a munitions foundry here. It was a good choice—the area had an existing iron industry and it was right on the Hudson. Cannons could be test-fired out over the river and then easily transported. The West Point Foundry was active for nearly a century; today the ruins are a historic district. Cold Spring is a very popular shopping destination. The well-preserved 19th-century downtown area is very walkable; it's

full of antiques shops, restaurants, and a number of interesting stores. Nearby is Boscobel, a restored historic mansion that is the summer home of the Hudson Valley Shakespeare Theater.

ULSTER COUNTY

One of the original 12 counties established in 1683, Ulster takes its name from the Irish province of the same name. The name was chosen not because the area had a large Irish population but because Ulster was an earldom of the Duke of York (later King James II), who personally owned the Hudson Valley region. Today Ulster County is large—1,161 square miles—and heavily populated, with about 180,000 residents. Most of the county is within the Catskill Park and the Shawangunk Ridge and falls outside the scope of this book. That still leaves a lot of the county, however, including the historic city of Kingston.

Kingston

Kingston's long history dates back to the earliest Dutch settlement in the early 1600s. Called Esopus at first, Kingston began as a tiny outpost conveniently located at the mouth of the Esopus Creek almost exactly halfway between Albany and Manhattan. As the village grew, Dutch farmers along the Esopus Creek came into conflict with the local Native Americans. When hostilities erupted in 1658, the settlers moved up to a nearby hill and built a stockade around their homes. To this day, the upper part of Kingston is called the Stockade District and contains many historic structures and stone houses. In 1777, Kingston was declared the first capital of New York State. On October 16, 1777, the town was burned to the ground by British troops. The old Dutch stone houses survived, as did the original Senate House. After the war, the town slowly began to grow. The lower portion of the town, on the Rondout Creek, was a natural harbor, and shipbuilding and the shipping industry grew in importance. After the Delaware & Hudson Canal was completed in 1828, shipping grew rapidly as cheap coal from the mines of Pennsylvania arrived at the canal's terminus in Kingston and had to be shipped on.

The growth of the railroads killed off a lot of river traffic, however, and although Kingston became an important railroad center, starting in the late 1800s the city lost industry and jobs and went into a decline. In the 1950s, however, IBM arrived and brought thousands of good jobs to the area. The good times lasted into the early 1990s, when IBM closed its Kingston plant. Today Kingston has recovered somewhat and has been fairly successful in attracting high-tech companies to replace IBM. The city now has a very lively art and music scene, a lot of good restaurants, and a great waterfront area along the Rondout Creek.

New Paltz

One of the oldest settlements in the region is New Paltz, founded in 1677 when French Huguenots, fleeing religious repression in their homeland, bought 40,000 acres from the Esopus tribe. They established a settlement along the Wallkill River and built houses from stone. Six of those houses still stand, and Huguenot Street is the oldest street in America. New Paltz remained a small, agricultural town for decades. In the second half of the 19th century, resort hotels, such as the famous Mohonk Mountain House, began to spring up. The natural beauty of the Wallkill River valley and the Shawangunk Ridge, combined with easy access up the Hudson by steamboat and rail, made tourism a major part of the economy from then on. Today the State University of New York at New Paltz is a major presence in town (and the largest employer in the county). Main Street is full of interesting bookstores, restaurants, and shops. The town's close proximity to the Shawangunk Ridge attracts many rock climbers to the area; it's also a great place for hiking and biking.

Saugerties

Saugerties sounds like it ought to be an Indian name, but in fact it's Dutch, from the word meaning sawyer. By the time the town was officially founded in 1677, a number of sawmills were in operation. In the 19th century, Saugerties became well known for its extensive bluestone quarries. In the second half of the 20th century,

one of those old quarries became the distinctive work of environmental art called Opus 40. The town lost a lot of its industry starting in the 1950s. When IBM closed its nearby Kingston facility in the early 1990s, Saugerties suffered. The town has made a major comeback, however, helped along in the summer by the presence of Horse Shows in the Sun, which brings huge crowds to the area to see competitive riding events. Another major annual event is the Hudson Valley Garlic Festival in late September. Antiques stores and a number of good restaurants have been joined by some interesting new shops and some art galleries—with more anticipated.

Woodstock

The village of Woodstock isn't really in the Hudson Valley. In fact, it's inside the Catskill Park and really shouldn't be in this book at all. It's simply impossible to leave out a place that's so closely associated with the area, and besides, Woodstock is fun. It's a very individual place with a distinct countercultural feel. The village dates its fame as a haven for artists back to 1903, when the Byrdcliffe arts and crafts colony was founded in Woodstock by a wealthy Englishman named Ralph Radcliffe Whitehead. Byrdcliffe exists to this day—and is considered the oldest arts colony in the country. Today Woodstock and the surrounding area are full of art galleries and studios. The village itself is now a major tourism destination. Some 70 retail shops—not one of them a chain store—are crammed into just a few streets, along with restaurants and galleries. On a summer weekend and during the Woodstock Film Festival in October, this can be a very crowded and lively place. **Note:** The famed Woodstock Festival in 1969 didn't happen here. It was 50 miles away on a farm in Bethel, in Sullivan County.

Hudson Valley Tourism

Tourism is a major industry in the mid–Hudson Valley. Local government and non-profit organizations in the region are happy to provide tons of free information to anyone planning a visit.

Regional

Catskill Mountain Foundation
7970 Main Street
Hunter, NY 12442
(518) 263-2000
www.catskillmtn.org

Hudson River Valley National Heritage Area
Capitol Building, Room 254
Albany, NY 12224
(518) 473-3835
www.hudsonrivervalley.com

Hudson Valley Tourism
124 Main Street
Goshen, NY 10924
(845) 291-2136
(800) 232-4782
www.travelhudsonvalley.org

I♥NY
(800) CALL-NYS
www.iloveny.com

County/Town

Columbia County

Columbia County Department of Tourism
401 State Street
Hudson, NY 12534
(518) 828-3375
(800) 724-1846
www.bestcountryroads.com

Dutchess County

Dutchess County Tourism
3 Neptune Road
Poughkeepsie, NY 12601
(845) 463-4000
(800) 445-3131
www.dutchesstourism.com

Greene County

Greene County Resort and Hospitality Association
Box 332
Cairo, NY 12413
www.thecatskills.com

Greene County Tourism Office
Box 527
Catskill, NY 12414
(518) 993-3223
(800) 355-CATS
www.greenetourism.com

Orange County

Orange County Tourism
124 Main Street
Goshen, NY 10924
(845) 615-3860
www.orangetourism.org

Putnam County

Putnam County Visitors Bureau
110 Old Route 6, Building 3
Carmel, NY 10512
(845) 225-0381
(800) 470-4854
www.visitputnam.org

Ulster County

Ulster County Tourism
10 Westbrook Lane
Kingston, NY 12401
(845) 340-3566
(800) 342-5826
www.ulstertourism.info

GETTING HERE, GETTING AROUND

Long before Henry Hudson arrived in 1609, the Hudson River was a water highway for the Native Americans of the region. The river remained the main transportation route up and down the Hudson Valley for centuries after Hudson, gradually giving way first to railroads and then to automobiles. Today two major transportation hubs—New York City and Albany—bracket the region. In between is a road and bridge network that ties together both sides of the Hudson and connects the valley to the nearby metro regions. The region is also well served by an extensive rail and commuter bus system, although more local public transportation is limited. It's relatively easy to use public transit to get to the cities and larger towns of the region (see the Web site www.nyrides.com for a good overview), but once there, a car is almost a necessity.

ROADWAYS

The road network in the region covered by this book is bounded on the east by the Taconic State Parkway and on west by the New York State Thruway—which also happen to be the main north-south routes to, through, and from the region. Within those boundaries, several state highways are main north-south and also east-west routes through the region.

Construction began on the historic Taconic State Parkway back in 1927. The parkway was originally designed to extend the Bronx River Parkway and provide a scenic and rapid route to the Bear Mountain Bridge and points beyond. The portion that goes through Putnam and southern Dutchess counties was built between 1932 and 1938. The road was further extended through Dutchess and Columbia Counties starting in 1955. In November 1963, the parkway was officially declared complete. In all, the Taconic State Parkway is 105.3 miles long and passes through some of the most scenic parts of the region. In Westchester, the Taconic is now a six-lane expressway; it narrows down to two lanes in each direction after Yorktown. The parkway concepts of naturalistic landscaping, native stone construction, limited interchanges, and no commercial traffic make the Taconic a beautiful road

to drive—the scenery and views are magnificent at almost any given point. Those same parkway concepts of narrow lanes, narrow shoulders, and curves that follow the natural terrain can also make the Taconic a challenge for drivers, especially in bad weather. Locals know to avoid the Taconic in heavy rain and even light snowfall if possible. Even so, this beautiful and historic road is the main north-south express route through Putnam, Dutchess, and Columbia Counties and the best way to intersect with U.S. Route 90 (Mass Pike) to get to the Albany area and eastern Massachusetts. There are no rest areas along the Taconic—services such as food, gas, and accommodations are in towns off the parkway and are indicated by icons on exit signs. For safety reasons most of the scenic overlooks on the Taconic were closed long ago, but two (one northbound, one southbound) remain in Columbia County between Harlemville and Philmont. If time permits, stop to enjoy views clear across the Hudson Valley to the Catskills.

i For real-time travel information on the interstate and state highways and bridges of the mid–Hudson Valley region, check the New York State Department of Transportation Web site at www.nysdot.gov.

The other major north-south route on the east side of the Hudson is U.S. Route 9. This road is even more historic than the Taconic, though today it is considerably less scenic. Route 9 in New York State begins in the center of the George Washington Bridge in Manhattan. It follows a path north, paralleling the Hudson, all the way to the town of Champlain, just south of the Canadian border along Lake Champlain. Route 9 is the longest north-south U.S. highway in the state. The portion that passes through the eastern mid-Hudson region incorporates large portions of the historic old Albany Post Road, a path that dates back to colonial times. Route 9 takes you through all the many towns that are along the east bank of the Hudson. The road varies from two to four lanes all along the way. Today it's largely lined with strip malls and shopping centers, although the stretches that run through countryside and offer nice views across the river increase the further north the road goes. U.S. Route 9 has a confusing number of lettered state highways that are offshoots or spurs—Route 9G, for instance, diverges from Route 9 in Poughkeepsie and runs north more or less parallel to Route 9, though further to the east, until it intersects Route 9 again near Rhinebeck and then runs parallel some more, this time to the west along the Hudson. It's all very confusing—the best advice is to carry a good map.

On the west side of the Hudson, the Governor Thomas E. Dewey Thruway, better known as the New York State Thruway or Interstate 87, begins at the New York–New Jersey border near Suffern in Rockland County, then quickly enters Orange County and heads north, ending nearly 500 miles away in Buffalo. The Thruway was built in the 1950s as a way to connect the major cities in New York with a limited access highway. The Thruway is the longest toll road in the United States. For most of the region in this book, the road runs parallel to the Hudson River but well inland, generally anywhere from 5 to 10 miles. The Thruway passes near or through just about every west-side city and town mentioned in this book. It's in many ways the exact opposite of the Taconic State Parkway—a soulless, six- or eight-lane road full of semitrailers and trucks, with standard-issue service areas along the way. U.S. Route 9W is the other major north-south route on the west side. It runs parallel to the Hudson starting at Cornwall in Orange County and follows the river north all the way to the Albany area. It's mostly two lanes; though large portions are lined with strip malls and other commercial structures, many other portions pass through lovely rolling countryside. Traffic can back up badly on this road if there's an accident or severe weather; call (800) 847-8929 for road conditions.

> **i** Having an EZ Pass receiver in your car allows you to zip through tollbooths anywhere in New York State without having to stop—the toll is automatically billed to your account. EZ Pass works in 11 other states, including New Jersey and Massachusetts, but not in Connecticut and Vermont. For details, check www.ezpassny.com or call (800) 333-TOLL.

THE HUDSON RIVER BRIDGES

The major east-west roads in the Hudson Valley all lead to five major bridges that cross the river and link the region. For information on the Hudson River bridges in the region, contact the New York State Bridge Authority at www.nysba.state.ny.us or call (845) 691-7245. The toll on all the regional bridges is $1. All the bridges have walkways—there is no charge for pedestrians and bike riders.

BEAR MOUNTAIN BRIDGE
Connects US 6 (Orange County) and US 202 (Westchester County near Peekskill)
The southernmost bridge in the region is the Bear Mountain Bridge, included here because technically part of the toll plaza on the western side of the Hudson is in Orange County. It's also included because when it was opened in 1924 it was the longest main suspension span in the world (eclipsed just two years later by the Benjamin Franklin Bridge across the Delaware River in Philadelphia).

NEWBURGH-BEACON BRIDGE
Carries NY 52 and I-84 between Newburgh and Beacon

Officially, this is the Hamilton Fish Newburgh-Beacon Bridge, named for a long-serving local member of Congress. It opened in 1964, and a second parallel span was opened in 1980. The bridge provides connections on the west side to the NYS Thruway, Stewart Airport, and US 9W. On the east side, the bridge connects to US 9 in Fishkill. I-84 interchanges with the Taconic State Parkway further to the east in East Fishkill at exit 15.

MID-HUDSON BRIDGE
Carries NY Routes 44 and 55 between Poughkeepsie and Highland

When this bridge was opened in 1930, Franklin Delano Roosevelt was governor of New York State; his family home was in nearby Hyde Park. The bridge is named for him, so officially it's the Franklin Delano Roosevelt Mid-Hudson Bridge. When it was completed, it was the sixth-longest suspension bridge in the world. A fun feature of this bridge is that it has an LED lighting system that is used to decorate it with colors for holidays. If you're lucky, you might see one of the peregrine falcons that nest on the bridge. On the west side, the bridge connects with the NYS Thruway and Route 9W; on both sides, Routes 44 and 55 are major east-west routes. On the east, Routes 44 and 55 both interchange with the Taconic State Parkway.

i Gas is expensive and commuting is tiring. Why not share the burden by van pooling, ridesharing, or car pooling? MetroPool, sponsored by the New York State Department of Transportation, can hook you up with others in your area. Call (800) FIND-RIDE or go to www.metropool.com.

KINGSTON-RHINECLIFF BRIDGE
Carries Route 199 between Kingston and Rhinecliff

This bridge is officially the George Clinton Memorial Bridge, named for the first governor of New York State. When it was opened in 1957, the bridge replaced the quaint but unreliable Kingston-Rhinecliff ferry service, and the official name quickly fell into disuse. The views from the bridge up and down the Hudson are wonderful. To the west, the bridge takes you into Kingston and connects to the NYS Thruway, U.S. Route 209 (a local highway that heads into the Wallkill Valley and the Catskills), and US 32 and US 9W, north-south local highways that parallel the river. On the east, the bridge connects to Route 199, a major east-west route across northern Dutchess County, and to Route 9, heading north-south parallel to the river.

RIP VAN WINKLE BRIDGE
Carries Route 23 between Hudson and Catskill

Opened in 1935, the Rip Van Winkle Bridge is named for the famous Catskills character in the 1819 story by Washington Irving. On the west side, the bridge connects with the NYS Thruway, US 9W, and NY 385. On the east side, it connects with NY 9G.

AIRPORTS

STEWART INTERNATIONAL AIRPORT
1180 First Street
New Windsor
(845) 564-7200
www.panynj.gov

Stewart International Airport began life in the 1930s as a military base to train cadets from nearby West Point. Today it has a dual existence, serving as a military airfield for the New York National Guard and the U.S. Marine Corps Reserve and also as a major passenger airport. In November 2007, after much wrangling, the Port Authority of New York and New Jersey took control of the airport. The goal is to make Stewart the fourth airport for the New York City metro region, to relieve congestion at JFK, La Guardia, and Newark-Liberty. This is a goal not universally appreciated in the region, where many residents are concerned about the additional congestion, development, and noise the airport will bring.

Although the runway at Stewart is long enough to accommodate the space shuttle, this is still a small airport with only two runways. Airlines flying limited flights from here are AirTran, Delta, JetBlue, Northwest, and US Airways. Parking has the great advantage of being nearby, plentiful, and relatively inexpensive. Recent construction has created a new interchange on I-84 at Drury Lane, making road access to the airport very direct. Access from nearby I-87 (New York State Thruway) is also fairly direct. A direct rail link from the metro area is still in the early planning stages. By public transportation, take MetroNorth to Beacon in southern Dutchess County and take the Leprechaun Bus Line to the airport (845-565-7900). Rental car agencies at the airport are Avis, Budget, Enterprise, and Hertz.

ALBANY INTERNATIONAL AIRPORT
737 Albany-Shaker Road
Albany
(518) 242-2200
www.albanyairport.com
Albany International Airport is the major air center for the Capital Region, western New England, and northeastern New York. It's a large and very

---

Cruising the Hudson

Several charter boats offer a variety of cruises on the Hudson River. Passengers can go on dinner cruises, lighthouse tours, scenic tours, school trips—the cruise companies offer several options, including private charters for parties. Schedules, routes, and fees vary enormously. Call ahead for details and reservations (information on the Web sites is bound to change).

Hudson River Adventures
Newburgh
(845) 220-2120
www.prideofthehudson.com
The 130-passenger *Pride of the Hudson* and the small *Pollepel* depart from Newburgh Landing.

Hudson Cruises, Inc.
Hudson
(518) 822-1014
www.primebuys.com/hudsoncruises
Sail on the 150-passenger *Hudson Spirit* or the *Lil Spirit*. Most cruises leave from Hudson or Waryas Park in Poughkeepsie.

Hudson Maritime Services
Beacon
(845) 265-7621
www.hudsonriver.cjb.net
Sail on the 25-foot sloop *Manitou* or the 19-foot powerboat *Orion*.

Hudson River Cruises
Kingston
(845) 340-4700
www.hudsonrivercruises.com
The 300-passenger *Rip Van Winkle* sails from Rondout Landing at the foot of Broadway in Kingston.

North River Cruises
Kingston
(845) 679-8205
www.northrivercruises.com
The motor yacht *Teal* departs from Rondout Landing at the foot of Broadway in Kingston.

River Rose
Newburgh
(845) 401-6400
www.commcomm.net/riverrose.htm
An authentic paddle wheeler, *River Rose* accommodates 150 passengers and departs from Newburgh Landing at the foot of Broadway in Newburgh.

modern airport with three concourses. Numerous major airlines fly from here, including American, Northwest, United, Delta, US Airways, Air Canada, Continental, and Southwest. It's easy to get to: The airport is located pretty much at the junction of I-87 and I-90 northwest of the city of Albany. Parking in nearby garages with walkways leading directly into the terminal make Albany International a very manageable airport. The terminal has a business center and meeting rooms as well as a number of shops and restaurants. Rental car agencies at the airport are Avis, Budget, Enterprise, Hertz, National/Alamo, and Thrifty.

RAIL

AMTRAK
(800) 872-7245
www.amtrak.com
Passenger rail service in the mid–Hudson Valley is available only on the east side of the river. Amtrak trains depart from Penn Station in New York and travel north straight up the Hudson (when northbound, sit on the left-hand side of the train for spectacular views) to Poughkeepsie, Rhinecliff, Hudson, and Albany. Where they go after that depends—Empire Service trains end at Niagara Falls, while Adirondack Line trains end in Montreal, for example. Amtrak trains are comfortable, with roomy airline-style seats, lots of luggage space, and usually a snack bar car. Tickets are relatively expensive—the fare from Penn Station to Hudson, for instance, ranges between $32 and $48, depending on what time of day you're traveling. Reservations aren't required, but they're recommended, especially if you're traveling at a peak period. Get your ticket before boarding, because prices on the train are much higher. Amtrak trains are speedy—it's only two hours from Penn Station to Hudson. Check the Web site for detailed schedules and reservations information.

METRO-NORTH
(800) 638-7646
www.mta.info
Metro-North is the commuter rail line serving the

east side of the Hudson Valley. The Hudson Line heads straight up the river from Grand Central Station, with beautiful views all along the way. Garrison in Putnam County is the first stop in the mid-Hudson region; after that the stops are Cold Spring, Beacon, New Hamburg, and Poughkeepsie (final stop). The trip from Grand Central Station to Poughkeepsie is 1 hour, 40 minutes. The trains run frequently, including on weekends. Metro-North is more efficient than cushy—the seats are comfortable but don't recline—and every train has restroom facilities. Fares vary depending on where you're going and the time of day—off-peak (non-rush hour) prices are lower. The typical one-way peak fare from Grand Central to Poughkeepsie is $15.25. It's $5 more if you buy it on the train, so use the handy kiosks at the station to get your ticket in advance. Metro-North runs some special excursions to the mid-Hudson region. The Roosevelt Ride, for example, goes to Poughkeepsie, where a van takes visitors to the Roosevelt home and other sites in nearby Hyde Park and returns to the station in time for a return train. Check the Web site for schedules, travel packages, and travel advisories.

BUS LINES

ADIRONDACK TRAILWAYS (PINEHILL TRAILWAYS)
(800) 225-6815
www.trailwaysny.com
Serving Ulster and Orange Counties and the Albany area.

ARTHUR F. MULLIGAN, INC. (FORMERLY ARROW BUS LINE)
(845) 658-8600
Serving Ulster and Dutchess Counties.

COACH USA/SHORTLINE/ROCKLAND COACH
(800) 631-8405
www.coachusa.com, www.shortlinebus.com
Serving Orange, Dutchess, and Ulster Counties.

LEPRECHAUN LINES
(800) 624-4217
www.leprechaunlines.com
Serving Dutchess, Putnam, and Orange Counties; shuttle from Beacon train station to Stewart Airport.

i The Newburgh-Beacon commuter ferry meets the morning and evening commuter trains at the Beacon Metro-North train station and crosses the river to the Front Street marina in Newburgh. The ride takes about 10 minutes and costs $1.

LOCAL PUBLIC TRANSIT

DUTCHESS COUNTY LOOP BUS SYSTEM
(845) 485-4690
www.dutchessny.gov

KINGSTON CITIBUS
(845) 331-3725
www.ci.kingston.ny.us

POUGHKEEPSIE TRANSIT
(845) 451-4118
www.cityofpoughkeepsie.com

PUTNAM AREA RAPID TRANSIT (PART)
(845) 878-RIDE
www.putnamcountyny.com

UCAT (ULSTER COUNTY AREA TRANSIT)
(845) 340-3333
www.co.ulster.ny.us

HUDSON VALLEY HISTORY

For 10,000 years or more, the Hudson Valley region was home to Algonquian-speaking Indians, mostly members of the Munsee and Mahican groups. These Native Americans are often referred to as Woodland Indians, because the area was heavily forested and their lifeways revolved around the woods and the mighty river that flowed through their lands. In the Mahican dialect, the river was called Muhheakantuck, meaning "river that flows two ways."

The description was apt, because the Hudson River, from its mouth in New York Harbor to the city of Troy 153 miles away, is a tidal estuary. The river flows northward as the tide comes in and south as it goes out. The water is very salty at the mouth, where it mingles with the Atlantic Ocean, and is brackish as far north as Newburgh. The source of the Hudson is a tiny pond perched high on the southwest side of Mt. Marcy—at 5,344 feet, New York State's highest mountain. From this spot, poetically named Lake Tear of the Clouds, the water flows into tributaries that eventually flow into the Hudson. As mighty rivers go, the Hudson isn't particularly lengthy. From Lake Tear of the Clouds to the Battery is a distance of only 315 miles. The Rhine, to which the Hudson is often compared, is the longest river in Europe at 820 miles.

HENRY HUDSON EXPLORES

European exploration of the Hudson began with Giovanni da Verrazano, who in 1524 discovered the mouth of the Hudson and apparently sailed a short way upriver. He noted that it was a broad waterway that seemed to head north from the vast bay he had explored. In 1609, Henry Hudson, an English sea captain working for the Dutch East India Company, was dispatched by his employers to search for the fabled Northwest Passage—the sea route that supposedly led through the North American continent and on to the riches of the Indies.

Hudson and his crew of 20 sailed from Amsterdam in April 1609 on the *Half Moon,* a square-rigged wooden ship that was only 65 feet long and 17 feet wide. They sailed as far south as the Chesapeake and Delaware Bays, then turned north again and arrived in New York Bay in early September. On September 12, Hudson began sailing upriver. Because the water remained salty as he headed north, he was hopeful that he had indeed found the Northwest Passage.

Hudson and his crew were astonished by the river. The tides, the magnificent and unspoiled scenery, the abundance of timber, fish, waterfowl, and game, and, above all, the pure air awed them. The *Half Moon* sailed as far as present-day Albany, when it became clear that, spectacular though the river was, it wasn't the Northwest Passage after all. The *Half Moon* sailed back downriver and on October 4 departed for the voyage home.

Hudson didn't find what he was looking for, but he discovered something that was far more important: the potential for a hugely lucrative fur trade with the Native Americans of the region, centered on the magnificent natural harbor of New York Bay. The Indians Hudson met along the river were happy to trade beaver, mink, and otter pelts for what the Dutch considered trifles— beads, knives, ax heads, needles, and cloth.

COLONIZATION BEGINS

Soon after Hudson's voyage up the river, the Dutch claimed the region as a province for trade and settlement. Dutch colonization of New Netherland started very soon after. By 1624 a small band of 18 families had settled at Fort Orange (later Albany); in 1624, 30 Dutch colonists landed on Manhattan. The river became a water highway connecting the growing commercial center of New Amsterdam on the tip of Manhattan with the fur-trading center of Fort Orange. In between, fur traders, timber merchants, farmers, and others began small riverside settlements.

To encourage the population of the area, in 1629 the Dutch West India Company began making huge land grants to patroons—wealthy stockholders who were given almost feudal rights over the land. The patroons were obligated to bring over colonists who would settle on their land as tenant farmers. In the mid-Hudson region, the patroon was Robert Livingston, the first of many distinguished Roberts in the family. His patronship of Livingston Manor covered 160,000 acres.

In 1664, the situation in the region changed abruptly. As part of the ongoing Anglo-Dutch warfare, New Amsterdam was seized by the English in a near-bloodless takeover. (The Dutch colonists so hated their governor, Peter Stuyvesant, that they wouldn't rally to defend their settlement.) The name of the colony was changed to New York.

i The New Netherland Institute is a nonprofit organization dedicated to studying Dutch history in the New World and the Dutch heritage in America. The organization sponsors the New Netherland Project, which translates and studies the many historic documents from that period that are in the New York State Library and state archives. The NNI Web site has a lot of good information about Dutch North America: www.nnp.org.

The Dutch were no longer in charge, but they remained very much in evidence. Dutch settlements were well established in the region and Dutch influence remained very powerful for decades, as shown by the many Dutch place names up and down the valley. The town of Kinderhook in Columbia County, for instance, takes its name from Henry Hudson himself, who called it Kinderhoeck, Dutch for "children's corner,"

because so many curious Mahican children came to gaze at his ship there. Martin Van Buren, the eighth president, was a resident of Kinderhook. He grew up speaking Dutch and spoke English with a noticeable Dutch accent.

Under English control, the region continued to grow. Instead of huge land grants to Dutch patroons, huge land patents were granted or sold to English colonists. The land grants were divided into townships, and parcels were sold off to new settlers and farmers moving in from the rocky, unproductive farms of New England. Even so, many of the original families, such as the Livingstons, held onto their land and had vast estates.

The area also attracted colonists seeking religious freedom in the New World. Huguenots—Protestants from France and the Netherlands—settled the New Paltz area starting in the 1670s. Germans fleeing religious upheaval in the Palatine region arrived in the area starting in the early 1700s.

THE HUDSON AND THE REVOLUTION

During the Revolutionary War, control of the Hudson was a key strategic goal for both sides. Control by the British would isolate the New England colonies from the rest of the states and be a stranglehold on the commerce of New York. The British quickly got the upper hand at the start of the war by capturing New York in 1776. They held onto the city for the rest of the war, but the struggle to control the river seesawed back and forth. In 1776 the Americans stretched a chain across the river between Fort Montgomery on the west and Fort Clinton on the east (near the current Bear Mountain Bridge) to keep British ships from sailing upriver. The British captured both forts, removed the chain, and sent ships upriver to raid as far north as Kingston, the capital of the new state of New York. Kingston was burned to the ground. A later, much larger chain at West Point was installed in 1778. The British never tried to run it.

Further north on the Hudson, the Battle of Saratoga in the autumn of 1777 was a major turning point of the war. The British plan was to send an army under General John Burgoyne south from Canada down the Hudson. At the same time, General William Howe in New York City would march north up the river with his army. The goal was to cut the New England colonies off from the rest of the states. The British plan fell apart when Howe decided to head south and attack Philadelphia instead, leaving Burgoyne on his own. American militia under General Horatio Gates fought the British to a draw at Saratoga on September 19 and won a decisive victory in the second battle on October 7. Burgoyne surrendered his entire army a few days later. The impressive victory at Saratoga meant that further attack from Canada was unlikely, which kept New England from being isolated. More importantly, the success persuaded the French to enter the war on the American side.

Saratoga did not end the strategic importance of the Hudson Valley. After the French and American victory at Yorktown in 1781 in Virginia, General Washington led 7,000 troops to New Windsor, near Newburgh in Orange County. He wanted to be in position for another attack on New York City, if necessary. In fact, although there was some skirmishing in the area, the troops were never sent into battle again. In 1783, Washington issued his final "cessation of hostilities" order from his farmhouse headquarters in Newburgh.

After Independence, the Hudson Valley resumed its slow growth. In addition to farming, iron and timber production became important industries, as did fishing on the river, especially during the spectacular shad runs in the spring. Hundreds of Hudson River sloops—broadbeamed, single-masted ships designed to deal with the river's tricky tides and currents—sailed up and down, while numerous ferries crossed the river at strategic points.

ROBERT FULTON AND THE *CLERMONT*

From 1801 to 1804, the sixth Robert Livingston of Clermont in Columbia County was U.S. Minister to France. Livingston had been a member of the committee to draft the Declaration of Independence, had served as foreign minister during the Revolutionary War, and as Chancellor of the State of New York had administered the oath of office to George Washington. While in France, Livingston met an enterprising young American named Robert Fulton, who had come to Paris to study painting. Fulton was soon sidetracked into an exciting new technology, the steamboat. Livingston became equally enthusiastic, and the two were soon experimenting with steamboats on the Seine. They made their first successful voyage in 1803. Both returned to America in 1804, where they built another steamboat in New York City. Christened the *North River* (later the *Clermont* in honor of Livingston), this ship made the first commercial steamboat voyage, leaving Manhattan on August 17, 1807 and arriving at Livingston's Clermont Manor, 100 miles upriver, 24 hours later. Fulton spent the night and then sailed on to Albany, arriving 12 hours later. A trip that had once taken a week by sloop could now be completed in 36 hours. The placid life on the Hudson was changed forever.

ART AND INDUSTRY

As the new American nation found its identity, writers such as Washington Irving, James Fenimore Cooper, and Nathaniel Hawthorne wrote about American topics and earned acclaim not only at home but in Europe. Irving was the first American to be an international best-selling author. His tales of the Catskills, including the famous stories about Rip Van Winkle and the Headless Horseman in "The Legend of Sleepy Hollow," were published in 1819. They brought the natural beauty of the Hudson Valley to national and international attention.

Almost simultaneously, American artists were discovering the sublime beauty of their homeland. The first was Thomas Cole. Born in

i Washington Irving's Hudson Valley tales are in *The Sketch Book of Geoffrey Crayon, Gent.*, first published in 1819 and never out of print since.

Reading about the River

Want to know more about the Hudson River? A good starting point is *The Hudson: An Illustrated Guide to the Living River,* by Stephen P. Stanne, Roger G. Panetta, and Brian E. Forist (Rutgers University Press, 1996). A classic book is *The Hudson* by Carl Carmer, first published in 1939 and still valuable and fun to read today. A modern edition is published by Fordham University Press. Another very valuable title is Robert H. Boyle's *The Hudson River: A Natural and Unnatural History* (Norton, 1979). It's out of print, but inexpensive used copies are easy to find. For a literary take on the river, a good choice is *The Hudson River in Literature: An Anthology,* edited by Arthur G. Adam (Fordham University Press, 1988). For architecture and historic homes, try the beautifully illustrated *Historic Houses of the Hudson River Valley* by Gregory Long (Rizzoli, 2004). The Hudson River School and individual artists are discussed in many titles; a nicely illustrated starting point is *All That Is Glorious Around Us: Paintings from the Hudson River School,* by John Paul Driscoll (Cornell University Press, 1997). And for a beautiful look at the river today, try *Hudson River Journey,* with photos by Hardie Truesdale and text by Joanne Michaels (The Countryman Press, 2003).

the eastern Catskills made a deep impression on him. His paintings capturing the area landscapes were well received by critics and a public ready to cast off classical European influence in favor of a new style with American themes. Over the next half-century, many other artists traveled to the Hudson Valley region, the Catskills, and the Adirondacks. Their work, though often idealized, presented a romantic yet realistic depiction of the landscape, designed to evoke the sublime in nature. Collectively, the works of Cole and Asher Durand, followed later by Cole's pupil Frederic Edwin Church and by Albert Bierstadt, Jasper Cropsey, William Hart, and many others, came to be called the Hudson River School. Their work made the Hudson Valley the landscape that defined the nation.

INDUSTRY ON THE HUDSON

Even as the Hudson River School artists were celebrating the unspoiled wilderness, the Hudson River Valley region was rapidly industrializing. The opening of the Erie Canal in 1825 brought a huge increase in water traffic onto the Hudson. Riverfront towns such as Kingston, Newburgh, Poughkeepsie, and Beacon became important shipbuilding sites and coaling stations. The easy access to cheap transportation also led to rapid industrial growth, and manufacturing of all sorts—including ice harvesting, quarrying, and brick making—grew quickly. When railroads joined the transportation mix starting in the 1830s, growth came even faster. Railroads ran up and the down the banks of the Hudson and criss crossed the region. The famed Poughkeepsie Railroad-Highland Bridge, completed in 1888, was the longest railroad bridge in the world at the time and was the first and only rail crossing of the Hudson River south of Albany.

The easy transportation upriver from Manhattan led to another growth area: The Hudson Valley became the place for the wealthy to build their showcase country homes. Starting in the 1860s, mansion after mansion went up along the riverfront, built by Astors, Vanderbilts, Livingstons, and other fabulously wealthy families.

England in 1801, Cole came to America in 1818. The turning point of his artistic career was a steamboat ride up the Hudson to Catskill in the autumn of 1825. The brilliant fall colors and spectacular scenery he saw along the way and then in

(Franklin Roosevelt's family mansion in Hyde Park is modest compared to the massive Vanderbilt mansion a few miles away.) Times change, however, and starting in the 1900s many of those homes were eventually sold, torn down, burned (accidentally), or converted to orphanages, nursing homes, and other charitable institutions. A significant number, however, were donated to local historical organizations, New York State, or the federal government. Their architecture, furnishings, and grounds are preserved today as historic sites open to the public and are a major tourism draw.

The wealthy weren't the only ones to enjoy the Hudson Valley. Inexpensive steamboat excursions from New York regularly chugged upriver to Beacon, where tourists disembarked and went to ride the inclined railroad up nearby Mt. Beacon. Others went on to Poughkeepsie and points north to enjoy picnics and walks in the countryside. They began a steady flow of tourism that has continued ever since. In 1885, the New York State Legislature established the Forest Preserve of New York State, setting aside land in the Adirondacks and the Catskills to be protected as "forever wild." The Catskills became even more of a tourism and vacation destination, and many resort hotels, such as the Catskill Mountain House, reached by boat or train, sprang up.

CHANGING TIMES

As steamboats inevitably gave way to the railroads, passenger car, and trucks, the Hudson River shipping industry—and the towns that depended on it—declined. The Delaware & Hudson Canal in Kingston, for example, closed down in 1898, and the city lost a major source of employment. The Cornell Steamboat Company of Kingston, founded in 1847, became the largest tugboat company in America—but was out of business by the 1960s. Similarly, Newburgh, once a major shipbuilding center, faded to a depressed shadow of its former elegant self by the 1950s.

Not every city suffered. Poughkeepsie, for example, became famous for its breweries, hat

factories, paper mills, and Smith Brothers cough drops. Nabisco and Texaco had major plants in Beacon. There were foundries in Cold Spring as far back as the Revolutionary War; the famous Parrott gun of the Civil War was made here. Cold Spring was also the home of the Marathon Battery Company. From 1952 to 1979, this company manufactured nickel-cadmium batteries, mostly for military use. The end result was massive metal pollution of the Foundry Cove area by the plant and a hugely expensive cleanup that took two years and wasn't completed until 1994.

SAVING THE RIVER

Major water pollution issues were nothing new on the Hudson. For many decades, all that industry in the region sent waste products and effluent flowing into the water with little regulation, where it joined untreated sewage from the riverside communities. The river had become little more than sewer. By the 1960s, as environmental awareness grew, the plight of the Hudson became an important regional concern. The fledgling environmental movement in the valley was galvanized into action in 1962 when Consolidated Edison proposed a massive hydroelectric power plant that would be carved into the side of Storm King Mountain, an emblematic peak in the magnificent Hudson Highlands portion of the river. Citizens mobilized to oppose the plan, forming an organization called Scenic Hudson Preservation Conference. (This wonderful organization, now called just Scenic Hudson, is still in existence and remains active in preserving the natural beauty of the area.) The group raised a number of important issues about the proposed plant, but there was nothing in the law at the time to make Con Ed even consider the environmental impact of the plant, much less listen to the concerns of the people who would be affected by it. Scenic Hudson challenged Con Ed in a legal battle that continued for 17 years and set many crucial precedents that have guided environmental law ever since. Among other things, the struggle established the right of citizens to participate in environmental disputes and laid the groundwork for federal and state regulation of the environment. (The creation of the U.S. Environmental Protection Agency and the pathbreaking federal Clean Water Act of 1977 are direct outgrowths of the Scenic Hudson case.) For all practical purposes, the Scenic Hudson case was the birth of the modern environmental movement.

The Sloop *Clearwater*

As part of the Storm King struggle, famed folksinger Pete Seeger raised the funds to build the sloop *Clearwater*. A faithful wooden reproduction of the broad-beamed Hudson River sloops that once carried the commerce of the region, the *Clearwater* is 106 feet long and 108 feet high, with 4,000 square feet of sail area. She was launched on May 17, 1969. Since then, the *Clearwater* has been part of every significant battle to protect the Hudson, providing advocacy and leadership and taking legal action when necessary. Today the *Clearwater* cruises from Albany to New York Harbor and Long Island Sound, bringing environmental awareness and activism to anyone willing to listen. More than 500,000 people have participated in the sloop's onboard environmental education programs. The *Clearwater* mission continues to this day, still very actively supported by Pete Seeger. The *Clearwater's* annual Great Hudson River Revival Festival at Croton Point every June is a major event attracting some 20,000 people. To learn more about the sloop (including how to go for a sail), contact: Hudson River Sloop *Clearwater*, 112 Little Market Street, Poughkeepsie, NY 12601, (845) 454-7673, www.clearwater.org.

Today the Hudson River still faces important long-term pollution, environmental, and development issues, but it is markedly cleaner than it was in the 1960s. The river is once again a place for recreation. There are now many more public access points, and sailing, kayaking, canoeing, and fishing are popular. The river is swimmable; there are public swimming beaches in Beacon, Kingston, and the town of Ulster and plans for more beaches in the future.

DEPRESSION AND RESURGENCE

Much of the manufacturing in the region gradually moved out as the 20th century continued. Smith Brothers stopped making cough drops in Poughkeepsie in 1972. The growth of IBM in Poughkeepsie and elsewhere in the mid-Hudson region compensated for some of the job loss—and IBM remains today a major employer. But many of the mid-Hudson towns were suffering through a difficult transitional period starting in the 1960s.

Fortunately, the region's good transportation and easy access to New York City gradually helped bring prosperity back. The tourism industry in the area was always a major part of the economy, and the region is ideally located for weekend getaways and short vacations for metro-area residents. At the same time, the region is far enough away from the metro area to keep it from becoming a suburb and many areas remain largely rural. The mid–Hudson Valley has become the land of the weekend house and the weekend getaway—and a large service industry built around weekenders.

The empty storefronts and large, old industrial buildings in places such as Beacon, Hudson, and Kingston created a vacuum that began to be filled starting in the 1980s. As studio space for artists became increasingly expensive and unavailable in New York City, artists looked up the river and saw airy, well-lit, cheap space. They moved in and were joined by others who renovated buildings, opened restaurants and shops, and began a revitalization in the Hudson Valley that continues with great success. Dia:Beacon, the museum of contemporary art, opened in the former Nabisco printing plant in Beacon in 2003—a major symbol of the vibrant cultural scene in the region. High-tech industry continues to be a growing presence, and farmers are benefiting from the resurgence of interest in locally grown produce and from strong community support for open space. While serious issues of overdevelopment and pollution remain, the mid–Hudson Valley moves forward today with renewed vigor.

HUDSON VALLEY MANSIONS AND HISTORIC SITES: EAST SIDE OF THE HUDSON

The history of the Hudson Valley is very much the history of America, from the earliest explorers to the present day. Henry Hudson first sailed up the great river that now bears his name in 1607. Dutch and English settlement followed soon after. By the late 1600s the Hudson was a busy commercial highway, lined with prosperous farms and industrious villages. By the 1700s the Hudson had become militarily important as a route to Canada. During the Revolutionary War, the Hudson Valley was strategically crucial. It was the site of numerous military engagements, including the Battle of Saratoga in 1777 (a major turning point). After the war, growth continued. The long-term impact of historic land grants during the Dutch and English colonial period, along with easy access to the river on the east side, made this side of the river into an area of large agricultural estates. As railroads and steamboats made the area easily accessible from New York City, the mid–Hudson Valley became fashionable among the wealthy of New York City, who built summer homes here.

A surprising number of historic structures remain in the area, and of those, a surprising number are open to the public on a regular basis, making historic tourism one of the biggest draws in the mid–Hudson Valley. On the east bank in Columbia, Dutchess, and Putnam Counties, the Valley contains some of the oldest homes in the country. The Madam Brett Homestead in Beacon, for instance, dates back to 1709. Numerous Revolutionary War sites, such as Mount Gulian and the Van Wyck Homestead, dot the region. Historic mansions, such as Clermont, Montgomery Place, and the Franklin D. Roosevelt home, line the river, and well-preserved historic districts, such as the village of Kinderhook, let visitors walk in the footsteps of history.

Price Code

Most of the historic sites in the region charge visitors a nominal fee. Few ask for more than $5 per person. In many cases kids, students, and seniors can enter for a reduced fee; be sure to ask when paying. In the entries below, the absence of a dollar sign means the site is free or asks only for a voluntary donation.

$	$5 or less
$$	over $5 to $10
$$$	over $10

Access

Almost all the places listed here are fully accessible for those with mobility handicaps. Sites that have only partial or limited access are noted.

COLUMBIA COUNTY

Austerlitz

STEEPLETOP
East Hill Road
(518) 392-3103
www.millaysociety.org
My candle burns at both ends/It will not last the night;/But ah, my foes, and oh, my friends—/It gives a lovely light. Poet Edna St. Vincent Millay wrote those famous lines in 1920, when she was just

28 and already famed for both her poetry and her often scandalous personal life. She won the Pulitzer Prize for poetry in 1923 and purchased Steepletop, a 600-acre old farm in the hamlet of Austerlitz, in 1925. With her husband Eugene Boissevain (who died in 1949), Millay created beautiful gardens on the grounds, including a lovely sunken rose garden. Millay died at Steepletop in 1950 and is buried on the grounds. The property is now a National Historic Landmark. In 2006, New York State acquired more than 400 acres of the Steepletop land and protected them as part of the Harvey Mountain State Forest. A pilgrimage here gives real insight into a major source of Millay's poetry. The house and grounds are preserved much as Millay left them, but the buildings aren't open to the public. The grounds and gardens, including The Poetry Trail leading to the grave site, are—but call first.

Germantown

CLERMONT STATE HISTORIC SITE $
One Clermont Avenue
(518) 537-4240
www.friendsofclermont.org

The Clermont estate goes back to 1728, when Robert Livingston Jr. inherited a tract of 13,000 acres along the Hudson from his father. The Manor of Livingston, as it was known, was the second-largest private landholding in colonial America. It was enlarged even more when Robert's only child, Robert R. Livingston, married Margaret Beekman, heiress to vast tracts in Dutchess and Ulster Counties. Robert and Margaret produced the most famous Livingston of all: Robert R. Livingston Jr., who was a member of the committee that helped draft the Declaration of Independence. As Chancellor of the State of New York, he administered the oath of office to George Washington and later served as the first Secretary of State. Chancellor Livingston was the financial backer for Robert Fulton's experiments in steam power. In 1897, Fulton's boat *Clermont* sailed from New York City to Albany in 36 hours (with an overnight stop at the manor), beginning a transportation revolution. The original Georgian

manor at Clermont was burned during the Revolutionary War; between 1779 and 1782, Margaret had it rebuilt. After her death in 1800, the house underwent a number of additions and alterations over the next 120 years, culminating in a Colonial Revival remodeling in 1920. In 1962, Alice Delafield Clarkson Livingston, the last Mrs. Livingston to live on the estate, deeded the house and most of the property to the State of New York; an additional 71 acres were deeded to the state by her daughter in 1991, bringing the total to about 500 acres. Clermont today is a National Historic Landmark. The home appears much as it did in the 1930s, decorated with three centuries' worth of Livingston possessions, including fine furniture, art, china, and many other lovely objects. The gardens at Clermont are as historic as the house. The gardens on the east side of the house incorporate the terrace where Margaret Beekman Livingston had her garden in the 18th century; the Lilac Walk was planted by Edward P. Livingston in the 1820s. The four formal gardens are the creation of Alice Delafield Clarkson Livingston. They're in various states of restoration—the Walled Garden and the Wilderness Garden are complete, but work by volunteers continues on the South Spring Garden and the Cutting Garden. Clermont hosts the Chancellor's Sheep and Wool Showcase every April along with a number of other special events and exhibits throughout the year. The house at Clermont is open by guided tour only on Saturdays and Sundays, 11:00 a.m. to 4:00 p.m. between November and March and from 11:00 a.m. to 5:00 p.m. every day except Monday between April and October. The last tour starts 30 minutes before closing time. The grounds are open every day from 8:30 a.m. to sunset.

Hudson

FASNY MUSEUM OF FIREFIGHTING
117 Harry Howard Avenue
(877) 347-3687
www.fasnyfiremuseum.com

Visitors to the Museum of Firefighting experience 300 years of firefighting in just a few hours. The museum was founded in 1923 with 2,600 square feet of exhibit space and four antique fire engines. After several additions over the years, the museum has grown to 50,000 square feet and one of the largest collections of firefighting apparatus, equipment, gear, and memorabilia in the world. Kids love this museum because they can climb onto some of the equipment and are allowed to handle some objects and even ring fire bells. If you don't have kids in tow, the museum is still well worth a visit to see the beautifully restored fire apparatus and excellent displays. Open seven days a week from 10:00 a.m. to 5:00 p.m.; closed Easter, Thanksgiving, and Christmas.

OLANA STATE HISTORIC SITE

The Moorish-style home of Hudson River School painter Frederic Church is open to the public. See the Art in the Valley chapter for details.

Kinderhook

COLUMBIA COUNTY MUSEUM
5 Albany Avenue
(518) 758-9265
www.cchsny.org

The sites managed by the Columbia County Historical Society cover four centuries of history. The Columbia County Museum is the youngest—it was originally a Masonic temple built in 1916. Today the building houses the offices of the Columbia County Historical Society, a research library, and exhibition spaces. The exhibits on local history are well executed and provide a useful background for visiting the other sites— Van Alen House, Ichabod Crane Schoolhouse, and Vanderpoel House. Open seasonally from Memorial Day weekend through the first week in November, Monday, Thursday, Friday, and Saturday, 10:00 a.m. to 4:00 p.m., and Sunday noon to 4:00 p.m.

JAMES VANDERPOEL HOUSE $
16 Broad Street (Route 9)
(518) 758-9265
www.cchsny.org

Built around 1820, the Vanderpoel House is a

The historic and charming village of Kinderhook dates back to the early 1600s, soon after Henry Hudson first explored the area in 1609. The central area of the village contains an exceptionally well-preserved collection of 18th- and 19th-century architecture that was placed on the National Register of Historic Places in 1974. Information for a self-guided walking tour of the village is available at www.kinderhookconnection.com. For a driving tour, check www.kinderhook-ny.gov.

distinguished example of the Federal period architecture that displaced the earlier Dutch style in the Hudson Valley. The house is beautifully proportioned, with an elegant curved staircase in the entry hall. James Vanderpoel was a prominent local lawyer and politician. The house and its furnishings preserve the fashionable lifestyle of a prosperous family in the early 19th century. Open seasonally from Memorial Day weekend to Labor Day weekend, Thursday through Saturday, 10:00 a.m. to 4:00 p.m., and Sunday noon to 4:00 p.m.

LUYKAS VAN ALEN HOUSE AND
ICHABOD CRANE SCHOOLHOUSE $
Route 9H, just south of the village
(518) 758-9265
www.cchsny.org

The Dutch heritage of the Hudson Valley is preserved in this 18th-century rural farmhouse. The traditional Dutch architecture features parapet gables, Dutch doors, entrance stoops, and large fireplaces in every room. The site was designated a National Historic Landmark in 1968. The Ichabod Crane Schoolhouse is a 19th-century building that was in use into the 1940s. It takes its name from the schoolteacher in Washington Irving's famous 1820 story "The Legend of Sleepy Hollow." The character was said to be modeled on a Kinderhook schoolteacher named Jesse Merwin, who was a friend of Irving. The one-room schoolhouse was moved to the Van Alen property in 1974 and is restored to its 1920s appearance. Open seasonally from Memorial Day weekend to Labor Day weekend, Thursday through Saturday, 10:00 a.m. to 4:00 p.m., and Sunday noon to 4:00 p.m.

MARTIN VAN BUREN NATIONAL HISTORIC SITE $

Route 9H

(518) 758-9689

www.nps.gov/mava

The first U.S. president to be born under the flag of the United States, Martin Van Buren was born in Kinderhook in 1782 into a family of Dutch farmers. Starting out as a lawyer in 1804, he rose through the ranks of local politics and became a U.S. senator for New York in 1821. He helped form the Democratic Party, managed Andrew Jackson's successful 1828 presidential campaign, and served as vice president under Jackson from 1833 to 1837. Elected as the eighth president in 1836, Van Buren continued Jackson's policies of opposition to the extension of slavery. He lost to William Henry Harrison in the election of 1840. In 1848 he ran for president again as the Free-Soil candidate. His defeat was the end of his political career. After leaving the presidency, Van Buren came back to Kinderhook to Lindenwald, an estate of more than 220 acres he had purchased in 1839. The house started out in 1797 with Georgian-style architecture but was extensively remodeled over the years by Van Buren, including an elaborate new Romanesque front porch, a four-story brick tower at the back, and a mural-like hunting scene in the front hall made with 51 imported French wallpaper panels. Van Buren lived at Lindenwald until his death in 1862. The property changed hands many times after that and ended up as a National Historic Site in the 1970s. Though many of the original furnishings were scattered, the house is restored to the period of Van Buren's occupancy. Open seasonally from mid-May to the end of October, every day from 9:00 a.m. to 4:00 p.m. Guided tours begin on the hour. The grounds are open at no charge every day year-round from 7:00 a.m. to dusk.

Old Chatham

SHAKER MUSEUM AND LIBRARY $

88 Shaker Museum Road

(518) 794-9100

www.shakermuseumandlibrary.org

The Shakers were a Christian sect founded in England by Ann Lee in 1772. In 1774, Lee and her followers moved to New York; the New Lebanon colony near Old Chatham was founded in 1787 and soon became the physical and spiritual center of Shaker life. By 1860, some 600 followers lived here in more than 120 buildings spread over 600 acres. Over the years, however, the sect lost members and by the 1950s much of the property at New Lebanon was sold off. (Only a few followers remain and they have decided not to accept new members.) In 1950, surviving members of the colony donated thousands of objects and documents to the newly formed Shaker Museum and Library in Old Chatham. The artifacts represent more than two centuries of Shaker history, including furniture, decorative arts, textiles, and many objects from daily life and work. All show the beautiful simplicity and fine crafting that characterize Shaker culture. Today the museum holds more than 28,000 objects representing every Shaker community, making it by far the finest collection in the world. Some of the original structures in New Lebanon are dilapidated but still standing, including the remarkable 1859 Stone Barn and the 1824 Second Meeting House. Declared a National Historic Landmark District, the Mount Lebanon Shaker Village site is being restored under the auspices of the museum's Mount Lebanon Project and will eventually be open to the public. For the foreseeable future, it's closed due to construction and safety issues. The museum is open seasonally from Memorial Day weekend to mid-October. Hours are 10:00 a.m. to 5:00 p.m. daily; closed Tuesdays.

DUTCHESS COUNTY

Amenia

WETHERSFIELD ESTATE AND GARDENS
214 Pugsley Hill Road (off County Road 86)
(845) 373-8037

A little-known jewel, Wethersfield is tucked away—if it's possible to tuck 1,200 acres—in the hilly northeastern corner of Dutchess County. The estate is the former home of Chauncey Devereux Stillman. A wealthy investor and philanthropist, he was also a dedicated conservationist and *very* serious gardener. Starting with the original property (an old farm) in 1939, Stillman practiced sustainable agricultural and reforestation, bought additional land, and developed beautiful gardens in a variety of styles until his death in 1989. His art-filled Georgian brick home is in the center of a 10-acre classical Italian formal garden, complete with Renaissance sculptures. The estate grounds are open June through September on Wednesday, Friday, and Saturday, noon to 5:00 p.m. A reservation is needed to tour the house and the estate's carriage museum, but it's best to call before planning any visit—the schedule is subject to change.

i An excellent free guide detailing six historic and scenic driving tours is available from Dutchess County Tourism: (800) 445-3131; www.DutchessTourism.com.

Annandale-on-Hudson

MONTGOMERY PLACE $$
Annandale Road and Route 9G
(845) 758-5461
www.hudsonvalley.org

The landscaping genius of Andrew Jackson Downing and the architectural genius of Alexander Jackson Davis combined in 1842 to make Montgomery Place a magnificent showplace of American vernacular design. The story begins much earlier, however. In 1775 General Richard Montgomery, a Hudson Valley native, was killed in the battle for Quebec, thus becoming the first hero of the American Revolution. In 1802, his widow Janet bought a working farm on the Hudson near Red Hook and built herself a Federal-style house she called Chateau de Montgomery. The house was located at the end of a half-mile-long allée of trees. Janet built the farm into a prosperous enterprise. When she died in 1828 the property passed to her brother Edward Livingston, who was, among other accomplishments, Secretary of State under Andrew Jackson. Edward and his wife Louise renamed the estate Montgomery Place and used it as a summer residence. During the 40 years Louise presided over the estate, she oversaw a major renovation beginning in 1842, and her daughter, Coralie Livingston Barton, oversaw a second renovation starting in 1860. Andrew Jackson Davis was hired both times to expand and rebuild the original house. Davis added two wings, verandas, and details such as balustrades, converting Janet's original design into a more contemporary and romantic look. Davis also added a number of informal outbuildings. Also in the 1840s, famed landscape architect Andrew Jackson Downing was brought in to consult on the gardens and grounds. Under his direction, walkways were laid out and statuary, rustic benches, water features, and numerous specimen plants were installed. After the death of Coralie in 1873, Montgomery Place was occupied by a series of Livingston relatives. In 1921 the estate passed to General John Ross Delafield and his wife Violetta, who thoroughly renovated the house and made extensive changes and additions to the gardens and grounds. In 1986, Delafield descendants turned the estate, along with 434 acres of gardens and orchards, over to the preservation organization Historic Hudson Valley. It was opened to the public in 1988. Today Montgomery Place is considered one of the finest and best-preserved of all the famed Hudson River great estates. The historic house is filled with fine furniture, antiques, artwork, and two centuries of Livingston family memorabilia. The grounds are simply magnificent, with unparalleled views of the Hudson. In 2006, the house was closed for

 **Close-up**

Davis and Downing in the Hudson Valley

Alexander Jackson Davis (1803–1892) and Andrew Jackson Downing (1815–1852) were two of the most successful and influential architects of the 19th century. The two AJDs combined forces in the 1840s and had a massive and lasting impact on American home and landscape design. Davis began his career in New York City as an architectural illustrator and transitioned into designing buildings, typically in the classical Greek Revival style. In 1835 Davis wrote and illustrated *Rural Residences,* an architectural pattern book that contained plans for Gothic Revival homes. The book was very influential—Gothic Revival, with its gables, verandas, and towers, became very fashionable. (Because the decorative trim designs could be created by a skilled woodworker, the style also came to be called Carpenter Gothic.) Downing, a Newburgh native, began his career as a landscape architect—in fact, he is considered the originator of the profession. Downing created naturalistic landscapes that incorporated features of the terrain, such as rock outcroppings, and artfully designed vistas that improved on nature. His 1841 book, *Treatise and Practice of Landscape Gardening,* was very influential; it moved American garden and landscape design away from more formal classical styles and toward a simpler vernacular approach. The book brought him not only fame but many landscaping commissions. For his next book, Downing teamed up with Davis to write and illustrate *Cottage Residences,* a powerfully influential book that has remained in print to this day. The Gothic Revival style they advocated was highly decorative, with elaborate gables and chimneys and plenty of gingerbread work, but it was also practical. The designs utilized simple building materials (batten and board, for example) and methods that were readily accessible to people of modest means. The homes were airy and incorporated modern conveniences; they were designed to harmonize with, not dominate, rural environments. Downing died young in a tragic steamboat accident, but not before he had recruited the young Calvert Vaux as his assistant. Vaux and his partner Frederic Law Olmstead went on to incorporate Downing's ideas into their landscape designs, most notably Central Park in New York City and the grounds of the White House. The Hudson Valley still abounds in Davis and Downing buildings and landscapes. Many are in private hands, but a number are now historic sites open to the public. In the mid–Hudson Valley, the most notable are Montgomery Place in Annandale-on-Hudson, Locust Grove and Springside in Poughkeepsie, and the Dutch Reformed Church in Newburgh. Davis's masterful Lyndhurst, considered one of the finest extant Gothic Revival residences, is in Tarrytown in Westchester County. Easily visible but not open to the public are the Delamater House in Rhinebeck and Blithewood Mansion (now the Levy Economics Institute) and the gatehouse on Annandale Road at Bard College in Annandale-on-Hudson.

needed restoration and a complete reinterpretation of its history and exhibits; it will reopen in 2010. The grounds and outbuildings remain open and are well worth visiting even if you can't go into the house. Picnicking is encouraged. In season, you can purchase fresh fruit from the estate at the Montgomery Place Orchards farm stand. Montgomery Place is open May to October, Saturday and Sunday only, from 10:00 a.m. to 5:00 p.m.

Beacon

HOWLAND CULTURAL CENTER
477 Main Street
(845) 831-4988
www.howlandculturalcenter.org
Noted American architect Richard Morris Hunt (best known for designing the Metropolitan Museum of Art in New York City and a number of mansions in Newport, Rhode Island) designed the Howland Cultural Center, completed in 1872.

From the start, Civil War general Joseph I Iowland and other community leaders planned it as a public library and community cultural resource for the village of Matteawan (as Beacon was then called). The building is a good example of Stick Style, a highly decorative style influenced by medieval architecture—it became very popular in Victorian times largely because of Hunt's influence. Howland has six gables, a blue slate roof, and walls of elaborately decorative brick. An unusual interior dome soars to nearly 34 feet. The beautifully crafted wooden floors, walls, and ceiling of the dome make this space acoustically excellent, with a wonderful warm sound that's particularly well suited for chamber music. On its centennial in 1972, the building was placed on the National Register of Historic Places. Today the center offers an active program of concerts, recitals, plays, readings, and other cultural events (the books were moved to a new library in 1976). The building is usually open during regular business hours and for events, but check the online schedule or call first to be sure you can get in.

MADAM BRETT HOMESTEAD $
50 Van Nydeck Avenue
(845) 831-6533

The original portion of the Madam Brett Homestead dates back to about 1709, making it the oldest home in Dutchess County. It was built by Catheryna and Roger Brett. Madam Brett was the daughter of Francis Rombout, one of the three original Dutch patentees in what's now southern Dutchess County. Madam Brett was widowed at a young age, but she raised two sons and became a successful businesswoman, living to the age of 77 and dying in 1764. The homestead was occupied for nearly 250 years by seven successive generations of Brett descendants. During the Revolutionary War, the house was a depot for supplies and a shelter for soldiers; George Washington, the Marquis de Lafayette, and Baron von Steuben all visited. By 1954, however, the house was scheduled for demolition to make way for a supermarket. It was rescued by the local chapter of the Daughters of the American Revolution and turned into a museum. The 17-room house has

a roof of handmade scalloped wood shingles, sloped dormers, and a native stone foundation. Inside, the original furnishings include porcelain and 18th- and 19th-century furniture. The grounds include an herb garden and a formal garden. Open April through October, Wednesday through Monday, 10:00 a.m. to 5:00 p.m.; open in November on weekends, 10:00 a.m. to 4:30 p.m., and the first two weekends in December, noon to 5:00 p.m.

MOUNT GULIAN HISTORIC SITE $
145 Sterling Street
(845) 831-8172
www.mountgulian.org

Mount Gulian is the restored colonial homestead of the Verplanck family. Abraham Verplanck arrived in New Netherlands from Holland sometime between 1633 and 1638. He prospered as a trader in fur, tobacco, and other products. In 1683, his son Gulian and two partners purchased 85,000 acres in the Hudson Valley around what is now Fishkill and Beacon from the local Wappinger Indians. Around 1730, the family built a country retreat on the land overlooking the river and named it Mount Gulian in honor of their illustrious for bear. During the Revolutionary War, the Verplancks turned the home over to the Continental Army, and it became the headquarters for General Friedrich von Steuben. At the war's end, von Steuben and some other officers created the Society of the Cincinnati—America's first fraternal veterans' association. Over the years the house underwent expansion and renovation with the addition of new wings, barns and other outbuildings, and extensive gardens. It was occupied continuously by members of the Verplanck family until 1931, when the house was destroyed by an arson fire. Many of the furnishings and other valuables were saved and kept by family members, but the house remained an overgrown ruin until 1965, when a restoration project began with the assistance of Verplanck family members, local residents, and members of the Society of the Cincinnati. Today the house, with its graceful gambrel roof and four capped chimneys, looks much as it did in 1783, when it was von Steuben's headquarters. Historical exhibits and some original furnishings fill the rooms. A restored 18th-century Dutch barn is near the house. Volunteers are slowly restoring the gardens to their former glory; an easy 1.5-mile loop trail runs through the grounds and offers great views over the Hudson. To time your visit with one of the Revolutionary War historical reenactment events held at the site, check the calendar for schedules. Open for tours from the end of April to the end of October, Wednesday, Thursday, Friday, and Sunday, 1:00 to 5:00 p.m. The last tour starts at 4:00 p.m. **Note:** Mount Gulian is in the middle of the Hudson View Park Apartments complex—to get to the site, drive through the complex, ignoring the signs about private property.

i The Society of the Cincinnati was founded at Mount Gulian on May 13, 1783, as America's first veterans' association. The first members were all commissioned officers of the Continental Army and Navy. George Washington was the Society's President General from 1783 until his death in 1799. The Society lives on as an organization for direct male descendants of the original officers. Today it is a nonprofit organization supporting educational, cultural, and literary activities and promoting the ideals of liberty, heritage, and constitutional government.

Fishkill
VAN WYCK HOMESTEAD MUSEUM
504 Route 9
(845) 896-9560

In 1732 Cornelius Van Wyck purchased 959 acres in Fishkill from the redoubtable Madam Brett (see Madam Brett Homestead listing earlier in this chapter). He built a three-room Dutch-style house on the land; later he added another wing. During the Revolutionary War, the house was used as a military headquarters and supply center; 70 acres around the house were used as an encampment for more than 2,000 troops. Many notables spent

the night, including George Washington, John Jay, and Alexander Hamilton. After the war, the Van Wycks returned; descendants lived in the house for another 150 years while its history gradually faded. The house was sold out of the family in 1882. In 1962, the owners donated the building—the last remaining structure of the old encampment—and an acre of land to the Fishkill Historical Society. The house was placed on the National Register of Historic Places in 1972. In 1974, the encampment area around the house became the Dutchess Mall. The history wasn't entirely lost, however. Archaeological excavations and the mall construction turned up numerous artifacts; many are now on display at the restored house. Open Memorial Day through October on Saturday and Sunday, 1:00 to 4:00 p.m.

Hyde Park
HOME OF FRANKLIN D. ROOSEVELT
NATIONAL HISTORIC SITE $$$
4097 Albany Post Road (Route 9)
(845) 229-9115
www.nps.gov/hofr

The family home of Franklin Delano Roosevelt is one of the most significant and moving historic sites in the Hudson Valley. A visit here provides insight into the life and times of the extraordinary man who led America through the Great Depression and World War II. Roosevelt donated Springwood, the house where he was born and raised, and where he returned often throughout his life, to the nation in 1943. Springwood is preserved today much as it appeared at Roosevelt's death in 1945. Although the Roosevelt family was wealthy and the house is substantial, it is modest and unostentatious, particularly in comparison to the neighboring Vanderbilt estate (also listed in this chapter). The entrance is through a columned portico flanked by a fieldstone terrace with balustrade. Roosevelt stood on this terrace four times to acknowledge the crowds that came after each presidential election (although he never carried staunchly Republican Dutchess County or even the town of Hyde Park). The ground floor rooms include the art-filled entry hall, Dresden Room parlor, and formal dining room, along with the large combined living room and library that was the real center of life at Springwood. Roosevelt often worked at a desk in this room. Upstairs are several bedrooms, including Roosevelt's boyhood room, and rooms where notables such as Winston Churchill and King George VI stayed. In Roosevelt's lifetime, Springwood was operated as a working farm. On his income tax forms, Roosevelt always listed his occupation as tree farmer. The grounds today cover 290 acres, including some fields that are still cut for hay. The Rose Garden near the house contains the simple graves of both Franklin and Eleanor. Tiny tombstones mark the graves of Roosevelt's beloved dogs Chief and Fala. A visit to the FDR Home begins with the purchase of a ticket at the **Henry A. Wallace Visitor and Education Center**. (Wallace was secretary of agriculture from 1933 to 1940 and vice president during FDR's third term.) The ticket includes admission to the house and the FDR Presidential Library and Museum (the next listing). An attractive, airy building with fieldstone walls and high wooden gables, the center is a modern (2003) version of traditional Hudson Valley architecture. A movie theater shows an excellent short film about FDR. The center also has the New Deal Store, with an outstanding offering of books related to FDR, and Mrs. Nesbitt's Café, a very pleasant spot for lunch or a snack. (Mrs. Henrietta Nesbitt, a Hyde Park native, was the Roosevelts' cook for 12 years at the White House.) Look for the delightful bronze statue of Eleanor and Franklin on the terrace near the cafe. The site is open year-round, seven days a week; it's closed Thanksgiving, Christmas, and New Year's Day. The buildings are open from 9:00 a.m. to 5:00 p.m.; the grounds are open dawn to dusk. Springwood can be seen only by guided tours led by park rangers. The tour takes about an hour; the last tour of the day starts at 4:00 p.m. A tram shuttle is offered seasonally from May through October. The cafe is open every day from April through October, 10:00 a.m. to 4:00 p.m. The FDR site is very popular. During the peak months of July, August, and October and on holiday weekends, the tours often sell out. Make an advance reservation if you can: (877) 444-6777 or www.recreation.gov.

FRANKLIN D. ROOSEVELT PRESIDENTIAL LIBRARY AND MUSEUM $$$
4079 Albany Post Road (Route 9)
(800) FDR-VISIT or (845) 486-7770
www.fdrlibrary.marist.edu

The first presidential library, and the only one to be used by a sitting president, the FDR Library and Museum was designed by FDR himself and opened in 1941. The Dutch Colonial–style building contains FDR's private study, preserved as he left it in 1945. Displays in the museum portion of the building detail Roosevelt's life, including material from his early years, and outstanding exhibits on the Great Depression, New Deal, and World War II. The Eleanor Roosevelt Gallery details the inspiring life of the woman often called "First Lady of the World." A highlight is FDR's 1936 Ford Phaeton, specially outfitted with hand controls that allowed the president to drive despite his paralyzed legs. The library portion of the building contains more than 17 million pages of documents, including the papers of President and Mrs. Roosevelt and many of their associates, along with an extensive collection of photos and audiovisual materials and a significant collection of books related to the Roosevelts. The library and museum are open from 9:00 a.m. to 5:00 p.m. every day except Thanksgiving, Christmas, and New Year's Day. Admission is by ticket purchased at the Wallace Center—see the previous listing for the Home of Franklin D. Roosevelt for details.

TOP COTTAGE $$
FDR built Top Cottage in 1938 on a hilltop at the easternmost end of his estate. Designed by FDR himself in the Dutch Colonial style, it was his private retreat. It is quite possibly the first home in America designed from the start to be wheelchair accessible. In 1939, FDR famously hosted a cookout here for King George VI, Queen Elizabeth, and 150 other dignitaries. Hot dogs were served— on silver trays. After Franklin's death, the cottage passed through various hands until it was acquired by the Beaverkill Conservancy in 1996.

It became part of the Home of FDR National Historic Site in 2001. Top Cottage is open to visitors from May to October, Thursday through Monday. Access to the site is by shuttle bus only. Purchase tickets and board the shuttle bus at the Wallace Center (see the listing for the Home of FDR).

i The modest headquarters for the National Park Service at the FDR home is Bellefield, the former home of Thomas and Sarah Newbold (the property is now part of the historic site campus). The garden at Bellefield was designed in 1912 by Beatrix Farrand, one of the finest American landscape architects. Restored and maintained by volunteers, the charming garden, designed as three outdoor "rooms," is free and open to the public daily from dawn to dusk. For more information: (845) 229-5320; www.beatrixfarrandgarden.org.

VAL-KILL, ELEANOR ROOSEVELT NATIONAL HISTORIC SITE $$
Valkill Park Road and Route 9G
(845) 229-9422
www.nps.gov/elro

The only National Park Service site dedicated to a First Lady, Val-Kill was the home of Eleanor Roosevelt from 1945 to her death in 1962. The original Dutch Colonial–style stone cottage was built in 1925 on what was then the Roosevelt estate as a residence for Eleanor's friends Nancy Cook and Marion Dickerman. The house was christened Val-Kill after the Dutch name of nearby Fall Creek. In 1926 a larger building went up to house Val-Kill Industries, a small factory that employed local residents to manufacture replicas of Early American furniture. When the operation folded in 1936 under the weight of the Great Depression, the factory was converted to an apartment and several guest rooms to accommodate the overflow at Springwood, the main Roosevelt home, and as a refuge for Eleanor during the hectic presidential years. After FDR's death in 1945, Eleanor converted Val-Kill into a modest home and moved in permanently. It

was the only home that was ever entirely hers. During the rest of her active life, Eleanor traveled widely on behalf of the United Nations and humanitarian causes. She entertained many notables at Val-Kill, including Nikita Khrushchev, Jawaharlal Nehru, and John F. Kennedy. After her death, the furniture and contents of the cottage were dispersed and the property changed hands several times. In 1970, concerned citizens in the area united to preserve the property; it became a national historical site in 1977. Today the cottage has been restored to its appearance in 1962. Many of the original furnishings have been returned, including the 1950s Philco television, several pieces of Val-Kill furniture, and many mementoes of Eleanor's career and family. Val-Kill is open daily, May through October, from 9:00 a.m. to 5:00 p.m. From November through April, the site is closed on Tuesday and Wednesday. It is closed on Thanksgiving, Christmas, and New Year's Day. The house is seen only by guided tour, which takes about 45 minutes. The last tour of the day is at 4:00 p.m. Visitors can drive to Val-Kill directly (it's about 2 miles from the FDR home) or

i Thursday through Monday between May and October, Metro-North and the National Park Service join forces to offer a convenient package deal for visiting the Roosevelt sites in Hyde Park. Visitors take the Metro-North Hudson Line to the Poughkeepsie station, where a NPS van meets them at 11:00 a.m. and takes them to the nearby Roosevelt home and museum. In the afternoon, the van goes to Val-Kill and Top Cottage and then brings visitors back to the train station in time to catch the 5:30 p.m. departure to Grand Central Terminal. The entire trip is wheelchair accessible. The cost is $22 per person; kids under 16 are free. Note that the fee includes admission to all sites but does not cover train fare or lunch. For more information and to make a reservation, contact the NPS at (845) 229-5320 or visit the Web site of Historic Hyde Park at www.historichydepark.org.

take a free shuttle bus from the Wallace Center at the FDR home (see separate listing). The grounds are open at no charge daily year-round from dawn to dusk.

VANDERBILT MANSION NATIONAL HISTORIC SITE $$
Route 9
(845) 229-9115
www.nps.gov/vama

In 1895, Frederick William Vanderbilt (grandson of the shipping magnate Cornelius Vanderbilt) and his wife Louise bought 600 acres of land along the Hudson River in Hyde Park. They brought in the famed architectural firm of McKim, Mead and White (architects of, among other things, the original Penn Station) to build them a new mansion. The end result in 1898 was a 54-room, 55,000-square-foot masterpiece that is a perfect example of the Beaux Arts architectural style. It was also the first home in the town of Hyde Park to have electricity, generated by a hydroelectric power plant on Crum Elbow Creek. The furnishings are preserved intact—to visit here is to step back into the Gilded Age, circa 1906. It's hard to know where to look first when touring the house— everything is astonishingly ornate, starting with the arresting green and white marble cornices and pilasters of the elliptically shaped reception hall. The rooms are filled with antique furniture, tapes-tries, artwork, and *objets,* all imported from Europe and ranging over centuries of styles. Everything is on a grand scale. The dining room measures 30 by 50 feet; the floor is covered by a magnificent Ispahan oriental rug that measures 20 by 40 feet and is more than 300 years old. Visitors go up the aptly named Grand Stairway to the second floor. The highlight here is Mrs. Vanderbilt's bedroom, a reproduction of a French queen's bedroom of the Louis XV period. Commentary is superfluous. Louise died unexpectedly in 1926; Frederick lived on at the house as a near recluse, occupying some rooms on the third floor with the servants and spending most of his time indulging his love of horticulture in the formal Italianate-style gardens. He died on the estate in 1938. The Vanderbilts

were childless; the property was inherited by their niece, Margaret Van Alen. She promptly donated the mansion, furnishings, and about 220 acres of the land to the National Park Service in 1939. For decades after Frederick's death, his gardens were neglected. In 1984, volunteers began restoring the gardens to their former glory. It's an ongoing project that has accomplished a great deal—the gardens are blooming once again as an integral part of the estate. The grounds are magnificent, with sweeping carriage roads, numerous speci-men trees, and wonderful views of the Catskills across the Hudson. Vanderbilt Mansion is open to the public every day by guided tour from 9:00 a.m. to 5:00 p.m. The last tour of the day starts at 4:00 p.m. The site is closed on Thanksgiving, Christmas, and New Year's Day. The grounds are open every day at no charge from 7:00 a.m. to dusk.

Millbrook

INNISFREE GARDEN $
Tyrell Road
(845) 677-8000
www.innisfreegarden.org

Combine the ancient art of Chinese landscape design with the hilly topography of the Hudson Valley and you get Innisfree: a 150-acre public garden full of streams, waterfalls, retaining walls and berms, natural stone, and Chinese-inspired cup gardens (smaller gardens set within the larger garden), surrounding a 40-acre glacial lake. The integration of the plantings, water fea-tures, and landforms is especially impressive and beautiful. Innisfree began as the private garden of Walter and Marion Beck. In 1960 the prop-erty became the Innisfree Foundation and was opened to the public. The garden has a separate picnic area, making this a great spot for lunch and a stroll. However, the garden is not fully wheel-chair accessible. Innisfree's season runs from early May to mid-October. Hours are Wednesday, Thursday, and Friday, 10:00 a.m. to 4:00 p.m., and Saturday, Sunday, and legal holidays, 11:00 a.m. to 5:00 p.m. Closed Monday and Tuesday, except legal holidays. Dogs are not allowed.

[i] The Garden Conservancy's Open Days Program lets visitors to the Hudson Valley enjoy the many lush private gardens in the area. Participating owners open their property on selected days; the sites are chosen to be fairly close together so that several can be seen comfortably in a day. Admission to each garden is $5; reservations aren't needed. The proceeds support the national preservation work of the nonprofit Garden Conservancy. For more information: (845) 265-2029; www.garden conservancy.org.

Poughkeepsie

LOCUST GROVE, THE SAMUEL MORSE HISTORIC SITE $$

2683 South Road (Route 9)

(845) 454-4500

www.morsehistoricsite.org

One of the most handsome of the Hudson River estates, Locust Grove was the home of Samuel Finley Breese Morse, the man who invented the telegraph and the system of dots and dashes, better known as Morse code, which made the telegraph work. The 25-room Italianate mansion was designed by Alexander Jackson Davis and contains an extensive collection of American and European decorative arts and fine art. The house is situated on 150 rolling acres overlooking the river. In 1963, it became the first National Historic Site in Dutchess County. The original house at Locust Grove dates back to 1830, when the land was a farm. Morse purchased it in 1847 and hired Davis to remodel and expand the house in 1851. As might be expected from an inventor, Morse spent the rest of his life improving the landscape around the house. After he died in 1872, the family rented the house out. In 1901 it was sold to William and Martha Young, a wealthy couple from Poughkeepsie. The Youngs, aware of the historic importance of the house, preserved it very much as it had looked in Morse's time, but also added their own important collections of furniture, paintings, and ceramics. In 1975, Annette Young, William and Martha's daughter,

passed away after living 80 of her 90 years at Locust Grove. She left the house, its contents, and the land to a trust that would preserve it for the public. In 1979, Locust Grove indeed opened to the public; a visitor center was added in 2001. The 25 display rooms of Locust Grove have changed very little over the last century—the house is a time capsule of upper-crust Edwardian style. The grounds and gardens at Locust Grove are a reflection of Samuel Morse's artistic eye. He created a natural landscape in the romantic 19th-century

Queen City of the Hudson

Poughkeepsie was founded in 1687 by Dutch settlers. From 1777 to 1783, it was the capital of New York State, and in 1788 it was the site of the ratification of the U.S. Constitution by New York. Two interesting colonial structures can be visited here. The redbrick Glebe House at 635 Main Street, built in 1767, is today the headquarters of the Dutchess County Historical Society, which also owns the Clinton State House State Historic Site at 549 Main Street, a gabled fieldstone house dating to 1765 that was the center of state activity during the capital period. The house is named in tribute to George Clinton, the first governor of New York, who lived in Poughkeepsie for 21 years. Glebe House open-house days are offered throughout the year; the Clinton State House is open year-round, Tuesday through Friday, 10:00 a.m. to 3:00 p.m., by appointment only. The society also sponsors the annual Silver Ribbon Tour of historic sites and private homes every June; tickets are $35. For details: (845) 471-1630; www.dutchesscountyhistoricalsociety.org.

tradition, with stone walls, framed vistas, and places to sit and enjoy the view. (The spectacular multicolored bluff across the river is called Blue Point.) Close to the house are Victorian-style decorative gardens, a large perennial garden, and a kitchen garden that has been producing food for the estate for more than 200 years. Locust Grove hosts numerous events throughout the year, including free garden tours, concerts on the lawn, antique car shows, Civil War reenactments, and programs for kids. The schedule varies, so call or check the Web site for details. The house is open for guided tours every day from May to November, 10:00 a.m. to 3:00 p.m. The gardens and grounds are open every day year-round from 8:00 a.m. to dusk. The entire site is closed on Thanksgiving, Christmas, and New Year's Day.

Rhinebeck

WILDERSTEIN HISTORIC SITE

330 Morton Road

(845) 876-4818

www.wilderstein.org

Looking at the fanciful Queen Anne design of Wilderstein, it's hard to believe that this house started out as a restrained Italianate villa in 1852. In 1888, Robert Suckley and his wife Catherine renovated the house into its current elaborate design, adding a five-story tower topped with a candle-snuffer turret, a polychromatic paint scheme, stained-glass windows, a porte cochere, and a wide veranda that wraps around three sides of the house. The house is just as elaborate inside. It was decorated by Joseph Burr Tiffany in an eclectic (some might say chaotic) mix of historical styles, ranging from the Louis XVI salon to the Colonial Revival parlor. The grounds at Wilderstein were laid out by Calvert Vaux. He designed a planting scheme and laid out trails that take in the many spectacular Hudson views. Three generations of Suckleys lived at Wilderstein. Perhaps the most famous was Margaret "Daisy" Suckley. A confidante (and perhaps more) of her distant cousin Franklin Roosevelt, she presented Fala, FDR's beloved Scottie, to him and spent months at a time at the White House. In 1983

Daisy donated the house, its contents, and about 40 acres to Wilderstein Preservation. She lived on at the house, often greeting the many visitors, until her death in 1991 at age 99. The mansion is open from May to October, Thursday through Sunday, noon to 4:00 p.m., and on weekends in December. Try to time a visit for the annual Fala Gala in mid-September, when hundreds of Scotties and their owners converge here. The grounds and trails are open daily during daylight hours.

i The Quitman House and Palatine Farmstead in Rhinebeck preserve the early history of this historic town. In the early 1700s, German refugees from the war-wracked Palatine region (along the Rhine near the French border) emigrated to the mid–Hudson Valley area. The Palatine Homestead on Route 9 north of Rhinebeck is a farmhouse dating back to 1727; it is one of the very few surviving structures dating back to the Palatine immigrants. The nearby Quitman House was once the manse for the austerely beautiful Stone Church. It dates back to 1798 and is now the home of the Museum of History at Rhinebeck. The farmstead is being restored and is open by appointment; the Quitman House is open weekends from 2:00 to 4:00 p.m. For information: (845) 871-1798; www.quitmanpreservation.org.

Staatsburg

STAATSBURGH STATE HISTORIC SITE $

Old Post Road

(845) 889-8851

www.staatsburgh.org

A Beaux Art mansion of 65 rooms, 14 bathrooms, and 23 fireplaces, Staatsburgh was the home of Ruth Livingston Mills and her husband Ogden Mills, a noted financier and philanthropist. (In older guidebooks, this site is called Mills Mansion.) The home was designed in 1895 by McKim, Mead and White (the same firm that designed the slightly smaller Vanderbilt Mansion in Hyde Park). It was a remodeling and expansion of an existing Greek Revival house of a mere 25 rooms. The white stucco exterior is quite impressive, with a massive portico and embellishments of balustrades, pilasters, and floral swags. The interior is equally impressive. It's filled with elaborate furniture, oriental rugs, silk fabrics, and an extensive collection of antiques and *objets* from around the world. Restoration, both inside and out, is ongoing at Staatsburgh. The beautiful grounds and trails offer visitors a rare opportunity to get right down to the river. The railroad tracks that cut off many other sites run here in an inland cutting. The back lawn at Staatsburgh slopes gently down toward the Hudson; it's a favorite local spot for sledding. Staatsburgh is especially fabulous in December, when the theme is A Gilded Age Christmas—the home is elaborately decorated as it was in the Millses' time. In 1938, Gladys Mills Phipps donated the house, its contents, and 192 acres to the State of New York. The mansion is open by guided tour only from April 1 to October 31, Tuesday through Saturday, 10:00 a.m. to 5:00 p.m., and Sunday from noon to 5:00 p.m. From January 1 to March 31, the mansion is open Saturday and Sunday only, 11:00 a.m. to 4:00 p.m. From the Friday after Thanksgiving through December, call or check the Web site for the holiday schedule. The last tour begins half an hour before closing. The grounds are open daily year-round at no charge, 8:00 a.m. to dusk; picnicking is allowed. The mansion is partially accessible to those with limited mobility; the picnic areas, gift shop, and scenic vistas are fully accessible.

PUTNAM COUNTY

Cold Spring

STONECROP GARDENS $$
81 Stonecrop Lane
(845) 365-2000
www.stonecrop.org
A little-known gem, Stonecrop Gardens covers approximately 12 acres on a windswept bluff 1,100 feet high in the Hudson Highlands. The numerous display gardens are quite diverse and include woodland and water gardens, a grass

---

Springside National Historic Site

Springside National Historic Site (Route 9 and Academy Street, Poughkeepsie) preserves the remnants of one of Andrew Jackson Downing's last landscape designs, a property designed for Matthew Vassar in 1851. Downing incorporated natural landscape elements into a parklike area with curving pathways that direct the eye to scenic views. The grand villa Downing designed for the property was never built. Numerous other structures in the Gothic Revival style, with board-and-batten siding, gables, steep roofs, and ornamental chimneys, were constructed. Of them all, only the Gatehouse remains; somewhat modified from its original design, it is now a private residence. Twenty acres of Springside were saved from development in 1984. Much of the landscaping was overgrown, but volunteers have cleared the walkways and are slowly restoring the design. The site is free and open to the public daily, 8:00 a.m. to dusk. For information about guided tours, contact Springside Landscape Restoration (845-454-2060; www.home.att .net/~hannahb/springside).

---

garden, a gravel garden, and an enclosed English-style flower garden. Stonecrop is an enjoyable place to stroll and admire. It's also a serious educational resource with a staff of professional horticulturists. Stonecrop is open to visitors April 1 through October 31, Monday through Friday, the first and third Saturdays, and selected Sundays, 10:00 a.m. to 5:00 p.m.

Garrison

BOSCOBEL RESTORATION $$

1601 Route 9D
(845) 265-3638
www.boscobel.org

Boscobel is an elegant Federal-style mansion filled with one of the nation's leading collections of furniture and decorative arts from the Federal period (see the Art in the Valley chapter for more information). The house was originally located in Montrose, about 15 miles south of the present location. When a Veterans Administration hospital was built on the property in the 1950s, the mansion was declared surplus and sold at auction to a demolition contractor for $35. The beautiful front façade and many other exterior and interior architectural details were torn out and sold. In a last-ditch effort, funds were raised to purchase the remains of the house, repurchase the parts that had been sold, and disassemble and store the whole thing. In 1956, Boscobel Restoration purchased 25 acres with a sweeping view of the Hudson in Garrison. The house was reassembled at its new home and opened to the public in 1961. A major redecoration in the 1970s transformed Boscobel into the historically accurate showcase it is today. The grounds here offer breathtaking views of the Hudson River and

ℹ️ Hudson River Heritage is a nonprofit organization committed to preserving the historic architecture and landscapes of the mid–Hudson Valley. HRH is the steward for the Hudson River National Historic Landmark District, a 32-square-mile area that stretches 20 miles from Staatsburg to Clermont. In early October HRH sponsors the annual Country Seats Tour. The self-guided tour is a rare opportunity to see some of the historic private homes in the area. Tickets are $50 and sell out quickly. For details, contact HRH: (845) 876-2474; www.hudsonriverheritage.org.

Hudson Highlands. On the second Tuesday of each month, Boscobel opens its grounds to artists and photographers at no charge. Boscobel is also the home of the Hudson Valley Shakespeare Theater (see the Performing Arts and Film chapter for details).

MANITOGA/THE RUSSEL WRIGHT DESIGN CENTER $$$

584 Route 9D
(845) 424-3812
www.russelwrightcenter.org

Russel Wright was one of the leading designers of the 20th century. His inexpensive, mass-produced housewares, including furniture, dinnerware, appliances, and textiles, were innovative, attractive, informal, and very popular from the 1930s to the 1950s. Today they're still collected as decorative art objects. Russel Wright and his wife Mary purchased the 75 acres of former quarry that became Manitoga (Algonquin for "Place of the Great Spirit") in 1942. In 1952, after Mary's death, Russel began to restore and design the landscape while also slowly building his new home, Dragon Rock. The house is built into the quarry hillside and overlooks a pond that was once the quarry pit. Huge windows and terraces opening out from each room blend the indoors and the outdoors. A huge uncut cedar trunk supports the main roof. Dragon Rock and the area immediately around the house are open to the public by guided tour only from April through October, Thursday and Friday at 11:00 a.m. and Saturday and Sunday at 11:00 a.m. and 1:30 p.m. Tours are limited to 10 people and reservations are required. Because the tour involves walking on trails, wear comfortable shoes and dress appropriately. The site is not wheelchair accessible; visitors with mobility issues may have difficulty here. Four miles of hiking paths meander through the grounds at Manitoga and connect with the Appalachian Trail. For more on enjoying the grounds here, see the Parks and the Outdoors chapter.

HUDSON VALLEY MANSIONS AND HISTORIC SITES: WEST SIDE OF THE HUDSON

The west side of the Hudson River may not have the stately homes found across the river, but the area abounds in historic sites. Many, such as the stone houses found in New Paltz and elsewhere, reflect a rich Dutch and Huguenot heritage dating back to the late 1600s. Other sites, such as Washington's Headquarters in Newburgh, preserve the history of the Revolutionary War here. Others, such as the remains of the Delaware & Hudson Canal and several restored lighthouses, preserve the area's important industrial and shipping history. And some places, such as the historic city of Kingston, preserve the long, intricate story of the Hudson Valley, from the earliest settlement to this day. Visiting these historic sites along the Hudson River brings history alive, all against the backdrop of the beautiful Catskill Mountains.

Price Code

Most of the historic sites in the region charge visitors a nominal fee. Few ask for more than $5 per person. In many cases kids, students, and seniors can enter for a reduced fee; be sure to ask when paying. In the entries below, the absence of a dollar sign means the site is free or asks only for a voluntary donation.

$	$5 or less
$$	over $5 to $10
$$$	over $10

i The blue historical markers that are found in abundance along roadsides and in rest areas throughout the mid–Hudson Valley were placed by the New York Department of Education's state history office from 1926 to 1966. The markers commemorate important moments, often from Revolutionary times, in state history. For a database of signs organized by county, check the Web site of the New York State Museum in Albany at www.nysm.nysed.gov/historicmarkers.

Access

Almost all the places listed here are fully accessible for those with mobility handicaps. Sites that have only partial or limited access are noted.

GREENE COUNTY

Catskill

CEDAR GROVE, THE THOMAS COLE NATIONAL HISTORIC SITE $$
The Federal-style home of Thomas Cole, founder of the Hudson River School of Art, is open to the public. See the Art in the Valley chapter.

Coxsackie

BRONCK MUSEUM $
Pieter Bronck Road
(518) 731-6490
www.gchistory.org
The oldest surviving dwelling in the mid–Hudson Valley, the Pieter Bronck home is a typical Dutch farmstead dating back to 1663: It's built on land purchased from the local Mahican tribe by Pieter Bronck, a Swedish farmer, and his Dutch wife

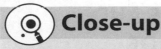 **Close-up**

The Revolutionary War in the Hudson Valley

Nearly one-third of the 300 or so battles and engagements of the Revolutionary War took place in New York State. Of those, a significant number took place in the Hudson Valley. After winning the Battle of Long Island in the spring of 1776, the British controlled New York City and Long Island. In 1777, they launched a three-pronged offensive designed to converge on Albany and gain control of the North River (as the Hudson was then called). The river was of critical strategic importance; controlling it would cut New England off from the rest of the colonies. The main attack sent General Burgoyne south from Canada through the Champlain Valley; a second prong sent Colonel Barry St. Leger east from Oswego along the Mohawk Valley; the third prong sent Sir Henry Clinton north, up the river. St. Leger ended up besieging Fort Stanwix, near present-day Rome, and was defeated by a relief column led by General Benedict Arnold (before he turned traitor). Sir Henry fought his way north up the Hudson. His ships broke through a chain laid across the river near West Point, then sailed on to Kingston and burned the town. Further north, on September 19, American troops under General Horatio Gates lost an engagement with the British under General Burgoyne at Saratoga. Three weeks later, on October 7, at what came to be called the Second Battle of Saratoga, the Americans decisively defeated the British, capturing an entire army of 9,000 men. Saratoga was the turning point of the Revolution. It was a great strategic victory and an important boost to morale—and it convinced the French to enter the war as allies of the Americans. After the final French and American victory at Yorktown in 1781 in Virginia, General Washington led 7,000 troops to their final winter encampment at New Windsor. From a farmhouse in Newburgh, Washington issued his final "cessation of hostilities" order in 1783. A number of Revolutionary War sites remain in the mid–Hudson Valley and are well worth visiting. Foremost among them, though slightly out of the range of this book, is the **Saratoga National Historic Park** (518-664-9821; www.nps.gov/sara), where visitors can retrace the action of this momentous engagement. An excellent free brochure about the **New York State Revolutionary War Heritage Trail** is available from Heritage New York (518-237-8643; www.heritageny.gov). Another excellent brochure on the topic comes from the **Hudson River Valley National Heritage Area** (845-452-4916; www.hudsonrivervalley.com). Driving tours of Revolutionary War sites in all of New York State and elsewhere can be found at www.revolutionaryday.com; the relevant tours for the mid–Hudson Valley are those for U.S. Route 9 and for U.S. Route 9W.

Helletje Jans. The original house was a simple single room constructed from local stone. The original massive beams, wide floorboards, and Dutch door are still in place. The Broncks prospered as farmers, and in 1738 Pieter's grandson Leendert built another house just a few feet away. Leendert's spacious, three-story house, with patterned brickwork and steep gables, was connected by a brick passageway to the original house. In the early 1800s, when wheat was the main crop, a large New World Dutch barn with a broad threshing floor and huge grain storage area was added. In the 1830s, the family switched to dairy farming and built an unusual 13-sided

hay barn. The Bronck family farmed their land continuously for 276 years. In 1939 the last family member donated the land and the 11 structures on it to the Greene County Historical Society. Today the Bronck Museum is a National Historic Landmark. The buildings are filled with period furniture, china, glass, silver, artwork, and antique tools and equipment. The old barns contain additional exhibits of agricultural equipment and horse-drawn vehicles and material on Greene County History, including a model of the famed Catskill Mountain House. The Bronck Museum is open by guided tour only from Memorial Day weekend to October 15, Wednesday, Thursday,

Catskill Mountain House

The Catskill Mountain House was a resort hotel near Palenville in the Catskills. It was built in 1824 on a plateau 1,600 feet high, with sweeping views up and down the Hudson. For the rest of the century, the resort was very popular with the rich and famous—and with artists such as Thomas Cole, who painted both the hotel and the view from it several times. Among other amenities, the hotel offered a cable-operated elevated railroad to spare guests the long coach ride it took to reach the summit. By the turn of the century, resorts in the Adirondack Mountain became more popular with the wealthy, and the Catskill Mountain House began to fade. The railroad was sold for scrap in 1918, and the hotel closed for good in 1941. The derelict property was acquired by New York State in 1962. In 1963, despite pleas from preservationists, it was burned down as part of the state mandate to keep the Catskill Park forever wild. Today the site—and the magnificent view—can still be seen on the very rugged Escarpment Trail, which can be picked up at the nearby North-South Lake State Campground.

ORANGE COUNTY

Cornwall

FORT MONTGOMERY STATE HISTORIC SITE $
Route 9W, ½ mile north of the
Bear Mountain Bridge
(845) 446-2134
www.nysparks.com

In October 1777, some 700 American soldiers made a heroic stand at Fort Montgomery and nearby Fort Clinton, holding off 2,100 British and Loyalists troops long enough to disrupt their march north up the Hudson. Although the Americans lost the forts, and hundreds were killed, wounded, or taken prisoner, in the bigger picture their resistance helped defeat the British strategy to gain control of the Hudson River. The 14-acre site preserves the ruins of the fort. There's a spectacular view from the remains of the Grand Battery, where huge cannons once guarded an iron chain across the river. (During the battle, the first British ship to hit the chain snapped it—a later, stronger chain was more effective.) To reach the former site of Fort Clinton, now the Trailside Museum and Zoo in Bear Mountain State Park, follow the marked trail south over the suspension bridge crossing the Popolopen Creek; it's about half a mile. The site and trail are not suitable for people with limited mobility. The site is open daily year-round from sunrise to sunset; the visitor center (which is wheelchair accessible) is open Wednesday through Sunday, 9:00 a.m. to 5:00 p.m.

HUDSON HIGHLANDS NATURE MUSEUM $
Formerly known as the Museum of the Hudson Highlands, this museum is oriented toward environmental education for kids. See the Kidstuff chapter for more information.

Marlboro

GOMEZ MILL HOUSE AND HISTORIC SITE $$
11 Mill House Road
(845) 236-3126
www.gomez.org

and Friday from noon to 4:00 p.m., Saturday from 10:00 a.m. to 4:00 p.m., and Sunday from 1:00 to 4:00 p.m. On Memorial Day, Independence Day, Labor Day, and Columbus Day, hours are 10:00 a.m. to 4:00 p.m. The last tour of the day begins at 3:30 p.m.

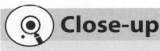 Close-up

Hudson River Lighthouses

The mighty Hudson River has been a major commercial waterway since the earliest days of European settlement in the 1600s. With the opening of the Erie Canal in 1825, the Hudson was connected with the interior of the nation, and traffic on the river exploded. The Delaware and Hudson Canal opened just three years later, transporting coal from Pennsylvania to Kingston and then onward up and down the river. As shipping grew, the demand for lighthouses to mark the many treacherous stretches on the river grew as well. Of the numerous lighthouses that were built along the river, only a handful remain. In the mid-Hudson region, the lighthouses at Esopus Meadows (near Port Ewen), the Rondout Creek in Kingston, Saugerties, and Hudson-Athens are still standing. The Esopus Meadows lighthouse dates back to 1838; the current dilapidated structure replaced it in 1871. The seven-room keeper's house has a mansard roof; it is the only remaining Hudson River lighthouse built with a wood frame and clapboard exterior. The Maid of the Meadows, as this lighthouse is affectionately called, was closed in 1965, replaced by a distinctly functional automated navigational aid on a pole outside the building. The Maid is being renovated by a volunteer group and is not currently open to the public. You can get good views of it from the Esopus Meadows Environmental Center on the west side of the river and from Norrie Point State Park from the east side. The Rondout Lighthouse, dating back only to 1915, is open to visitors seasonally through the Hudson River Maritime Museum (listed later in this chaper). The redbrick 1869 Saugerties lighthouse can be visited any time of the year—if you can time your visit for low tide (listed later in this chapter). Visitors can also spend the night here, making it one of the more spartan but interesting accommodations in the area. (See the Accommodations: West chapter for information on staying at the lighthouse.) The handsome Hudson–Athens lighthouse, built in the Second Empire style in 1873, is still a working light, although it was automated in 1949. It is being renovated by the Hudson–Athens Lighthouse Preservation Society. Boat trips to the lighthouse are offered several times a year for a modest fee; for details, contact HALPS at (518) 828-5294 or www .hudsonathenslighthouse.org. The Hudson River Lighthouse Coalition has information about all the remaining Hudson River lighthouses at www.hudsonlights.com.

One of the oldest continually occupied houses in the United States, and the earliest surviving Jewish residence in North America, the Gomez Mill House dates back to 1714. Its original builder, Luis Moses Gomez, fled the Spanish Inquisition in 1695 and ended up in the religiously tolerant colony of New York City in 1703. In 1705, he was granted an Act of Denization from Queen Anne, which allowed him the rights to conduct business, own property, and live freely within the British colonies. (The document is on view at the site.) Gomez became both a business and religious leader. He was the first president of Shearith Israel, the oldest synagogue in North America. He eventually purchased 6,900 acres in what is now Orange and Ulster Counties. A shrewd fur trader, he built the original one-story fieldstone house, with walls 3 feet thick, at a point where several

Indian trails converged. Gomez died in 1740. The next resident was Wolfert Acker, a patriot activist during the Revolution. Acker added the brick second story to the house and operated a sawmill and ferry. In 1835, the house passed to a gentleman farmer named William Henry Armstrong. Family members lived there until 1909, when the house was sold to Dard Hunter, a legendary artisan famed to this day for his work with handmade paper and printing. Hunter built a paper mill in the style of a Devonshire cottage. The house was sold to Martha Gruening, a social activist involved with the NAACP, in 1919; in 1947 the Starin family moved in and raised four children there. The Starins were instrumental in discovering and preserving the history of this unusual dwelling. It was placed on the National Register of Historic Sites in 1973; the Gomez

Foundation purchased the site in 1984. The site is really more moving for what it represents—religious, artistic, and personal freedom—than what it displays, but the exhibits are interesting. They range from early artifacts related to Gomez himself to Dard Hunter's original paper pulper—papermaking demonstrations are held regularly. The site is open for guided tours from April to October, Wednesday through Sunday, from 10:00 a.m. to 4:00 p.m. Tours begin at 10:00 a.m., 11:30 a.m., 1:00 p.m., and 2:30 p.m.

Newburgh

BANNERMAN'S CASTLE $$$
(845) 234-3204
www.bannermancastle.org

On the eastern bank of the Hudson near Fishkill, just 1,000 yards offshore, is a mysterious island with a tumbledown castle, complete with crenellated turrets and a six-story tower. (Passengers on MetroNorth or Amtrak get an excellent view.) It's Pollepel Island, and while the ruins look ancient, in fact they date back only to 1901. That's when Francis Bannerman, a Scottish-born arms dealer from New York City, bought the 6.5-acre island as a safe place to store his extensive inventory of weapons and ammunition. The castle was built as the arsenal; he also built a home for his family. In homage to his birthplace, the arsenal was modeled after a castle on the Isle of Skye, down to the moat, drawbridge, and portcullis. After Bannerman died in 1918, his sons carried on the business and used the house in the summers through the 1930s. By 1957, when the last superintendent of the arsenal retired, the business had long been moved from the island and the property was abandoned. In 1967, it was sold to the State of New York, which turned it over to the parks department. In 1969, a suspicious fire that burned for three days gutted the buildings. Starting in the late 1990s, the Bannerman Castle Trust, a volunteer group, has been stabilizing the ruins, clearing trails, and doing some restoration work. It's still largely off-limits to the public, but once a month, from May to October, the trust sponsors a boat ride to view the island. The *Pride of the Hudson* leaves from Torches

Landing in Newburgh (which is why the castle is listed here). For details and the schedule, contact the trust or Hudson River Adventures at (845) 220-2120 or www.prideofthehudson.com. The ride is pricey at $40 a head, but the spectacular views of the Hudson Highlands from the water, to say nothing of the up-close look at the island, make it worth the cost.

DAVID CRAWFORD HOUSE MUSEUM $
189 Montgomery Street
(845) 561-2585
www.newburghhistoricalsociety.com

A Neoclassical mansion dating back to 1834, the David Crawford House is now the home of the Historical Society of Newburgh Bay and the Highlands. Captain Crawford was a successful ship owner whose sloops and early steamboats sailed up and down the Hudson from his dock at the foot of Third Street. Today the house contains period detail and original furnishings, as well as a charming collection of scale model ships. The historical society runs an active program of exhibits and speakers at the house—call or check the Web site for the schedule. Open April through October on Sunday from 1:00 to 4:00 p.m.

WASHINGTON'S HEADQUARTERS
STATE HISTORIC SITE $
Liberty and Washington Streets
(845) 562-1195
www.nysparks.com

The Hasbrouck family's eight-room fieldstone farmhouse was the home of George and Martha Washington during the last months of the Revolutionary War, from April 1782 to August 1783. Hasbrouck House is the oldest house in the city of Newburgh. When the property was acquired by the State of New York, it also became the first publicly operated historic site in the nation. It was here that Washington rejected the idea that he should be king after the war. It was here that on April 19, 1783, he issued an order for the cessation of hostilities that formally ended the war, and it was here that he created and awarded the Badge of Military Merit, forerunner of the Purple Heart. The site, with its commanding view of the Hudson, preserves Hasbrouck House as it appeared in Washington's time. A museum and the Tower of Victory monument (it's not very towering—in fact, it's squat and ugly) built to commemorate the centennial of Washington's stay are also on the site. Open April through October, Monday and Wednesday through Saturday; closed Tuesday and Sunday. Hours are 10:00 a.m. to 5:00 p.m. The site is also open for special programs monthly throughout the year; call or check the Web site for events, especially on Presidents' Day weekend in February.

Vails Gate

KNOX'S HEADQUARTERS STATE HISTORIC SITE　$

Route 94 and Forge Hill Road
(845) 561-5498
www.nysparks.com

Major General Henry Knox, commander of the American artillery, had his military headquarters at New Windsor at Ellison House, a 1754 Georgian-style fieldstone manor. General Nathaniel Greene and General Horatio Gates, the victor at Saratoga, also spent time here. The elegant house has been restored to period style, including the slave quarters. Kids particularly enjoy the "hands-on" rooms, where they can touch reproductions of original furnishings and clothing. The remains of an old gristmill are also visible; a stone bridge that once carried the King's Highway passes over the Silver Stream gorge. On the grounds is the Jane Colden Native Plant Sanctuary, named for American's first female botanist. Jane Colden (1724–1766) was a keen observer of the native plant life around her; her botanical manuscripts are now in the British Museum in London. Living history programs take place here regularly—call or check the Web site for the schedule. The site is open mid-April

Andrew Jackson Downing of Newburgh

The city of Newburgh was the lifelong home of Andrew Jackson Downing (1815–1852), one of the most influential landscape architects of the 19th century and the father of the American park movement. Downing began his career working in his family's nursery business and gradually established a reputation for landscape design. In his short but very active life he wrote several highly influential books on both landscape and residential architecture and also edited the monthly journal *The Horticulturist*. In collaboration with Andrew Jackson Davis and Calvert Vaux, he designed picturesque landscapes for a number of Hudson River mansions (see the previous chapter for more on this). Downing was a strong supporter of his native Hudson Valley. Working with Davis and Vaux, he designed many Gothic Revival residences, including a number in the Newburgh area. (Those that remain are all in private hands and not open to the public; some good examples are found on Grand Street and Montgomery Street.) Downing died in the tragic burning of the Hudson River steamboat *Henry Clay* in 1852. At the time, he was supervising the construction of his designs for the grounds of the White House and the Mall in Washington, D.C. The lovely 35-acre Downing Park in the heart of Newburgh (845-565-5559) was designed in the 1890s as a memorial to Downing by Frederick Law Olmstead and Calvert Vaux. Opened in 1897, the park was the last collaboration by the designers of Central Park. Filled with hills and valleys, picturesque vistas, streams, a large pond, and winding walkways, it exemplifies Downing's vision of a park that brings the peace and beauty of the countryside to a city setting.

through late October, Wednesday through Saturday, from 10:00 a.m. to 5:00 p.m. and on Sunday from 1:00 to 5:00 p.m. It's also open Memorial Day, Independence Day, Labor Day, and Veterans Day.

NEW WINDSOR CANTONMENT STATE HISTORIC SITE AND NATIONAL PURPLE HEART HALL OF HONOR $
374 Temple Hill Road
(845) 561-1763
www.nysparks.com

Approximately 7,000 soldiers of the Continental Army, along with about 500 women and children, spent the last winter of the Revolutionary War here. Arriving in October 1782, they stayed through the summer of 1783. The soldiers built nearly 600 log huts, neatly aligned in rows a cantonment, or permanent camp. (The officers stayed in nearby homes.) They also built guardhouses, blacksmith shops, kitchens, a hospital, and other outbuildings, including a large assembly hall and chapel called the Temple of Virtue. After the war, the buildings were torn down. In 1936, the town of New Windsor acquired 167 acres of the site, including the area where most of the huts were. All that really remains of the original structures is the Mountainville Hut, said to have been built with logs from the cantonment. A reproduction of the Temple of Virtue is on the site; a museum was established in 1965. A good visitor center tells the story, and living history is presented by costumed interpreters who demonstrate musket drills, blacksmithing, medical care, and other aspects of life in the cantonment. In the Temple of Virtue that winter of 1783, Washington's officers met and awarded three particularly deserving soldiers a heart-shaped badge of purple cloth with the word "Merit" on it. In 1932, the Purple Heart was established in commemoration as a military decoration awarded to soldiers wounded or killed in action. The first medals were awarded here, but it wasn't until 2006 that the National Purple Heart Hall of Honor opened on the site. Covering 7,500 square feet, it tells the story of the medal through history. Historical reenactments take place at the cantonment regularly year-round—call or check the Web site

for details. The cantonment site is open mid-April through late October, Wednesday through Saturday, from 10:00 a.m. to 5:00 p.m. and on Sunday from 1:00 to 5:00 p.m. It's also open Memorial Day, Independence Day, Labor Day, and Veterans Day. The Hall of Honor is open year-round from Wednesday through Saturday, 10:00 a.m. to 5:00 p.m., Sunday 1:00 to 5:00 p.m., and Monday 10:00 a.m. to 5:00 p.m. It's closed Tuesday and Thanksgiving, Christmas, and New Year's Day.

i Visitors to the Revolutionary War state historic sites in the Newburgh area can purchase reduced-price combination tickets for Washington's Headquarters, New Windsor Cantonment, Knox's Headquarters, and the Last Encampment. Ask when paying at any of the sites.

West Point

UNITED STATES MILITARY ACADEMY AND MILITARY MUSEUM
2107 South Post Road
(845) 938-2638
www.usma.edu

In 1802, President Thomas Jefferson signed the act that created the military academy at West Point. The first class had two students. Today, some 4,400 cadets from every part of the country study here on a beautiful campus full of historic buildings, monuments, and spectacular views of the Hudson River. A visit to West Point starts at the Visitors Center and Military Museum. The Visitors Center features an exhibit about the Revolutionary War in the Hudson Valley and displays about student life, including a full-size model of a cadet's room. The Military Museum is the oldest, largest, and most diversified public collection of militaria in the country. It actually predates the academy—captured material was brought to West Point after the British defeat at Saratoga. The campus can be seen *only* by guided bus tour. (The fee is $10 to $12 for adults.) It's well worth doing for the architecture alone. West Point buildings were designed by the likes of Richard Morris Hunt and McKim, Mead, and White. Trophy Point is where ordnance from five wars is displayed, along with links from the massive iron chain that once blocked British ships from sailing up the Hudson. The moving monument to Union soldiers killed in the Civil War was designed by Stanford White. Cadet reviews (parades) are held regularly throughout the year and are open to the public. The schedule is subject to change, and reviews may be cancelled without prior notice, especially if the weather is bad. There's no fee, but definitely call ahead first. The famed USMA Band, comprised of soldier musicians (not cadets), is based at West Point and performs there regularly (the Music Under the Stars summer concerts are very enjoyable). Concerts are free and open to the public; for details, call the performance hotline at (845) 938-2617 or check the main USMA Web site. When planning your arrival at West Point, allow extra time for security checks. The Visitors Center is open every day from 9:00 a.m. to 4:45 p.m.; closed Thanksgiving, Christmas, and New Year's Day. The Military Museum is open every day from 10:30 a.m. to 4:15 p.m.; closed Thanksgiving, Christmas, and New Year's Day.

i The U.S. Military Academy at West Point is one of the top tourist attractions in New York—nearly three million people visit every year. The academy can be seen by guided bus/walking tour only. Tours are one to two hours; you walk for a bit more than half the time. The bus company accommodates mobility limitations. For security reasons, visitors 16 and older must provide a photo ID. The daily tours depart frequently from the Visitors Center, but the grounds or parts of the grounds are sometimes closed to outside visitors (during Graduation Week, for instance). Always call ahead before planning a visit and allow extra time for security checks. For the current schedule of tours and prices, contact West Point Tours, Inc. at (845) 446-4724 or www.westpointtours.com.

THE WARNER HOUSE $$
Constitution Island
(845) 446-8676
www.constitutionisland.org

Constitution Island is part of the U.S. Military Academy at West Point, even though the island is on the east side of the Hudson just offshore from Cold Spring in Putnam County. The island was the eastern end of an 80-ton iron chain that the Americans stretched across the Hudson in 1778. The chain, and the three redoubts and a battery built on the island, kept British warships from sailing upriver. (An earlier chain in 1777 was broken.) The Warner House on the island was the home of the Warner family from 1836 to 1915. Two sisters, Susan and Anna, lived there all their lives. Both were writers. Susan wrote *The Wide, Wide World* in 1850. The book was a huge best seller and stayed in print for decades, though its pious sentimentalism makes it almost unreadable today. Anna was best known for writing the words to the hymn "Jesus Loves Me." Both sisters taught Bible classes to West Point cadets for 40 years—they would row back and forth across the river. Today the Warner House is a living museum furnished with original Warner family possessions. It looks very much as Anna Warner left it when she died in 1915. The island itself is 280 acres and has numerous hiking trails leading to the ruins of Revolutionary War fortifications. The Constitution Island Association offers tours for the general public from mid-June to mid-October. On Wednesday and Thursday, visitors arrive by a boat that leaves from the South Dock at West Point at 1:00 p.m. and 2:00 p.m.; the tour lasts a bit more than two hours. The island is also open for special events, such as historic reenactments, on some Saturdays. Access then is from the gate at the south end of the parking lot at the MetroNorth station in Cold Spring; a free shuttle bus takes you onto the island. Contact the association for the schedule.

ULSTER COUNTY

Gardiner

LOCUST LAWN AND TERWILLIGER
HOUSE $$
400 Route 32S
(845) 255-1660
www.huguenotstreet.org

Owned and operated by Historic Huguenot Street, Locust Lawn is a Federal-style mansion built by Colonel Josiah Hasbrouck in 1814. Hasbrouck, a descendant of the original Dutch settlers in the area, served as a member of Congress under both Jefferson and Monroe. The house and its outbuildings represent a prosperous homestead farm of the time. They were donated to the historical society in 1958. One of those outbuildings is the 1738 Terwilliger House, an early stone building in the Dutch architectural tradition. The house was donated to the historical society in 1974. Both houses are preserved as museums with period furnishings. They're open weekends from June through October by guided tour only. Tours start every hour from 11:00 a.m. to 4:00 p.m. and last for about an hour.

High Falls

D&H CANAL HISTORICAL SOCIETY AND
MUSEUM $
Mohonk Road
(845) 687-9311
www.canalmuseum.org

The portion of the Delaware & Hudson Canal that passed through the High Falls area had five locks (numbers 16 through 20 out of a total of 108) that compensated for a drop of 70 feet in elevation. These locks were built in 1847 when the canal was enlarged. They're a remarkable feat of engineering—each lock lowers the level of the canal by about 12 feet. Their remains can still be seen on the Five Locks Walk, a trail maintained by the D&H Canal Historical Society (it starts across the street). The walk is a fascinating look into industrial history. At lock 16, for instance, the stonework is so precise that no mortar was needed. Deep rope burns from the tow ropes can be seen here on the corner of

the Depuy Canal House (now an excellent restaurant). The museum has an extensive collection of photos, artwork, and documents on the history of the D&H Canal. The exhibits are good, with dioramas, models (including a miniature working lock), and an interesting collection of artifacts such as snubbing posts and tools. The Five Locks Walk

The Delaware Hudson Canal

The **D&H Canal** was one of the man-made wonders of the world when it opened in 1828. Running 108 miles from the anthracite mines of Honesdale, Pennsylvania, to Eddyville on the Rondout Creek near Kingston, the canal brought cheap fuel to an emerging industrial nation. The canal was an amazing feat of engineering. It was 32 feet across at the top, 4 feet deep (later deepened to 6 feet), and contained 108 locks, 137 bridges (including four suspension aqueducts designed by John A. Roebling of Brooklyn Bridge fame), and 26 basins, dams, and reservoirs. The canal boats were pulled by mules. Moving at a rate of about 1 to 3 miles per hour, they made the round-trip in 7 to 10 days. The canal operated profitably until 1898, when the growth of railroads finally ended the canal era. The D&H was abandoned, although remnants of it can still be seen all along its former route. In the mid–Hudson Valley, the remains can be easily seen at High Falls and in the Kingston Rondout district. For a good list of all D&H Canal sites, see the National Park Service Web site at www.nps .gov/upde/d&hcanal.htm or the D&H Transportation Heritage Council Web site at www.dhthc.com.

is open year-round; it is not wheelchair accessible. The museum is accessible; it's open from the beginning of May to the end of October, Saturday and Sunday from 11:00 a.m. to 5:00 p.m.

Hurley

HURLEY HERITAGE SOCIETY MUSEUM
52 Main Street
(845) 338-1661
www.hurleyheritagesociety.org

The town of Hurley was founded in 1661 by 12 Huguenot and Dutch families. It became a thriving farming community. In 1777, after Kingston was burned by the British, Hurley became the temporary capital of New York State. In October 1783, General Washington himself visited the hamlet to thank the residents for their support. Hurley's Dutch and Huguenot heritage is still visible today in 26 well-preserved stone houses—the oldest and largest concentration of stone houses in the country. Hurley's history is explained in one of those houses, the Col. Jonathan Elmendorf House, now the museum of the Hurley Heritage Society. The house was built between 1783 and 1790. An ongoing exhibit about Hurley in the Revolutionary War is complemented by changing exhibits of local historic significance. Admission is free. The Hurley Heritage Society provides a free brochure for a self-guided walk/drive tour of the area and also offers guided

ℹ️ On the second Saturday in July every year, from 10:00 a.m. to 4:00 p.m. rain or shine, the owners of some of Hurley's historic stone houses open their doors to the public for Stone House Day. Costumed guides explain the history of the houses; the other festivities include a militia encampment reenactment and period music performances. Free buses take visitors to the houses not directly on Main Street. Tickets are $12; no reservations needed. Stone House Day is arranged and sponsored by the Hurley Reformed Church. For more information: (845) 331-4121 or www.stonehouseday.org.

walking tours of the village monthly between May and October; the charge is $3. Call or check the Web site for the schedule.

Kingston

FRED J. JOHNSTON MUSEUM AND FRIENDS OF HISTORIC KINGSTON MUSEUM $
63 Main Street
(845) 339-0720
www.fohk.org

Fred Johnston was both a nationally known antiques dealer and a passionate preservationist for the historic city of Kingston. On his death in 1993, he left his home and personal treasury of 18th- and 19th-century furnishings to the Friends of Historic Kingston (FOHK). Today, his collection is beautifully displayed in eight showcase room settings in his carefully restored 1812 Federal-style residence. The house is now a centerpiece of Kingston's historic Stockade District. In fact, it's the starting point for the Stockade walking tours offered by FOHK. The house was nearly lost in 1938, when it was scheduled to be demolished to make way for a gas station. Fred Johnston rescued the building and restored it to its original severe beauty and classic lines. The collection contains outstanding examples of American furniture, American glassware and pottery, Staffordshire porcelain, pictorial needlework, and other decorative arts. The Friends of Historic Kingston Museum is adjacent to the Johnston House and offers changing exhibitions on the history and heritage of the city. Both museums are open 1:00 to 4:00 p.m. Saturdays and Sundays from May through October and by appointment year-round. The Johnston House can be seen only by guided tour.

HUDSON RIVER MARITIME MUSEUM $
50 Rondout Landing
(845) 338-0071
www.hrmm.org

Surprisingly, given its importance, this is the only museum in New York State devoted to preserving the maritime history of the Hudson River. The museum is very appropriately located right on the Rondout Creek, where the old Delaware &

Hudson Canal terminated and the goods brought by canal boats were transferred to ships and railroad for transport up and down the Hudson. The museum has an extensive archive of documents and artifacts relating to Hudson River transportation, industry, and commerce. On exhibit inside are ice-harvesting tools, a variety of ship models, and displays about the river. The museum also has 380 feet of bulkhead on the creek for its collection of small craft, including a century-old shad boat, a life boat from the steamboat *Mary Powell*, a lighthouse tender, and several ice yachts. The museum's dock is also often visited by historic ship replicas such as the *Amistad* and the *Half Moon* and by ships such as the U.S. Coast Guard cutter *Eagle*, the only tall ship in active government service. The museum is open from the end of April to the end of October, Thursday through Monday, noon to 6:00 p.m.

RONDOUT LIGHTHOUSE   **$$**
(845) 338-0071
www.hrmm.org

The Hudson River Maritime Museum maintains the historic Rondout Lighthouse at the mouth of the Rondout Creek. The lighthouse, the third on that spot, was built in 1915 and occupied by a keeper and his family until 1946. It was abandoned and eventually turned over to the museum in 1988. The lighthouse has been restored and now contains period furnishings and exhibits documenting the history of all three Rondout lighthouses. The view of the Hudson from the top of the tower is spectacular. Access to the lighthouse is by a short boat ride provided by Mid-Hudson Estuarine Services (845-336-8145; www.kingstonlighthouse.com). The boat leaves from the nearby Rondout Creek Docks at One Broadway. The trips are available from Memorial Day weekend to Labor Day on Saturday and Sunday at 1:15 p.m. and 3:00 p.m. Call ahead to check the schedule.

KINGSTON HERITAGE AREA: THE RONDOUT
Bounded by Broadway, McEntee Street, West Strand and Abeel Street, and Home Street

The Rondout Creek was a major deepwater port for ships on the Hudson almost from the start

---

The Kingston Heritage Area

The Kingston Heritage Area (www .ci.kingston.ny.us) has two visitor centers to help you.

Rondout Waterfront
20 Broadway
(845) 331-7517

Exhibits, walking tour brochures, and information. Open year-round Monday through Friday, 9:00 a.m. to 5:00 p.m. Between May and October, also open Saturday and Sunday, 11:00 a.m. to 5:00 p.m.

Stockade District
308 Clinton Avenue
(845) 331-9506

Located in the 1837 Federal-style Thomas van Gaasbeek house. Exhibits, walking tour brochures, information, and restroom facilities. Open daily May through October, 11:00 a.m. to 5:00 p.m.

---

of European settlement in the 1650s, but there wasn't much of a community around it until the district known as Kingston Landing became the terminus of the Delaware & Hudson Canal in 1828. The village that became known as Rondout grew up around the canal and flourished as a shipping and boat-building center, reaching a peak of prosperity in the 1870s. In 1871, Rondout petitioned Albany to become a city; the village of Kingston countered by petitioning to include Rondout. Kingston won, and in 1872 the two villages were incorporated into the city of Kingston. The Rondout rose with the D&H Canal, and it crashed in 1898 when the canal was finally eclipsed by the railroads. The area went downhill and parts of it were thoughtlessly destroyed by urban renewal in the 1960s. Fortunately, many of the historic buildings on the west side were saved, and in 1974, the area was named to the National Register of Historic Places. Today the Rondout is a lively area of restored 19th-century architecture filled with restaurants, art galleries, shops, and marinas along the creek. The Friends of Historic Kingston provide an excellent free brochure to guide visitors on a walking tour of the area. The architecture here is eclectic and interesting. Many of the buildings, such as the seven Italianate buildings at 9 to 29 West Strand, feature cast-iron columns manufactured locally. The five churches in the area all feature variations on the Romanesque Revival style. The old Cornell Steamboat Company repair shop, with huge arched windows and large openings onto the Rondout Creek, can still be seen on East Strand. The Trolley Museum (listed later in this chapter) and the Hudson River Maritime Museum (listed earlier in this chapter) are fun and informative stops. The walking tour of the Rondout takes about 90 minutes—or longer if you stop at any of the many cafes, restaurants, and art galleries en route.

KINGSTON HERITAGE AREA: THE STOCKADE DISTRICT
Bounded by Clinton Avenue, North Front Street, Green Street, and Main Street

The earliest Dutch settlers of what is now the city of Kingston arrived in 1652. They settled along the Esopus Creek and began to farm, but soon came into conflict with the local Native Americans. In 1658, the governor of New Amsterdam, Peter Stuyvesant, stepped in and ordered the settlers to move to a bluff above the creek. They complied, literally tearing down their houses and barns and rebuilding them on the higher ground. In the space of three weeks, they also built a wall of tree trunks pounded into the ground, 1,200 feet by 1,300 feet, to enclose their settlement. The settlers lived within the Stockade, as it was called, leaving only to tend their fields, until 1664, when a peace treaty ended the Second Esopus War. Although the stockade eventually disappeared, the village streets within it stayed laid out as they were. The original wooden structures were replaced with substantial stone houses

of limestone and mortar. In 1777 Kingston was declared the first capital of New York State. The city hosted the State Senate and Assembly; the new state constitution was read to townspeople on April 22, 1777, from the front steps of what is now the Ulster County Courthouse. On October 16, 1777, the town was burned by British troops; more than 300 homes, barns, and other buildings were put to the torch. (The event is commemorated every two years in October in a reenactment—no actual burning takes place, but there's lots of marching around in historic costume.) The state government was forced to flee (it ended up in nearby Hurley). After the fire, however, the residents gradually returned and rebuilt their community. Today, 21 pre-Revolutionary stone houses are within Kingston's historic Stockade Area. They are still functioning homes and offices, making the Stockade one of the oldest neighborhoods in America. The best way to see the National Historic District Stockade Area is by foot, following the walking tour laid out in an excellent free brochure from the Friends of Historic Kingston. A fascinating highlight of the tour is The Four Corners at John and Crown Streets. This is the only intersection in the United States where 18th-century stone houses stand on all four corners. The Old Dutch Church at 272 Wall Street, built of native bluestone in 1852, is the home of a congregation that dates back to 1659. George Clinton, first governor of New York, is buried there. Other highlights include the Senate House State Historic Site (see listing on following page) and the Fred J. Johnston House (see the Art in the Valley chapter). A monument at the Ulster County Courthouse at 285 Wall Street commemorates Sojourner Truth, a local former slave. In 1828, a year after slavery was abolished in New York, she sued in that court for her son's freedom in Alabama—and won. A replica of the 14-foot-high stockade is at Frog Alley Park on North Front Street. The tour, mostly on quiet residential streets, takes about 90 minutes. The old slate sidewalks are sometimes narrow and uneven, but overall the walk is accessible for those with limited mobility.

SENATE HOUSE STATE HISTORIC SITE $

296 Fair Street
(845) 338-2786
www.nysparks.com

After the New York State Constitution was adopted in 1777, Kingston became the state's first capital. Merchant Abraham van Gaasbeek's simple 1676 stone house became the first meeting place of the State Senate. There, in an ordinary, rather bare room, the first 17 state senators met to form a new state government in September and October of 1777. They were forced to flee when the British attacked Kingston on October 16. Although it was used only briefly, the Senate House is a landmark site of American democracy—it is the oldest public building in America. The house was deeded to New York State in 1888. In 1927 the adjacent museum was built. It contains a major collection of the works of John Vanderlyn (1775–1852), a local artist whose landscapes, portraits, and historical paintings are found in many American museums. The Senate House museum also displays other furnishings and decorative arts and offers an active program of concerts, lectures, and other events, including demonstrations of colonial crafts on Saturday mornings. Open April 15 through October 31, Monday and Wednesday through Saturday from 10:00 a.m. to 5:00 p.m. and Sunday from 11:00 a.m. to 5:00 p.m. Also open Memorial Day, Independence Day, and Labor Day. The van Gaasbeek House can be seen by guided tour only; the last tour starts half an hour before closing. The house is fully accessible; the museum is only partially accessible.

TROLLEY MUSEUM OF NEW YORK $

89 East Strand
(845) 331-3399
www.tmny.org

Yes, the displays of trolley, subway, and rapid transit cars here illustrate the rich history of rail transportation in the Hudson Valley, and yes, the museum has a great visitor center located on the original site of the Ulster & Delaware Railroad yards. But the real fun here is taking an actual trolley ride. The museum operates a genuine trolley car on an excursion ride that runs 1.5 miles from West Strand Park at the foot of Broadway in downtown Kingston to picnic grounds at Kingston Point, stopping at the museum in between. Visitors can board at any of the locations; the fare is included in the admission fee. The museum is open from Memorial Day to Columbus Day, Saturday, Sunday, and holidays from noon to 5:00 p.m. The last trolley ride is at approximately 4:30 p.m.

VOLUNTEER FIREMEN'S HALL AND MUSEUM

265 Fair Street
(845) 338-1247

Located in the historic Stockade District, the museum is in the 1857 firehouse of the former volunteer Wiltwyck Hose Company. It features antique firefighting artifacts and apparatus, including an 1898 stream engine. Small but very friendly and accessible; kids love this place. Open April through October on Friday, 11:00 a.m. to 3:00 p.m., and Saturday, 10:00 a.m. to 4:00 p.m. From June through August, the museum is also open on Wednesday, 11:00 a.m. to 3:00 p.m.

i Kingston has two other historic districts: Chestnut Street and Fair Street. The Chestnut Street district was the home of the more affluent members of the Rondout community. The district takes in the top of the hill on West Chestnut Street. The houses here are in an interesting mix of 19th-century architectural styles—a separate walking tour booklet is available at the visitor center. The Fair Street district is just to the south of the Stockade area. It, too, was a residential neighborhood for the wealthy. The houses along this long block mostly date from around 1850 and range in architectural style from Italianate to Second Empire to Queen Anne and Colonial Revival.

New Paltz

HUGUENOT STREET STONE HOUSES $$
Huguenot Historical Society
18 Broadhead Avenue
(845) 255-1600
www.huguenotstreet.org

The village of New Paltz was founded in 1678 by a dozen Huguenot families who had fled religious persecution in northern France. The colonists purchased nearly 40,000 acres along the Wallkill River from the Esopus Indians and named their new town after die Pfalz, the region along the Rhine River where they had lived temporarily before leaving for the New World. The families began replacing their temporary homes with solid stone structures in the early 1700s. Today seven of those original homes survive as house museums owned and operated by the Huguenot Historical Society. The tree-lined street overlooking a bend in the Wallkill was declared a National Historic Landmark District in 1964. Four of the houses are very close to their original appearance; three others were modified in the 1830s, 1890s, and 1940, making three centuries of history visible almost at a glance on one of the oldest streets in America. The houses are open for tours from May through October, Monday through Sunday (closed Wednesday). Tours begin every hour from 10:00 a.m. to 4:00 p.m. at the DuBois Fort Visitors Center at 18 Broadhead Avenue (where you'll find very pleasant picnic facilities). The historic houses aren't wheelchair accessible, but special arrangements can be made—call ahead. Call or check the Web site for information about the extensive educational programs and special events organized by the Huguenot Historical Society.

Rosendale

A.J. SNYDER ESTATE $
668 Route 213
(845) 658-9900
www.centuryhouse.org

After a visit to the Cement Industry Museum at the A.J. Snyder Estate you may know more about cement than you really need, but this site is worth a visit, especially if you also go to the Widow Jane Mine on the property. The cement industry was once massively important here. Natural cement from the Rosendale area was used to build the Brooklyn Bridge, the Washington Monument, Grand Central Terminal, and many other major structures. The museum is in Century House, the 1809 home of A.J. Snyder (1889–1975), who owned the now defunct Century Cement Company. His large collection of carriages and sleighs is on exhibit in the carriage house. Today the old limestone mine is used, among other things, for musical performances and recording sessions. Open May through October, Saturday and Sunday, from 1:00 to 4:00 p.m. Call or check the Web site for events at the mine. Route 213 is a narrow road that winds along as it follows the Rondout Creek. Be careful entering and exiting this site.

Old New Paltz Day

The Huguenot Historical Society sponsors the annual Old New Paltz Day every September. The old stone houses are open for tours, and reenactors, period performers, Native American musicians and storytellers, craftspeople, exhibits, and children's activities are all on hand for an experience that brings history alive. Admission is $10 for adults, $5 for kids (6 and under are free). The Society also sponsors Haunted Huguenot Street weekend near the end of October. This Halloween tradition is very popular—advance reservations are strongly suggested. For more information: (845) 255-1660 or www.huguenotstreet.org.

Saugerties

SAUGERTIES LIGHTHOUSE $
168 Lighthouse Drive
(845) 247-0656
www.saugertieslighthouse.com
To get to the Saugerties Lighthouse, you have two choices—walk (it's the only Hudson River lighthouse accessible by land) or take a boat. If you're walking, the route is an easy half-mile nature trail that starts at the end of Lighthouse Drive just past the Coast Guard station in the village of Saugerties. The trail floods ankle-high or a bit more at high tide, so plan your visit accordingly—call ahead to ask about the tide table. Visitors can tour a small museum and the lighthouse itself, as well as picnic on the grounds and enjoy a swim in the river. You can also stay the night by advance reservation (see the Accommodations: West chapter). Tours are available from Memorial Day through Labor Day on weekends and holidays from 2:00 to 5:00 p.m.

ℹ️ Perrine's Bridge is a historic covered bridge spanning the Wallkill River between Esopus and Rosendale. Built in 1834, it is a single 138-foot span in the Burr arch truss design. It was authentically restored in 1969. A walk (no cars are allowed) across this bridge is a trip back in time, accompanied by the roar of traffic from the New York State Thruway bridge overhead. It's an interesting experience. The bridge is on Route 213 near Route 32.

Stone Ridge

BEVIER HOUSE MUSEUM $
2682 Route 209
(845) 338-5614
www.bevierhousemuseum.org
Andries Van Leuven, a Dutch settler, built the original one-room stone house here in the 1680s. In 1715, it was purchased by Louis Bevier. The house and surrounding lands remained in the Bevier family for 223 years and seven generations. The family expanded the house over the years and made a number of improvements between 1840 and 1890, turning it into the large, elegant stone structure, complete with widow's walk, it is today. In 1938, Bevier House became the home of the Ulster County Historical Society. Visitors to Bevier House today can learn how a Dutch farm family really lived. The first floor houses the original kitchen with 18th-century furnishings. The old scullery houses an extensive and extremely interesting tool collection covering three centuries. The parlors on the main floor are filled with late 19th-century Victorian furnishings. A room on the second floor is devoted to Civil War artifacts. The museum is open from mid-May through the end of October, Thursday through Monday, 1:00 to 5:00 p.m.

ℹ️ Ulster County is full of historic stone structures, including the largest collection of 17th- and 18th-century stone houses still standing in the United States. An excellent free booklet with driving tour directions, "Ulster County's Legacy in Stone," is available from Ulster County Tourism (800-342-5826 or www.ulster tourism.info).

Ulster Park

KLYNE ESOPUS MUSEUM
764 Route 9W
(845) 338-8109
www.klyneesopusmuseum.org
The former Ulster Park Reformed Church, built in 1827, is now the home of the Klyne Esopus Museum, whose mission is "Exhibiting the pride of Esopus." And what does Esopus have to be proud of? Well, it's a small museum, but it does have an interesting exhibit about Alton B. Parker, who ran for president against Teddy Roosevelt in 1904. He lost by a landslide and didn't even carry Ulster County. Other exhibits focus on two other famous Ulster Park residents, naturalist John Burroughs and abolitionist and former slave Sojourner Truth. The terrace in front is a nice spot for a picnic. Open June through December, Friday through Tuesday, 1:00 to 4:00 p.m.

ACCOMMODATIONS: EAST SIDE OF THE HUDSON

On the east side of the Hudson, small inns and bed-and-breakfast operations are fairly numerous, and there is a fair number of chain and individually owned motels, although the chain motels are mostly clustered in the southern part of Dutchess County (Poughkeepsie and Fishkill). Even so, rooms can be in short supply during the peak season from around May 1 to the end of October. On a peak season weekend with a major event, such as the Dutchess County Fair in Rhinebeck near the end of August, rooms may be almost impossible to find on short notice. If you're planning a visit during this period, book well in advance. Because winter is a little quieter in the area, rooms are easier to find; many establishments offer discounted prices and special getaway deals then.

There are so many fine accommodations in the area that this chapter can't begin to list them all. The establishments included here were selected because they're particularly comfortable, charming, and convenient. All the establishments listed here are open year-round and accept major credit cards; exceptions are noted. This chapter also includes a listing of local campgrounds and RV parks. Costs, amenities, and seasons vary so much for camping that details can't be provided here. Call ahead and make your reservations as far in advance as possible.

Some B&Bs are very family-friendly, but most aren't really equipped to accommodate younger kids. Call ahead—sometimes special arrangements can be made. Some B&Bs allow pets, often for an extra fee; again, call ahead. Resident dogs, cats, and other animals are part of what makes staying at a B&B fun, but if you have allergies, be sure to ask about animals when making reservations.

In New York, small inns and B&Bs are not required to be wheelchair accessible. Many will have at least one room that is at least partially accessible, usually in the sense of being on the ground floor, but only a few have rooms designed for full access. If you have special needs, call in advance. Innkeepers want their guests to be comfortable and will generally do what they can to help.

New York State law allows smoking in lodgings, but only in specially designated guest rooms—and small operations aren't required to provide smoking guest rooms. For all practical purposes, no B&B or small inn allows smoking in guest rooms or anywhere indoors. Chain hotels and motels usually offer smoking rooms; check when making reservations.

Check-in and check-out times, minimum stays, cancellation and no-show policies, and other house rules vary quite a bit from place to place. As a general rule, innkeepers are strict about their cancellation and no-show policies. They have to be—small operations simply can't afford unexpectedly empty rooms that can't be filled on short notice. The policies are usually clearly stated on the establishment's Web site and in its printed materials. The innkeepers will also be sure to explain them when you make your reservation. Most will try to accommodate guests with extended check-ins and so on, if possible—the more advance notice you can give, the better.

Price Code

The rates given here are for an overnight stay by two adults sharing a room on a weekend during the peak season, loosely defined as between April and November. Weekday rates and off-season rates are generally lower. The rates given here don't include state and local taxes. New York State tax is 8 percent; the county occupancy tax varies, but it's anywhere from 2 to 4 percent. The rates also don't include any additional charges.

$	less than $200
$$	$200 to $299
$$$	$300 to $450
$$$$	more than $450

i Many of the small inn and bed-and-breakfast establishments in the region belong to the Hudson Valley Lodging Association. The Web site at www.hudson-valleylodging.com is a good source of up-to-date information on lodgings options.

COLUMBIA COUNTY

Canaan

THE INN AT SILVER MAPLE FARM $–$$
Route 295
(518) 781-3600
www.silvermaplefarm.com
The Inn at Silver Maple Farm offers 11 spacious guest rooms set on 10 private acres in the Berkshire foothills. (The location is a bit out of the region covered in this book, but it is included because it is one of the nicest countryside inns in the county.) The rooms are simple yet elegant, with wide-plank pine floors, luxury bedding, and fantastic views from the windows. The Great Room, with cathedral ceiling and clerestory windows, offers guests a calming place to relax—it's also where the gourmet breakfast buffet is served every morning, and where tea and homemade chocolate chip cookies are served every afternoon. Children under 10 are welcome to stay in some rooms; older children can be accommodated in any guest room.

Claverack

WAGON WAY BED & BREAKFAST $
23 Rivenburg Lane
(518) 851-7524
www.wagonwaybb.com
A small and pleasant B&B, Wagon Way has four guest rooms. This inn is very kid-friendly. Two of the rooms have extra beds (bunk beds in the Trellis Room!), and the Gingham Room has a separate sleeping area with a full-size bed. All rooms have private baths. Wagon Way has an in-ground swimming pool for guests, set in a large, landscaped lawn. Breakfast is served in the sunroom and features home-baked muffins and breads and breakfast casseroles. Bonus: While you're staying at Wagon Way, you can take a ballroom dancing lesson at the on-site dance studio.

i More information about places to stay in Columbia County is available from the Columbia County Lodging Association at www.columbiacountylodging.com or (800) 558-8218.

Hudson

THE BALLOON BED & BREAKFAST $
73 Route 25
(518) 828-3735
www.balloonbedandbreakfast.com
The Balloon Bed & Breakfast takes its name from the hot-air balloon rides offered by the proprietors. Balloon rides usually take place at dawn or toward sunset, when the winds are gentlest and most predictable, so a B&B for people planning a flight makes a lot of sense. The Balloon has three guest rooms in a restored 1869 Victorian cottage. Each room is decorated with antiques and has a private bath, complete with claw-foot bathtub. A full breakfast is served every morning. No kids. Call well in advance to arrange a balloon flight (with or without an overnight stay).

THE COUNTRY SQUIRE BED & BREAKFAST $
251 Allen Street
(518) 822-9229
www.countrysquireny.com

Just a couple of blocks away from the lively scene on Warren Street, The Country Squire is located in a 21-room Queen Anne mansion built in 1900. The building began life as a rectory and later became a convent; in 1930 it was purchased by a family for use as a residence. Over the years, the house was converted into multiple residences, but the owners carefully preserved the original architectural details. When the house was again sold in 2004 to become The Country Squire, all the original features were restored. This jewel of a house has an imposing mahogany staircase, parquet floors, five fireplaces, stained glass, 10-foot ceilings, and the original pocket doors. The five guest rooms are decorated with a comfortable, uncluttered mixture of contemporary and vintage furnishings. All rooms have large private baths with windows and vintage claw-foot bathtubs. An abundant Continental breakfast is served every morning. Free Wi-Fi. Both on-street and off-street parking is available for guests.

HUDSON CITY BED & BREAKFAST $
326 Allen Street
(518) 828-9139
www.hudsoncitybnb.com

The city of Hudson is full of architectural gems, and the Hudson City Bed & Breakfast is one of them. This three-story Second Empire–style house was built by Joshua T. Waterman, a successful local businessman, in 1865. It has been beautifully restored and now has a range of guest rooms. There's a suite that's often used by honeymooners and nine other rooms, all with private baths. The rooms are all spacious and charming, with high ceilings, Victorian details, and vintage furnishings. Breakfast is served every morning in the elaborate dining room. The entire house is often rented out to family groups and wedding parties. Kids are welcome here. Free Wi-Fi.

THE INN AT BLUE STORES BED & BREAKFAST $$
2323 Route 9
(518) 537-4277
www.innatbluestores.com

Built in 1908 in a distinctive Spanish colonial style, the Inn at Blue Stores captures the design principles of the Arts and Crafts Movement of that time. The inn has clay tile roofs, a stucco exterior, stained-glass fixtures, an impressive leaded-glass entry hall, and distinctive black oak woodwork. It's a far cry from the more typical Dutch and American colonial architecture of the area, but somehow the house, once a gentleman's farm, fits its setting in the historic crossroads hamlet of Blue Stores. The inn is on a 100-acre working farm—it's a very quiet and relaxing place. Five guest rooms decorated with period furniture are available. The inn has a large porch and swimming pool for guests; the common areas include a recreation room and a sitting room, both with fireplaces. Guests are served a full gourmet breakfast every morning; afternoon tea is served in the garden or by the fireplace in the sitting room. Payment is by personal check or cash only. Kids over 10 are welcome. Pet cats are in residence.

INN AT CA'MEA $
333-335 Warren Street
(518) 822-0005
www.camearestaurant.com

The Inn at Ca'Mea is right across a courtyard from the Ca'Mea Ristorante, a top dining destination in Hudson (see Restaurants: East chapter for details). The slogan for the inn is "Come for the food, stay for the weekend, it's the Italian way." The inn offers four guest rooms, each with private bath; two of the rooms have private balconies overlooking the garden. The rooms have flat-screen TVs and Wi-Fi. The building is a historic Federal-style gem right across the street from the Hudson Opera House. Inn guests receive a 20 percent discount at the restaurant; they can also arrange for in-room dining through the restaurant. Accommodations for pets and children are limited—call in advance.

THE INN AT HUDSON $$
317 Allen Street
(518) 822-9322
www.theinnathudson.com

The building that is now The Inn at Hudson is one of the most architecturally important in a city chock-full of important architecture. The elegant 17-room house was designed in the Dutch/Jacobean style by the renowned Albany architect Marcus Reynolds in 1903 and completed in 1906. The owner was Morgan Jones, the heir to the Sapolio soap fortune (vintage Sapolio ads are collectors' items today). The structure was considered one of the city's finest residential mansions. It remained a single-family home until 1980, when it was converted to a nursing home. After the nursing home closed, the property was acquired in 2005 by Dini Lamot and his partner Windle Davis. They began a careful restoration of the building, which, among other things, uncovered the magnificent stained-glass window and painted frieze in the imposing wood-paneled entry hall. The inn today offers four large guest rooms, all meticulously restored and furnished with vintage antiques—some, provided by a local antiques dealer, are also for sale. Cable TV and Wi-Fi are in every guest room. Breakfast is served in the astonishing dining room; guests gather for afternoon drinks and snacks in the restored library. The inn is also available for business meetings, whole-house rentals, and wedding parties.

MOUNT MERINO MANOR $$$
4317 Route 23
(518) 828-5583
www.mountmerinomanor.com

Set on more than 100 very private acres of unspoiled woodlands, and with stunning views out over the Hudson, Mount Merino Manor is right next door to Olana State Historic Site, home of artist Frederic Church (see the Art in the Valley chapter for more about this site). The stately Victorian mansion was built in 1870 by Church's personal physician, Dr. Gustavus A. Sabine. Today the inn has seven guest rooms and suites, all beautifully restored. The rooms are furnished with period pieces; several have decorative fireplaces. All have spacious spa-style bathroom and feature luxury linens. A gourmet country breakfast is served every morning. Kids over 10 are welcome. The inn is available for business conferences, wedding parties, family reunions, and whole-house rentals.

ST. CHARLES HOTEL $
16-18 Park Place
(518) 822-9900
www.stcharleshotel.com

The newly renovated St. Charles Hotel offers affordable accommodations close to bustling Warren Street, the center of the action in Hudson. The hotel offers 34 rooms in a variety of configurations. All rooms have cable TV with 78 channels and free HBO and Wi-Fi access. The building has an elevator and is wheelchair accessible. Smoking rooms are available. A Continental breakfast is provided every morning for guests. Small pets are welcome—call in advance to make arrangements. The St. Charles also offers space for business meetings and events. The Boardroom can hold up to 20 people, while the Henry Hudson Ballroom can accommodate up to 100.

THYME IN THE COUNTRY $
671 Fish and Game Road
(518) 672-6166
www.thymeinthecountrybandb.com

An eco-friendly B&B, Thyme in the Country is a restored 1880s farmhouse on five peaceful acres. The three guest rooms, all with private baths, feature natural-fiber bedding, curtains, and rugs; only eco-friendly cleaning products and methods are used. The spacious, comfortable rooms are furnished with simple antiques. The Lavender Room can be converted to a suite with a second bedroom that's ideal for families traveling with kids. A delicious full breakfast is served every morning—the ingredients often come from the inn's own organic garden. Thyme in the Country is a model of ecological sensitivity. The renovations were done using recycled building materials; the house has solar panels that provide one-third of the electricity, a highly efficient zone heating system, and water-efficient appliances and bathroom fixtures. Not only does all this minimize the environmental impact, it makes the inn a good choice for guests with environmental sensitivities.

UNION STREET GUEST HOUSE $$$
349 Union Street
(518) 828-0958
www.unionstreetguesthouse.com

The Union Street Guest House is a Greek Revival structure that dates back to 1830. The elegantly proportioned, high-ceilinged rooms are spacious and comfortable. The inn offers six suites—three in the Main House and three in the adjoining Brick House, a historic structure dating back to the 1790s. The largest is the Gallery Suite, with three bedrooms, a large private sitting area, a reading room, a kitchenette area, and a private entrance with summer porch. Some of the other suites also offer kitchenettes and private entrances. All offer vintage furnishings, luxury linens, wireless Internet access, and a full cable TV package. Kids are welcome, although parental supervision is requested. Pets can sometimes be accommodated—call ahead.

Kinderhook

KINDERHOOK BED & BREAKFAST $
67 Broad Street
(518) 758-1850
www.kinderhookbandb.com

A center-hall Colonial built in the early 1900s, Kinderhook Bed & Breakfast is on more than an acre of land right in the historic village of Kinderhook. The property features beautiful perennial gardens. The four guest rooms here are spacious and comfortable. Two rooms are upstairs in the main house, and two rooms are on the ground floor in the Guest Cottage. Each room is uniquely decorated and has a private bath. The Great Room is decorated in traditional country style with Shaker influences. Look for the Shaker star motif in the Great Room, on the side fence, and throughout the house. Host Jayne Hester is nationally known for her rug hooking (she runs a rug-hooking school at the inn several times a year). A Continental breakfast is served in the Great Room every morning. Kids are welcome here. No pets, but you can play with Thurman, the resident standard poodle.

THE VAN SCHAACK HOUSE $$
20 Broad Street
(518) 758-6118
www.vanschaackhouse.com

The Van Schaack House is historic even for the village of Kinderhook. It's a former mansion that dates back to 1785. The original owner, Peter Van Schaack, was a distinguished legal scholar who took in small groups of students for training, giving his home a plausible claim to be the first law school in New York State. Distinguished guests in Van Schaack's lifetime (he died in 1832 at the age of 85) included John Jay, Gouverneur Morris, Aaron Burr, Washington Irving, and Martin Van Buren (whose own home is nearby—see the Mansions and Historic Sites: East chapter for details). Today The Van Schaack House is as elegant as it was more than two centuries ago. Period details, such as the spectacular stairway that leads to the guest rooms, have been beautifully restored, and the entire house is furnished with art and antiques. Four guest rooms are available, each with private bath, cable TV, luxury bedding, and period furnishings. A full breakfast is served every morning in the dining room. Guests are welcome to use the gym, library, computer room, and sitting rooms. Kids over 12 are welcome.

Stuyvesant

ROWDY GARDEN HOUSE AT
WEST WIND FARM $
545 Route 26A
(518) 758-6855
www.therowdygardenhouse.com

Set among stunning gardens created by host Vivian Cook, Rowdy Garden House is a relaxed and affordable B&B. The 10-acre property is just minutes from the banks of the Hudson River and offers sweeping Catskill views; the historic village of Kinderhook is just five minutes away. The house, a rambling country Cape, is furnished with an intriguing mixture of antique, vintage, and casual pieces. The common areas include the first-floor den and a dining room with a wood-burning fireplace. The guest rooms are on the second floor and include two large suites with queen-size beds and private baths and a twin room with bath across the hall. A family-style breakfast is served each morning, featuring local produce and homemade jams and herbal butters. Kids over 7 are welcome, with parental supervision. *Note:* There's a resident cat.

Valatie

NATHAN WILD HOUSE   **$**
3007 Main Street
(518) 758-9684
www.nathanwildhouse.com

The original part of this elegant B&B dates back to 1826, when Nathan Wild, a wealthy industrialist who made his fortune in textile mills, built a Federal-style house for his family. Nathan Wild was a good friend of President Martin Van Buren, who often rode over from Lindenwald to have breakfast (see the Mansions and Historic Sites: East chapter for more about Lindenwald). Around 1850 the interior was extensively remodeled in the popular Italianate style; additional wings and a ballroom were added over the following decades. Today, the Nathan Wild House is on the National Register of Historic Sites. Many of the original architectural details are still in place, including the beautifully proportioned main entrance hall with an elaborately carved walnut arch framing a three-sided bay window. The parlor has a marble Eastlake fireplace and is furnished with Federal and Victorian antiques. Nathan Wild House features three guest rooms— one in the Main House and two in the self-contained North Wing. The North Wing can also be rented as a guest house for stays of six nights or longer. It offers two elegant bedrooms, a sitting room, a dining room, and a kitchen. Breakfast is served to B&B guests in the Greek Revival dining room in the Main House. Guests have use of an in-ground swimming pool.

DUTCHESS COUNTY

Beacon

MT. BEACON BED & BREAKFAST   **$**
829 Wolcott Avenue (Route 9D)
(845) 831-0737
www.mtbeaconbedandbreakfast.com

A 1911 Colonial Revival mansion, Mt. Beacon Bed & Breakfast has been beautifully restored to its original elegance. The entrance foyer has a grand center staircase leading up to the three guest rooms on the second floor. All the rooms are decorated with charming vintage furnishings and all have newly renovated full baths featuring claw-foot tubs. The public areas include the spacious formal living room with a magnificent wood-burning fireplace. French doors lead from the living room to a covered patio and in-ground swimming pool. A three-course gourmet breakfast is served every morning in the dining room; guests who need an early start before 8:30 a.m. are offered a Continental breakfast. Free Wi-Fi.

Hopewell Junction

**BYKENHULLE HOUSE
BED & BREAKFAST**   **$$**
21 Bykenhulle Road
(845) 242-3260
www.bykenhullehouse.com

Bykenhulle House is a historic Georgian manor house dating back to 1841. The 17-room house features six guest rooms, along with two formal living rooms, a sunroom, patios, a ballroom, and spectacular gardens. The guest rooms are furnished with elegant antiques, period wallpaper and rugs, a sitting area, fireplaces, and comfortable beds with luxury linens. Every room has cable TV and Internet access. A full breakfast is served each morning in the dining room. Well-behaved children aged 12 and up are welcome. Bykenhulle House is a very popular spot for weddings and corporate events. Reservations should be made well in advance.

LE CHAMBORD $

2737 Route 52
(845) 221-1941
www.lechambord.com

Le Chambord combines the charm of a restored 1863 Georgian-style mansion set on 10 bucolic acres with four-star cuisine (see the Restaurants: East Side chapter for details on dining here). The elegant main Inn has nine large guest rooms, each with a comfortable sitting area, filled with antiques and period furnishings. Nearby Tara Hall has 16 spacious guest rooms for corporate clients; there's also a well-equipped conference center. Guests at Le Chambord enjoy luxury bedding and oversize bathrooms. All rooms are equipped with cable TV and high-speed Internet access. Not surprisingly, given the restaurant's well-deserved fame, the Continental breakfast served to guests each morning in the lovely dining room is a gourmet treat. Le Chambord is a popular site for weddings, banquets, and private and corporate events. Rooms at the Inn can fill up fast, especially during popular wedding months. Reserve as far ahead as possible.

Hyde Park

INN THE WOODS BED & BREAKFAST $

32 Howard Boulevard Extension
(845) 229-9331
www.innthewoods.com

Unusually for a B&B, Inn the Woods isn't a restored historic house. Instead, it's a spacious, light-filled contemporary home set among peaceful woods. The inn offers guests two options. The Tree Top Suite is the entire second story of the inn and has its own private entrance and private deck. An expansive, window-lined space, the suite has two full-size canopy beds, working fireplace, dining area and kitchenette, and sitting area with futons that can be converted to extra beds—up to six guests can stay here. The other choice at the inn is the Cliffside Room, with a luxurious king-size brass bed. A full three-course breakfast is served to guests each morning in the sunlit dining room. The inn has a resident dog and two cats. Kids over 13 are welcome.

JOURNEY INN BED & BREAKFAST $

1 Sherwood Place
(845) 229-8972
www.journeyinn.com

Located across the street from the Vanderbilt Mansion National Historic Site (see the Mansions and Historic Sites: East chapter for details), Journey Inn is conveniently located for visitors to any of the historic sites in Hyde Park. It's also close to the Culinary Institute of America—in fact, the inn offers special rates to guests taking continuing education courses there (call for details). Journey Inn has six guest rooms, including two suites. The rooms are spacious and individually decorated, with rare attention to comfortable seating and good light for reading. Free Wi-Fi. A full gourmet breakfast is served family-style daily at 8:30 a.m. in the Morning Room. The menu includes fresh baked goods, a fruit course with dishes such as Banana Chantilly, and a hot main course such as special pancakes or an egg dish. Kids over 9 are welcome.

LE PETIT CHATEAU INN $$

39 West Dorsey Lane
(845) 437-4688
www.lepetitchateauinn.com

Wine enthusiasts and gourmets will find Le Petit Chateau especially welcoming. Each of the inn's four rooms is named for a famous French wine region, and a welcome gift of cheese from France greets each guest. Each room also has an extensive library of books about wine. The inn is a restored farmhouse from 1900 set on a 40-acre estate. Only a quarter of a mile from the Culinary Institute of America, the inn features weekend food and wine seminars and culinary getaways with private cooking classes. Breakfast and the baked goods at Le Petit Chateau are prepared by student chefs from the CIA. They're eager to practice their skills and impress the guests, making breakfast here a special occasion. All rooms have fireplaces, cable TV, and Internet access. The inn is available for small conferences and corporate events. American Express is the only credit card accepted.

THE WILLOWS BED & BREAKFAST $
53 Travis Road
(845) 471-6115
www.willowsbnb.com

A small B&B with only two guest rooms, The Willows is a restored 1765 Colonial farmhouse set on a quiet country road. The rooms are furnished with country and Victorian antiques and collectibles; each is very comfortable, with private bath. Breakfast here is a hearty meal featuring local produce, homemade breads, homemade sausage and cheese, and even honey from the innkeeper's own hives. A dog and cat are in residence. Kids over 12 are welcome.

Millbrook

MILLBROOK COUNTRY HOUSE $$
3244 Sharon Turnpike
(845) 677-9570
www.millbrookcountryhouse.com

The Greek Revival–style home that is Millbrook Country House is nearly two centuries old. Despite its origins in early Dutchess County history, today the house is furnished with elegant Italian antiques. The Italian motif and the antiques are carried through in the four beautifully decorated guest rooms. Breakfast at Millbrook Country House is served in the dining room and includes seasonal fruit, homemade baked goods, and a specially prepared dish such as herb omelet. Afternoon tea is served in the parlor or outside in the gardens in nice weather. (The lovely gardens here are adorned with contemporary sculpture by two local artists, Tim Mark and Anthony Krauss.) On Friday nights, the inn offers a house-prepared prix-fixe dinner (make arrangements at least three days in advance). Guests can access free Wi-Fi, but the rooms have no TVs. As a general rule, the inn doesn't accomodate children, but exceptions can be made—call in advance. Three cats are in residence. Credit cards are accepted, but personal checks or cash are preferred.

THE PORTER HOUSE $$
17 Washington Avenue
(845) 677-3057
www.innsofmillbrook.com

Located in the center of the lovely village of Millbrook, Porter House was originally built as a private residence in 1912 by Italian stonemasons. Today the original period details are still in place, including hardwood floors and beautiful chestnut woodwork. The three two-room suites and two guest rooms are all decorated with simple country antiques, vintage pieces, and oriental carpets—and all have private baths. An extensive breakfast buffet is served in the dining room every morning. Kids over 12 are welcome.

Poughkeepsie

COPPER PENNY INN $
2406 New Hackensack Road (Route 376)
(845) 452-3045
www.copperpennyinn.com

Located within walking distance of Vassar College, Copper Penny Inn is a restored 1860s farmhouse set on 12 wooded acres laced with streams and a pond. The inn has four charming guest rooms that preserve many details of the original house; all rooms have private baths and Internet access. Public areas include a comfortable living room with wood-burning fireplace, a pantry with snacks and beverages, and a stone terrace and screened porch. A full breakfast is served daily in the dining room or on the terrace in warmer weather. Kids over 12 are welcome.

INN AT THE FALLS $
50 Red Oaks Mill Road
(845) 462-5770
www.innatthefalls.com

With seven king suites, five queen suites, and 24 double rooms, Inn at the Falls offers the charm and character of a small country inn with contemporary touches. No two rooms are the same here, but all are spacious, comfortable, and offer free Wi-Fi and cable TV with free HBO. The decor ranges from Asian antiques to contemporary American. Smoking rooms are available. The inn also offers a fitness room, a bar, a conference room, and a large living/dining room area. The Continental breakfast is complimentary. The inn offers a discount to IBM employees and corporate guests. Pets are welcome for an additional fee of $75 a night.

POUGHKEEPSIE GRAND HOTEL $
40 Civic Center Plaza
(845) 485-5300
www.pokgrand.com

Centrally located in the downtown area, the Poughkeepsie Grand is a full-service hotel with 200 guest rooms and suites. The hotel is a very popular venue for weddings (there are five bridal suites), banquets, conferences, and meetings. The hotel adjoins the Poughkeepsie Civic Center, which hosts many large conferences and trade shows. Business travelers get special consideration here with executive guest rooms that feature all the standard room amenities (refrigerator, free high-speed Internet access, complimentary *USA Today* newspaper) along with a generous supply of office products and a working desk with comfortable chair and good lighting. Smoking rooms are available. The hotel offers a special rate to IBM employees and corporate guests. The room rate includes a full breakfast. Room service through Cosimo's Restaurant is available from 6:30 a.m. to 10:00 p.m. daily.

Red Hook

GRAND DUTCHESS BED & BREAKFAST $
7571 Old Post Road
(845) 758-5818
www.granddutchess.com

A lovingly restored ornate Victorian mansion, the Grand Dutchess is on a quiet street in the quiet country village of Red Hook. The six guest rooms here are all large and airy—most are corner rooms that are flooded with light. All are furnished with period pieces and have private baths. The public spaces here include verandas, a great room on the third floor stocked with cold drinks, and two authentically furnished formal Victorian parlors. A very hearty breakfast is served every morning

in the exquisite dining room. Well-behaved kids over 6 are welcome.

RED HOOK COUNTRY INN $
7460 South Broadway
(845) 758-8445
www.theredhookinn.com

With six guest rooms and a private restaurant, the Red Hook Country Inn is a bit unusual. The guest rooms in this restored 1841 Federal-style mansion feature a nice mix of antique furnishings and modern comforts, including Wi-Fi, very comfortable beds with luxury linens, and whirlpool tubs in some baths. Guests can also enjoy an outdoor hot tub and lounging on the front veranda. A full breakfast is served every morning. What really sets the Red Hook Inn apart, however, is the Roasted Garlic Dining Room. Chef Nabil K. Ayoub, who was once personal chef to Jackie Onassis, now offers private, five-course prix-fixe dinners on Friday, Saturday, and Sunday evenings. Reservations are required at least 24 hours in advance. (Chef Ayoub is also certified to prepare kosher meals and will happily do so with advance notice.) The dinner service makes the Red Hook Inn a good choice for wedding parties, family groups, and corporate retreats. The two dining rooms at the inn can handle events for up to 200 people. Payment for lodgings and the prix-fixe dinner is by cash or personal check.

Rhinebeck

BECKRICK LODGE $
27 Beckrick Drive
(845) 876-5929
www.beckricklodge.com

A relaxed and child-friendly B&B, Beckrick Lodge offers three guest rooms. The Delft Room is an airy room with queen bed and hall bath. The Tuscan Suite features drive-up access, making it a good choice for guests with mobility issues. The Provence Pied à Terre is ideal for a traveling family—it has a king bed that can become two twins, a living area with loveseat and two chairs that convert to twin beds, an entertainment center with satellite TV, and a private deck area.

A hearty breakfast is served every morning in the dining room or on the screened-in porch in nice weather. The beautiful backyard is a certified backyard wildlife habitat. Guests are welcome to paddle around on the private pond or take a dip in the swimming pool. A cat is in residence.

BEEKMAN ARMS AND DELAMATER INN $$
6387 Mill Street (Route 9)
(845) 876-7077
www.beekmandelamaterinn.com

Located right in the middle of the charming and historic village of Rhinebeck, the Beekman Arms is the oldest continuously operated hotel in America, dating back to 1766. Guest accommodations are in the original building and in a number of nearby buildings. In all, the inn offers 73 rooms, including two that are fully wheelchair accessible. The Beekman Arms is the original inn. The 13 rooms and suites on the upper floors here date back to 1766, making a stay in this section of the Inn a unique historic experience. The rooms here are pleasantly old-fashioned—they've been recently redecorated with period-style furnishings, updated baths, and modern conveniences such as cable TV and Internet access. The Guest House, located behind the main inn, offers comfortable motel-style accommodations with contemporary decor. This is the pet-friendly section of the inn, but animal arrangements need to be made in advance. The Firehouse was once the village's fire hall. It is now a suite with exposed brick walls, high ceilings, and a comfortable living room area. The Townsend House next door has four deluxe rooms with king-size beds and gas fireplaces. The Delamater Inn complex, just a block away, offers 50 modern rooms surrounding an elegant garden courtyard. The original Delamater House, designed in 1844 by the famed architect Andrew Jackson Davis, is in the ornate American Gothic style. It offers seven guest rooms and a living room. The Germond House, dating back to around 1850, offers four junior suites, each with a bedroom and a separate sitting room. The Courtyard Rooms are in several newer buildings; all offer working fireplaces. The Delamater Inn offers full modern facilities for small conferences and corporate meetings. A distinctive touch here is the complimentary flask of sherry in every guest room. A complimentary Continental breakfast is served daily. The outstanding Tavern at the Beekman Arms is located in the main inn (see the Restaurants: East chapter for details). The Beekman Arms and Delamater Inn are very popular, especially with wedding parties and during the many events that take place at the nearby Dutchess County Fairgrounds. Make reservations as far in advance as possible.

THE GABLES AT RHINEBECK $
6358 Mill Street
(845) 876-7577

Fifteen gables adorn this rambling 1860 Gothic Revival house in the heart of the village of Rhinebeck. The gables and the interesting angles they form with the walls give each of the three guest rooms a unique design, complemented by the traditional country decor. Each room is furnished with a queen size bed and luxury linens and has an updated private bath. The Cottage Rose Suite has a sitting room and can accommodate a third person with advance notice. Guests can enjoy the living room on the main floor and the wraparound porches; an amenities room on the third floor is stocked with beverages. A full gourmet breakfast, featuring local produce, is served every morning. Kids over 12 are welcome. The inn has a resident dog.

HIDEAWAY SUITES $$
439 Lake Drive
(845) 266-5673
www.ehideawaysuites.com

Nestled in seven acres of woods a few miles outside Rhinebeck, Hideaway Suites is quiet and private. The inn offers three full suites, each with a sitting room, fireplace, and whirlpool tub; the Woodland Suite has a king-size four-poster bed and private deck overlooking the woods. Hideaway Suites also offers three spacious and well-appointed guest rooms, all with luxurious private baths. A full breakfast is served every morning. Hideaway Suites provides special rates for participants at the nearby Omega Institute—ask when making reservations. Children over 12 are welcome.

THE LOOKING GLASS BED & BREAKFAST $
28-30 Chestnut Street
(845) 876-8986
www.thelookingglassbandb.com
The Looking Glass is an apt name for a B&B located in an unusual mirror Victorian house. Built circa 1889 and located on one of Rhinebeck's most gracious streets, the house is really a twin structure—two identical houses adjacent to each other. One house contains the four guest rooms, along with the dining room, formal parlor, and den. The other is living quarters for the innkeepers. The Looking Glass has been impeccably restored with period wallpapers and fabrics and in an authentic color palette both inside and out. Many original architectural details are still in place, including the exterior fish scale shingles. The guest rooms are decorated in period style with queen-size beds; antiques and fresh flowers adorn every room. A four-course breakfast is served on weekends; during the week, a Continental breakfast, including homemade breads, is offered. There are no TVs in the rooms, but guests can watch the television in the den; free Wi-Fi is available throughout the house. Payment by cash or check is preferred.

OLDE RHINEBECK INN $$
340 Wurtemburg Road
(845) 871-1745
www.rhinebeckinn.com
An early American farmhouse dating back to around 1745, Olde Rhinebeck Inn has been lovingly restored and updated to include modern amenities such as private baths and satellite TV in every room. The inn offers four guest rooms, including the two-room Ryefield Suite. Decorated in a huntsman motif, the suite has a dramatic queen-size canopy bed and a twin bed in the adjoining sitting room. A full breakfast is served daily on an authentic trestle table in the dining room. Local and homegrown produce is featured, including fresh eggs from the inn's own chickens. Payment by check, cash, or debit card is preferred.

PRIMROSE HILL BED & BREAKFAST $
567 Ackert Hook Road
(845) 698-0370
www.primrosehillbb.com
With only two guest rooms and set on three peaceful acres, Primrose Hill is very private and quiet. The Reflections room has a vaulted ceiling and a canopied four-poster bed; Traveler's Rest has an English sleigh bed and wicker furniture from the Caribbean. Both rooms have full modern baths, cable TV, and wireless Internet access. The common areas include the living room with wood-burning fireplace, a spacious wraparound front porch, and a shaded back deck. A four-course breakfast is served in the sunny dining room, complete with home-baked breads and pastries and a choice of entrees. Children can't be accommodated easily—call ahead to discuss.

STONE CHURCH ROAD BED & BREAKFAST $
339 Stone Church Road
(845) 758-2427
www.stonechurchroadbedandbreakfast.com
Set on eight acres of rolling woodlands and overlooking the famed Rhinebeck Aerodrome, Stone Church Road offers four affordable guest rooms in a country contemporary house. All the rooms are on the second floor with scenic views. They're decorated with a comfortable mixture of modern and antique furnishings; all have queen-size beds. Two rooms share a full bath; the other two have private baths. A hearty breakfast, including home-baked breads and pastries, is served every morning. This is a family-friendly B&B, with rollaway beds or air mattresses available to accommodate a third person in the room.

VERANDA HOUSE BED AND BREAKFAST $$
6487 Montgomery Street
(845) 876-4133
www.verandahouse.com
A historic house set in the heart of a historic

village, Veranda House dates back to 1842. The house, including the five guest rooms, is furnished with a wonderful collection of American and English antiques and fine art. The guest rooms are decorated with authentic period wallpaper, lace curtains, and elegant antiques; all rooms have private baths. A full gourmet breakfast, featuring homemade pastries and a variety of hot entrees, is served in the exquisite dining room every morning; in warmer weather, guests can enjoy their breakfast on the terrace overlooking the garden. Kids over 12 are welcome.

WHISTLEWOOD FARM BED & BREAKFAST $$
52 Pells Road
(845) 876-6838
www.whistlewood.com
WhistleWood Farm is set on a hilltop overlooking wildflower gardens, pastures filled with grazing horses, and the rolling countryside so characteristic of the mid-Hudson region. The guest rooms here are in two locations. The main lodge has four spacious and eclectically decorated rooms featuring beamed ceilings, antiques, and oriental rugs. The common areas include a living room with fieldstone fireplace, a sunny front porch, a solarium, and decks overlooking the fields and woods. Guests at the main lodge enjoy a hearty buffet breakfast in the morning (a Continental breakfast is available for early risers) and homemade pie and cake in the afternoon. The Carriage House, just a short walk from the main lodge, has three guest rooms with a shared kitchen/sitting area. Each room has a private bluestone patio. The rooms can be booked individually or the entire cottage can be booked for a group. Guests here are welcome to come to the main lodge for the dessert table. Free Wi-Fi is available for all guests. WhistleWood Farm's hilltop setting is very popular for weddings, private parties, family groups, and corporate events. It's also available for film shoots. Rooms fill fast—reserve ahead as far as possible. Small, well-behaved pets are accepted at an extra charge; an outdoor kennel is also available. (You can also board your horse at the farm.)

Rhinecliff

THE RHINECLIFF $$
4 Grinnell Street
(845) 876-0590
www.therhinecliff.com
The historic hamlet of Rhinecliff was long home to the Rhinecliff Hotel, a much-beloved local landmark and popular night spot located just to the south of the rail station. The old hotel was built in 1854, however, and time had taken its toll. It was closed down in 2003. In the summer of 2008, after $5 million in renovations, the hotel reopened as The Rhinecliff. The new hotel is beautifully done. The ground floor offers an excellent brasserie-style restaurant and bar (including the original Victorian oak bar from the old hotel); the restaurant has a bluestone patio overlooking the river. The Riverview Room, a banquet room with a wraparound balcony and sweeping river views, is available for weddings, parties, and corporate events. The second and third floors now have nine large guest rooms. Furnished with king-size beds, luxury linens, flat-screen TVs, and country elegant decor, the rooms have baths with double-size whirlpool tubs. Every room has a private balcony with spectacular views of the Hudson River. The Bridal Suite has a four-poster bed, a private sun deck, and a luxurious open bath. A complimentary breakfast is included for overnight guests. Throughout the hotel, many of the original architectural details have been preserved or reused. Among other touches, the original porches that once ran the length of the building on the first and second floors have been restored, and the guest room floors are made from the original antique floorboards.

Staatsburg

BELVEDERE MANSION $$$
10 Old Route 9
(845) 889-8000
www.belvederemansion.com
Set on a 15-acre country estate looking out over the Hudson River and the Catskills, the Belvedere Mansion is a National Historic Landmark dating to 1900. (The Neoclassical mansion replaced a

historic older house from the 1760s that burned down.) The Belvedere has 33 guest rooms in all, eight in the Neoclassical mansion and the rest in three different nearby buildings. Staying the night in the mansion is like taking a step back into the Gilded Age. Each guest room here has ornate moldings, 19th-century French and Italian period furnishings and fabrics, and a marble bath. The queen-size French Empire beds have luxury linens, down pillows, and beautiful down comforters. In the nearby Carriage House, rooms are decorated in Hudson Valley primitive, with king-size beds, fireplaces, and marble baths. Each room here has its own private entrance. The Hunt Lodge, decorated in the style of an Adirondack camp, features spacious rooms with fireplaces, balconies or terraces, and private entrances. Rooms in the Zen Lodge are smaller and simply decorated with muted earth tones and Asian fabrics; each room has a queen-size bed and Manchurian slate bathroom. French doors open onto a cedar wraparound terrace. Relaxation is the goal at Belvedere—which means there are no phones or TVs in the guest rooms. A large-screen TV is available in the guests' sitting area, and free Wi-Fi is available throughout the inn. A lovely swimming pool, a tennis court, and beautiful gardens are open to guests. A complimentary country gourmet breakfast is served in the lovely breakfast room in the main building. Belvedere Mansion is noted for its fine dining (see the Restaurants: East chapter for details). It is an extremely popular site for weddings, private functions, and corporate events. Book as far in advance as possible.

Stanfordville

JENNY'S COUNTRY MANOR LODGE $
1639 Route 199
(845) 876-1151
www.jennysmanor.com
The 14 guest rooms at Jenny's Country Manor Lodge are simply decorated and comfortably furnished; several also have kitchenettes. What gives this affordable inn its special fun feel is the owners' collection of Chevrolets from the 1940s and 1950s, along with the extensive collection of die-cast model cars of all makes on display in the restaurant (Jenny's Bar-B-Q). A full country breakfast is served to guests on weekends.

Tivoli

HARMONY HILL OF CLERMONT $
29 LeGrand Avenue
(845) 489-4706
www.harmonyhillny.com
A relaxed and homelike atmosphere that is very welcoming of kids sets Harmony Hill apart from many other B&Bs. The inn offers two guest rooms and two suites. All are comfortably furnished with modern baths; most rooms have great Catskills views. The entire inn is available for small groups and family groups. A stay here includes a light meal on the night of arrival, a full home-style breakfast, daytime snacks, and a simple evening meal for each night of your stay. Small, well-behaved dogs are welcome. Payment is by cash or personal check only.

HOTEL MADALIN $$
53 Broadway
(845) 757-2100
www.madalinhotel.com
In 2006, the original 1909 Madalin Hotel was completely restored by new owners. The building still has many of its original period details, including the ornate, 19-foot carved wooden bar. Madalin's Table, the restaurant on the ground floor, is one of the area's finest dining experiences (see the Restaurants: East chapter for details). The 11 guest rooms upstairs have been fully renovated with period antiques, mostly in the Eastlake style. The rooms have also been fully updated with amenities such as king- or queen-size four-poster beds, flat-screen TVs, and wireless Internet access. The rooms were styled by set designer Ben Schecter and television producer George Barimo, who also redecorated the famed Chelsea Hotel in Manhattan.

PUTNAM COUNTY

Cold Spring

HUDSON HOUSE RIVER INN   **$$**
2 Main Street
(845) 265-9355
www.hudsonhouseinn.com

Located on the riverfront in the charming village of Cold Spring, Hudson House River Inn offers 12 guest rooms and one large suite. The historic, three-story clapboard structure was built in 1832 and is the second-oldest continuously operating inn in New York State (the first is The Beekman Arms in Rhinebeck, listed earlier in this chapter). The restaurant in the inn is one of the best places to eat in the area (see the Restaurants: East chapter for details). The rooms here are spacious and comfortably furnished; each has a lovely view of the Hudson River, Main Street, or the Storm King Mountain and West Point across the river. Some rooms have full balconies or walk-out terraces. During the week, guests are served a complimentary Continental breakfast; a full breakfast is offered Saturday and Sunday.

THE PIG HILL INN   **$$**
75 Main Street
(845) 265-9247
www.pighillinn.com

The historic 1825 brick building that is The Pig Hill Inn is in the center of Cold Spring, within easy walking distance of all the antiques shops, restaurants, and other attractions of this lively village. The three-story inn has nine guest rooms, each individually decorated with antiques and high-quality reproduction period pieces. With a few exceptions, the antiques in the rooms are for sale—after all, this is Cold Spring, antiques capital of the lower Hudson Valley. Breakfast here is a full meal served in the glass Victorian conservatory or on the garden terrace in the warmer weather. Guests who prefer to have breakfast in bed are indulged by the innkeepers. A Continental breakfast is available for guests who need to depart before 8:30 a.m. Free Wi-Fi is available throughout the inn. Children over 7 are welcome.

i The Putnam County Visitors Bureau has current listings of accommodations in the area. Check the Web site at www.visitputnam.org or call (845) 225-0381.

PLUMBUSH INN   **$$**
1656 Route 9D
(845) 265-3904
www.plumbushinn.net

Plumbush Inn is well-known in the region as a wonderfully romantic place for lunch or dinner (see the Restaurants: East chapter for details). The original property was owned by the Marquise Agnes Rizzo dei Ritii, born in America as plain Agnes Shewan; early in the 1800s she named it Plumbush after a nearby farm. The building that is now the inn dates back to 1865 and was built for Robert Parker Parrott, the inventor of the Parrott gun used during the Civil War. The house was designed in the Gothic Revival style by George Harney, a local architect who was much influenced by Andrew Jackson Downing. Today many of the period details remain; the two wings added when the house was converted to the inn were sensitively designed and placed out of sight. The interior maintains many of the charming period details. While the restaurant remains the main focus here, Plumbush Inn also offers three beautiful, spacious guest rooms, all furnished with antiques. A Continental breakfast is brought up to the guest rooms each morning. Overnight guests also receive a $50 dinner credit at the restaurant.

Garrison

THE GARRISON INN   **$$**
Route 9
(845) 424-4747
www.thegarrison.com

The Garrison resort has a spectacular golf course (see the Golf chapter) and the Valley restaurant (see the Restaurants: East chapter). It also offers four intimate guest rooms with relaxed but elegant contemporary decor. Each room has a king-size bed, luxury linens, plasma TV, high-speed Internet access, and a marble and mosaic tile bath. Guests are served a complimentary

Continental breakfast. The inn offers several good weekend getaway packages, including a golf getaway, a wellness getaway with spa rejuvenation package, and a stay-and-dine package. All getaways include dinner at the Valley restaurant. With only four rooms, the inn fills up very quickly, especially in the peak season; reservations several months in advance are suggested.

CHAIN HOTELS AND MOTELS

Beacon/Fishkill Area

COURTYARD BY MARRIOTT
Route 9 and I-84
(845) 897-2400
www.courtyard.com

HAMPTON INN
2515 Route 9
(845) 896-4000
www.hamptoninn.com

HILTON GARDEN INN
25 Westage Drive
(845) 896-7100
www.hiltongardeninn.com

HOLIDAY INN EXPRESS
21 Schuyler Boulevard
(845) 896-4001
www.hiexpress.com

HOLIDAY INN OF FISHKILL
Route 9 and I-84
(845) 896-6281
www.holidayinn.com

MAINSTAY SUITES
25 Merritt Boulevard
(800) 660-6246
www.mainstaysuites.com

MARRIOTT RESIDENCE INN
Route 9 and I-84
(845) 896-5210
www.residenceinn.com

QUALITY INN AND SUITES FISHKILL
849 Route 52
(845) 897-9300
www.qualityinn.com

RAMADA FISHKILL
20 Schuyler Boulevard
(845) 896-4995
www.ramada.com

RESIDENCE INN
2481 Route 9
(845) 896-5210
www.residenceinn.com

SIERRA SUITES
100 Westage Business Center Drive
(845) 897-5757
www.sierrasuites.com

Poughkeepsie Area

BEST WESTERN INN AND CONFERENCE CENTER
679 South Road (Route 9)
(845) 462-4600
www.bestwestern.com

COURTYARD BY MARRIOTT
408 South Road (Route 9)
(845) 485-6336
www.courtyard.com

DAYS INN
536 Haight Avenue
(845) 454-1010
www.daysinn.com

ECONO LODGE
418 South Road (Route 9)
(845) 452-6600
www.econolodge.com

HOLIDAY INN EXPRESS
341 South Road (Route 9)
(845) 473-1151
www.hiexpress.com

SHERATON HOTEL
40 Civic Center Plaza
(845) 485-5300
www.sheraton.com

SUPER 8 MOTEL HYDE PARK
528 Route 9
(845) 229-0088
www.super8.com

CAMPGROUNDS AND RV PARKS

On the east side of the Hudson Valley, campgrounds are a bit on the scarce side. Of the campgrounds that are available, several are excellent (and inexpensive) state sites. Fees for camping vary widely, depending on the time of year and the type of campsite. The camping season is generally from April 15 to October 15, though some sites are open a bit longer. All the sites listed here provide the usual campground amenities, including water, electric, and sewer hookups, dump stations, fire rings, picnic tables, and laundry rooms—some even offer free Wi-Fi. Many sites have recreational facilities, including swimming pools, playgrounds, and game rooms. Some sites also offer rental cabins. Sites fill up *very* quickly, especially around events such as the Dutchess County Fair in late August. Advance reservations are essential. Check ahead with the campground for details on pet policies, check-in and check-out times, minimum and maximum stays, and cancellation policies. Most sites can accommodate even the largest RVs, but check ahead to be sure.

For an accurate, town-by-town listing of campgrounds in New York State, go to www.campgrounds.com.

Columbia

BROOK N WOOD FAMILY CAMPGROUND
1947 County Road 8
Elizaville
(518) 537-6896
www.brooknwood.com

DUTCHESS

INTERLAKE RV PARK
428 Lake Drive
Rhinebeck
(845) 266-5388
www.interlakervpark.com

MARGARET LEWIS NORRIE STATE PARK
Old Post Road
Staatsburg
(845) 889-4646
www.nysparks.com/parks

WILCOX MEMORIAL PARK
Route 199
Stanfordville
(845) 758-6100
www.co.dutchess.ny.us/CountyGov/
Departments/DPW-Parks/PPwilcox.htm

Putnam

CLARENCE FAHNESTOCK STATE PARK
1498 Route 301
Carmel
(845) 225-7207
www.nysparks.com/parks

ACCOMMODATIONS: WEST SIDE OF THE HUDSON

The mid–Hudson Valley region is a year-round tourist destination, which creates a steady demand for accommodations. In addition, there are many events throughout the year that bring people flooding into the region and create peak demand periods. Even the dead of winter can be busy—that's when the Catskills ski resorts, such as Hunter Mountain and Windham, are in full swing. In recent years the relative lack of hotel space on the west side of the Hudson has improved. A number of chains have put up new sites in Kingston, Newburgh (near Stewart Airport), and elsewhere that have helped relieve the room shortage. The west side also has some small inns and many B&Bs. They can book up fast—reserve in advance. This chapter also includes a listing of local campgrounds and RV parks. Because fees, amenities, and seasons vary so much, details are not provided here. Call ahead and make your reservations as far in advance as possible. Campgrounds can fill up very, very quickly during the summer season.

A few points to bear in mind: This chapter is by no means comprehensive—there simply isn't room to list all the many fine accommodations in the area. The establishments listed here were chosen because they're particularly well known for their comfort and hospitality. Almost all the establishments in this chapter accept major credit cards; exceptions are noted. Almost all are open year-round and every day—the rare exceptions are noted. While some B&Bs are very welcoming of kids and families, others aren't really equipped to accommodate younger kids. The rules are noted, but rules can sometimes bend. Call ahead. Some B&Bs allow well-behaved dogs, often for a small extra fee. Again, call ahead. On the other hand, some B&Bs have resident dogs, cats, and other animals. If you have allergies, be sure to ask about resident pets when making reservations.

In New York, small inns and B&Bs are not required to be wheelchair accessible. Many will have at least one room that is at least partially accessible, usually in the sense of being on the ground floor, but only a few have rooms designed for full access. If you have special needs, call in advance. Innkeepers want their guests to be comfortable and will generally do what they can to help.

New York State law allows smoking in lodgings, but only in specially designated guest rooms—and small operations aren't required to provide smoking rooms. For all practical purposes, no B&B or small inn allows smoking in guest rooms or anywhere indoors. Chain hotels and motels usually offer smoking rooms—check when making reservations.

Check-in and check-out times, minimum stays, cancellation and no-show policies, and other house rules vary quite a bit from place to place. The policies are usually clearly stated on the establishment's Web site and in their printed materials. The innkeepers will also be sure to explain them when you make your reservation. Cancellations and no-shows are a real problem for small establishments, because they can't fill an empty room quickly. If you must cancel, do so as far in advance as possible to avoid fees. Most innkeepers will try to accommodate guests with extended check-ins and so on, if possible—the more advance notice you can give, the better.

Price Code

The rates given here are for an overnight stay by two adults sharing a room on a weekend during the peak season, loosely defined as between April and November. Weekday rates and off-season rates are generally lower. The rates given here don't include state and local taxes. New York State tax is 8 percent; the county occupancy tax varies, but it's anywhere from 2 to 4 percent. The rates also don't include any additional charges.

$	less than $200
$$	$200 to $299
$$$	$300 to $450
$$$$	more than $450

GREENE COUNTY

Athens

THE STEWART HOUSE $-$$
2 North Water Street
(518) 945-1357
www.stewarthouse.com

Stewart House has a strong claim to being one of the most romantic spots on the Hudson River. The landmark inn dates back to around 1883 and was extensively renovated in recent years. Seven rooms and two suites, all decorated in period antiques, are available. The Meryl Streep Room is a favorite with guests—it's the room where she died in the movie *Ironweed*. The room has wonderful views to the south and west and is furnished with a Queen Anne bed. The Dakota Room is named for Dakota Fanning, who stayed here while filming *War of the Worlds* in 2004. The room has a Queen Anne bed, a decorative fireplace, and a large and comfy walnut sofa. The spacious Garden Penthouse suite has a four-poster Queen Anne bed, full kitchen, and fireplace. It's available with two extra beds as a family suite. The Stewart House Restaurant offers fine dining (see the Restaurants: West chapter for details). Free Wi-Fi.

Catskill

CALEB STREET'S INN $
251 Main Street
(518) 943-0246
www.calebstreetsinn.com

Caleb Street's Inn was built in 1785 right in the center of the historic little town of Catskill. This small, friendly B&B offers two rooms (with shared bath) and two suites with kitchenettes (ideal for families and extended stays). The rooms are comfortably furnished with an early 1800s feel. A candlelight breakfast is served in the period dining room on fine china complemented with crystal and silver. In nice weather, the Charleston veranda overlooking the Catskill Marina is a great place to relax. Free Wi-Fi.

THE KAATERSKILL $
424 High Falls Road Extension
(518) 678-0026
www.portraitsandpaintings.net/farm/site01.html

A former estate now converted into a luxury inn, The Kaaterskill takes its name from the famed Kaaterskill Creek, a scenic waterway famed for the double-drop Kaaterskill Falls near Palenville. The falls were immortalized in 1826 by the artist Thomas Cole (whose house can be visited in Catskill—see the Mansions and Historic Sites: West chapter for details) and by many other Hudson River School artists after him. Today, The Kaaterskill gives visitors a sense of what these artists saw nearly two centuries ago—sweeping views of the Catskill Mountains and 32 acres of untouched woodlands and winding streams. The main building here is a beautifully restored Dutch barn. The inn offers six luxury suites, all with fireplaces, private patios, small kitchenettes, luxury bedding, and private baths with spas. The rooms and common areas are decorated with fine art and Asian antiques.

ORANGE COUNTY

Cornwall

CROMWELL MANOR HISTORIC INN   **$–$$$**
174 Angola Road
(845) 534-7136
www.cromwellmanor.com
Ranked as one of the finest inns in New York State, Cromwell Manor is on seven beautiful country acres with formal gardens and spectacular mountain views. The main building is the historic Manor House, a brick mansion dating back to 1820. It contains nine romantic guest rooms, all decorated with period antiques and fine furnishings. Many rooms have wood-burning fireplaces; all have private baths. The finest suite at The Manor House is the Oliver Cromwell Suite, which takes up the entire first floor of the 1840 addition. The room is furnished with a king-size poster bed and has a large sitting area. The large multi level bathroom features an oversized spa for two. Notable among the other rooms is The Wellington, a spacious first-floor room with pine floors, a wood-burning fireplace, a four-poster queen-size bed, and large private bath. Both the room and bath are fully wheelchair accessible. Also on the property is The Chimneys Cottage, built in 1764 and containing four guest rooms with private baths. The cottage is frequently booked in its entirety for parties, small groups traveling together, and family gatherings. All guests have a gourmet breakfast served at their private table; a 24-hour Continental breakfast is also available. Free Wi-Fi is available throughout The Manor House.

i Check the Web site of the Orange County Bed & Breakfast Association at www.new-york-inns.com for more information about accommodations in the area.

Mountainville

THE STORM KING LODGE   **$–$$**
100 Pleasant Hill Road
(845) 534-9421
www.stormkinglodge.com

Converted from an early 1800s post-and-beam barn, the Storm King Lodge offers six comfortable guest rooms, all with private baths, and a guest cottage with fully equipped kitchen that's ideal for two couples or family stays. All guests are welcome to use the large and beautiful swimming pool in the garden. There's also a Great Room with roaring fireplace and a lovely veranda for enjoying the stunning views in warmer weather. A healthy, home-baked buffet breakfast is served every morning.

Newburgh

GOLDSMITH DENNISTON HOUSE   **$**
227 Montgomery Street
(845) 562-8076
www.dennistonbb.com
A grand Federal-style home overlooking the Hudson in Newburgh's historic district, the Goldsmith Denniston House was built around 1820. It's been lovingly restored to its original elegance, down to the plaster moldings and marble mantelpieces, and furnished with antiques and fine art. Guests are accommodated in four rooms, all with private baths and queen-size beds. The room styles range from Federal to Victorian. Breakfast is served in an elegant, high-ceilinged dining room, complete with period chandelier and magnificent fireplace. A full professional kitchen in on-site—catered dinners and guest parties can be arranged.

West Point

THE THAYER HOTEL   **$$–$$$**
674 Thayer Road
(845) 446-4731
www.thethayerhotel.com
The majestic Gothic-style Thayer Hotel is located at the south entrance to the United States Military Academy. It's named for Colonel Sylvanus Thayer, Superintendent of the Academy from 1817 to 1833. The granite building dates back to 1926 and is listed on the National Register of Historic Places. Today the Thayer offers 151 beautiful guest rooms, 10 meeting rooms, and a charming old-fashioned dining room well known for its cuisine (see the Restaurants: West chapter

for details). Extensive renovation of the hotel in 2003 and 2004 modernized the rooms and facilities while keeping the 1920s charm. Every room has a magnificent view out over the Hudson River or the Hudson Highlands. The famed Eisenhower and MacArthur presidential suites have housed presidents, foreign dignitaries, and many celebrities. The suites offer a private bedroom and bath, living room, kitchenette with bar, dining room, and half bath. You don't have to be famous to stay in these suites—they're often booked for receptions, small social events, and meetings. Most guests stay in the comfortably furnished standard and deluxe rooms—all have king- or queen-size beds and spacious bathrooms. During some times of the year, such as West Point graduation, rooms at the Thayer are booked years in advance. This is also a very popular venue for weddings, especially in the warmer months. At some times of year, however, especially in the winter months, rooms are much more available. The Thayer offers some attractively priced weekend and holiday specials—check the Web site for updates.

ULSTER COUNTY

Gardiner

BLUEBERRY INN ON KIERNAN FARM   **$$**
1308 Bruynswick Road
(845) 255-8998
www.blueberry-inn.com
The attractive old Dutch-style farmhouse at Blueberry Inn (it dates back to around 1790) is on its own 15 acres within a 140-acre working farm. The views of the Shawangunks, especially the landmarks Gertrude's Nose and Millbrook Mountain, are spectacular. The four guest rooms here are pleasant, with queen-size beds, period-style

> **i** The Ulster B&B Alliance Web site (www.hudsonvalleybandbs.com) is an excellent source of information on charming places to stay in the area. The site features more than 40 B&Bs and country inns, along with an online availability hotline.

furnishings, and handmade quilts. Not all rooms have private baths. A full breakfast, featuring freshly baked blueberry (of course) muffins, is served to guests in the large country kitchen.

CEDAR HILL FARM   **$$**
287 McKinstry Road
(845) 255-0554
www.culinarybandb.com
Cedar Hill Farm calls itself a culinary bed-and-breakfast, both because the food prepared by chef Jennifer Stack is exceptionally good, and because over the winter Chef Stack offers culinary adventure weekends, where guests can spend at least four hours learning new techniques and recipes from her in a professionally equipped kitchen. Chef Stack is an advocate of sustainable agriculture; she features local foods on her menus and in the culinary workshops. The breakfast menu includes items such as smoked salmon omelet with local goat cheese and dill or chocolate-stuffed French toast with raspberry sauce. This is a small place, with only three very elegant rooms, and only four guests can participate in each culinary weekend—book far in advance. Overnight accommodations are offered only Thursday through Sunday.

MINNEWASKA LODGE   **$-$$**
3116 Route 44/55
(845) 255-1110
www.minnewaskalodge.com
Luxurious but intimate, Minnewaska Lodge is a 26-room mountain inn located on 17 acres near the magnificent Shawangunk Mountains and right next to Minnewaska State Park. It's widely seen as one of the best B&Bs in the Hudson Valley. The rooms have Mission-style decor with contemporary amenities, including spacious bathrooms, cable TV, and free Wi-Fi. All rooms feature lovely views of the mountains or forest; many rooms also feature a private deck and cathedral ceilings. A hearty Continental breakfast is served every morning in the beautiful Great Room. Minnewaska Lodge is popular with family groups enjoying the many recreational opportunities

in the area. It's also popular for small groups, wedding parties, and corporate retreats. Rooms can fill quickly during peak periods, especially between May and October. Reserve early.

High Falls

INN AT CANAL HOUSE $
Route 213
(845) 687-7700
www.depuycanalhouse.net

The Depuy Canal House is one of the finest restaurants in the region (see the Restaurants: West chapter for details). Because guests come from miles away to eat here, it makes sense that there's also a small inn across the street in the Locktender Cottage. The inn offers two suites and two double rooms. The South Garden Suite has a queen-size bed, full kitchen and dinette, full bath with spa, and an outside garden patio. The smaller North Suite has a queen-size bed, sitting area, and full bath with spa. The double rooms have standard beds, with private full baths. All the rooms have period furnishing and a nice airy feel. Children are welcome.

Highland

FOX HILL BED AND BREAKFAST $
55 South Chodikee Lake Road
(845) 691-8151
www.foxhillbandb.com

Guests at this traditional B&B can choose from three different rooms, all with queen-size beds, private sitting areas, and private baths. The ground-floor Tropic Room also has a gas fireplace. On the second floor, the Heritage Room is a spacious suite with antique oak furnishings, while the Garden Room suite has French doors that open onto a private sitting area with daybed. A full breakfast is served on weekends; during the week, breakfast is country Continental. Guests have the use of an in-ground swimming pool, spacious sun deck, gazebo with hot tub, and an air-conditioned fitness center. Wi-Fi is available. Fox Hill is fully smoke-free and uses only nontoxic cleansers in the house and for the linens—environmentally sensitive guests will find this a welcoming place.

HIGHLAND MANOR BED AND BREAKFAST $
2 Windsor Hills Road
(845) 691-9080
www.highlandmanorbandb.com

Built in 2001, this country inn offers five beautiful rooms, all with private baths. The Garden Room is a guest favorite. It's airy and very large, with wonderful views over the landscaped gardens, a queen-size bed, fireplace, in-room spa, TV with basic cable and DVD player, and private bath. All rooms offer plush featherbeds and pillows. The common areas include an extensive porch; a gazebo with a hammock swing; a guest sitting room with fireplace, library, and games; and a recreational area with pool table, foosball, and darts. A different gourmet full breakfast is served each morning in the elegant dining room, featuring fresh-baked muffins and scones and fruit from local farms. Children over 14 are welcome.

INN AT TWAALFSKILL $
144 Vineyard Avenue
(845) 691-3605
www.innattwaalfskill.com

The Inn at Twaalfskill takes its name from the bubbling Twaalfskill Creek, which meanders across the front of the spacious property. The house was originally built in 1902 as the home of Harcourt Pratt, a prominent local businessman who served in Congress. In 2005, the inn was extensively modernized, with careful attention to retaining the original turn-of-the-century architectural details. The decor is a rich, warm blend of European and American country style, pulled together with coordinated fabrics and period furnishings. There are three large main rooms here, all with private baths, queen-size beds, cable TV, and wireless Internet connection. (A fourth bedroom on the first floor is available for groups renting the entire inn.) Breakfast is served in the sunny conservatory. Guests can also enjoy cozy common areas, a large shady yard with century-old oak trees, a breezy porch, and a peaceful garden terrace.

Kingston

RONDOUT INN $

79 Broadway

(845) 399-2902

www.rondoutinn.com

Rondout Inn offers the privacy of an apartment suite with the charm of a bed-and-breakfast. It's located in a historic 1820s Federal-style building right in the historic Rondout waterfront district. The suites are above the owners' antiques shop. Each suite—the Wiltwyck and the Esopus—is a one-bedroom apartment with a large living room and fully furnished kitchen. The kitchens are stocked with everything needed for a Continental breakfast and light snacks. The proprietors offer midweek specials and getaway weekends—check the Web site for details. Free Wi-Fi.

SCHWARTZ'S INN $

70 North Front Street

(845) 389-9918

www.schwartzsinn.com

Schwartz's Inn is located in the heart of Kingston's historic Stockade District, close to all the landmarks and many restaurants and galleries in the area. This is a small but very pleasant place, with only two rooms, both with double beds. Kids are welcome, so it's a good choice for a family trip. Free Wi-Fi.

THREE OAKS BED AND BREAKFAST $$

110 Fairview Avenue

(845) 339-1115

www.threeoaks.us

Set in a quiet neighborhood near the Stockade District, Three Oaks Bed and Breakfast is in a 1905 colonial home. The inn offers two airy bedrooms with hardwood floors, each with access to the private living room. Guests often rent the entire suite for family groups—kids and well-behaved dogs are welcome here. There's also a furnished one-bedroom apartment available for short-term, extended-stay, or vacation rental.

Milton

BUTTERMILK FALLS INN AND SPA $$–$$$$

220 North Road

(845) 795-1310

www.buttermilkfallsinn.com

Originally a trading post dating back to 1680, the main guest house at Buttermilk Falls Inn is a family homestead built in 1764. A recent renovation and expansion has updated this outstanding inn while retaining the historic features and colonial charm. Buttermilk Falls offers 10 guest rooms in the main building and another three in renovated carriage houses on the landscaped 70-acre grounds. Each guest room offers a fireplace, private bath (many with spas), cable TV, high-speed Internet, and fantastic views out over the Hudson River. The rooms are furnished with canopy beds, antiques, and fine artwork. Breakfast here is a full buffet featuring fresh produce and eggs from the inn's own gardens, orchards, and hens; afternoon tea is served daily, featuring finger sandwiches and freshly baked treats. In addition to the guest rooms, Buttermilk Falls offers an unusual eco-friendly spa experience. The spa uses only naturally crafted and organic products, and the sauna, steam room, and mineral pool are heated using solar and geothermal energy. Buttermilk Falls offers some excellent midweek packages—check the Web site for details.

New Paltz

LEFÈVRE HOUSE BED & BREAKFAST $–$$

14 Southside Avenue

(845) 255-4747

www.lefevrehouse.com

A "painted lady" Victorian dating back to the 1870s, Lefèvre House preserves the historical features of the house while providing up-to-date services. The decor here is best described as eclectic, a mixture of contemporary and antique furnishings. Each of the nine bedrooms features a different color theme, accented by luxurious Versace bedding. There's also a two-bedroom suite that sleeps up to six, with a full kitchen and sitting room. Breakfast here is a three-course gourmet treat, served on china and crisp linen.

Lefèvre House doubles as an art gallery—the paintings and sculptures that decorate the rooms are for exhibit and sale. Because of its location in downtown New Paltz, Lefèvre House is a favorite for visitors to SUNY New Paltz. Kids and dogs (no cats) are welcome; there's an additional fee for the pooch. The inn offers some good package deals—check the Web site for details. Free Wi-Fi.

MAPLESTONE INN $–$$
541 Route 32 South
(845) 255-6861
www.maplestoneinn.com
The guest rooms at Maplestone Inn are unusually spacious, with private baths. The inn is a renovated stone farmhouse from the 1790s; it's located on seven peaceful acres of lawns and gardens. The Hunter Room on the first floor has a king-size bed and a private porch. The Tucker Room on the second floor offers a huge bath with spectacular views. The Jenkins Suite is three rooms with a bedroom fireplace, bathroom with claw-foot tub and private steam unit, and a sitting room with pull-out sofa for two additional guests. Guests choose between a Continental breakfast served in their room or the full chef's breakfast served in the dining room. Kids over 12 are welcome; no pets. Free Wi-Fi.

MOHONK MOUNTAIN HOUSE $$$$
1000 Mountain Rest Road
(845) 255-1000
www.mohonk.com
There are places to stay in the region that are older than the Mohonk Mountain House, but this world-famous hotel is a trip back in time to the graciousness of the Victorian era. A grand 265-room Victorian castle, the resort sprawls along the edge of the spectacularly beautiful Lake Mohonk. Half a mile long, 60 feet deep, and lined with majestic rock formations, the mountain lake looks today very much as it did when Albert Smiley first laid eyes on it in 1869. He envisioned a peaceful retreat where visitors could enjoy the beauty of nature and renew their spirits. That vision remains the guiding principle at Mohonk Mountain House today, carried on

by their descendants—this is one of the oldest family-owned resorts in America. It was named a National Historic Landmark in 1986. Surrounded by stunning gardens and sweeping lawns, and secluded among 26,000 acres of pristine woodlands and mountains, Mohonk Mountain House is a genuine retreat, a place to enjoy 19th-century charm with 21st-century amenities. Because Mohonk Mountain House is a full American plan resort, the rates include accommodations, three meals daily prepared by award-winning chefs, and afternoon tea, all served in the spectacular main dining room or smaller side rooms. The rates also include most recreational activities, including hiking, swimming in the heated indoor pool or Lake Mohonk, a well-equipped fitness center, tennis, midweek golf, boating, croquet, lawn bowling, and even shuffleboard. In the winter, there's cross-country skiing on 35 miles of groomed trails, along with sledding, snowshoeing, and ice-skating. Other activities, such as rock climbing, mountain biking, and horseback riding, are available for an additional fee. Evening entertainment includes movies, nature shows, dancing, sing alongs, and other events. Mohonk has recently opened an award-winning 30,000-square-foot spa wing, featuring 16 treatment rooms, sauna and steam rooms, a beauty salon, and an outdoor heated mineral pool, along with a comprehensive fitness center, yoga studio, and an indoor heated swimming pool. Mohonk Mountain House is a touch on the formal side. Resort casual attire is appropriate during the day. Dinner is more formal, with jackets suggested for gentlemen over 12; women should dress accordingly. For decades, alcohol wasn't served at Mohonk. Today, the resort has an outstanding wine list; drinks are available in the dining room at lunch and dinner, and the Carriage Lounge is open daily from 5:00 to 11:00 p.m. No alcohol is served anywhere else, although guests may have alcohol in their rooms. The rooms here are all large and comfortable, featuring Victorian, Edwardian, and Craftsman decor. Many rooms have balconies and fireplaces. All have Wi-Fi; none have televisions. A number of rooms are fully wheelchair accessible.

Mohonk has a well-deserved reputation for being expensive, but the many packages and theme programs here can be excellent values. Because these programs are very popular, and because Mohonk is a favorite spot for family reunions, weddings, and other events, reservations well in advance are an absolute must.

MOONDANCE RIDGE BED AND BREAKFAST $$
55 Shivertown Road
(800) 641-5618
www.moondanceridge.com

Moondance Ridge combines Craftsman design from the early 1900s with Hollywood elegance in the five guest rooms. It's a good mix—the Starry Night suite, for instance, is modeled after Jean Harlow's actual bedroom, including a four-poster bed with draperies. (This room is also wheelchair accessible, as are all the common areas.) The Moondance Suite is decorated in the style of Humphrey Bogart and Lauren Bacall, with a four-poster king-size bed, dramatic Hollywood vanity, fireplace, balcony, and bath with heated double whirlpool overlooking a private wooded area. All rooms have private baths with whirlpool tubs and showers. Weekend rates include a three-course gourmet breakfast; on weekdays, a full country breakfast is served.

Rosendale

CREEK LOCKS BED & BREAKFAST $
1046 Creek Locks Road
(845) 331-5889
www.creeklocksbedandbreakfast.com

The three guest rooms at Creek Locks are in a newly renovated 1866 Gothic Revival farmhouse. The inn is on four wooded acres along the Rondout Creek, with frontage on what was once part of the historic Delaware & Hudson Canal. The rooms here are large and bright, with the original wide plank floors, antique armoires, TVs with DVD players, Wi-Fi, and private baths. The inn welcomes children. Small, well-behaved pets are also welcome for an additional fee—call ahead to make arrangements. Creek Locks has a resident dog. Breakfast here is a full meal served in the dining room or on the porch in nice weather.

HARDENBERGH HOUSE BED & BREAKFAST $
118 Maple Hill Drive
(845) 658-9147
www.hardenberghouse.com

With only two elegant guest rooms, Hardenbergh House is small but welcoming. The house is a meticulously restored Victorian filled with authentic decor and fine antiques. The stunning parlor and dining room are like stepping back into the 19th century. The guest rooms are similarly elegant. The Grand Room has a romantic fireplace and separate entrance; the Asia Room is stunningly decorated with chinoiserie. The European-style breakfast features freshly baked goods prepared by a Culinary Institute–trained pastry chef. Ingredients come from the many local farms and other producers whenever possible.

Saugerties

BARCLAY HEIGHTS BED & BREAKFAST $–$$
158 Burt Street
(845) 246-3788
www.outstandinghospitality.com

Barclay Heights Bed & Breakfast offers six guest rooms, all with cozy sitting areas and private baths, in an 1890 Victorian shingle-style cottage. The rooms are furnished with an eclectic mix of antiques and period pieces and feature handwoven antique oriental rugs, gilt mirrors, stained-glass lamps, and all-natural bedding. The location—on the Esopus Creek with a view of Overlook Mountain and adjacent to the Saugerties Lighthouse wetlands preserve—is beautiful. It's a great spot for nature lovers, who can enjoy birding and watching wildlife in the preserve. Breakfast here is a special treat. Owner David Smythe is a professional chef who teaches at the Culinary Institute, and his wife Justine is a Culinary Institute–trained chef. They prepare a personalized breakfast for every guest, served in the contemporary dining room or on the deck in pleasant weather.

THE INN AT CAFÉ TAMAYO $
89 Partition Street
(845) 246-9571
www.cafetamayo.com
The building that houses The Inn at Café Tamayo has been providing fine food and lodging ever since it was built in 1864. Today the ground floor houses Café Tamayo, one of the finest restaurants in the region (see the Restaurants: West chapter for details). The inn upstairs has three bedrooms and one two-bedroom suite with sitting room, all beautifully restored with many of the decorative features of the original building. The rooms are bright and airy, with plenty of windows. Each room is furnished with antique tables and lamps; period paintings and prints hang on the walls. Each room has a private bath. The inn is located in the center of Saugerties, but guests have access to off-street parking in a private lot. Payment is by cash or check.

THE MONTGOMERY BED & BREAKFAST $
76 Montgomery Street
(845) 234-0083
www.montgomerybandb.com
Located in the heart of the charming village of Saugerties, The Montgomery has four spacious guest rooms, all with private baths and cable TV. There's also a deluxe suite with kitchen, living room with sleeper sofa, four-poster California king bed, and private entrance. Each guest room is decorated in a different style—Deco, for instance—and has period furnishings and luxurious bedding. A country breakfast is served in the bright dining area; guests can also enjoy the spacious parlor, patio, and old-fashioned back porch. Off-street parking is provided for guests.

THE RENWICK CLIFTON HOUSE BED & BREAKFAST $–$$
27 Barclay Street
(845) 246-0552
www.renwickclifton.com
A Southern-style mansion dating back to 1812, the Renwick Clifton House is right on the Hudson River. The four guest rooms here are named, appropriately enough, after famous steamboats that once sailed on the river and used the nearby Saugerties Lighthouse for navigation. Each room—the Mary Powell, Chancellor Livingston, Clermont, and Ansonia—is beautifully decorated with replica antiques and features cable TV on a plasma screen, Wi-Fi, and modern baths tiled in Italian marble. On weekends, guests are served a four-course gourmet breakfast; during the week the menu is a hearty country breakfast. Children over 14 are welcome.

SAUGERTIES LIGHTHOUSE $
Lighthouse Drive
(845) 247-0656
www.saugertieslighthouse.com
A stay at the restored Saugerties Lighthouse is a great opportunity to experience a bit of history firsthand (see the Hudson Valley Mansions and Historic Sites: West Side chapter for more information about the lighthouse). Arranging a visit here is a little complicated, however. Guests who arrive by boat can tie up at the lighthouse dock any time, but guests who come from the shore have to time their arrival and departure for the period between high tides when the half-mile trail to the lighthouse isn't underwater. Staying here is a fairly bare-bones experience. The lighthouse has two second-floor bedrooms, each with a double bed. Kids are welcome here (dogs too), and cots are available. The large bedroom windows offer spectacular views. There's only one bathroom, a shared facility on the first floor that has a sink, shower, and composting toilet (always a hit with kids, less popular with adults). A hearty breakfast, cooked by the lighthouse keeper, is provided. The kitchen is available for guests to use to prepare other meals, and guests can also use the outdoor barbecue grill. The lighthouse is open all year. Weekends book up quickly year-round; between April and October, demand is strong even on weekdays. Reserve early.

Stone Ridge

THE INN AT STONE RIDGE $$-$$$
3805 Main Street
(845) 687-0736
www.innatstoneridge.com

The Inn at Stone Ridge is the 18th-century Has-brouck House, a Dutch colonial mansion. The oldest section of the restored bluestone house dates back to 1757. The inn is set on 150 acres of lawns, gardens, a working apple orchard, and woodland. The rooms here are very spacious and are decorated in period antiques, updated with modern amenities. Public areas include a huge living room and dining area. The Inn at Stone Ridge can accommodate up to 20 people in one three-room and two two-room suites, two one-bedroom suites, and two complete two-bedroom apartments in the Carriage House. Family groups sometimes rent the entire inn as a private guest house, but most of the time it's available to individual guests on a bed-and-breakfast basis. Kids are welcome—the one-bedroom suites are set up with sleeping accommodations for them. Chefs/owners Dan and Suzanne Hauspurg prepare a gourmet breakfast every morning. They're also available to cater memorable meals, ranging from five-course dinners celebrating special events to barbecues on the lawn. Whenever possible, they use local produce from their own orchard and from nearby farmers.

THE 1712 HOUSE $
93 Mill Dam Road
(845) 687-7167
www.1712house.com

Settlement on the property that's now The 1712 House dates back to the mid-1600s, when the Hardenbergh family received a land grant of almost 250 square miles. The original farm was where the house is now. In the 1700s, a dam was constructed and one of the earliest watermills in the region was built next to it. The mill is long gone, but the pond remains, along with a large Dutch barn with a slate roof that's a local landmark. The 1712 House is unique. Built in modern times but faithful to the style of the 1700s, the house has bluestone walls, wide board floors, hand-hewn beams, and custom-made colonial-style furniture. It's set on 80 unspoiled acres. Guests at The 1712 House are accommodated in six bedrooms, all featuring a handmade colonial-style king- or queen-size bed. Every room has a beautiful view from the windows; a dining area, high-speed Internet, and cable TV are also in every room. The common areas include a guest living/dining room, a bluestone patio, and a spacious wraparound deck. Breakfast is made to order every morning and is served in the dining room or in the privacy of your own room. Kids over 12 are welcome here during the week, but on weekends it's grown-ups only.

SPARROW HAWK BED & BREAKFAST $-$$
4496 Route 209
(845) 687-4492
www.sparrowhawkbandb.com

Sparrow Hawk Bed & Breakfast is a beautifully restored brick colonial structure dating back to 1770 and set among black locust trees that are more than 200 years old. The house still has its original wide plank floors and a number of the original fireplaces. All five guest rooms are large and comfy, furnished with period antiques, and have private baths. Behind the old house is the soaring Grand Room, with cathedral windows and a balcony, where guests are welcome to relax. A full gourmet breakfast is served by the fireplace here every morning—except in the nice weather, when breakfast is served on the bluestone patio. Kids over 12 are welcome. Sparrow Hawk offers a number of good packages and specials, including their weekend innkeepers seminar on how to run a B&B. Check the Web site for details.

Woodstock

EMERSON RESORT AND SPA $$$-$$$$
5340 Route 28
Mount Tremper
(877) 688-2828
www.emersonplace.com

Guests at the elegant Emerson Resort and Spa

can choose between two very distinctive types of accommodations. The Inn consists of 25 luxury suites for adults only. Each suite has spectacular views from the oversized windows and private decks. All feature canopy beds, Asian-influenced decor, lounge areas, gas fireplaces, and spacious baths with whirlpool tubs and Swiss showers. The Lodge is a separate structure with 27 rooms, including many multiroom suites. The Lodge is family-oriented, although it's still very private, and singles and couples won't feel out of place. The accommodations here are luxurious and spacious. The largest accommodations here are the family suites, which hold six people very comfortably. Each family suite has a private sitting room with a queen-size sofa bed and flat-screen TV, two bedrooms and two full bathrooms, and a balcony overlooking the rushing Esopus Creek. Pets are welcome at The Lodge for an additional $25 fee per day. Emerson offers fine dining at the Phoenix restaurant. The Spa is a full-service facility, with 10 treatment rooms and more than 40 treatment options. The resort offers a number of attractive packages and specials year-round—check the Web site for updates.

ENCHANTED MANOR OF WOODSTOCK $-$$
23 Rowe Road
(845) 679-9012
www.enchantedmanorinn.com
Enchanted Manor is an elegant sight, with majestic columns, a circular driveway, a large pond, and beautifully landscaped grounds adorned with sculptures. The inn offers three beautifully decorated guest rooms, all with private bath, and a two-room suite with a spacious Roman bathroom featuring a sunken spa for two. For even more privacy, there's the Cottage, cozily set off by itself in the woods. A major attraction at Enchanted Manor is the spectacular outdoor saltwater pool. Surrounded by a cypress deck, the in-ground pool is heated and chlorine-free. The six-person outdoor hot tub next to the pool overlooks a waterfall. Indoors, guests can relax by

the fireplace in the living room or watch wildlife through the large picture windows in the dining area. Breakfast at Enchanted Manor during the week is a full self-serve buffet. Sunday breakfast features pancakes, omelets, and assorted pastries. The owners are very accommodating of vegetarian and vegan dietary needs. *Note:* Enchanted Manor is a shoe-free environment. Slippers are provided, or bring your own.

TWIN GABLES GUEST HOME $
73 Tinker Street
(845) 679-9479
www.twingableswoodstockny.com
A Woodstock landmark, Twin Gables Guest Home is right in the heart of the village. It's been a popular guest house for well more than 50 years. The accommodations here are affordable, very clean, and fairly basic—only three of the nine guest rooms have private baths, and the Continental breakfast is simple but good. The rooms are comfortably furnished with antiques and handmade rugs. Artwork by Woodstock artists hangs on the walls. Guests can relax in the cozy common parlor. Limited off-street parking is available. Credit cards accepted; no personal checks.

THE WILD ROSE INN $$
66 Rock City Road
(845) 679-8783
www.thewildroseinn.com
The Wild Rose Inn is a restored Victorian mansion dating back to 1898, complete with upscale detailing and period decor. Two guest rooms, one full suite, and two spacious junior suites make this a good choice for families. Kids are welcome here, and most rooms have sleeper sofas. The rooms are furnished with period antiques and floral carpeting. All have cable TV and private baths with whirlpool tubs. Brandy is complimentary! Breakfast at The Wild Rose features home-baked pastries, fresh fruit, and a wide assortment of other choices. There's a $25 charge each for the third and fourth persons in the room. Personal checks not accepted less than 14 days prior to arrival.

WOODSTOCK COUNTRY INN $-$$
185 Cooper Lake Road
(845) 679-9380
www.woodstockcountryinn.com
What could be more appropriate for a stay in Woodstock than the former home of famed artist Jo Cantine? When Cantine died in 1987 at the age of 94, her 19th-century farmhouse residence was renovated and became the Woodstock Country Inn. Today several of Cantine's wonderful paintings and her hand-painted furniture are on display in the common rooms and guest rooms of the inn. Four lovely guest rooms are available, each offering mountain views, luxurious bedding, a private porch or deck, and a spacious full bath. A heated swimming pool, set in a wildflower meadow with mountain views, is open to guests from May to October. A full breakfast featuring organic eggs and produce is served every morning. Kids over 12 are welcome.

**WOODSTOCK INN ON THE
MILLSTREAM** $-$$
48 Tannery Brook Road
(845) 679-8211
www.woodstock-inn-ny.com
The Woodstock Inn offers 18 guest rooms in three buildings, set among beautiful gardens and manicured lawns. The lovely Millstream cascades through the three-acre property. Accommodations here are affordable and convenient—the inn is only a short walk from the heart of Woodstock. The 10 standard rooms all have private entrances and private baths with showers (no kids in these rooms). The remaining rooms are more luxurious studios, complete with kitchenettes and full baths with spa tubs—they're ideal for family stays. All rooms have cable TV and free Wi-Fi. A lavish Continental breakfast is served buffet-style every morning in the lobby.

CHAIN HOTELS AND MOTELS
Athens/Catksill/Coxsackie Area
BEST WESTERN NEW BALTIMORE
12600 Route 9W
(518) 731-8100
www.bestwestern.com

BUDGET INN AND SUITES
9809 Route 9W
(518) 943-2350

QUALITY INN AND CONFERENCE CENTER
704 Route 23B
(518) 943-5800
www.qualityinn.com

Kingston Area
COURTYARD BY MARRIOTT
500 Frank Sottile Boulevard
(845) 382-2300
www.courtyard.com

HOLIDAY INN
503 Washington Avenue
(845) 338-0400
www.hikingston.com

QUALITY INN & SUITES
114 Route 28
(845) 339-3900
www.qualityinn.com

RAMADA INN
Route 28 Exit NYS Thruway
(845) 339-3900
www.ramada.com

SUPER 8 MOTEL
487 Washington Avenue
(845) 338-3078
www.super8.com

Newburgh Area

COMFORT INN NEWBURGH
5 Lakeside Drive
(845) 567-0567
www.comfortinn.com

COURTYARD BY MARRIOTT NEWBURGH AIRPORT
4 Governor Drive
(845) 567-4800
www.courtyard.com

DAYS INN
915 Union Avenue
(845) 564-7550
www.daysinn.com

ECONOMY INN
483 Route 9W
(845) 562-6170

HAMPTON INN
1054 Union Avenue
(845) 567-9100
www.hamptoninn.com

HILTON GARDEN INN
15 Crossroads Court
(845) 567-9500
www.hiltongardeninn.com

HOWARD JOHNSON INN
95 Route 17K
(845) 564-4000
www.hojo.com

QUALITY INN & SUITES
90 Route 17K
(845) 564-9020
www.qualityinn.com

RAMADA INN WEST POINT
1289 Route 300
(845) 564-4500
www.ramada.com

SUPER 8 MOTEL
1287 Route 300
(845) 654-5700
www.super8.com

New Paltz Area

ECONO LODGE NEW PALTZ
530 Main Street
(845) 255-6200
www.econolodge.com

RODEWAY INN AND SUITES
601 Main Street
(845) 883-7373
www.rodewayinnandsuitesnp.com

SUPER 8 MOTEL
7 Terwilliger Lane
(845) 255-8865
www.super8.com

Saugerties Area

COMFORT INN
2790 Route 32
(845) 246-1565
www.comfortinn.com

HOWARD JOHNSON INN
2764 Route 32
(845) 246-9511
www.hojo.com

CAMPGROUNDS AND RV PARKS

The west side of the Hudson Valley offers a number of private and state campgrounds and RV parks. Many more are found to the west in the Catskills, an area that's outside the scope of this book. Fees for camping vary so much, depending on the place, the time of year, and the type of campsite, that it's impossible to give a meaningful range. All the sites listed here provide the usual amenities for campers, including water, electric, and sewer hookups, dump stations, fire rings, picnic tables, Wi-Fi, and laundry rooms.

Many sites have recreational facilities, including swimming pools, playgrounds, and game rooms. Some sites also offer rental cabins. The camping season is generally from April 15 to October 15. Sites fill up very quickly—advance reservations are essential. Check with the campsite for details on pet policies. Almost all allow dogs, but some have size limits—and some have dog recreation areas. Most sites can accommodate even the largest RVs, but check ahead to be sure. Also check ahead for details on check-in and check-out times, minimum stays, and cancellation policies.

Detailed information on state and private campgrounds can be found on the I Love NY Web site at www.iloveny.com/Outdoors.aspx.

Greene

BROOKSIDE CAMPGROUNDS
4952 Route 32
Catskill
(800) 390-4412
www.campingfriend.com/brooksidecampground

CEDAR GROVE CAMPGROUND
Schoharie Turnpike
Athens
(518) 945-1451

EARLTON HILL FAMILY CAMPGROUND
600 Medway-Earlton Road
Earlton
(518) 731-2751

INDIAN RIDGE CAMPSITES
1446 Leeds Athens Road
Leeds
(518) 943-3516

WOODS ROAD CAMPSITE
152 Vedder Road
Catskill

(518) 943-9118

Orange

NEWBURGH KOA
Freetown Highway
Newburgh
(845) 564-2836
www.newburghkoa.com

Ulster

HIDDEN VALLEY LAKE CAMPGROUND
290 Whiteport Road
Kingston
(845) 338-4616

RIP VAN WINKLE CAMPGROUNDS
149 Blue Mountain Road
Saugerties
(888) 720-1232
www.ripvanwinklecampgrounds.com

RONDOUT VALLEY RESORT
105 Mettacahonts Road
Accord
(845) 626-5521
www.rondoutvalley.com

SAUGERTIES/WOODSTOCK KOA
882 Route 212
Saugerties
(800) 562-4081
www.saugertieskoa.com

YOGI BEAR'S JELLYSTONE PARK™ CAMP RESORT AT LAZY RIVER
50 Bevier Road
Gardiner
(845) 255-5193
www.lazyriverny.com

RESTAURANTS: EAST SIDE OF THE HUDSON

The mid–Hudson Valley region has long been both a popular tourism destination and also home to a sophisticated population of adventurous eaters. In addition, the famed Culinary Institute of America, the training ground for many of the nation's top chefs, is right in the middle of the region in Hyde Park. The many graduates of the CIA who have learned to love the scenic beauty and bountiful local produce of the Hudson Valley have stayed here and gone to work in local restaurants or opened places of their own. The end result is that a *lot* of good restaurants are found in the mid–Hudson Valley. They boast outstanding chefs and creative cuisine. More and more, they also proudly emphasize their use of local suppliers. Hudson Valley farmers and artisans fill out the menus with sustainably raised produce, meats, poultry, eggs, cheese, wine, and other fine foods.

On the east side of the Hudson, several towns are particularly full of good places to eat. Hudson in Columbia County; Rhinebeck, Millbrook, Poughkeepsie, and Beacon in Dutchess County; and Cold Spring in Putnam County all have numerous places to get a great meal. But don't overlook the many fine restaurants in the other charming towns of the region—they're well worth visiting.

To keep this chapter (and the next one on restaurants on the west side of the Hudson) to a barely manageable length, only restaurants that offer full dinner service are listed. Many but not all of these restaurants also offer lunch and Sunday brunch—if they do, the listings say so. The open days are listed, but because hours may vary seasonally, they're not given unless the restaurant has unusual hours—the kitchen is open very late, for instance. If in doubt, call ahead for information.

This chapter is organized first by county, then alphabetically by town, and then alphabetically by restaurant name. With some very rare exceptions, every restaurant here accepts all major credit cards. Also with some very rare exceptions, every restaurant here has a liquor license and offers at least beer and wine; most have full bars.

Where reservations are important, the listing says so—and where a restaurant doesn't accept reservations, the listing says that as well. As a general rule, however, even places that don't ordinarily take reservations ask you to reserve for larger parties of six or more. When in doubt, call ahead—and ask if there's a private room for your group. A surprising number of restaurants have them. At particularly busy times (in the summer, on weekends, on major holidays) you may need to call a few days in advance for a reservation. Usually, however, you can be accommodated if you call the day before or early on the same day.

New York State law requires that all restaurants be fully wheelchair accessible. In the very few cases where accessibility may be problem, it's noted. Again, if in doubt, call ahead. And New York State law forbids smoking in restaurants and bars.

Price Code

The prices at the restaurants listed here range from moderate to very expensive indeed. The price code below gives the average price for dinner entrees for two. That's entrees only—the price excludes cocktails, wine, beer, beverages, appetizers, desserts, tax, and tip. As a general rule, prices at lunch are lower than those at dinner, but the menu may be limited. Some restaurants offer prix-fixe dinners or have special nights with fixed prices. These offerings can be a very good value, especially if you're dining out on a weeknight.

$	less than $30
$$	$31 to $50
$$$	$51 to $65
$$$$	$66 or higher

Hudson Valley Restaurant Weeks

The restaurants of the Hudson Valley get to show themselves off every March during Hudson Valley Restaurant Weeks. Nearly 80 restaurants in seven counties, including Putnam, Dutchess, Orange, Ulster, and Columbia, participate by serving specially priced three-course lunch and dinner menus any night but Saturday in mid-March. Presented by *The Valley Table*, a free, five-times-a-year magazine focusing on Hudson Valley food and restaurants, the event always showcases locally grown products. It's a great way to try out a new restaurant. For more information, call (845) 561-2022 or check www. HudsonValleyRestaurantWeek.com.

COLUMBIA COUNTY

Chatham

BLUE PLATE RESTAURANT $$
1 Kinderhook Street
(518) 392-7711
www.chathamblueplate.net

Located on a historic corner in the center of town, the Blue Plate is a lot like Kinderhook itself—small and charming. Striped awnings shade the Victorian entrance; inside, the welcoming staff seats guests in an airy, casual dining room. The menu here is American bistro, with standards and seasonal specials that revolve around local Hudson Valley produce, including lamb from the nearby Old Chatham Sheepherding Company farm. The highlight of the menu is the famous Blue Plate Meat Loaf, topped with bacon and served with garlic mashed potatoes and gravy. But don't think vegetarian dishes are an afterthought here—the regular menu always includes at least two vegetarian dishes, such as pasta with broccoli rabe, sun-dried tomatoes, onions, pignolis, and olives, and there's always at least one meatless dish on the specials list. For a small neighborhood restaurant, the Blue Plate has a surprisingly broad and well-chosen wine list, although most are sold by the bottle only. The beer list is equally interesting. On Wednesday nights, the Blue Plate offers live music (mostly folk, jazz, and bluegrass). Open for dinner every night except Monday.

LIPPERA'S AT THE CHATHAM HOUSE/
THE CHATHAM HOUSE TAVERN $$
29 Hudson Avenue
(518) 392-6600
www.thechathamhouse.com

Years ago, The Chatham House was a railroad hotel with a rather dubious reputation. The days when Chatham was a major railroad junction are long past, however, and the building had fallen into disrepair when Butch and Monica Lippera bought it in the 1990s. They've since restored the 1859 structure, including the fabulous wraparound porches, and created two restaurants, along with retail and gallery space on the upper

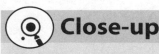 **Close-up**

Local Diners

This book covers six counties, so when it comes to diners, only a handful of standouts can be listed. It's a given here that all the diners offer good food, reasonable prices, and are open long hours, though not all are open 24/7.

COLUMBIA COUNTY

O's Eatery
309 Rigor Hill Road
Chatham
(518) 392-1001
www.oseatery.com
The only diner for the entire length of the Taconic Parkway; classic 1952 Colonial-style Fodero design.

DUTCHESS COUNTY

Daily Planet
1202 Route 55
LaGrangeville
(845) 452-0110
www.dailyplanetdiner.com
You can order Kryptonite Sticks here (OK, they're really deep-fried mozzarella). A 1940s look and lots of TV nostalgia on the menu. Kids love this place.

Dutchess Diner
1950 South Road
Poughkeepsie
(845) 297-8100
www.dutchessdiner.com
Open 24/7, good bakery, salad bar.

Eveready Diner
4189 Albany Post Road (Route 9)
Hyde Park
(845) 229-8100
Classic retro diner. Open until 2:00 a.m.

"Historic" Red Hook Diner
7550 North Broadway (Route 9)
Red Hook
(845) 758-6232
www.historic-village-diner.com
Authentic Silk City design from the 1950s, so historic it's listed on the National Register of Historic Places.

Palace Diner
194 Washington Street
Poughkeepsie
(845) 473-1576
www.thepalacediner.com
A classic family-operated Greek diner, handy to Marist College and St. Francis Hospital.

GREENE COUNTY

Ursula's Riverside Diner
6 South Water Street
Athens
(518) 945-3402
The Hudson River is right across the street. Very friendly staff and customers.

ULSTER COUNTY

College Diner
500 Main Street
New Paltz
(845) 255-5040
Open 24/7, in the heart of New Paltz.

Dietz Stadium Diner
127 North Front Street
Kingston
(845) 331-5321
Open 24/7. Loyal local clientele.

Michael's Diner
1071 Ulster Avenue
Kingston
(845) 336-6514
Open 24/7. Friendly staff even in the wee hours.

Plaza Diner
27 New Paltz Plaza
New Paltz
(845) 255-1030
Open 24/7. Good daily specials. Convenient location in central New Paltz.

floor. The Lipperas are charter members of the Columbia County Farm to Plate program, meaning they get most of their ingredients from local farms and dairies. The dinner menu is locally inspired and changes with the season. On a typical winter evening it might include homemade country-style pâté, braised short ribs, or classic cheese manicotti. The Tavern offers lunch, dinner, and bar food in a more informal atmosphere, including burgers, wraps, sandwiches, and pizza along with comfort food entrees such as macaroni and cheese. Caution: The warm, homemade potato chips with dill dip are highly addictive. Dinner at Lippera's is served every evening; reservations are strongly suggested. Lunch in the Tavern is served Monday to Saturday. Both restaurants are closed on Tuesdays between September and April.

i Restaurant meals in New York State are taxed. In Columbia County, the tax is 8 percent. In Dutchess County, it's $8^1/_8$ percent. In Putnam County, it's $8^3/_8$ percent. When calculating your tip, use the pretax total.

Germantown

RESTAURANT $$
2 Church Avenue
(518) 537-2160

Yes, this restaurant really is named just Restaurant. The food here is eclectic with a decidedly Italian leaning. The menu changes weekly to accommodate seasonal local produce. Enjoyable as the entrees such as pan-roasted lemon chicken are, what makes Restaurant really stand out are the individual artisanal pizzas. Thin-crusted and baked in a wood-fired oven, the pizzas come in a variety of interesting combinations. The Nana, for instance, combines arugula and tomatoes with mozzarella, while the Gaspar is a cheeseless pizza made with tomatoes, anchovies, capers, and olives. The dining room at Restaurant is lovely. The sage green walls are warm and intimate, and the tables are just far enough apart to make for easy conversation without feeling isolated. Open

for lunch on Saturday and Sunday only; dinner is served Thursday through Sunday.

Hudson

CA'MEA RISTORANTE $$
333 Warren Street
(518) 822-0005
www.camearestaurant.com

Authentic northern Italian cuisine is featured at this well-established Hudson favorite. The ravioli and pastas are homemade and the wine list is outstanding. At dinner, try the ravioli dello chef—homemade sweet potato and ricotta cheese, served with fresh sage, butter, and truffle oil—and the other excellent pasta dishes. The menu also features beautifully prepared entrees such as petto d'anatra al balsamico (pan-seared duck breast with sesame and pine nuts in a balsamic sauce). The lunch menu offers panini, a daily special omelet, and a small but select range of pasta dishes and entrees. It's all served in a spacious, contemporary dining room with coffered mahogany ceilings; a very pleasant back garden is open seasonally for outdoor dining. Reservations required. Closed Mondays.

DA | BA $$$
225 Warren Street
(518) 249-4631
www.dabahudson.com

Not for the faint of heart (or palate), DA | BA is one the more interesting restaurants in the Hudson Valley. It is definitely the only restaurant that lists the salads on the menu under the heading "Roughage." Appetizers such as salt-baked duck with seaweed salad and mushroom tea are listed under "Essentials." Entrees are listed under "Sustenance" and include dishes such grilled filet mignon with red wine reduction, chanterelle potato puree, and serrano-wrapped asparagus, and lamb rack with white wine cherry sauce, sautéed fruit, potato fondant, and spiced sausage. For less adventurous eaters, the restaurant also offers pub fare—a classic burger or BLT, with homemade fries. Dinner every day but Sunday; reservations a must.

ℹ️ New York State says: No smoking any-where in restaurants or bars! It's the law—no exceptions.

MEXICAN RADIO $

537 Warren Street

(518) 828-7770

www.mexrad.com

Fun if a little on the noisy side, Mexican Radio is the Hudson outpost of the parent restaurant in Man-hattan. The food here manages to be both authen-tically Mexican and highly original. The Mexican spring rolls, for instance, are made with corn, mush-rooms, peppers, lettuce, and guacamole rolled in spring roll wrappers and served with raspberry peanut chipotle dipping sauce. Not exactly tradi-tional—but delicious. Enjoy the best margaritas for many, many miles around and have the wonderful flan for dessert. Open daily until 11:00 p.m.

MUDDY CUP COFFEE HOUSE $

742 Warren Street

(518) 828-2210

www.muddycup.com

The Muddy Cup coffee houses aren't exactly a chain of lookalike stores, but there are now seven of them in the Hudson Valley, reaching as far north as Schenectady. Owners Jim Svetz and Brian Woodward began on Staten Island and opened their first Hudson Valley store in Hudson in 2001. Each store is in remodeled space in an existing building, which means each store is different in a funky sort of way. All feature an interesting variety of fresh-brewed coffee and tea drinks, along with locally baked snacks. Each store is also closely involved with the local arts community, offering wall space for art exhibits and performance space for musicians and writers. They're all excellent spots for some relaxation and refreshment during a long day of antiquing and gallery hopping. All stores are open every day from 6:00 or 7:00 a.m. to 11:00 p.m. or later. Other locations are: **Bea-con,** 129 Main Street, (845) 440-8855; **Catskill,** 410 Main Street, (518) 303-9228; **Kingston,** 516 Broadway, (845) 338-3881; **New Paltz,** 58 Main Street, (845) 255-5801; Saugerties, **66 Partition St.,** (845) 246-5775.

RED DOT RESTAURANT AND BAR $$

321 Warren Street

(518) 828-3657

Entering the dining room of this storefront bistro is a bit of a shock. The building is faded Victorian on the outside but strikingly modern on the inside, with 10-foot ceilings and an arresting black-and-red color scheme. A lovely walled gar-den in the back is open for seasonal dining. Red Dot offers good food and drink in a pleasantly relaxed atmosphere. The menu is eclectic, but the most popular entrees are traditional fish and chips and homemade chicken pot pie. Open for dinner Wednesday through Sunday; lunch on Saturday and Sunday only.

SWOON KITCHENBAR $$$

340 Warren Street

(518) 822-8938

www.swoonkitchenbar.com

The outstanding New American cuisine cre-ated here by chef-owner Jeff Gimmel is indeed enough to make you swoon—and that's before you encounter the creations of his wife and pastry chef Nina Gimmel. The menu features homemade charcuterie and dishes prepared with local ingredients whenever possible, so the menu changes often, depending on what's in season. Typical dinner dishes are an appetizer of Sky Farms arugula salad with gorgonzola soufflé and an entree of Stone Church Farm duck confit, served with grilled endive and wild porcini sauce. The lunch menu features salads, panini, pasta, and a handful of entrees. It's all served up in a relaxed, flower-filled dining room. Definitely make dinner reservations. Lunch Thursday through Monday, dinner every day but Wednesday.

VICO RESTAURANT AND BAR $$$

136 Warren Street

(518) 828-6529

www.vico-restaurant.com

Traditional Tuscan cuisine meets locally grown Hudson Valley ingredients at this very hospitable restaurant. The menu offers a wonderful range of authentic Tuscan dishes such as lasagne al cinghiale (lasagna made with wild boar ragù and béchamel sauce). A dinner menu highlight is the bistecca Fiorentina, made with locally raised organic beef. It's a 22-ounce porterhouse steak, grilled with olive oil in the Florentine style, and served with Tuscan fries seasoned with rosemary and sage. The wine list offers an excellent selection of Italian wines to accompany your meal. Reservations suggested. Dinner every evening except Tuesday; lunch Friday, Saturday, and Sunday only.

DUTCHESS COUNTY

Amenia

SEREVAN RESTAURANT $$$
6 Autumn Lane (Route 44)
(845) 373-9800
www.serevan.com
Although Amenia is in eastern Dutchess County and technically not in the Hudson Valley, it's included here because otherwise one of the area's finest restaurants would have to be omitted. Chef Serge Madikians brings his Armenian ancestry and broad culinary experience to Serevan. His cuisine is an artful blend of the Middle East and the Mediterranean, all served in a restored 1880s farmhouse. The menu changes weekly here, depending on what Chef Serge can source from local providers. Entrees on a typical week might range from pan-seared branzino with cumin-scented hummus and preserved lemons to breast of duck with parsnip puree and brussels sprouts. Desserts here are in keeping with the cuisine, which means they're not the usual fare. Try chilled watermelon with warm Greek feta cheese dumpling and cilantro syrup or the caramel cashew tart with curry crème Anglaise and cassis ice cream. The Sunday brunch menu features panini and omelets; like the dinner menu, it varies weekly. Reservations strongly suggested. Open for dinner Thursday through Monday; Sunday brunch.

Bangall

RED DEVON MARKET AND CAFE $
108 Hunns Lake Road
(845) 868-3175

Red Devon is a restaurant with a mission: to support local agriculture and be a model green business. It succeeds nicely on both counts. The cafe serves locally grown food, including beef from the owners' own herd of Red Devon cattle; humanely grown meat, poultry, and eggs from local producers; and cheese, vegetables, and fruits from nearby farms. Local products and baked goods are also sold in the attached market. All the baking is done on the premises, using seasonal ingredients. The food here is imaginative and carefully prepared; needless to say, the menu varies quite a bit according to the availability of local produce. Old-timers who remember when the building was the Stage Stop restaurant, owned by actor Jimmy Cagney, will hardly recognize it today, although the elaborate bar remains. The building has been extensively renovated using green methods, including recycled wood from old barns, a rooftop solar system for hot water, and a geothermal heating/cooling system. Even the takeout food from the market side is sold in compostable containers. The market at Red Devon is open daily from 8:00 a.m. to 6:00 p.m.; closed Tuesday and Wednesday. The cafe is open for breakfast and lunch every day except Tuesday and Wednesday; dinner is served Thursday through Sunday.

Beacon

CAFÉ AMARCORD $$
276 Main Street
(845) 440-0050
www.cafeamarcord.net
Classic Italian mingles with New American at this enjoyable cafe. On the starters menu at dinner, for instance, the classic side is represented by dishes such as shaved fennel salad with picholine olives; on the New American side are dishes such as herbed goat cheese terrine with roasted baby beets. Likewise for the entrees: Parmesan-encrusted chicken breast with mushrooms and escarole are on the menu next to seared sea scallops with apple-smoked bacon butter and spinach soufflé. The pastas include homemade potato gnocchi with roasted lobster in a lobster

basil mint cream sauce—a long name for a really good dish. Several specials every evening add to the relatively short menu. Closed Mondays.

CUP & SAUCER TEA ROOM $
165 Main Street
(845) 831-6287
www.cupandsaucertearoom.com

After a long morning or afternoon of looking at art in Beacon, a cup of tea and a sandwich or hot dish is just what's needed—and this is just the place for it. Cup & Saucer is quiet, unhurried, and moderately priced. Grilled sandwiches are on the menu, along with hot dishes such as traditional cottage pie (your choice of beef, chicken, or sausage and onions) and macaroni and cheese. There's also a full afternoon tea, complete with scones, assorted tea sandwiches, and dessert. In addition to the restaurant, the Designer Boutique features eclectic giftware and tea accessories. Open daily 11:00 a.m. to 5:00 p.m.; closed Tuesday.

Homespun Foods

Places that serve good, quick, moderately priced lunches are hard to find, which makes Homespun Foods, at 232 Main Street in Beacon (845) 831-5096; www.homespunfoods.com), that much more of a local asset. Choose from homemade soups and imaginative sandwiches, have a classic Greek salad platter—or check the blackboard and select something interesting from the daily specials. Eat at one of the indoor tables or on the patio out back, or take your meal home with you. Open every day, 8:00 a.m. to 5:00 p.m; until 7:00 p.m on Friday and Saturday.

PIGGY BANK $$
448 Main Street
(845) 838-0028
www.piggybankrestaurant.com

The Piggy Bank actually once was a real bank—the vault is still there behind the bar, but now it holds the wine collection. Other remnants of the 1880s building, including the high tin ceiling and big windows, along with the open kitchen, make this a very open and airy restaurant. The specialty here is Southern-style smokehouse barbeque. Ribs are marinated overnight in a special spice blend, slow-cooked over hickory wood, then finished either dry on the grill or basted with barbeque sauce, and served with your choice of two side dishes. Barbeque chicken gets a similar treatment. Other items on the menu include pulled pork, steak, and fried catfish. A few token vegetarian dishes are on the menu, but this is a restaurant for hungry carnivores. Rack-Attack Tuesdays offer an all-you-can-eat rib extravaganza. Open every day for lunch and dinner.

SUKHOTHAI $
516 Main Street
(845) 790-5375
www.sukhothainy.net

Authentic ethnic cuisine is in comparatively short supply in the mid–Hudson Valley, so a genuine Thai restaurant is something of a rarity. The menu here is large and diverse, covering a range of Thai regional styles. House specials include a number of well-prepared duck dishes, include a fiery roasted duck in red curry and crispy Sukhothai duck served in the restaurant's special sauce with steamed vegetables. For dessert, try the grilled banana split—a Thai take on an American classic—or, in summer, the sticky rice and mango. Closed Mondays.

Fishkill
COPPER $$
1111 Main Street
(845) 896-1000
www.copperrestaurantbar.com

Located in the heart of historic Fishkill, Copper

features New American cuisine in an old American building dating back to 1875. (This restaurant used to be the North Street Grill.) The menu is varied and extensive, starting with interesting salads such as five-spiced chicken and including pasta offerings such as seafood manicotti and house specialties such as Louisiana gumbo. Open for lunch and dinner every day. **Note:** Three steps up into the restaurant could be an issue for guests with mobility handicaps.

HUDSON'S RIBS & FISH $$$
1099 Route 9
(845) 297-5002
www.hudsonsribsandfish.com
There's nothing innovative on the menu here, just choice meats and fresh seafood, making this one of the best steak and seafood houses in the Hudson Valley. Not only that, meals here are an excellent value. All dinners include Hudson's signature hot popovers with strawberry butter, a family-style Caesar salad, a fresh-cut vegetable tray, and a choice of rice or potatoes in various styles (the garlic steak fries are particularly good). In addition to the menu items, the specials always include three different fresh seafood choices. Open every day for dinner only.

IL BARILOTTO $$$
1113 Main Street
(845) 897-4300
www.ilbarilottorestaurant.com
Contemporary Italian cuisine is the specialty at Il Barilotto, which means the menu is fairly sophisticated. Not too many other restaurants in the region serve grilled baby octopus as an appetizer, for instance. The homemade pastas and entrees are equally interesting and authentic. Several specials, based on seasonal local produce, are offered every evening. The extensive all-Italian wine list offers an unusual number of choices by the glass or half bottle—a nice touch that gives diners a chance to match the wine individually to their meals and explore new vintages. It's all served in a lovely restored brick carriage house; an impressive granite bar with mahogany moldings dominates the romantic main dining room.

Reservations suggested. Lunch and dinner every day but Sunday.

SAPORE STEAKHOUSE $$$
1108 Main Street
(845) 897-3300
http://cena2000.com/sapore
A contemporary upscale steakhouse, Sapore offers prime, dry-aged beef and fairly standard—and very well prepared—entrees, such as grilled Cornish hen. The pasta and seafood dishes, such as papadelle hunter style with duck, quail, and pheasant ragù, move the menu in a more adventurous direction, but where it gets really interesting is the grilled game section. Sapore is probably the only restaurant in the region to offer premium-cut tenderloin of ostrich or grilled medallions of elk along with the more traditional grilled venison medallions and veal loin chops. An outstanding international wine list is offered. Dinner every evening; lunch on weekdays only.

TANJORE $
992 Main Street Plaza (Route 52)
(845) 896-6659
www.tanjoreindiancuisine.com
Tanjore offers an extensive menu of well-prepared, flavorful dishes with authentic Indian flavors. This is one of the rare restaurants in the region to really show off the remarkable sophistication and variety of Indian food. The appetizer and bread listings on the menu are extensive; try the bread basket, which offers your choice of any three breads on the menu. The entrees are varied and include interesting dishes such as dhansak, lamb cooked in an onion sauce with yellow lentils and flavored with fennel seeds. Tanjore has an outstanding selection of vegetarian dishes such as Kerala avial, made with potatoes, carrots, yam, eggplant, and squash flavored with coconut, cumin, and curry leaves. This is one restaurant where vegetarians don't feel like second-class citizens. The dining room at Tanjore is far from elegant, but the good service, reasonable prices, and great food more than make up for the ordinary setting. Open for lunch and dinner every day.

VIA NOVE $$
1166 Main Street
(845) 896-2255
www.via-nove.com

Traditional Italian/Mediterranean cuisine is on the menu here, all beautifully prepared. The menu offers few surprises, but that's the point—in classic cuisine, it's the preparation and presentation that count, and Via Nove does that very well. An excellent wine list complements the menu. The restaurant is lovely, with a spacious interior decorated with contemporary art—it's like eating in a gallery—and a beautiful bar and lounge area. Open every day for lunch and dinner.

Hopewell Junction

THE BLUE FOUNTAIN $$
826 Route 376
(845) 226-3570
www.thebluefountain.com

This is one of the prettier restaurants in the region—nicely landscaped grounds lead to the entrance, and the spacious dining room has lots of windows that give it an open feeling. The food here is classic Italian in generous portions—even the brick oven personal pizzas are enough for two. The standard pastas are all homemade. The entrees, such as veal Sorrentino and chicken marsala, are also standard and unsurprising but always well prepared. Good food and moderate prices make The Blue Fountain quite popular— reservations are a good idea, especially on weekends or for groups of six or more. Open for dinner every evening; lunch on weekdays only.

LE CHAMBORD $$$$
2737 Route 52
(845) 221-1941
www.lechambord.com

Four-star dining in the luxurious French style is the hallmark at Le Chambord. A meal here is a real experience in luxury, starting with your arrival on the beautifully landscaped 10-acre grounds. The restaurant is in a pillared 1863 Georgian-style mansion. The elegant dining room is decorated with art from host Roy Benich's extensive collection. The cuisine is classic French, featuring perfectly prepared dishes such as roast rack of lamb for two, carved tableside by the well-trained staff, and tournedos Rossini (pan-seared beef tenderloin with Hudson Valley foie gras). The menu changes with the seasons, and the chef offers nightly specials. The outstanding wine list includes more than 600 choices. Open for lunch Monday through Friday; open for dinner every evening. Reservations and appropriate attire a must. In addition to the restaurant, Le Chambord also offers one of the finest small hotels in the region—see the Accommodations: East chapter for details.

PEZA $
2539 Route 52 (Heritage Square)
(845) 223-8040
www.peza.biz

This small restaurant offers hardwood-grilled pizzas, hearth-baked paninis, a variety of pastas, and a handful of good, mostly Italian entrees. As the name suggests, pizza is prominently featured on the menu. The fun part comes as you build your own pizza, selecting the dough (traditional or honey wheat), the sauce (tomato basil, clam velouté, chipotle BBQ), and the cheese and toppings (way too numerous to list here). The bar specializes in martinis. Open for dinner every day; lunch on weekdays only; closed Monday.

Hyde Park

TWIST $$$
4290 Route 9
(845) 229-7094
www.letstwist.com

The management at Twist describe it as a casual American restaurant, but that doesn't really convey how good this restaurant is. The menu is short but well thought out. It focuses on locally sourced New American cuisine such as sautéed Hudson Valley duck breast served with bacon-wrapped fingerling potatoes, Swiss chard, and red onion marmalade, but it also ranges into such

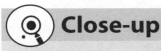 Close-up

The Great Chefs of the Future Start Here

The Culinary Institute of America (CIA) in Hyde Park is the premier culinary college in America. As part of the training program for future chefs, the college operates five student-staffed restaurants on the campus. Each restaurant focuses on a different cuisine and style—and each restaurant is a wonderful dining experience. The students achieve a very high professional level, so much so that you don't mind paying to let them practice on you. The CIA came to Hyde Park in 1972—and not surprisingly, the restaurant renaissance of the Hudson Valley, fueled by highly trained graduates, began soon after. In any given year, more than 2,400 students are enrolled in degree programs, and thousands more come to attend professional development programs and take courses for food enthusiasts.

American Bounty Restaurant   **$$$**
Imaginative New American cuisine featuring regional specialties prepared with Hudson Valley ingredients. Lunch and dinner Tuesday through Saturday.

Apple Pie Bakery Café   **$**
The showcase for baking and pastry arts students. The cafe offers baked goods and cafe cuisine for dining in and take out. Monday through Friday, 8:00 a.m. to 6:30 p.m.

Escoffier Restaurant   **$$$$**
Traditional French cuisine, updated to contemporary taste and served with panache in an elegant dining room. Lunch and dinner Tuesday through Saturday.

Ristorante Caterina de' Medici   **$$$**
Italian cuisine featuring seasonal ingredients in a stunning Tuscan villa setting. Lunch and dinner Monday through Friday.

St. Andrew's Café   **$$**
A casual, family-friendly cafe atmosphere offering salads, sandwiches, wood-fired pizzas, and seasonal entrees. Lunch and dinner Monday through Friday.

All the restaurants are on the CIA campus on Route 9 at St. Andrew's Road in Hyde Park. The vast Gothic building and extensive campus along the Hudson was once a Jesuit seminary. Reservations are recommended for all restaurants except the Apple Pie Bakery Café. Because the restaurants are so popular, advance planning is needed, especially for a Friday or Saturday and in the months of September and October. Weekday reservations are a little easier to get— sometimes even the same day—and during the winter you might get lucky with a same-day reservation on a weekend. Call (845) 471-6608 or go to www.ciachef.edu for reservations. The restaurants are closed during student vacation periods. Except for the cafes, the dress code is business or country-club casual.

interesting territory as Thai fish soup (actually an entree). For the less adventurous, Twist offers excellent steaks with your choice of side dishes and sauces. Outstanding homemade desserts and a bar with a variety of unusual bottled beers round out the dining experience. Open for dinner only; closed Monday and Tuesday.

Milan

LA CIENEGA $
1215 Route 199
(845) 758-8333
Located just a couple of miles west of the Taconic Parkway in the rural town of Milan, La Cienega offers freshly made, authentic Mexican food at

reasonable prices. While Mexican food isn't exactly native to the Hudson Valley, this unpretentious restaurant still sources as many ingredients as possible from local farmers. Specialties here include tacos and burritos with a wide range of fillings, tequila lime chicken, and grilled shrimp with a cilantro citrus sauce. The desserts are very good—try the chocolate chili ice cream. The pleasant dining room is nicely decorated in a country style accented by Mexican folk art. Open for dinner every night; closed Monday and Tuesday.

Millbrook

CAFÉ LES BAUX $$$
152 Church Street
(845) 677-8166
www.cafelesbaux.com

Café Les Baux has that real French bistro feel—a bit crowded but with an excellent menu featuring classic bistro dishes such as steak frites and duck breast in port wine sauce and tarte Tatin for dessert. And in true bistro fashion, the menu also features daily specials based on what's available at local markets. This is a popular spot for lunch and dinner in Millbrook; dinner reservations are a good idea. The entrance to the unpretentious dining room is up three steps, which could be an issue for guests with mobility handicaps. Closed Tuesday.

CHARLOTTE'S $$$
4258 Route 44
(845) 677-5888
www.charlottesny.com

Longtime Valley residents will remember Charlotte's as Allyn's, a favorite spot for special-occasion dining. The name has changed, but the ambiance and food remain as beautiful as ever. Charlotte's is in a restored mansion set in the middle of lovely gardens, with views out over the Millbrook countryside. Each of the four dining rooms has an ornate working fireplace. In the summer there's outdoor dining on the patio. The menu here is fairly standard New American, featuring well-prepared dishes such as salmon

in lime dill beurre blanc and smoked pork chop with dirty mashed potatoes. The menu incorporates local ingredients and changes seasonally. Game specialties are offered in the winter. The wine cellar at Charlotte's has won local awards. Open for dinner every evening; brunch on weekends. Reservations strongly suggested.

LA PUERTA AZUL $$
2510 Route 44
(845) 677-2985
www.lapuertaazul.com

Don't let the strip mall setting of this restaurant put you off. The minute you walk through the blue door, you're transported to sunny Mexico. This is a handsome but still informal dining room, decorated in deep blue and earth tones. The food at La Puerta Azul is carefully crafted traditional Mexican. The handmade guacamole, prepared tableside, is a favorite appetizer here. Move on to any of the main course dishes, such as camarones al pastor (seared shrimp flavored with achiote, diced pineapple, and onions) or the unusual cordero al vapor (smoked lamb shank coated with chiles and garlic and steamed in avocado leaves). The bar offers a wide selection of bottled beer and more than 80 different tequilas. Reservations recommended. Open for lunch and dinner every day except Monday, with live music on weekends.

PICOLO RESTAURANT $
3279 Franklin Avenue
(845) 677-2853
www.picolorestaurant.tripod.com

A casual, family-friendly restaurant in the heart of the village of Millbrook, Picolo offers home-style cooking with an Italian slant. Pastas such as fettuccini carbonaro are always on the menu, as are good fish dishes such as pan-roasted salmon filet. If you're in the mood for something more casual, try the individual pizzas—a favorite with kids. Open for dinner every evening; brunch on weekends only. Closed Monday and Tuesday.

Pine Plains

STISSING HOUSE RESTAURANT AND
TAVERN $$$
3812 Route 199 (at Route 82)
(518) 398-8800
www.stissinghouse.com
The original Stissing tavern in the unspoiled town of Pine Plains dates back to 1782—George Washington ate here. It's been serving food ever since, making Stissing House, as it's called today, America's oldest and longest-operated restaurant. In 2005 the restaurant was taken over by Michel and Patricia Jean, who have turned it into one of the region's destination restaurants. The food here is outstanding—simple brasserie dishes, such as the double-cut pork chop or hanger steak, are perfectly prepared using the wood-fired grill, and there are always several daily specials using local, seasonal ingredients. Fabulous thin-crust pizzas are made in a wood-fired oven. The building has been nicely restored to its Dutch Colonial origins, making the surroundings as interesting as the food. Stissing House is casual and kid-friendly, but it can get crowded on the weekends, especially in the summer. Reservations are strongly suggested. Open for dinner only; closed Tuesday and Wednesday.

Poughkeepsie

THE ARTIST'S PALATE $$$
307 Main Street
(845) 483-8074
www.theartistspalate.biz
The Artist's Palate is very much in tune with the vibrant arts scene in Poughkeepsie. Works by local artists are on display here, and this bistro-style restaurant sees its food as works of art too. The Artist's Palate is located conveniently close to the Bardavon Opera House and offers a nice pre-theater dinner on show nights. Open for lunch weekdays only; dinner every night except Sunday.

BABYCAKES CAFE $
1-3 Collegeview Avenue
(845) 485-8411
www.babycakescafe.com

Located near Vassar College in the Arlington business district, Babycakes began as a tiny European-style bakery and cafe in 2002. Today it's expanded into a 65-seat full-service restaurant—but the baked goods are still homemade and still fabulous. The restaurant offers a complete dinner menu that also includes signature sandwiches such as the portobello eggplant wrap and vegetarian muffaletta; entrees vary with the season and include dishes such as orange five-spice salmon and chicken Provençal linguine. Babycakes Cafe is open every day except Monday. Dinner service is Wednesday through Saturday, 6:00 to 10:00 p.m..

BEECH TREE GRILL $$
1 Collegeview Avenue
(845) 471-7279
www.beechtreegrill.com
Located just next to Vassar College, Beech Tree Grill offers an American bistro atmosphere—comfortable, friendly, and unpretentious. The restaurant serves pastas, salads, a rotating selection of hot entrees and daily specials, and great sandwiches (even at dinner). Top it off with a homemade dessert from the ever-changing daily list—this is just about the only restaurant in the area to offer a genuine root beer float. Adding to the enjoyment of the food is one of the better selections of local and imported beers. Open for dinner only on Monday; lunch and dinner the rest of the week; Sunday brunch.

BUSY BEE CAFÉ $$
138 South Avenue
(845) 452-6800
This small restaurant, tucked into a residential neighborhood near Vassar Brothers Hospital, is often—and rightly—described as a hidden gem. It's hard to describe a typical dish at Busy Bee, though, because the eclectic menu changes frequently. Suffice it to say that the food here is excellent, with imaginative influences from Asian, Italian, and Cajun cooking and outstanding desserts. On Wednesdays and Thursdays, the restaurant offers a three-course prix-fixe dinner, paired with a glass of wine, for under $30. Parking

is available at the Good Dog Pub across the street—don't bother trying to find street parking. Open for lunch Monday through Friday; dinner Wednesday through Saturday.

COSIMO'S POUGHKEEPSIE $$
120 Delafield Street
(845) 485-7172
www.cosimospoughkeepsie.com

Tuscan cuisine with a New World touch is the focus at this attractive and spacious restaurant. Thin-crusted pizzas and calzones—from the menu or create your own—come hot from the wood-fired brick oven. There's a broad range of traditional Italian appetizers, such as the house-made mozzarella with roasted peppers. Pastas here are nicely prepared and served in generous portions. The entrees are excellent— try the chicken Valvostana, a chicken breast rolled around mushrooms and Fontina cheese and served with a marsala reduction along with spinach and roasted potatoes. Open every day for lunch and dinner.

COYOTE GRILL $$
2629 South Road
(845) 471-3900
www.coyotegrillny.com

Although the name strongly suggests a Mexican restaurant, Coyote Grill is much more eclectic than that. Mexican specialties such as fajitas are indeed on the menu, but so are American classics such as chicken and biscuits with country gravy, oven-roasted turkey with all the trimmings, and an array of burgers. And so are dishes from around the globe, such as Thai hanger steak served with jasmine rice and tamarind sauce. The martini lounge offers 15 different custom-made martinis with your choice of olives hand-stuffed with bleu cheese, anchovy, jalapeño, pimento, and garlic. Open every day for lunch and dinner. This is one the very few restaurants in the region to serve dinner late—the kitchen is open until midnight on weeknights and until 1:00 a.m. on weekends.

LE PAVILLON $$$
230 Salt Point Turnpike
(845) 473-2525
www.lepavillonrestaurant.com

French cuisine with a Normandy accent is created here by master chef Claude Guermont, formerly the Chef-Instructor at the Escoffier Restaurant at the Culinary Institute of America. The setting for this well-established restaurant is perfect: a restored farmhouse with three pleasant dining rooms, set back from a quiet country road. The menu features classic French entrees such as cassoulet, coq au vin, and roasted duck with blackberry sauce. Save room for a fabulous dessert soufflé. It's all served by a very professional staff. Reservations suggested. Open for dinner Tuesday through Saturday.

SPANKY'S $$
85 Main Street
(845) 485-2294
www.spankysrestaurantpok.com

Southern-style and Cajun cooking are the themes at Spanky's, located by the Poughkeepsie train station. Another theme here is celebration: The Catfish Festival is held every September, the Crawfish Festival is from late April to early May, and the Oyster Festival is in November. The menu features the dishes of Savannah and the Charleston area during Savannah Summer, running from mid-June to the end of August. Year-round, check out the Southern specialties, like the crab-and-jalapeño-stuffed hush puppies appetizer, and entrees such as buttermilk fried chicken, served with waffles and collards, and Low Country shrimp and grits. Open for lunch Tuesday through Friday, for dinner Tuesday through Sunday. Closed Monday.

Red Hook

MAX'S MEMPHIS BARBEQUE $$
136 South Broadway
(845) 758-MAXS
www.maxsbbq.com

It's easy to describe this restaurant: the best barbecue in the Hudson Valley. It's made Memphis-style, which means a dry rub and slow smoking over a hickory fire. As befits a barbecue restaurant, Max's is friendly, informal, relatively inexpensive, and has a great bar. The traditional dinners are not only delicious, they're an excellent value. Generous portions of barbecue favorites such as Max's signature dish, hand-rubbed barbecue pulled pork, slow-smoked beef brisket, and St. Louis cut slow-smoked barbecue pork ribs are served with your choice of two sides (the traditional collards are fabulous). Max's offers an unusually good kids' menu—it's smaller portions of the adult food, not the usual chicken fingers and fries. Dinner only; closed Monday.

i Ice-cream lovers will love Holy Cow at 7270 Broadway (845-758-5959) in Red Hook. The ice cream here is homemade—it's rich and delicious and comes in a wide variety of flavors. The line is often out the door on hot summer nights. Open every day, but hours are seasonal.

MERCATO $$
61 East Market Street
(845) 758-5879
The chef at this small, friendly, excellent restaurant is Giovanni Buitoni, a seventh-generation descendant of the famed Italian pasta manufacturing family. His cooking is classic Italian with a contemporary touch—and it's outstanding. The menu here is short and changes daily, based on the seasonal availability of local produce. It's limited to just a handful of appetizers, some pastas, a single risotto, and several entrees each evening, along with a couple of daily specials. All are beautifully prepared and served by a friendly staff. The front room can get a little noisy; the back room has a large table for big groups and is quieter. Lunch and dinner Tuesday through Saturday.

FLATIRON STEAK HOUSE $$
7488 South Broadway
(845) 758-6260
www.flatironsteakhouse.com
Flatiron Steak House offers casual dining from a simple but sophisticated menu. The emphasis is on steaks, seafood, and outstanding burgers, including one made with duck. The restaurant uses local ingredients whenever possible, including locally raised beef and lamb. The signature dish here is the flatiron steak, a shoulder cut that's available in a 5- or 8-ounce portion. All steaks come with a choice of seven different homemade sauces, including a flavorful house-made ketchup. Additional entrees are based on seasonally available ingredients and vary depending on the time of year. Side dishes include a sumptuous truffle mac and cheese. At the bar, beers from nearby breweries are featured. The thoughtful wine list includes local vintages along with a good selection from further afield. Open for dinner Tuesday through Saturday; closed Monday. Brunch is served on Sunday from noon to 3:00 p.m. Reservations recommended.

Rhinebeck
AGRA TANDOOR $
5856 Route 9
(845) 876-7510
One of the better ethnic choices in the region, Agra Tandoor isn't much to look at from the outside. It's nicer inside, with Indian decor and a spacious, quiet dining area. The food here has been reliably authentic and reasonably priced for a number of years. The restaurant has recently come under the same management as Tanjore in Fishkill (listed previously) and the already good food has improved. The wide-ranging menu contains a large number of well-prepared vegetarian dishes. Open for lunch and dinner every day. The dinner buffet served Wednesday, Friday, and Sunday is an excellent value.

i The Rhinebeck branch of the Bread Alone Café and Bakery sells the company's namesake artisanal breads and also offers outstanding pastries, panini, and sandwiches to eat there or to go. (See the Restaurants: West chapter for more information.) The store is at 43 East Market Street (845-876-3108; www.breadalone .com). Hours are 7:00 a.m. to 5:00 or 6:00 p.m. daily.

ARIELLE $$
51 East Market Street
(845) 876-5666
www.ariellerhinebeck.com

A newcomer to the lively Rhinebeck restaurant scene, Arielle offers a Mediterranean menu with distinctive French touches. The menu varies seasonally and depending on what the local farmers have to offer, but it reliably includes a good selection of interesting hors d'oeuvres such as grilled sardines and pistou, a Provençal vegetable soup with basil pesto. The main menu features market-fresh seafood, entrees such as pork Milanese, and pasta dishes, including homemade herb gnocchi. The less adventurous can try the steak menu, which offers a choice of traditional steak frites, New York strip, and rib eye steak. An unusual dish here is côte de boeuf for two. The brunch menu is interesting as well, with dishes such as buckwheat crepes and lobster BLT on a brioche. Open for dinner Tuesday through Sunday. Brunch on Sunday is served from noon to 4:00 p.m.

AROI THAI RESTAURANT $
55 East Market Street
(845) 876-1114
www.aroirestaurant.com

Thai food finally arrived in Rhinebeck in 2008 when Aroi opened. This pleasant restaurant offers an interesting and authentic traditional Thai menu; outdoor dining in a small garden area is available in nice weather. There's a good selection of Thai-style curries. Among the traditional entrees, the pla lad prik, a whole deep-fried fish with a curry sauce, is a good choice. Desserts here are on the unusual side and include jackfruit ice cream and taro pearls in coconut cream. Aroi is open for dinner every night. Lunch is served Thursday through Monday from 11:30 a.m. to 3:00 p.m.; the lunch specials are a good value.

CALICO RESTAURANT AND PATISSERIE $$$
6384 Mill Street
(845) 876-2749
www.calicorhinebeck.com

This is quite possibly the smallest restaurant in the entire mid-Hudson region, with just seven tables in a tiny storefront. Don't let the dimensions fool you, though—this is also one of the best restaurants in the region. Chef Anthony Balassone serves outstanding bistro-style food with a European accent. Try the award-winning garlic soup and follow it up with one of the European-accented entrees, such as the roasted pork tenderloin with a brandy-infused brown sauce. Be sure to save a *lot* of room for dessert, because the other half of Calico is a wonderful patisserie featuring the creations of pastry chef Leslie Balassone (Anthony's wife). The pastry list is the dessert menu for the restaurant. Reservations are a must here. Lunch and dinner every day except Monday and Tuesday. The bakery is open starting at 8:00 a.m. **Note:** Three steps up from the street may be a problem for those with mobility handicaps.

DIASPORA $$
1094 Route 308
(845) 758-9601
www.diasporacuisine.com

The Mediterranean cuisine of Diaspora has a delightful Greek accent, with some Italian touches. The menu offers a long selection of well-prepared traditional Greek appetizers such as taramosalata (fish roe spread) and saganaki (fried kasseri cheese). Entrees are very nicely done here, with special emphasis on seafood. Dishes such as lithrini sti skara (grilled red snapper with lemon and olive oil) are made with fresh ingredients and prepared simply but very skillfully. The wine list here offers a good opportunity to explore the interesting world of Greek vintages. This is a very pleasant restaurant, with high ceilings that keep the noise level down even when the dining room is crowded. Diaspora is a bit out of the way on the eastern outskirts of Rhinebeck, but the bucolic setting among horse farms make the 10-minute drive from town worthwhile. Open for dinner only; closed on Monday and Tuesday.

DOUBLE O GRILL $$
6595 Route 9
(845) 876-0800
www.doubleogrill.com

The original Double O Grill is in southern Dutchess

County in Wappingers Falls (see listing there). The Rhinebeck restaurant offers the same menu and the same late-night hours.

GIGI TRATTORIA $$$
6422 Montgomery Street
(845) 876-1007
www.gigitrattoria.com

The great food at Gigi Trattoria is what happens when the Italian insistence on fresh ingredients and clean flavors meets fabulous Hudson Valley produce. (Owner Laura Pensiero has become a major player on the local foodie scene—see the entry for Gigi Market in the Farm Markets and Wineries chapter.) The menu here changes often, varying with the season and the availability of local products. Try the Gigi skizzas—crispy "pizzas" made on a flatbread base and topped with a great combination of ingredients. The Bianca, for instance, marries Coach Farm goat cheese with mozzarella, rosemary preserved figs, pears, arugula, and white truffle oil. Equally excellent antipasti, salads, soups, and pastas are on the menu, along with a daily risotto. Entrees include Gigi's take on Italian classics such as saltimbocca along with imaginative daily specials. On Tuesday, Wednesday, and Thursday evenings, Gigi offers a four-course prix-fixe menu—an excellent value. Gigi is very popular, especially on weekends, and it can get noisy. In true trattoria fashion, reservations aren't taken for groups smaller than six, so you may end up waiting a bit for a table. The food is worth the wait. (The Cucina Room in the back has a huge table for large groups and private parties.) Lunch Friday through Sunday; dinner Tuesday through Sunday. Closed Monday.

LE PETIT BISTRO $$$
8 East Market Street
(845) 876-7400
www.lepetitbistro.com

A long-running fixture in the center of Rhinebeck, Le Petit Bistro is one the finest traditional French restaurants in the region. It's an intimate (OK, some would say crowded) restaurant with excellent service, wonderful food, and a good wine list. The menu offers classic French dishes such

as coquilles St. Jacques, roast rack of lamb, and even frog's legs, all cooked perfectly. Chef Joseph Dalu also presents daily seafood specials and daily chef's specials, often with a Mediterranean touch. The homemade desserts are outstanding as well. Reservations are recommended. Dinner only; closed Tuesday and Wednesday.

OSAKA $$
22 Garden Street
(845) 876-7338
www.osakasushi.net

The smaller but equally good outpost of the original Osaka in Tivoli. (See page 101.)

SABROSO $$$
22 Garden Street
(845) 876-8688
www.sabrosoplatos.com

A meal at Sabroso is an eye-opening, palate-expanding experience—this restaurant features fusion cuisine based on the flavors of Central and South America. The menu is divided into tapas, or appetizers, and platos, or entrees. Both halves are full of intriguing choices, such as the tapas dish of grilled shrimp skewered on sugarcane and served over field greens with hearts of palm. On the platos menu are dishes such as the classic Argentinean entrana (skirt steak) with chimichurri sauce. Daily seafood and chef's specials round out the offerings. The well-chosen wine list explores the vintages of Spain, Portugal, Argentina, and Chile. This is a fun restaurant, with attractive contemporary decor and good service. Reservations strongly suggested. Open for dinner every day but Tuesday.

STARR PLACE $$
6417 Montgomery Street
(845) 876-2924
www.starrplace.com

A relatively new addition to the Rhinebeck restaurant scene, Starr Place offers an American bistro menu, a good, reasonably priced by-the-glass wine list, a contemporary design, and live entertainment in the lounge on weekends. The menu features local produce and changes so frequently with the seasons and availability that it's hard to pick a typical dish. French bread pizzas are a somewhat off beat (but very good) offering. Among the appetizers are choices such as flash-fried seasonal mushrooms and mussel pots. Entrees are generally typical bistro food, such as braised short ribs and baked salmon. Seasonal specials are offered daily. It's all cooked up by Roberto Mosconi, considered one of the area's most promising chefs. Lunch and dinner every day except Wednesday.

THE TAVERN AT THE BEEKMAN ARMS $$$$
6387 Mill Street
(845) 876-1766
www.beekmanandelamaterinn.com

The Tavern is the restaurant at the famed Beekman Arms, the oldest inn in America (see the Accommodations: East chapter for more on this historic place). When you eat here, you're in the company of presidents, including George Washington and Franklin D. Roosevelt. The menu offers well-prepared American classics such as Hudson Valley duck breast and Black Angus prime rib au jus, served by a very capable staff. The Tavern offers several different dining rooms, including the garden greenhouse. The most interesting is the Tap Room, which dates back to colonial times and features overhead beams and an open-hearth fireplace. The Tavern is a favorite spot for family groups celebrating special occasions. Reservations are suggested. Open for lunch and dinner daily; Sunday brunch is very popular.

TERRAPIN $$$
6425 Montgomery Street
(845) 876-3330
www.terrapinrestaurant.com

Many critics have called Terrapin one of the finest restaurants in the entire region—and they're right. The outstanding food here is served in a wonderful setting by an excellent staff. It all makes for a memorable meal. Terrapin is in a restored former church that dates back to 1825. The beautiful renovation has created two elegant and distinct areas: the main dining room and the

informal bistro room. The menu is eclectic. Chef Josh Kroner combines flavors from around the world with the finest ingredients, drawn from local suppliers whenever possible. A good example is the wontons filled with goat cheese—an appetizer that is surprising and delicious. Another example: the golden nugget squash soup made with coconut milk and lemongrass. The entrees and daily specials are equally imaginative—and always perfectly prepared and beautifully presented. Terrapin is one of the few restaurants of its class to routinely include vegetarian choices on the menu. Reservations strongly suggested. Lunch and dinner every day.

Rhinecliff

CHINA ROSE $
1 Schatzell Avenue (next to Amtrak station)
(845) 876-7442

China Rose serves authentic, well-prepared Chinese food—something that is scarce in the mid–Hudson Valley. The menu offers a good choice of both traditional and spicier dishes, and the daily specials are usually interesting. The specialty of the house, however, is the sake margaritas. This is a busy place that has a high decibel level when it's crowded (and it usually is). In nice weather, eat outdoors on the terrace and enjoy the sweeping views of the Hudson River. China Rose doesn't take reservations, so you may have to wait to get in. The margaritas are worth it. Dinner only. Closed Tuesday. *Note:* Not wheelchair accessible.

Staatsburg

BELVEDERE MANSION $$$$
10 Old Route 9
(845) 889-8000
www.belvederemansion.com

The Belvedere Mansion is a lovely small hotel (see the Accommodations: East chapter for details). It also happens to have a very good restaurant. The antique-filled dining room features a wood-burning fireplace and great views of the Hudson Valley. The food here is French-inspired American cuisine. The menu changes with the seasons, and includes appetizers such as fricassee of rabbit with

French lentils and entrees such as pan-seared duck breast with tarragon-mustard gnocchi. It's all served in a luxurious atmosphere that's perfect for a romantic evening. Reservations required. Dinner only, Thursday through Sunday.

PORTOFINO $$
57 Old Post Road
(845) 889-4711
www.portofinorest.com

This popular restaurant is a bit out of the way but well worth the trip—as the crowds on weekends prove. The food here is classic Italian, well prepared and served in generous portions. The extensive menu offers an unusually good selection of pasta dishes and favorite entrees, along with daily specials. Reservations aren't taken here, so be prepared for a wait on weekends. Enjoy a drink at the pleasant, old-fashioned bar while you wait. Dinner every night except Monday.

Tivoli

LUNA 61 $
55 Broadway
(845) 758-0061
www.luna61.com

Luna 61 is one of the very rare vegetarian restaurants where confirmed carnivores leave satisfied. And because most menu items made with cheese can be made with alternative ingredients for those who don't eat any animal products, Luna 61 is the even rarer restaurant where vegans can enjoy excellent food. The wholesome and hearty cooking draws on the vegetarian traditions of the world, ranging from barbecued tempeh served with quinoa to seitan fajitas to traditional ravioli in a sauce with sage and pecans. The food here is strictly organic (even the beer and wine), and much of it comes from local farmers. It's skillfully prepared and served in a pleasant, very relaxed dining room. Accessibility warning: Guests are served in the downstairs part of the restaurant, but the main dining room is up a spiral staircase. Dinner Tuesday through Sunday; Sunday brunch.

MADALIN'S TABLE $$$
53 Broadway
(845) 757-2100
www.madalinhotel.com

Madalin's Table is the restaurant for the Madalin Hotel (see the Accommodations: East chapter for details). The restaurant is in two rooms on the ground floor of this restored 1909 building. One room is the romantic dining room, the other a taproom with tables arranged around the ornate wooden bar. The food in both rooms is the same, and it's outstanding. It ranges from simple bar food such as burgers and fish and chips to traditional but sophisticated entrees such as roasted black cod with horseradish-creamed leeks and roasted corn salad. The menu changes with the seasons and makes extensive use of local ingredients. Dinner only; closed Tuesday.

OSAKA $$
74 Broadway
(845) 757-5055
www.osakasushi.net

Sushi is the specialty at Osaka, both at the original Tivoli location and the Rhinebeck location (previously listed). Both restaurants also serve traditional Japanese dishes such as salmon teriyaki and very good bento box lunches. The sushi here is notably fresh, varied, and well prepared, making both restaurants very popular among local aficionados. The Tivoli restaurant is the more spacious; the Rhinebeck spot is smaller and can get crowded. At either location, the staff is friendly and attentive. Open for lunch and dinner every day.

SANTA FE $$
52 Broadway
(845) 757-4100
www.santafetivoli.com

Fresh, well-prepared, sophisticated Mexican food is featured at this fun (and often noisy) restaurant. The menu offers dishes such as grilled Oaxacan tacos, made with char-grilled chicken in a spicy mole poblano sauce and enchiladas de San Miguel (stacked enchiladas with mushrooms, spinach, feta cheese, sun-dried tomatoes, and cheddar cheese). This isn't your typical Mexican restaurant! Even the kids' menu is authentic, offering kid-size portions of quesadillas and tacos. Reservations strongly suggested. Dinner only; closed Monday.

Wappingers Falls

AROMA OSTERIA $$
114 Old Post Road
(845) 298-6790
www.aromaosteriarestaurant.com
Aroma Osteria features rustic Italian cooking served in an upscale setting, starting with the dramatic granite bar at the entrance. The dining room is equally dramatic, rising two stories in the center and with a huge mural of an Italian grape harvest on one wall. The food here draws on all regions of Italy but focuses most closely on the robust dishes of southern Italy, with an excellent selection of pastas. The outstanding wine list showcases Italian wines from every region, with many choices available by the glass. Reservations strongly suggested. Lunch Tuesday through Sunday; dinner Tuesday through Saturday.

DOUBLE O GRILL $$
1536 Route 9
(845) 297-7625
www.doubleogrill.com
Both Double O restaurants (the Rhinebeck outpost is listed previously in this chapter) offer good food, home-baked breads and desserts, and well-stocked bars. They also offer late-owl hours, serving dinner until midnight and beyond. The menus are extensive, with plenty of good appetizers that double as bar food, such as Asian lettuce wraps and sweet corn tamale cakes. The entrees include an excellent selection of seafood, gourmet salads, and traditional dishes such as Madeira chicken and oven-roasted turkey. The sandwich menu is extensive, including a range of burgers and including interesting choices such as a crab cake hoagie. Open for lunch and dinner every day.

MOJO GRILL $$
942 Route 376 (Samerlin Plaza)
(845) 226-1111
www.mojogrill.net
The food at Mojo Grill is hard to describe. The menu offers an eclectic assortment of dishes with Italian, Latin, and Asian influences, but it also offers classic dishes such as homemade meat loaf. The categories don't really matter, though, because the menu changes so often that there aren't really any signature dishes. (There *is* a signature drink, a very good house margarita.) The dishes are always interesting and well prepared, so this restaurant is worth checking out. Reservations suggested. Open every day for lunch and dinner.

PUTNAM COUNTY

Cold Spring

BRASSERIE LE BOUCHON $$
76 Main Street
(845) 265-7676
Located in a century-old house in the heart of Cold Spring, Brasserie Le Bouchon is within easy walking distance of the MetroNorth train station. It's a relaxed restaurant with a sort of funky feel—this is good French food without any fuss. All the traditional favorites, from onion soup to steak frites to cassoulet, are on the menu. Daily specials are based on fresh local produce; the specials and the menu change with the seasons. The main dining room features an ornate fireplace. In nice weather you can eat on the porch or in the garden out back. Reservations suggested. Open for lunch and dinner every day except Tuesday. *Note:* Two steps up from the street may be a problem for guests with mobility handicaps.

CATHRYN'S TUSCAN GRILL $$$
91 Main Street
(845) 265-5582
www.tuscangrill.com

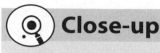

Close-up

Waterfront Dining: East Side

Dining while looking out over the majestic Hudson River is one of the great pleasures of the region. There are several good choices on the east side of the river. **Hudson House River Inn** (2 Main Street, Cold Spring, 845-265-9355, www.hudsonhouseinn.com; $$$) offers a lovely dining room with wide plank floors and farmhouse antiques; an outdoor patio overlooks the river. (For more about the inn part, see the Accommodations: East chapter.) The food here is traditional American, beautifully prepared and served, and the wine list has a broad selection of American wines, including many local vintages. The prix-fixe dinner menu (served Sunday through Friday) is an excellent value. Open for lunch and dinner every day. **Riverview Restaurant** (45 Fair Street, Cold Spring, 845-265-4778, www.riverdining.com; $$) is a local favorite for American cuisine with an Italian bent—the brick-oven pizzas are really good. The river view is only from the outdoor terrace and they only take cash, but it's still a good spot for a casual family meal. Open for lunch and dinner Tuesday through Sunday. **Shadows on the Hudson** (176 Rinaldi Boulevard, Poughkeepsie, 845-486-9500, www.shadowsonthehudson .com; $$) is perched on a cliff 40 feet above the Hudson—the views up and down the river from here are fabulous. The food is simple and well prepared, focusing on seafood, steaks, and burgers. The real action at Shadows takes place in the bar at night—there's a wide selection of gourmet cocktails and a huge TV wall. Open every day for lunch, dinner, and late-night snacks. **River Station** (1 Water Street, Poughkeepsie, 845-452-9207, www.riverstationrest.com; $) is the oldest continuously operated restaurant in the city—it began as a saloon in 1866. Lovely views of the river and Mid-Hudson Bridge from the glassed-in upper level and outdoor patio. The menu is mostly steak and seafood with additional eclectic offerings, including a chowder bar. Open every day for lunch and dinner; Sunday brunch.

Cathryn's Tuscan Grill is set back in a quiet courtyard off Cold Spring's main drag, within easy walking distance from the MetroNorth train station. It's a good spot for a meal after a long day of exploring the village. Classic northern Italian cuisine fills the extensive menu, with a good selection of pastas and a daily risotto. Entrees include grilled pheasant and grilled rack of venison in addition to traditional dishes such as veal scaloppini. The wine list offers a broad selection of Italian vintages. Reservations recommended. Open for lunch and dinner every day.

COLD SPRING DEPOT $$
1 Depot Square
(845) 265-5000
www.coldspringdepot.com
Cold Spring Depot manages a difficult feat: It's both very family-friendly and the sort of place where a grown-up actually wants to eat. The restaurant really is a restored train depot dating

back to 1893. Today nearly 70 trains go past the depot every day. Sitting out on the patio and watching the trains go by is a lot of fun for kids and parents alike. The food here is good and reasonably priced, especially the daily specials such as Meatloaf Madness on Monday and the Tuesday evening Pot Pie Party. Open daily for lunch and dinner.

PLUMBUSH INN $$$$
1656 Route 9D (at Route 301)
(845) 265-3904
www.plumbushinn.net
Plumbush Inn offers a very good restaurant in addition to the romantic accommodations (see the Accommodations: East chapter for details). The menu here features rustic American cuisine in a casually elegant setting—a great spot for celebrating a special occasion. The dishes are based on the classics, ranging from wild mushroom bisque to Plumbush's own beef

Wellington. Daily and seasonal specials draw on Hudson Valley bounty to round out the menu. Reservations strongly suggested. Open daily for lunch and dinner.

Garrison

BIRD AND BOTTLE INN $$$$
1123 Old Albany Post Road
(Indian Brook Road)
(845) 424-2333
www.thebirdandbottleinn.com

There's been an inn at this location since 1761. In the old days it was a coach stop on the route from New York City to Albany, and it's still a convenient stopping point for those headed in either direction—you can even stay overnight. The building has been lovingly restored to its early appearance. While the decor of the dining room transports you back a couple centuries, the menu is strictly contemporary, with dishes such as grilled free-range seven-spice chicken, served with mashed potatoes and chicken jus. The dinner menu offers a choice of a la carte or prix fixe. An excellent spot for a romantic weekend to celebrate something special. Reservations strongly recommended. Open for lunch Saturday and Sunday; dinner Thursday through Sunday.

TAVERN AT HIGHLANDS
COUNTRY CLUB $$
955 Route 9D
(845) 424-3254
www.highlandscountryclub.net

Tavern takes local sourcing for ingredients very seriously. The meats, poultry, and eggs come from local pasture-raised animals and are hormone- and antibiotic-free; the vegetables are from local organic growers. The superior flavor of these products comes out in the excellent seasonal menus with a New American twist. The menu changes often, but typical dishes include roasted sweet potato soup garnished with homemade beef jerky and locally made pork sausage with baby beets. An unusual menu item is raclette, Swiss cheese that is scraped off a melting chunk and served with potatoes, cornichons, and pickled onion. The casually elegant dining room in the setting of the beautiful Highlands Country Club adds to the enjoyment of a meal here. Reservations suggested. Open in the fall and winter for lunch and dinner, Wednesday through Sunday; every day in spring and summer.

VALLEY RESTAURANT AT THE
GARRISON $$$
2015 Route 9 (Snake Hill Road)
(845) 424-3604
www.thegarrison.com

Valley restaurant at The Garrison may have the most spectacular view of any restaurant in the region. The contemporary architecture of the resort looks out over the Hudson River and Hudson Highlands and across at Storm King Mountain. (You can stay here overnight—see the Accommodations: East chapter for details.) The restaurant has a very open and spacious feel, especially when the weather is good and the doors to the dining area on the terrace are open. Executive Chef Jeff Raider has created a constantly changing menu of seasonal American cuisine. Each dish has his unique touch. Sautéed soft-shell crabs, for instance, are served with a salad of smoked bacon, tomatoes, fingerling potatoes, and ramps—not your usual presentation. Raider is a big believer in local produce, to the point of growing a large vegetable garden out behind the restaurant. Reservations recommended. Open every day for lunch and dinner.

RESTAURANTS: WEST SIDE OF THE HUDSON

The mid–Hudson Valley restaurant scene is as lively on the west side of the river as it is on the east. Diners here will find many interesting spots serving great food—and much of that food is likely to come from nearby farms. Today more and more restaurant owners and chefs in the area have a deep and growing commitment to supporting local agriculture. In turn, local growers and food artisans are coming up with more and more options and ideas for the chefs. It's an exciting time to be an adventurous eater!

On the west side of the Hudson, Kingston and New Paltz in Ulster County and Newburgh in Orange County are major restaurant centers. But don't forget the restaurants in other places, such as the Depuy Canal House in High Falls, owned by the pioneering chef John Novi. They may be a bit off the beaten path, but they're still very accessible. The rural setting has many advantages. The scenery en route is beautiful, and diners enjoy big-city quality and service at country prices and in a relaxed, unfrenzied atmosphere. And the parking is usually near the door and free!

To keep this chapter from getting totally out of hand, only restaurants that offer sit-down dinner service are listed. Many but not all of these restaurants also offer lunch and Sunday brunch—if they do, the listings say so. The open days are listed, but because hours may vary seasonally, hours are not given unless the restaurant has unusual hours—the kitchen is open very late, for instance. If in doubt, call ahead for information.

This chapter is organized first by county, then alphabetically by town, and then alphabetically by restaurant name. With some very rare exceptions, every restaurant here accepts all major credit cards. Also with some very rare exceptions, every restaurant here has a liquor license and offers at least beer and wine; most have full bars.

Where reservations are important, the listings say so—and where a restaurant doesn't accept reservations, the listing says that as well. As a general rule, however, even places that don't ordinarily take reservations ask you to reserve for parties of six or more. When in doubt, call ahead—and ask if there's a private room for your group. A surprising number of restaurants have them. At particularly busy times (in the summer, on weekends, on major holidays) you may need to call a few days in advance for a reservation. Usually, however, you can be accommodated if you call the day before or early on the same day.

New York State law requires that all restaurants be fully wheelchair accessible. In the very few cases where accessibility may be problem, it's noted. Again, if in doubt, call ahead. And New York State law forbids smoking in restaurants and bars.

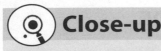

Close-up

Waterfront Dining: West Side

The beautiful Hudson River is the backdrop for many good restaurants in the region. Many are near marinas and docks, allowing boaters to tie up and enjoy a good meal just steps away.

GREENE COUNTY

Athens offers the stunning **River Tavern at Stewart House,** a restored 1883 landmark building. In nice weather, enjoy the traditional casual menu outside in the River Garden (2 North Water Street, 518-945-1357, www.stewarthouse.com; $$). Reservations suggested; open daily for dinner. In Catskill, **Catskill Point** (7 Main Street, 518-943-3173, www.catskillpoint.com; $$) has great views from the riverside dining room. The food is standard pub fare and entrees; live jazz and blues at Stella's Lounge. Lunch and dinner served every day.

ORANGE COUNTY

The revitalized waterfront of the river town of Newburgh has given birth to a number of good places to eat (and drink). The **Front Street Marina,** for instance, is now the home to six restaurants. The **Big Easy Bistro** (40 Front Street, 845-565-3939, www.bigeasybistro.com; $$) offers New Orleans cuisine such as seafood gumbo, but is also famed for the build-your-own Big Easy Burger. Open every day for lunch and dinner. The upscale **Blue Martini** (50 Front Street, 845-562-7111; $$) has a good menu, with emphasis on sushi and fish dishes, but the 25 specialty martinis are the main draw. Open every day for lunch and dinner; the bar stays open late on weekends. **Café Pitti** (40 Front Street, 845-565-1444, http://cena2000.com/cafepitti; $) is for casual dining with an Italian accent. The menu features panini and thin-crust pizzas from the wood-burning oven. Open for lunch and dinner every day. **Cena 2000** (50 Front Street, 845-561-7676, http://cena2000.com; $$) is a beautiful restaurant that serves expertly prepared Northern Italian food, including a good selection of homemade pastas. Enjoy outdoor dining and an outdoor bar in warmer weather. Open every day for lunch and dinner. **Havana 59** (50 Front Street, 845-562-7767, www.havana59newburgh.com; $$) has a menu with nicely made Mexican-style dishes. The outdoor patio is a good place to enjoy one of the restaurant's special mojitos. The **River Grill** (40 Front Street, 845-561-6308, www.therivergrill.com; $$$) offers a Continental menu featuring well-prepared standards. The elegant dining room has nice views and good service. Open for lunch and dinner every day.

Price Code

The prices at the restaurants listed here range from moderate to very expensive indeed. The price code below gives the average price for dinner entrees for two. That's entrees only—the price excludes cocktails, wine, beer, beverages, appetizers, desserts, tax, and tip. As a general rule, prices at lunch are lower than those at dinner, but the menu may be limited. Some restaurants offer prix-fixe dinners or have special nights with fixed prices. These offerings can be a very good value, especially if you're dining out on a weeknight.

$	less than $30
$$	$31 to $50
$$$	$51 to $65
$$$$	$66 or higher

GREENE COUNTY

Catskill

BELL'S CAFÉ $
387 Main Street
(518) 943-4070
www.bellscafeny.net

Pamela's on the Hudson is in the Newburgh Yacht Club (1 Park Place, 845-562-4505, www.pamelastravelingfeast.com; $$). This stunning restaurant offers a Continental menu, good service, and a great view of the river and the Newburgh-Beacon Bridge. A good choice for celebrating something special. Reservations suggested. Open for lunch and dinner every day except Monday.

Torches on the Hudson (120 Front Street, 845-568-0100, www.torchesonthehudson.com; $$$) is a large restaurant right on the water. If you tire of the river view through the floor-to-ceiling windows, you can watch the fish in the massive 6,000-gallon saltwater aquarium in the bar area. The food here is nicely prepared eclectic American. The food and the lively bar make this a destination restaurant for a night out.

ULSTER COUNTY

The Rondout waterfront in Kingston was once an active seaport and shipbuilding center. Times have changed, and today the boats in the area are mostly recreational. Sailors' bars have given way to family restaurants. **Mariner's Harbor** (1 Broadway, 845-340-8051, www.marinersharbor.com; $$) is a long-established favorite for seafood, with a famous raw bar. Fish-haters can enjoy steaks and burgers. The patio overlooks the Rondout Creek. Open every day for lunch and dinner. **Ship to Shore** (15 West Strand, 845-334-8887, www.menuexplorer.com/shiptoshore; $$) is located in a restored building fronting on the Rondout Creek. The cuisine in this cozy restaurant is imaginative New American, with an emphasis on fresh seafood. The prix-fixe lunch and early-bird dinner menus are good values. Reservations suggested. Lunch and dinner served every day. **Steel House** (100 Rondout Landing, 845-338-7847, www.steelhouse.us; $$) is located in a renovated 19th-century structure that once housed the Cornell Steamboat Company. Today it's a large, lively restaurant featuring Italian cuisine, including a large selection of thin-crust pizzas from the brick oven. The soaring, four-story dining area, topped with a clerestory roof, is stunning. On Thursday nights, the space is turned over to country line dancing, hosted by a local radio personality. Open for lunch and dinner every day.

In Highland near the Mid-Hudson Bridge, **Frank Guido's Mariner's Landing** on the Hudson (46 River Road, 845-691-6011; $$) offers docking facilities and a good Italian-American menu. Open for lunch and dinner every day.

Small and charming, Bell's Café serves well-crafted food with authentic Middle Eastern accents. Appetizers like Moroccan fish cake in a roasted tomato harissa puree and entrees like Lebanese-style lamb shank over pureed Jerusalem artichokes aren't found on many menus in the region. The less adventurous can sample classic cassoulet or have a specialty hamburger, such as the Blue Burger made with bleu cheese and roasted garlic spread. Dinner Wednesday through Saturday; brunch Saturday and Sunday. Closed Monday and Tuesday.

ORANGE COUNTY

Cornwall

CANTERBURY BROOK INN $$
331 Main Street
(845) 534-9658
www.thecanterburybrookinn.com
Continental cuisine with a Swiss flavor is the specialty at Canterbury Brook Inn. This is a very attractive place, with several dining rooms (each with a fireplace) and a terrace overlooking Canterbury Brook. The menu offers classic Wiener schnitzel,

grilled Swiss bratwurst, and other well-prepared dishes. Candlelight and attentive service make this a nice place for a romantic dinner. The complete three-course dinner special offered on Tuesday, Wednesday, and Thursday is an excellent value. Reservations suggested. Lunch and dinner served Tuesday through Saturday.

i No ifs, ands, or butts: Smoking isn't allowed in restaurants and bars in New York State.

PAINTERS' $
266 Hudson Street
(845) 534-2109
www.painters-restaurant.com

Painters' offers casual dining from an eclectic menu, including a good selection of focaccia and weekly blackboard specials, but the real reason to eat here is the astonishing beer selection—the list has more than 100 international beers. Overnight accommodations are available at the attached inn. Open for lunch and dinner every day; Sunday brunch.

THE RIVER BANK $$
3 River Avenue
(845) 534-3046
www.theriverbank.biz

The food here is fairly standard American, including good thin-crust pizzas and a nice selection of well-prepared entrees such as grilled strip steak with peppercorn sauce. It's the decor that makes this family-friendly restaurant fun: It's in an old bank and uses a money theme. The former bank vault is now a wine cellar; the dining room walls are the green color of money and the bar is copper-topped. An antique cash register by the door dispenses chocolate coins. Open for lunch and dinner every day except Tuesday.

Newburgh

BEEB'S $$$
30 Plank Road
(845) 568-6102
www.beebsbistro.com

Woody's All Natural

Woody's All Natural (30 Quaker Avenue, Cornwall, 845-534-1111, www.woodysallnatural.com; $) offers a family-friendly, simple menu of mostly burgers, hot dogs, and grilled cheese. What sets this place apart is that the meat comes from locally raised, grass-fed beef, and the other ingredients come from local sources whenever possible. The shakes and malts are made with great ice cream from Jane's in Kingston. Open from 11:30 a.m. to 8:30 p.m. every day but Sunday and Monday.

Beeb's is a romantic bistro set in a lovely old Victorian building that was once a stagecoach stop on the way to the Newburgh waterfront. The menu varies with the seasons but focuses on standard New American dishes such as pan-seared pork chops and the unusual lobster and shrimp shepherd's pie. There's a patio for outdoor dining. The food and service are excellent, making Beeb's a good choice for a special meal. Reservations suggested. Open for lunch weekdays only; dinner Monday through Saturday. Closed Sunday and on major holidays.

i Exploring Newburgh and Beacon across the river can make you hungry. Caffé Macchiato in downtown Newburgh (99 Liberty Street, 845-565-4616, www.caffemacchiatonewburgh.com; $) is a good place to stop for lunch or a snack. The menu includes great homemade baked goods, salads, and a good selection of panini and sandwiches, along with a daily special. Open 10:00 a.m. to 4:00 p.m. Tuesday through Friday, and 9:00 a.m. to 4:00 p.m. Saturday and Sunday; closed Monday.

IL CENÀCOLO $$$$
228 South Plank Road (Route 52)
(845) 564-4464
http://cena2000.com/main.htm

Widely considered one of the finest Italian restaurants in the region, Il Cenàcolo is deceptively unattractive from the outside. Step inside from the strip-mall setting, however, and you're in a lovely Tuscan-style dining room, with pale-yellow walls and linen-draped tables. There's a menu here, but you can safely ignore it. Instead, discuss the numerous daily specials with the well-trained waitstaff and then make your selection from what they offer. Ditto for the wine—the wine list is excellent. A meal here is about as expensive as it gets in the mid–Hudson Valley, but it's worth it for a special occasion. Reservations a must. Open for lunch Monday, Wednesday, and Friday only; dinner every night except Tuesday. **Note:** The few steps down into the entrance area and the narrow passageway to the dining room may be a problem for those with mobility handicaps.

COSIMO'S ON UNION $$
1217 Union Avenue (Route 300)
(845) 567-1556
www.cosimosonunion.com

A sister restaurant to Cosimo's Kingston (listed later in this chapter), Cosimo's on Union offers the same good Italian food, including a wide range of pizza choices made in the wood-fired brick oven. The casual trattoria setting is a restored turn-of-the-century house with exposed stone walls. Open for lunch and dinner every day.

West Point

THAYER HOTEL $$$
674 Thayer Road
(845) 446-4731
www.thethayerhotel.com

The main dining room at the Thayer Hotel next to the United States Military Academy at West Point is lovely, with high gothic windows looking out onto manicured grounds. (For more about the hotel, see the Accommodations: West chapter.) The food here is standard Continental—as befits

---

Have You Ever Tried Peruvian Cuisine?

Machu Picchu (301 Broadway, Newburgh, 845-562-6478, www.machupicchurest.com; $) bills itself as the only authentic Peruvian restaurant in Orange County. In fact, it may be the only authentic Peruvian restaurant in the entire region. Good food, interesting flavors (try the Peruvian rotisserie chicken), and reasonable prices. Takeout is very popular here. Full bar. Open 10:00 a.m. to 10:00 p.m. weekdays and Sunday, 10:00 a.m. to 11:30 p.m. Friday and Saturday; closed Tuesday.

---

the surroundings—and quite good. It's a destination restaurant for the area. Saturday night is date night at The Thayer, with dinner and dancing in the main dining room. On Sunday, crowds arrive for the famed Champagne brunch buffet. Reservations strongly suggested. Open for breakfast, lunch, and dinner every day.

ULSTER COUNTY

Bearsville

BEAR CAFÉ $$$$
295 Tinker Street (Route 212)
(845) 679-5555
www.bearcafe.com

Right on the edge of the town of Woodstock, the Bear Café is a longtime favorite for its excellent New American cooking and delightful location alongside a bubbling stream. The restaurant is located in the Bearsville Theater complex (see the Nightlife chapter for details). The Bear was created in 1971 by Albert Grossman, a music industry power who was the personal manager for many pioneering artists, including Bob Dylan and Janis Joplin. Today it's owned and run by

Peter Cantine with chef Eric Mann. The oil paintings on the walls are the works of the noted artist Jo Cantine, Peter's grandmother. A visit to the Bear Café is always worthwhile for both the food and the award-winning wine list, along with the chance of catching a glimpse of a celebrity. Reservations are a must. Open for dinner every night except Tuesday.

i Restaurant meals in New York State are taxed. In Greene County, the tax is 8 percent. In Orange County, it's $8^1/8$ percent. In Ulster County, it's 8 percent. Use the pretax total when figuring out how much to tip.

THE LITTLE BEAR $$
295 Tinker Street (Route 212)
(845) 679-8899

The Little Bear is just next door to the Bear Café (see previous listing) and is equally scenic. A bit surprisingly, the cuisine here is Chinese, with an extensive menu offering a lot of interesting specials, such as scallops with black bean sauce. The food is authentic and quite good. As befits the Woodstock area, the menu offers a wide variety of well-prepared vegetarian selections. The Little Bear is casual and family-friendly, but reservations are recommended. Open for lunch and dinner every day.

Kingston

ARMADILLO BAR AND GRILL $$
97 Abeel Street
(845) 339-1550
www.armadillos.net

The Southwest comes to the Rondout waterfront area at this very welcoming bar and grill. It's a fun place, starting with beckoning cacti in the front window. Inside, the decor is faux Spanish tile work, including the individual painted tabletops. There's a big bluestone patio in the back for outdoor dining in warm weather. The food is a well-made combination of Southwestern and

Bread Alone

The Bread Alone Café and Bakery on Route 28 in Boiceville (845-769-3328) is the home base for this famed European-style bakery. Bread here is made using organic ingredients and baked in wood-fired brick ovens, but despite the name, bread isn't the only thing they bake. The cafe serves hand-crafted pastries and offers fabulous panini and sandwiches (on their artisan bread, of course) at lunch time. Bread Alone has two other locations: in nearby Woodstock at 22 Mill Hill Road (845-679-2108) and across the Hudson in Rhinebeck at 43 East Market Street (845-876-3108). Hours are 7:00 a.m. to 5:00 or 6:00 p.m. every day. Bread Alone products are also available at many farmers markets in the area and in New York City Greenmarket locations. For more info, check the Web site at www.breadalone.com.

Mexican influence with local products, including vegetables and cheeses. The grilled fish and fajitas are locally famous, as are the margaritas (frozen in the summer). Armadillo is owned by Merle Borenstein, who is also a community activist and dog lover. This is the only restaurant in the region that has an adjoining dog play area, open to all good dogs in good weather. Open for dinner Tuesday through Sunday, lunch on weekends only.

LE CANARD ENCHAINÉ $$$
276 Fair Street
(845) 339-2003
www.le-canardenchaine.com

One of the best French restaurants in a region

(Q) Close-Up

John Novi and His Restaurants

Chef John Novi is often called the father of New American cuisine, and for good reason. As a very young chef, he bought a derelict 1797 building on the historic Delaware & Hudson Canal, renovated it on a shoestring, and opened a restaurant in it in 1969. His innovative use of local ingredients and new flavor combinations earned the Depuy Canal House a four-star rating from the *New York Times* just a year later. He's maintained the same high culinary level ever since. Today, Novi operates three restaurants under one roof in the tiny hamlet of High Falls. First and foremost is the **Depuy Canal House Restaurant.** Novi has restored the building impeccably and filled the cozy dining rooms with antiques. The setting, the food, and the service combine to make a meal here a truly memorable experience. The menu is large and changes often, based on the seasons and what's available from local producers. In addition to a la carte choices, the restaurant offers five-course and eight-course tasting menus. If you dine here, be sure to walk up to the second-floor balcony that overlooks the kitchen and watch the chefs at work.

For a less formal (and less expensive) meal, try **Chef's on Fire,** the bistro-style restaurant located in the stone cellar of the Canal House. The wood-fired oven here is used to make wonderful pizzas. Other menu items include salads, panini, and quesadillas.

Also under the Canal House roof—actually, in the wine cellar—is **Amici Sushi.** Not surprisingly, this Japanese restaurant under master chef Makio Idesako has an excellent reputation for outstanding and authentic sushi, sashimi, and rolls.

Depuy Canal House Restaurant   **$$$$**
Route 213 (Main Street)
High Falls
(845) 687-7700
www.depuycanalhouse.com
Reservations a must. Dinner Friday, Saturday, and Sunday only. Saturday breakfast and Sunday brunch.

Chef's on Fire   **$$**
(845) 687-7778
Reservations suggested. Breakfast, lunch, and dinner Thursday through Sunday.

Amici Sushi   **$$**
(845) 687-7778
Reservations suggested. Seasonal hours, but dinner usually Thursday through Sunday.

that has several very good choices, Le Canard Enchainé was opened by owner/chef Jean-Jacques Carquillat in 1996. The food here is classic French with a pinch of New American. Standard French dishes such as cassoulet and roast duck are on the same menu as Cajun tilapia. Chef Jean-Jacques doesn't like to be bored, however, so on the first Friday of every month he offers Moroccan Night with authentic cuisine—accompanied by authentic belly dancers. Le Canard is noted not just for great food but also for a great wine list and piano bar. Locals are well aware of the excellent value of its prix-fixe meals. They're offered at lunch every day and for dinner on weeknights (cash only). Reservations are a must. Open every day for lunch and dinner.

i Jane's Restaurant, at 305 Wall Street (845-338-8315) in Kingston's Stockade district, is a good, inexpensive place for a quick meal, but the real attraction here is the excellent homemade ice cream. No credit cards; closed Sunday.

COSIMO'S KINGSTON $$
14 Thomas Street (at Broadway)
(845) 340-0550
www.cosimoskingston.com
Cosimo's offers good, affordable Italian cuisine in an interestingly restored building in midtown Kingston. The exposed brick walls and pressed tin ceiling are nice enough, but the Hudson Valley bluestone floor and stairs, and the ornate mahogany bar, give this restaurant a bit of an extra glow. Cosimo's specialties include 16 different pizzas—or design your own—made in a wood-fired brick oven. Appetizers and entrees that feature the house-crafted mozzarella, such as the grilled chicken penne, are standouts. Desserts are very good here—try the tiramisu. Open for lunch and dinner every day.

THE EGG'S NEST $$
Route 213 (Main Street)
(845) 687-7255
www.theeggsnest.com
The decor at The Egg's Nest can kindly be described as eclectic, with lots of paintings right on the walls and even on the furniture. The reasonably priced and very good food is eclectic too. The cuisine has a Southwestern slant, with offerings such as quesadillas and some creative wraps, as well as burgers and over stuffed sandwiches. The most interesting items on the menu, however, are the praeseux (pronounced pray-sue), or tortilla-crusted pizzas (sort of), with your choice of Mexican, Greek, or vegetarian toppings. They're definitely different and worth a try. Open every day from 11:30 a.m. to 11:00 p.m. *Note:* Cash and personal checks only—no credit cards.

Highland
DOWNTOWN CAFÉ $$
1 West Strand
(845) 331-5904
http://home.hvc.rr.com/nine44/downtown/homepage.html
After a few hours of enjoying the galleries and sights of the Rondout district, Downtown Café is a welcome oasis for a good, reasonably priced meal at any time of day. The cuisine here is Italian fusion, if there is such a thing. In addition to thin-crust grilled pizzas, the dinner menu offers handmade pasta dishes, such as malfatti (spinach-ricotta dumplings) in Roquefort cream sauce, that go way beyond ordinary. Chef Graziano Tecchio's imaginative daily specials feature whatever's good at the local markets. The lunch menu offers salads, a pared-down pasta list, pizzas, and really good wraps and sandwiches. Downtown Café is open for breakfast as well, featuring a variety of three-egg omelet. In the summer, enjoy your meal in the outdoor courtyard. Open Monday through Thursday, 10:00 a.m. to 10:00 p.m.; Friday and Saturday, 10 a.m. to 11:00 p.m.; and Sunday, 9:00 a.m. to 9:00 p.m.

ELEPHANT $$$
310 Wall Street
(845) 338-9310
www.elephantwinebar.com
Because Elephant is more of a wine bar than a restaurant, it offers a terrific tapas (small servings of a variety of Spanish-style dishes) menu. This is one place where there's a very good chance you'll try something delicious that you've never eaten—or drunk—before. The menu includes charcuterie listings under "Swine of the Week" and an assortment of unusual European cheeses under "Dairy Bar." Most desserts are house-made, and they're as good as everything else on the menu. It's all beautifully prepared and served with panache. The wine list is equally interesting, consisting of lesser-known but well-chosen European bottles. Open Tuesday through Thursday, 3:00 to 10:00 p.m., Friday and Saturday, 3:00 p.m. to midnight; closed Sunday and Monday.

HOFFMAN HOUSE $$
94 Front Street
(845) 338-2626
www.hoffmanhousetavern.com
Hoffman House is in the heart of Kingston's historic Stockade district, and it fits right in. The restaurant is in an old stone building that dates back to 1679 and is registered as a National Historic Landmark. The building has been extensively and

authentically restored and features the original random-width planked floors and a fireplace in each of the main dining rooms. Many original interior features, such as the molding and baseboards and even some door handles, are still in place. Hoffman House serves traditional Continental cuisine, well prepared and expertly served by an experienced staff. This is a great place for a meal to celebrate something special. Reservations strongly suggested. Open for lunch and dinner Monday through Saturday.

THE UGLY GUS CAFÉ & BAR   **$$**
11 Main Street
(845) 334-UGLY
www.uglygus.com
Don't let the name put you off—Ugly Gus offers excellent food in a relaxed atmosphere. The menu is mostly traditional American, offering entrees such as baked stuffed shrimp, turkey pot pie, and a charbroiled Philly steak sandwich. Big Ugly Burgers are also on the menu. The cafe is in the old City Hotel, a Kingston landmark dating back to 1905. The decor preserves the turn-of-the-century feel. Front and back dining areas here are casual and friendly; the restaurant is a popular lunch spot for workers in uptown Kingston. Despite the convivial bar (or maybe because of it) Ugly Gus is family-friendly. Telling you about the hilarious kids' menu, however, would spoil the fun. Lunch weekdays only; dinner Monday through Saturday. Closed Sunday.

THE WOULD   **$$$**
120 North Road
(845) 691-9883
www.thewould.com
The Would began its life in the 1920s as part of an Italian-oriented summer resort. The original bocce court is still out back, and it's still in regular use in warm weather. Diners can watch from the tables on the porch. In the winter, dine indoors by the wood-burning fireplace. The food here diverged away from Italian in 1994 when new owners took over. (The owners are Claire Winslow and Debra Dooley—a rare female duo in the male-dominated restaurant world.) The

menu features New American cuisine served in a bistro setting. Favorites here are the poultry dishes made with free-range organic chickens—a good example is the pan-seared chicken with locally grown chard sautéed with mustard cream. Reservations suggested. Open nightly for dinner. Lunch is served seasonally—call for hours.

Marlboro

RACCOON SALOON & RESTAURANT   **$$**
1330 Main Street (Route 9W)
(845) 236-7872
www.raccoonsaloon.com
Raccoon Saloon offers family dining with a bit of an Irish accent. The menu is well-prepared traditional American, but the real reason for a visit here is to have an outstandingly good hamburger at a reasonable price. The burgers here are so generously sized that there's a petite version on the menu, and even that is on the hefty side. They're served on toasted buns with homemade ketchup and your choice of french fries, sweet potato fries, or onion rings. The Raccoon is in a restored pre-Revolutionary building that was a speakeasy during Prohibition. Ask to be seated in the east dining room—the windows overlook a spectacular 235-foot waterfall formed by Old Man's Kill as it flows toward the Hudson River. Open for lunch and dinner every day.

New Paltz

BARNABYS   **$**
16 North Chestnut Street (Route 32 North)
(845) 255-2433
The two-story brick building that houses Barnabys was built in the 1860s and has been a New Paltz landmark ever since. Over the decades it has been many things, including a vaudeville house and move theater. Starting in the 1960s, a traditional pub filled the downstairs, while the upstairs was an art movie venue. In 2003 new owners renovated the building and converted it into a large and bustling two-story restaurant. Downstairs, Barnabys is a snug bar and small dining area; upstairs, the nicely designed large dining room has the original tin ceiling and

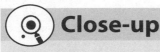

Close-up

Brew pubs

Brewpubs combine homemade beer with good food. What could be better? Several brewpubs operate in the region. In Dutchess County, there's the **Hyde Park Brewing Company** (4076 Albany Post Road, Hyde Park, 845-229-8277, www.hydeparkbrewing.moonfruit.com; $$). Eight microbrews are made here, including Mary P's Porter, Von Schtupp's Black Lager, and Winkle Lager. The menu is American regional steakhouse, offering steaks and fresh seafood. Open for lunch every day but Sunday; open for dinner every night; taps open until midnight Monday through Thursday, until 1:00 a.m. on Friday and Saturday, and until 11:00 p.m. on Sunday. The brewmaster for Hyde Park Brewing is also the brewmaster for **Skytop Steak House and Brewing Company** in Kingston in Ulster County (237 Forest Hill Drive, 845-340-4277, www .skytopsteakhouse.com; $$). Skytop offers eight home-brews, including Cliffside Black Lager and Highland Diesel Black Ale. Steak is the specialty of the house; the dinner specials are a good value. Skytop is a very attractive place—a large, chalet-style building perched on a hilltop with great views. Open for dinner every night. **Keegan Ales** in uptown Kingston (20 St. James Street, 845-331-BREW, www.keeganales.com; $) offers three home-brews: Old Capitol (ale), Mother's Milk (stout), and Hurricane Kitty (India pale ale). Beers from other local producers are also on tap. The food here is simple pub grub: bar snacks, sandwiches, panini. Open Monday through Thursday, 4:00 to 10:00 p.m., Friday and Saturday from noon to midnight; closed Sunday. Live music on Friday and Saturday nights; no cover. In New Paltz, the **Gilded Otter** (3 Main Street, 845-256-1700, www.gildedotter.com; $$), named for a ship that brought Huguenot refugees to New Paltz in the 1600s, has seven home-brews, including Rail Trail Pale Ale and Sonte House Imperial Stout. The Gilded Otter is a large, stone-and-wood, lodge-like building along the Wallkill River. The menu is extensive and includes both bar snacks and more substantial entrees such as jambalaya, meat loaf, and hearty sandwiches. Live music on Friday and Saturday nights. Open every day for lunch and dinner.

comfortable booths. The menu here is broad, offering a wide array of sandwiches (including wraps and paninis), salads, and burgers, along with a wide assortment of fairly standard appetizers, including quesadillas and eggplant rollatini, and dinner entrees that range from simple grilled steaks to market-fresh fish. The portions here are substantial and the food is well prepared. Open every day for lunch, dinner, and late-night snacks. Breakfast is served on Sundays from 10:00 a.m. to 2:00 p.m.

BESO $$

46 Main Street

(845) 255-1426

www.beso-restaurant.com

Beso serves modern American cuisine, beautifully prepared and presented. The menu changes often, based on the season and what's available from local farmers and other local suppliers. There's no typical dish—just trust the imaginative and skillful cooking of chef Chad Greer. His wife Tammy Ogeltree bakes the excellent desserts. Beso has a contemporary decor with an open feeling, but it can get a little noisy, especially on a weekend evening. Reservations strongly suggested. Open for dinner only; closed Tuesday. Accessibility warning: The entrance to Beso is five

i Good Turkish restaurants aren't very common, which makes Anatolia (62 Main Street, New Paltz, 845-255-3700; $) that much more interesting. Try the famed lentil soup. Other options include salads, sandwiches, hot entrees, and a wide variety of vegetarian dishes. Open daily 11:00 a.m. to 11:00 p.m.

steps up from the street. Dinner is served in the bar area on the ground floor, but the main dining room is up a flight of stairs.

GADALETO'S SEAFOOD $$
246 Main Street
(845) 255-1717
www.gadaletos.com

Gadaleto's Seafood Market has been selling fish in the Hudson Valley since 1945. The store moved to New Paltz in 1980. A few years later, a wayward car plowed a big hole in the side of the building, and Gadaleto's take-out window was born. In 1996, the full-service family-style restaurant opened. It's far from upscale, but what matters is that Gadaleto's serves the freshest seafood in the region. In addition to the signature entrees such as lobster pot pie and pecan-crusted tilapia, diners can choose any fish dish they want. Check the daily list for what's available, then ask for it however you want it prepared—blackened, jerked, fried, baked, broiled, grilled, or steamed. Your fish comes with vegetables and your choice of a side dish. Seasonal special nights, such as the Thursday Lobster Lounge, are a good value. Reservations aren't accepted, so there may a wait on weekends. Open for lunch and dinner every day.

HARVEST CAFÉ $$
Water Street Market (10 Main Street)
(845) 255-4205
www.harvestcafenp.com

The Harvest Café is open year-round, but a major attraction is outdoor dining on the second-story deck, with spectacular views of the Shawangunk Ridge and Wallkill River. The New American menu here is seasonally inspired and draws heavily on ingredients from local farmers and artisans. The menu is short and rounded out by daily specials. Vegetarians get equal treatment at Harvest cafe—there's always at least two meatless entrées, such as potato and Cheddar cheese pierogies served with homemade apple chutney and sour cream, on the menu. Open for lunch and dinner every day but Tuesday.

LOCUST TREE $$$
215 Huguenot Street
(845) 255-7888
www.locusttree.com

The romantic setting of the Locust Tree—a restored 1759 house in the heart of the historic Huguenot district—combined with the outstanding food make this restaurant a regional standout. Chef Barbara Bogart's menu emphasizes northern European cuisine, including signature dishes such as Normandy duck breast with crepe ribbons. Seasonal products and free-range, grassfed meats from local farms are featured here. The restaurant has three indoor dining rooms, each with a working fireplace, and a lovely outdoor patio. Private rooms are also available. Reservations strongly suggested. Dinner Wednesday through Sunday, plus Sunday brunch. Closed Monday and Tuesday. *Note:* American Express, cash, and personal checks only.

i **Breakfast all day and Friday pasta night are the two main attractions at Main Street Bistro (59 Main Street, 845-255-7766, www.mainstreetbistro.com). Other reasons to eat at this small, eclectic restaurant are the reasonable prices and good vegetarian choices.**

MOHONK MOUNTAIN HOUSE $$$$
1000 Mountain Rest Road
(845) 256-2056
www.mohonk.com

Day guests, as they're called at this traditional resort, are welcome to eat in the Mohonk Mountain House dining room. Be aware before you go, however, that there's a strict dress code. Neat sports attire is appropriate during the day for breakfast and lunch. Jackets and ties are suggested for gentlemen at the evening meal; ladies should wear dresses, skirts, or evening slacks. The menu here is modern American cuisine. It's good, and the setting is very pleasant, but food has never been the main attraction at Mohonk (see the Accommodations: West chapter for more on this historic hotel). The best deal here may be the Sunday brunch, which includes entrance to the spectacular grounds and parking. Reservations a must. Open for breakfast, lunch, and dinner every day. Hours vary slightly with the seasons.

ℹ️ Hiking the Wallkill Rail Trail can make you hungry. La Stazione Ristorante, located in the restored train station right on the trail at 5 Main Street in New Paltz (opposite the Water Street Market), solves that problem with good Italian food at moderate prices (845-256-9447; $$). Open for lunch and dinner every day.

SURUCHI $
5 Church Street
(845) 255-2772
www.suruchiindian.com
Suruchi means "good taste" in Sanskrit. The food here lives up to the name. Suruchi offers an organic and mostly vegetarian and vegan menu, with some dishes made with free-range, organic chicken or wild shrimp. Even the yogurt and cheeses are homemade using organic local milk. The good food is served in a very calm atmosphere. For a more authentic experience, sit in one of the Indian-style cushioned platform booths. Open for dinner only. Closed Monday and Tuesday.

VILLAGE TEAROOM $
10 Plattekill Avenue
(845) 255-3434
www.villagetearoom.com
Despite the name, the Village Tearoom actually serves breakfast, lunch, and dinner. The food here is good overall at any meal—the dinner entrees feature homey comfort foods such as chicken pot pie—but the real attraction is the homemade baked goods. The restaurant itself is charming. It's in a building dating back to the 1830s, with low ceilings and hand-hewn beams. Inside, there are three small dining areas; in mild weather, the tree-shaded outdoor patio in the back is delightful, while the front patio offers

good views of the Shawangunks. Families with kids can enjoy a seating area with a chalkboard wall and toys. Open Tuesday to Friday, 8:00 a.m. to 9:00 p.m.; Saturday and Sunday, 9:00 a.m. to 9:00 p.m. Closed Monday.

Rosendale

BYWATER BISTRO $$
419 Main Street
(845) 658-3210
www.bywaterbistro.com
This pleasant bistro is called Bywater because the beautiful Rondout Creek flows through the property behind the building. In mild weather, you can enjoy the view from the lovely garden dining area. The food here is mostly American bistro fare, such as hanger steak with a red wine and shallot sauce, made with local ingredients whenever possible. The menu also offers vegetarian choices and daily specials. The desserts, such as banana rice pudding, are all house-made. Bywater offers a good rotating selection of microbrews and a wine list. Reservations suggested on weekends. Open for dinner every night except Tuesday and Wednesday.

ROSENDALE CAFÉ $
434 Main Street
(845) 658-9048
www.rosendalecafe.com
Vegetarian food and a great performance space come together at Rosendale Café. The varied menu here is vegetarian and vegan, all made with strictly organic ingredients, and very reasonably priced. The cafe is a local favorite for music lovers. Weekend concerts feature jazz, blues, world, and experimental music. Every other Tuesday is Community Music Night, showcasing local musicians. Open for lunch every day except for Monday; open for dinner every night.

Saugerties

CAFÉ TAMAYO $$$
89 Partition Street (Route 9W)
(845) 246-9571
www.cafetamayo.com

Café Tamayo features ethnically influenced American food. What that means is that chef-owner James Tamayo uses local ingredients from regional farmers in highly creative ways—many dishes are prepared over a wood-burning grill. The menu here changes so often with the seasons and the availability of local products that there's no typical dish, but there is a house specialty that shouldn't be missed: a wonderful duck confit. The excellent wine list offers many by-the-glass choices and features New York State wines. Café Tamayo is a lovely restaurant, with an amazingly ornate antique mahogany bar and a delightful back patio. Reservations recommended on weekends. Open for dinner only Wednesday through Sunday.

MISS LUCY'S KITCHEN $$
90 Partition Street (Route 9W)
(845) 246-9240
www.misslucyskitchen.com

Local providers are the mainstay of Miss Lucy's Kitchen. The restaurant uses only local, all-natural dairy products, eggs, poultry, meat, and produce. In season, many of the herbs and vegetables come from the restaurant's own garden. All that great food goes into a menu that changes daily, depending on the market. Whatever's on for the day is mostly traditional European-American, such as the cassoulet or the homemade ravioli. The excellent ice cream is house-made. The pleasant country dining room is adorned with antique kitchen utensils. The atmosphere here is relaxed and family-friendly, helped along by the inexpensive kids' menu. Open for lunch and dinner Wednesday through Sunday.

NEW WORLD HOME COOKING $$$
1411 Route 212 (Glasco Turnpike)
(845) 246-0900
www.ricorlando.com

Chef Ric Orlando cooks up what he calls "global heritage cuisine" at this well-regarded restaurant. What that really means is that he's a talented chef who enjoys the assertive flavors of ethnic cuisines of every sort, including all those that make up the American melting pot. Be warned: By *assertive*, Chef Ric usually means hot! The extensive menu changes with the seasons and the market, depending on what's available from local suppliers. The specials menu every night offers at least two soups, four appetizers, and four entrees. Vegetarians and vegans are taken seriously here—there are always several entrees to choose from. The three-course prix-fixe meal, offered until 7:00 p.m. every night except Saturday and holidays, is a genuine bargain. No matter what else you order, be sure to try the blackened string beans. With funky decor and a $6 kids' menu, this is a relaxed and family-friendly place. Reservations very strongly recommended. Lunch every day except Monday. Dinner nightly, but closed Monday and Tuesday from November through April, except for Monday holidays.

THE RED ONION $$$
1654 Route 212 (Glasco Turnpike)
(845) 679-1223
www.redonionrestaurant.com

The outstanding cocktail list, extensive wine list, and sophisticated menu of New American dishes tell you this restaurant, located in a restored 1850s farmhouse, is a place for grown-ups. The menu is revised daily, depending on what's available from local suppliers, but fresh mussels, good salads (the smoked trout salad is wonderful), and house-made pastas are always there to complement the well-prepared entrees. Reservations strongly suggested, especially on weekends and holidays. Open for dinner every night but Wednesday. Sunday brunch.

Stone Ridge

THE FRENCH CORNER $$$$
3407 Cooper Street
(845) 687-0810
www.frcorner.com

Chef Jacques Qualin formerly headed the kitchen of Le Pèrigord, one of Manhattan's most respected restaurants. Chef Jacques has brought his talent to his own restaurant, making The French Corner a regional standout. The food here is updated classic French, such as braised pork shank with lentils and foie gras sauce, perfectly prepared and served. At under $30 and available every evening, the rustic prix-fixe dinners at The French Corner are an amazing bargain—the menu changes often, and includes appetizers such as butternut squash soup with wild mushrooms and entrees such as hazelnut crusted chicken with homemade fettuccini. Reservations suggested. Dinner is served Thursday through Sunday; Sunday brunch.

West Park

THE GLOBAL PALATE $$$
1746 Route 9W
(845) 384-6590
www.globalpalaterestaurant.com

At the Global Palate local ingredients are taken seriously. The meat, fish, and poultry are all-natural and come from local suppliers, as does the produce. All that local bounty goes into New American dishes with a global accent, such as shrimp and pear potstickers, served as an appetizer. The menu here changes with the seasons—a typical autumn dish might be seared sea scallops served with a smoked haddock potato cake and sautéed pea shoots. Desserts here, prepared by pastry chef Jessica Winchell, are very special. The maple flan is outstanding and Cookies and Crème—vanilla ice cream sandwiched between fresh-baked chocolate chip cookies—is well worth the 10-minute wait while it bakes. Reservations suggested. Open for dinner Wednesday through Sunday; Sunday brunch.

Woodstock

CUCINA $$
109 Mill Hill Road
(845) 679-9800
www.cucinawoodstock.com

Contemporary classics fill the interesting menu at Cucina. Small bites such as olive oil roasted almonds with paprika open the menu; salads such as roasted beets with goat cheese and appetizers such as old-fashioned chicken soup

follow. The menu also offers a choice of individual thin-crust pizzas, a variety of pastas (including the risottos of the day), and a good choice of main courses. Options here include lamb shanks braised in red wine and served with polenta, and market fish of the day. The dining room has a clean, contemporary look with an attractive full bar. Dinner is served Tuesday through Sunday; in addition, brunch is served on weekends. Closed Monday.

ORIOLE 9 $$
17 Tinker Street
(845) 679-5763
www.oriole9.com

With good food, moderate prices, a relaxed atmosphere, and a location in the heart of Woodstock, Oriole 9 is a great place to start or end a visit to this historic town. The food has a definite European slant, even at breakfast—you can have eggs in many styles, or French toast Belle Helene (with chocolate sauce, whipped cream, and pear). The lunch menu has interesting sandwich selections, such as the Thai crab cakes sandwich, served with avocado, tomato, and wasabi yogurt. Breakfast and lunch are served until 4:30 daily. At dinner, the menu branches out into entrees such as Asian-style Cornish game hens with black rice and tatsoi. Daily specials expand the offerings. The multicourse tasting menus, with matched wines, are a good value. Dinner reservations suggested. Open from 8:30 a.m. to 4:30 p.m. Sunday through Tuesday; 8:30 a.m. to 10:00 p.m. Wednesday through Saturday.

VIOLETTE $$
85 Mill Hill Road
(845) 679-5300
www.violettewoodstock.com

The French bistro cuisine served here matches nicely with the cozy setting—an old brick house with a small garden in front, a big bay window, and wood-burning fireplaces and a beamed ceiling inside. The menu offers classic French dishes such as homemade pâté and chicken paillard. There's also a daily risotto and other daily specials. The wine list is excellent, with a lot of good European and American choices. The good, reasonably priced lunch menu offers interesting sandwiches, such as brie and apple on ciabatta bread. A cup of soup comes with all lunch items, making this one of the better buys in the area. Reservations suggested for dinner. In the summer, open for lunch and dinner every day except Wednesday; Sunday brunch. Winter hours are shorter—call first to check.

NIGHTLIFE

The Hudson Valley is a very musical place—and all the musicians come out at night. Leaving aside the thriving classical music scene covered in the Performing Arts and Film chapter, the region also has an active rock, jazz, and folk scene. Several famous venues for musicians, including the Bearsville Theater in Woodstock and The Chance in Poughkeepsie, offer regular concert performances. In addition, there's a lively and varied music scene at local bars and restaurants.

In fact, the entire mid-Hudson region abounds with good bars—with and without restaurants attached. There are far too many to include them all here—and many great restaurants with lounges are already covered in the two Restaurant chapters. This chapter focuses on the standouts—the places that showcase local musicians or have some other claim to fame, like being a great sports bar or an authentic Irish pub. Where cover fees are usual, they're listed, but be aware that not every venue has a cover for every performance, and that the fee may vary. Likewise, the price of drinks and bar food varies considerably from place to place—and then there are all those happy hours, half-price nights, and promotional events. Prices vary so much that there's no point in putting in a price code, though price ranges are given where relevant.

Some important reminders: The legal drinking age in New York State is 21; most bars will not allow underage patrons to enter after 8:00 p.m., if they let them in at all. New York State law says that anyone under 16 attending a music event must be accompanied by a parent or legal guardian. In Putnam County, the official closing time for bars is 3:00 a.m.; everywhere else in the region, it's 4:00 a.m. No smoking in any bar or restaurant in New York State!

MUSIC VENUES

BARDAVON
35 Market Street
Poughkeepsie
(845) 473-2072
www.bardavon.org

A historic venue with a great auditorium (see the Performing Arts and Film chapter for details), the Bardavon presents top headliners such as Sinead O'Connor, Mickey Hart, Manhattan Transfer, Smokey Robinson, and Kenny Loggins. Ticket prices are in the $45 range. Purchase tickets through the box office or through TicketMaster at (845) 454-3388 or www.ticketmaster.com. Parking is in nearby municipal lots.

BEARSVILLE THEATER
291 Tinker Street (Route 212)
Woodstock
(845) 679-4406
www.bearsvilletheater.com

One of the places that makes Woodstock Woodstock, the Bearsville Theater is the creation of Albert Grossman. A music industry genius who early recognized the talent of artists such as Bob Dylan, Janis Joplin, and The Band, Grossman envisioned a beautiful, intimate theater (just 250 seats) where musicians could perform away from the pressures of more commercial settings. Grossman died in 1986, two years before the theater opened. Today his widow Sally Grossman runs the facilities, including the famed Bearsville recording studios. The roster of performers here is amazingly varied: Fleetwood Mac, Warren Zevon, Natalie Merchant, Jefferson Starship, Donald Fagen, and Eddie Palmieri. Concert tickets are in the range of $15 to $50 or more—it all depends on who's playing. Tickets can be purchased online or by calling the box office. In addition to concerts, the Bearsville Theater regularly hosts dance parties; the cover is usually $10.

THE CHANCE
6 Crannell Street
Poughkeepsie
(845) 471-1966
www.thechancecomplex.com

One of the premier music venues in the Hudson Valley, The Chance was opened in 1970. The performers and audience from those early days reads like a rock Who's Who: Muddy Waters, Ozzy Osbourne, and Lionel Hampton on stage, Jerry Garcia and Bob Dylan in the audience. The Chance is known as a place where talented groups get off the ground—The Police played here when they were still totally unknown. Nationally known musicians, emerging musicians, brand-new musicians all get a chance (get it?) here. The main club is an intimate space that was once a movie palace in downtown Poughkeepsie; the 1920s feel is still there in the decor, especially the Egyptian mummy cases that flank the stage. The acoustics are excellent, aided by a state-of-the-art sound system. In addition to the main theater, The Chance also offers performances in The Loft and in Club Crannell Street around the corner. Ticket prices range from $7 to $25 and occasionally more. Tickets can be purchased through the box office or through TicketWeb at www.ticketweb.com. Doors for all shows open at 8:30 p.m. unless otherwise noted. *Note:* To avoid towing, park in the inexpensive nearby municipal lot.

i For the latest info on who's playing where in the region, check the excellent Hudson Valley Music Web site at www.hvmusic.com.

EISENHOWER HALL THEATRE
United States Military Academy
West Point
(845) 938-4159
www.ikehall.com

The acoustics and sight lines at Ike Hall are unusually good. Combine that with the great roster of performers here and you have one of the best venues in the region for a major concert (there's more about this fabulous theater in the Performing Arts and Film chapter). The lineup here has included Sinbad, the Dave Mathews Band, Trisha Yearwood, and Lord of the Dance. Ticket prices are in the $25 to $50 range. Tickets can be purchased from the box office or from Telecharge. *Note:* Because Eisenhower Hall is on the USMA campus, allow at least an hour before curtain time for security; everyone over 16 needs a photo ID.

LEVON HELM STUDIOS
160 Plochman Lane
Woodstock
(845) 679-2744
www.levonhelm.com

Legendary musician Levon Helm lives and works in Woodstock. He holds regular Midnight Ramble Sessions with the Levon Helm Band at the recording studio attached to his home. Guest artists are often booked to appear with the band, but other musicians who happen to be around often turn up and perform. The ambience in the studio is relaxed and friendly, with a clean family atmosphere. There's a small stage, a big open fireplace, and lots of good seats. Doors open at 7:00 p.m. and the show starts at 8:00 p.m. Levon Helm loves to play music for an audience—concerts usually last a good four hours. There's a zero tolerance policy for alcohol here. No alcohol or food is served, although free soft drinks and water are available. Phone reservations for shows are an absolute must. Call as far in advance as possible. Seating is on a first-come basis, so it's best to arrive early.

MAIR THEATER
Mid-Hudson Civic Center
14 Civic Center Plaza
Poughkeepsie
(845) 454-5800
www.midhudsonciviccenter.com
OK, it's a big 3,000-seat auditorium, and you're not likely to hear history being made as a great new musician debuts, but for your standard rock or pop concert, Mair Theater does just fine. It's got a solid stage and sound system and books great headliners. Recent performers here include Clay Aiken, B.B. King, the Goo Goo Dolls, and Melissa Etheridge. Tickets are generally in the $35 to $60 range. Purchase tickets from the box office or from Ticketmaster at www.ticketmaster.com. Parking is in the lot of the nearby Sheraton Hotel or in the municipal lot across the street.

TOWNE CRIER CAFÉ
130 Route 22
Pawling
(845) 855-1300
www.townecrier.com
Although this venue technically isn't in the Hudson Valley region covered by this book, it's such a well-known spot for great music that it has to be included. The Towne Crier was founded in 1972, which makes it one of the oldest ongoing venues of its type in America. Ever since it opened, the Towne Crier has put the music first and has consistently presented an amazing lineup of live music ranging from blues to zydeco, with everything in between, including jazz, folk, world, and Celtic. Well-known performers to grace the stage here include Lucy Kaplansky, Suzanne Vega, Andy Summers of The Police, Kate and Anna McGarrigle, Ellis Paul, and Dar Williams. The cafe is a good place for lunch or dinner even if you're not also seeing a show. Show times are Friday and Saturday nights at 9:00 p.m.; Sunday and weekdays 8:00 p.m. Open mic night is Wednesday at 7:00 p.m. Ticket prices range from $4 for open mic night to $40 for some of the more popular performers; the average is around $20. Tickets are more expensive at the door, so call ahead for reservations.

ULSTER PERFORMING ARTS CENTER (UPAC)
601 Broadway
Kingston
(845) 331-6088
www.upac.org
In 2006, UPAC, a 1,500-seat venue, merged with Bardavon in Poughkeepsie (see the Performing Arts and Film chapter for more on this theater). The combined strength of the two groups means that UPAC now books fabulous shows featuring performers such as Kenny Loggins, Blondie, and Queen Latifah. Tickets are $45 to $80. Tickets can be purchased through the box office or through TicketMaster. Parking is in inexpensive nearby municipal lots or at meters on the street.

> **i** Radio Woodstock, WDST at 100.1 FM, is a major concert promoter in the region. Check the Web site at www.wdst.com for details and to order tickets.

BARS

Columbia County

Chatham

PEINT O GWRW TAFARN
36 Main Street
(518) 392-2337
A low-key local establishment, the Peint o Gwrw is a little piece of Wales set in bucolic Columbia County. The name in Welsh means "Pint of Ale Tavern," and that's pretty much the main reason to stop by here. The bar has a wide variety of

> **i** New York State frowns on driving under the influence. Many bars and restaurants in the region participate in safe ride programs, which usually means a free taxi ride home for patrons who shouldn't be driving. At other establishments, bartenders will call taxis for patrons on request or when they feel it's necessary. Just about every bar will give designated drivers free soft drinks all evening long.

beers on tap, and it's an outlet for locally brewed beers from the nearby Chatham Brewing Company. The food is standard pub grub; live music on Friday night.

Hudson

STRAY BAR
521 Warren Street
(518) 828-7303
www.straybar.com

Stray Bar has a little bit of everything you'd want from a bar: a pool table, a dance floor complete with disco ball, an ornate bar, and a stage for live music (left over from the days when the space really was a theater). The music starts at 9:00 p.m. on weekends; covers are in the $8 range. There's a DJ every Friday and Saturday night—no cover after the show. Wednesday is open mic night, starting at 9:00 p.m.—no cover. Stray Bar is open seven days a week from 4:00 p.m. to 4:00 a.m. Accessibility warning: Stray Bar is up a flight of stairs.

Dutchess County

Beacon

THE BARKING FROG
436 Fishkill Avenue
(845) 831-1337

OK, frog's legs really are on the menu here—and they're surprisingly good, especially with the house hot dipping sauce. Have them with the Barking Frog cocktail, a potent mixture that gets its bright-green color from a dose of Midori liqueur. There's also a pretty good selection of bar food, burgers, and entrees such as Asian-style grilled chicken, plus a small late-night menu for the midnight munchies. The friendly fun here includes two pool tables, six big-screen TVs, a foosball table, steel-tip and electric dartboards, and karaoke on Wednesday night at 9:00 p.m. Local bands such as Chowderhead appear on weekend evenings, and dance parties happen once or twice a month on Saturday night. Performances and dancing usually start at 10:00 p.m.

MAX'S ON MAIN
246 Main Street
(845) 838-6297
www.maxsonmain.com

The nightlife headquarters of Beacon, Max's on Main is also the latest incarnation (since 2006) of the oldest bar in town. As befits a sort of historic establishment, there's a long, ornate wooden bar and a wide selection of beers on tap. Friendly bartenders mix up the Maxtini, the house cocktail—a Cosmopolitan made with grapefruit juice. The food is good and very reasonably priced. Max's is a good place for lunch or dinner, but the place really comes alive later in the evening—the entertainment begins at 9:30 p.m. There's never a cover to see the local and regional groups that play on weekends. Karaoke night is Thursday (also no cover), the bar has NFL season ticket football, and dance parties happen here pretty regularly. Max's is open daily for lunch and dinner; cocktails until closing.

Fishkill

THE KELTIC HOUSE
1004 Main Street
(845) 896-1110
www.thekeltichouse.com

The Keltic House brings the authentic Irish pub experience to the Hudson Valley, complete with lots of dark wood and imported Irish bartenders pulling the pints. The menu includes standard pub grub such as burgers, fish and chips, and Irish eggs, but it also extends to good hot sandwiches and entrees such as herb-roasted pork loin. Live music at The Keltic House happens not just on weekend nights but also some weeknights. The authentic Irish theme doesn't carry over into the entertainment. The bands are mostly local and regional groups such as The Benjamins and Amish Outlaws—not exactly the sorts of band for Irish step dancing. The bar offers large-screen plasma TVs and Wi-Fi Internet access.

MICHAEL'S SPORTS CAFÉ
738 Route 9
(845) 896-5766
www.michaelsportscafe.com

Michael's calls itself a sports cafe, and it is true that the bar has 18 television screens for watching your favorite teams—the entire NFL package is available during football season—along with darts and pool. But the sports part of the name is also a little misleading, because Michael's is a popular music venue. There's live entertainment here four nights a week. Tuesday is acoustic night, Thursday night is karaoke, Friday night is always a dance party, and every Saturday night hosts a different local band, such as Nuts in a Blender. The menu here is well-prepared standard pub fare, heavy on the wings and burgers.

Hopewell Junction

GOODFELLAS INN
2550 Route 52
(845) 226-6003
www.goodfellasinn.com

Beer lovers love this bar—it has 32 taps and carries more than 150 bottle brews from all over the country and the world. In fact, GoodFellas claims to have the most tap beers in six counties, which means it has the most tap beers of any place in this book. The beer menu has many interesting, unusual, and hard-to-find brews, such as Hitachino Nest red rice ale from Japan. The building is a lovely old converted house on spacious grounds. Enjoy your beer inside or outside on a large deck in the backyard.

Hyde Park

BLEACHERS SPORTS BAR
547 Violet Avenue
(845) 452-4575

A relative newcomer to the area, Bleachers Sports Bar offers multiple screens showing a variety of sports—this is a bar for sports lovers of every type. Sports memorabilia cover the walls in the bar area. Bleachers offers karaoke on Friday nights and is starting to tap into the local music scene

on Saturday evenings. It's a late-night place—on weekdays there's a second happy hour from 10:00 p.m. to midnight, and the bar routinely stays open until 4:00 a.m. on Friday and Saturday.

Millbrook

SEANY B.'S
3624 Franklin Avenue
(845) 677-2282
www.myspace.com/seany_bs101

Beer and music go together nicely at Seany B.'s, a fairly new incarnation of an older British-style pub in quiet Millbrook. The slogan at Seany B.'s is "If you don't know how to drink we'll school you." What you'll learn is how to enjoy a good beer—the bar offers more than 100 domestic and imported bottled and draft beers. Local groups play here every Friday and Saturday night—no cover—and have quickly made this bar a popular nightspot. Karaoke night is every other Friday, and open mic night is every Thursday.

Poughkeepsie

BANANAS COMEDY CLUB
2170 Route 9 (Best Western)
(845) 462-3333
www.angelfire.com/comics/mikeirwin/index
.html

Bananas Comedy Club has been making people laugh since 1986. At the original Poughkeepsie club (there's another in Hasbrouck Heights in New Jersey), three shows every weekend bring in enthusiastic crowds. In addition to newcomers and emerging comics, the club boasts headliners that have included Sinbad, Bobcat Goldthwait, Jamie Foxx, Caroline Rhea, and Robert Klein. This is the club that gave Jimmy Fallon of *Saturday Night Live* and *Late Night* fame his start, back when he was a 17-year-old senior at Saugerties High School. Reservations are strongly recommended. Phone reservations are taken starting the Sunday before the show. Advance tickets can also be purchased through TicketWeb at (866) 468-7619 or www.ticketweb.com. The Friday night show starts at 9:30 p.m.; tickets are $12. Saturday night shows start at 8:00 p.m. and 10:30

p.m.; tickets are $15. Seating begins one hour before the early show and half an hour before the late show. Seating is on a first-come, first-served basis. Bananas offers a dinner package at Harper's Café for an additional $20—a good value. Proper attire is required—no tank tops, cutoffs, or hats. Guests must be 16 or older.

THE DUBLINER IRISH PUB
796 Main Street
(845) 454-7322
www.dublinerpubny.com

The Victorian-style interior of this establishment is cozy and comfortable, with an open fireplace and an old-fashioned snug. The Dubliner offers 23 different draft beers, served in 20-ounce imperial pints. The menu features Irish specialties. In 2007 the Dubliner was voted Best of the Hudson Valley for nightlife by readers of *Hudson Valley* magazine. Two things are big attractions here: sports from Ireland on the big screen, including rugby and soccer matches, and a great lineup of traditional Irish music from local performers (no cover). Other local musicians also play gigs here—check the Web site to see who's on when. Those who enjoy live music but don't like late nights can come out for brunch on weekends. Karaoke night is every Wednesday at 10:00 p.m.

MAHONEY'S IRISH PUB AND RESTAURANT
35 Main Street
(845) 471-3027
www.mahoneysirishpub.com

Located right next to the Poughkeepsie train station, Mahoney's is more than just a place for a quick drink after getting off a commuter train. The bar is in a restored factory building, but it doesn't look industrial at all. The place has a relaxed feel, with exposed ceiling beams and comfy leather armchairs by an open fire near the bar. The bar itself opens up to two stories; the upper level is ringed with a balcony area for dining. Mahoney's is a popular local nightspot, with Stump! trivia night every Monday, pub games on Tuesday, karaoke on Wednesday, and even a Thursday night bowling league. On the weekends, Mahoney's breaks loose

and local and regional bands rock the house. The live music is followed by dancing with a DJ from 2:00 a.m. to closing at 4:00 a.m.

SHADOWS ON THE HUDSON
176 Rinaldi Boulevard
(845) 486-9500
www.shadowsonthehudson.com

Shadows is perched on a 40-foot bluff overlooking the Hudson—the views are spectacular (and the food is good). The bar scene here is very lively. The sleek indoor bar and cocktail lounge features a 14-foot-tall high-def video wall where up to nine different video sources can be shown at once. An outdoor bar on a deck overlooking the river is open in the warmer weather. Shadows is regionally famous for its amazing cocktails and long drinks. The recipes were created exclusively for Shadows by master mixologist Tobin Ellis. He also selected and trained the bar staff to the highest standard. Any drink here is a work of art, but to sample the finest at Shadows, try the Cucumber Cosmopolitan or the Bramble Martini.

Red Hook

TIN PAN ALLEY
7909 Old Post Road (Route 9)
(845) 758-4545
www.tinpanalleyrestaurant.com

The food at this attractive venue is good (great desserts!), with outdoor dining in the garden in good weather, and the bar is well stocked and staffed. The place comes alive on Friday and Saturday nights, when live music and performers take the stage. The slant is toward folk, soul and blues, and jazz; comedians also do occasional gigs.

Rhinebeck

THE FIREBIRD LOUNGE
6423 Montgomery Street
(off Garden Street)
(845) 876-8686
www.myspace.com/firebirdlounge

Firebird Lounge is right in the village of Rhinebeck, just behind Upstate Films. Although Rhinebeck is full of restaurants, and although most of them have good bars that even feature occasional live music, these establishments are still primarily restaurants. Firebird Lounge, on the other hand, is a bar (complete with pool table, dart boards, and foosball) that also happens to serve pretty good standard pub grub. The barroom has comfy leather chairs and a well-stocked jukebox and offers one of the best beer selections in Dutchess County—six on tap, more than 50 in the bottle. Friday night brings a dance party starting at 11:00 p.m. (no cover), and every Saturday night brings live music from local groups.

Tivoli

THE BLACK SWAN
66 Broadway
(845) 757-3777
A low-key Irish pub in the middle of the tiny village of Tivoli, The Black Swan is a great place for a quiet pint and a chat with friends. The food is good too, if a bit on the eclectic side of pub grub. In warmer weather, the very pleasant outdoor dining area is a good place for a casual meal. What makes The Black Swan a special place on a Saturday night is the seriously good music that happens here. Most of it is acoustic, and all of it is original. Refreshingly, the main requirement for performing here seems to be dedication to music, not the size of the amps. Local and regional groups perform, usually without a cover.

Greene County
Catskill

DOUBLES II
29 Church Street
(518) 697-8833
www.doublesii.com
A new incarnation of an old bar, Doubles II is a great dance venue—dance parties are every Friday and Saturday, all night. The resident DJs here draw big crowds. When the DJs aren't in charge, live music is. This is a late-night weekend spot—it's open Thursday 5:00 p.m. to midnight, Friday and Saturday 7:00 p.m. to 3:00 a.m.; closed the rest of the week.

STELLA'S LOUNGE AT CATSKILL POINT
7 Main Street
(518) 943-3173
www.catskillpoint.com
The restaurant at Catskill Point offers good food and fabulous river views, but there's an even better reason to come here: the live jazz, blues, and other music at Stella's Lounge. The lounge has a sort of 1950s Greenwich Village feel, with retro decor, a long bar, and red lighting—the only thing missing is the haze of cigarette smoke. The performers are mostly well-known locals, including the Betty MacDonald Trio and the Tequila Mockingbirds. Shows start at 8:30 p.m. Friday and Saturday nights; the cover is $10.

Orange County
Newburgh

BLUE MARTINI
50 Front Street
(845) 562-7111
As the name suggests, 25 specialty martinis, plus other specialty cocktails, are the main draw here (the food is good, too). The large front bar is complemented by outdoor patios and a tiki bar overlooking the Hudson. The crowd here tends to be lively—the bar stays open late on the weekends, and the dinner menu is available until 11:00 p.m. on Friday and Saturday.

THE GOLDEN RAIL ALE HOUSE
29 Old North Plank Road
(845) 565-BEER
www.thegoldenrail.com
As close as you can come to a typical English pub without leaving the Hudson Valley, the Golden Rail Ale House has been serving beer, and lots of it, since 1977. The bar offers 18 beers on tap and more than 70 bottled brews, both domestic and international. The Golden Rail also often gets small amounts of limited-quantity specialty brews that won't be easily found anywhere else. Entertainment comes from the vast collection in the digital jukebox, the pool table, darts, and foosball, and all the local teams on TV. Standard pub grub is available. There's also free Wi-Fi.

GULLY'S RESTAURANT
2 Washington Street
(845) 565-0077

Back in the 1980s, Con Edison wanted to get rid of a retired water barge. Ralph Risio bought it and converted it into a floating restaurant and bar—and a local favorite on the Newburgh waterfront was born. The lower level is the restaurant part, with good, moderately priced food, a very relaxed atmosphere (kids welcome), and great river views. The upper level is the bar. There's live music here just about every night, including well-known local DJs and bands such as Chowderhead and Replica. The crowd is friendly and there's never a cover. Gully's isn't expensive to begin with, and it runs a lot of promotional nights that make the drink prices very reasonable.

TORCHES ON THE HUDSON
120 Front Street
(845) 568-0100
www.torchesonthehudson.com

The Aqua Bar at Torches is truly awesome: It features a 6,000-gallon saltwater aquarium with 30 fish species. The rest of the bar is impressive, too, with mahogany woodwork and sea-themed lighting fixtures. It's one of the area's most popular late-night spots. The resident DJ and guests spin most nights, and there's live entertainment on weekends. In the warmer weather, when the patios overlooking the Hudson are open, the bar really jumps. Torches is also one of the best restaurants in the area. The gorgeous dining room has 25-foot floor-to-ceiling windows overlooking the Hudson.

Putnam County
Garrison
THE STADIUM
1308 Route 9
(845) 734-4000
www.stadiumbarrest.com

The Stadium is the ultimate sports bar in the region. One of the largest individual collections of sports memorabilia in the country is on display here, including treasures such as Mickey Mantle's 1956 Triple Crown trophy. Also on display is Paul Hornung's 1956 Heisman Trophy. (Hornung sold the trophy to owner Joe Walsh and used the money to endow a scholarship at Notre Dame. Walsh matched Hornung's contribution, doubling the size of the fund.) In all, more than 1,000 items related to football, hockey, baseball, and basketball are exhibited, making The Stadium the country's largest sports memorabilia restaurant. It's not all nostalgia here, however—the bar features 22 TV screens showing today's sports as they happen. The menu is standard American cuisine, carefully prepared. The dining room is open from 11:30 a.m. to 10:00 p.m.; the bar stays open until 3:00 a.m.

Ulster County
Kingston
BACKSTAGE PRODUCTIONS
323 Wall Street
(845) 338-8700
www.backstagestudios.net

An arts and entertainment complex right in the middle of uptown Kingston, Backstage Productions is a performance venue for music of all sorts. Originally built as a vaudeville theater in the late 1800s, the block-long building is being restored to contain performance spaces, studios, and classrooms. There's no food here (you can bring your own), but there is an excellent full bar. Live music shows happen on Friday and Saturday nights. Wednesday night is a dance party ($8 cover), and Thursday is Wide Open Mic night (no cover). Reservations are available for some events—call for details.

THE BRIDGEWATER BAR AND GRILL
50 Abeel Street
(845) 340-4272
www.bridgewaterbarandgrill.com

One of the more historically interesting bars in Kingston's historic Rondout District, the Bridgewater was originally a synagogue built in 1892. It was restored as a restaurant and bar in 1996 and renovated in 2005 (the previous incarnation was called West Strand Grill). Today it's a friendly bar with good food, beer served in pints, and a strong Irish flavor. Expect live music, usually Irish-themed, every Friday and Saturday night (no cover). Groups appearing here have included The Redeemers, The Wolftones, and Enter the Haggis. The kitchen is open with a full menu until 10:00 p.m., Wednesday through Saturday. Closed Monday and Tuesday.

HICKORY BBQ AND SMOKEHOUSE
743 Route 28
(845) 338-2424
www.hickoryrestaurant.com
The barbeque here is excellent, and it's a great place for a family-friendly dinner. On the weekends, though, it's time for the grown-ups to have some fun. The live music usually starts at 9:00 p.m. Friday and Saturday. It leans toward the country rock side, but at any given time, soul, blues, jazz, or roots rock might be on stage. The bar features a good beer selection.

RIVE GAUCHE
276 Fair Street
(845) 339-2003
www.le-canardenchaine.com
An extension of one of the finest French restaurants in the region (see the Restaurants: West chapter), Rive Gauche is a late-night club featuring music and dancing, and, of course, a full bar featuring French wines and cognacs. The club is open from 10:00 p.m. to 2:00 a.m., Friday through Sunday. Dance to a DJ Friday and Saturday nights. Alternative tea dances happen on Sunday, with drag shows on the first and third Sundays. Doors open at 7:00 p.m.; drag shows start at 9:00 p.m.; the cover is $5. Some other special events may also have a cover.

SNAPPER MAGEE'S
59 Front Street
(845) 339-3888
www.snappermagees.com
An Irish pub, more or less, Snapper Magee's is a popular hangout in uptown Kingston. Two things make this establishment stand out from an ordinary bar: the very cool pinball machine and the amazing jukebox. Offering an incredibly wide selection ranging from The Clash to Elvis Costello to The Ramones to the Dropkick Murphys, and updated every month, the jukebox is one of the most extensive and eclectic in the region. Open late every night.

New Paltz
BACCHUS
4 South Chestnut Street
(845) 255-8636
www.bacchusnewpaltz.com
Bacchus is a long-standing New Paltz favorite that's very popular with the many rock climbers, bikers, hikers, and other outdoor sorts found in abundance in the area. The food is good here, with a Southwestern accent. Enjoy dinner in the upstairs restaurant and then move downstairs to the tavern for an enjoyable evening sampling the more than 300 domestic and international bottled brews. Open daily; late-night appetizer menu at the bar. Bacchus has recently expanded to include a family-oriented billiards area with seven full-size tables, table tennis, foosball, and video and pinball games. The rate is $4 an hour per person.

CABALOOSA
58 Main Street
(845) 255-3400 or (845) 255-2400
www.cabaloosa.com
Cabaloosa is actually a family of three venues: Cabaloosa itself, which is billed as a live room and dance bar; Oasis Café, another music venue; and Katana Sake Bar, which is within the Oasis Café. At the Cabs Live Room, Thursday night is '70s and '80s dance night, with discounted drinks and free admission for ladies; Friday night is also a DJ dance party. The live music is on Saturday night, with local and regional indie bands; the cover is typically $5. Guests can be 18 and up (but, of course, only those over 21 can drink alcohol).

The Oasis Café is a late-night venue, opening at 7:00 p.m. every evening and closing at 4:00 a.m. There's entertainment almost every night: Tuesday is jazz night; Wednesday is open mic (plus free pool); and live bands play Thursday, Friday, and Saturday night. The Katana Sake Bar at Oasis Café is an even later nightspot, opening at 10:00 p.m. (5:00 p.m. on Friday) and closing at 4:00 a.m. The huge sake menu (more than 70 selections) and Asian specialty drinks make this one of the more interesting bars in the area.

MCGILLICUDDY'S RESTAURANT AND TAP HOUSE
84 Main Street
(845) 256-9289
www.cuddysny.com
McGillicuddy's is a nice mix of pub and club. During the week it's a local sports bar and restaurant serving well-prepared standard pub fare. A dozen TV screens carry the full NFL ticket and Yankees and Mets baseball. On weekends, McGillicuddy's turns into one long dance party, with live DJs on Thursday, Friday, and Saturday night. The cover is only $3, and the drink specials are good deals. The kitchen stays open until closing time at 4:00 a.m.

Rosendale
ROSENDALE CAFÉ
434 Main Street
(845) 658-9048
www.rosendalecafe.com
The vegetarian food is unusually good and interesting here (see the Restaurants: West chapter for more), just like the evening live music performances. The concerts are pretty low key, but they feature a wide range of performers in a relaxed and friendly atmosphere. Weekend concerts feature jazz, blues, world, and experimental music. Every other Tuesday is Community Music Night, showcasing local singer-songwriters. Prices for concerts vary from $10 to $20, with some free events. No reservations and no advance ticket sales; seating is on a first-come, first-served basis.

Dinner is served during the performances; there's a $5 per person minimum dinner order.

Saugerties
THE DUTCH ALE HOUSE
253 Main Street
(845) 247-BEER
www.dutchalehouse.com
A beer bar that opened in 2006, the Dutch Ale House offers more than 15 beers on tap, including standbys such as Coors Light and unusual microbrews such as Beamish Stout, Bare Knuckle Stout, and Tetley's Ale. The food here is hearty pub grub, including a great burger and a good selection of homemade soups. This is a warm and cozy place, with a great antique bar and free Wi-Fi. Open every day for lunch (except Monday) and dinner; the bar closes at 11:00 p.m.

DUTCH ARMS CHAPEL
16 John Street
(845) 943-6720
www.johnstjam.net
The historic Dutch Arms Chapel belongs to the Saugerties Reformed Church. It's now used as a sort of coffeehouse music venue featuring local musicians (in fact, back in the '60s, the building was a coffeehouse). The most popular regular event here is the John St. Jam. These concerts feature eclectic acoustic Americana, meaning pretty much anything from folk to blues to rock. The setting is very relaxed and intimate. The "stage" is just a big rug in the center of the floor surrounded by chairs. The audience is never more than a few feet from the musicians. John St. Jam concerts happen on the second and fifth Saturday of each month. Admission is $3; home-baked goodies, coffee, tea, and other nonalcoholic beverages are available. The doors open at 7:00 p.m.; the music starts at 7:30 p.m. The performances are two rounds of four players each, with an intermission in between. The space fills quickly, so arrive early for the best seats.

PIG BAR & GRILL
110 Partition Street
(845) 246-1058

A relative newcomer to the music scene, Pig Bar & Grill opened in 2007 (replacing an earlier establishment called the Chow Hound). Local jazz fans were relieved when the new owner decided to continue the popular Sunday night jazz jam sessions. Local performers, including singer Pamela Pentony and pianist Francesca Tanksley, jam from 7:30 to 10:30 p.m. On other nights, local indie bands such as popular The Gypsy Nomads perform here. The schedule varies—call for details.

THE COLONY CAFÉ
22 Rock City Road
(845) 679-5342
www.myspace.com/colonycafe

Built in the center of Woodstock as a hotel in 1929, the Colony Café today is an active and popular venue for live music. The cafe has a full bar and a fine art gallery (but no restaurant). Performers are on stage here every night, and the mix is impressive: reggae one night, indie rock the next, bluegrass after that. Dance parties, CD release parties, spoken word nights, and, of course, open mic nights round out an eclectic schedule. Most events have covers in the $5 to $10 range; some are free.

PERFORMING ARTS AND FILM

The Hudson Valley is packed with places to enjoy top-notch live theater, dance, and music. The region also has a very lively film scene, with many art houses and the famed Woodstock Film Festival.

Schedules and prices vary so much that it's impossible to give specifics here, although approximate dates and prices are given where relevant. Check with the box office or the venue's Web site for up-to-date information. The phone numbers given here are for the box office. Many but not all venues can take your ticket order in advance over the phone or through the Web site. A very few places also offer tickets through services such as Ticketmaster. Most but not all venues accept credit cards—those that don't are noted.

The prices or price ranges given here are for same-day purchases for adults. Just about every venue in this chapter offers reduced prices for seniors, students, kids, and groups of 10 or more. In some cases subscriptions are available, usually at a discount.

Note: Children under age 5 may not be admitted to live performances. Check with the box office in advance.

The places listed here are all wheelchair accessible. Infrared assistive listening devices are available at many venues. Check with the box office and ask about borrowing a receiver.

Unless otherwise noted, parking for all venues is free, plentiful, and on-site.

THEATERS AND THEATER COMPANIES

Columbia County

Chatham

THE MAC-HAYDN THEATRE
1925 Route 203
(518) 392-9292
www.machaydntheatre.org
Dedicated to presenting and preserving the great American musical, the nonprofit Mac-Haydn Theatre is an intimate, 350-seat theater-in-the-round. Every seat is less than 30 feet from the stage. Performances here are highly professional and encompass both new releases and the classic repertoire of Broadway's Golden Age. The theater presents a 15-week season every summer, with seven or eight fully staged musical shows, such as *My Fair Lady* and *Hairspray*, running for two weeks each. In addition, the theater produces four original children's musicals every year. Average yearly attendance is 38,000. Performance times and days vary a bit during the run of each show— check with the box office for details. Tickets are $27 and $28 for evening performances, $26 for all matinee seats, children under 12 with an adult $12. Advance purchase is recommended.

Ghent

WALKING THE DOG THEATER
39 Oak Hill Road
(518) 392-0131
www.wtdtheater.org
Walking the Dog Theater is a nonprofit organization dedicated to creating theater events that entertain and build community. To fulfill that mission, the company presents workshop productions and original, new, and classic plays at a variety of venues. The company also has a strong commitment to Shakespeare. In 1999 it created Shakespeare Alive!, an intensive summer theater

program for young people, and in 2004 the company developed its Shakespeare in Schools program. Since its founding in 1997, Walking the Dog Theater has given more than 600 performances that have reached more than 60,000 people. As the company moves forward, it is deepening its roots in Columbia County with collaborative programs with local artists and performances at local theaters such as the Hudson Opera House. Check the Web site to stay informed about upcoming performances and programs for kids.

Hudson

HUDSON OPERA HOUSE
327 Warren Street
(518) 822 1438
www.hudsonoperahouse.org
A nonprofit organization founded in 1991, the Hudson Opera House offers a year-round schedule of arts and cultural programming. The schedule includes concerts, readings, storytelling, theater and dance performances, workshops, and after-school programs. Because this is a community organization, the programming is mostly free or very low cost. Since the historic space was reopened late in 1997, the Hudson Opera House has presented more than 2,000 cultural and educational programs.

STAGEWORKS/HUDSON
41-A Cross Street
(518) 822-9667
www.stageworkshudson.org
Stageworks/Hudson is a not-for-profit Equity theater company dedicated to bringing high-quality theater and other productions to the region. The theater is located in a vast former warehouse that was once a factory making flypaper. The building was restored and the state-of-the-art, 100-seat Max and Lillian Katzman Theater was opened in 2004. Stageworks presents professional theater with an emphasis on new play development. The space is also home base for the Walking the Dog Theater company (previously listed). The performance schedule varies over the year—check the Web site for details. Tickets for preview

performances are $16; weekday, matinee, and Sunday performances are $22; and Friday and Saturday evening performances are $27. Advance purchase is recommended. Stageworks offers a special child-care program for performances on second and third Saturday evenings—it's $7 per hour per child. Call in advance to make arrangements. Parking for performances is in the inexpensive city parking lot off nearby Front Street, opposite the Amtrak station.

Spencertown

SPENCERTOWN ACADEMY ARTS CENTER
Route 203
(518) 392-3693
www.spencertownacademy.org
Located in tiny Spencertown near Austerlitz, the nonprofit Spencertown Academy Arts Center is a restored 1840s Greek Revival schoolhouse. It has a 110-seat auditorium that is used by a variety of performers to present classical, world, and traditional music concerts. The center also offers a variety of other events, including spoken word programs, performance art, small theater pieces, puppet shows, and a popular series called Cabaret in the Country. Admission to most events is $12 or less; some events are free.

Dutchess County
Annandale-on-Hudson

RICHARD B. FISHER CENTER FOR THE PERFORMING ARTS
Bard College
(845) 758-7900
www.fishercenter.bard.edu
Designed by the acclaimed architect Frank Gehry, the astonishing Fisher Center at Bard College incorporates two theaters. The Sosnoff Theater is a surprisingly intimate, 900-seat theater with an orchestra pit. It's an outstanding space that can accommodate just about any form of the performing arts. An acoustic shell turns the theater into an outstanding concert hall for opera, symphonic performances, and chamber music. Theater Two is a smaller, flexible space that's used mostly for the college's dance and theater

programs during the academic year. Throughout the year, the Sosnoff Theater offers an extensive program of professional theater, dance, concerts, and other performances. The Fisher Center is home to the annual Bard Music Festival, which focuses on the works and times of a particular composer through a year long program of concerts, other performances, and lectures. Bard SummerScape, a festival of opera, theater, and dance, occurs every summer at the Fisher Center (see sidebar for more information). Average ticket prices range from $20 to $75. Tickets tend to sell out quickly, especially for SummerScape programs, so order in advance when possible.

Beacon

HOWLAND CULTURAL CENTER
477 Main Street
(845) 831-4988
www.howlandculturalcenter.org

Bard SummerScape

The annual Bard SummerScape is an acclaimed interdisciplinary arts series that focuses on the life, times, and artistic connections of a single composer such as Franz Schubert or Sergei Prokofiev, to take two recent examples. The performances take place at Bard College in the amazing Richard B. Fisher Center for the Performing Arts, designed by architect Frank Gehry. SummerScape events include the full spectrum of performing arts, including opera, dance, music, theater, and film. When the performances are over, enjoy the wonderful Spiegeltent (a temporary but very ornate pavilion) for drinks, dinner, late-night cabaret-style entertainment, and afternoon family programs. SummerScape runs from the beginning of July to the middle of August.

The beautiful Richard Morris Hunt building that houses the Howland Cultural Center is described in the Mansions and Historic Sites: East chapter. Because of its unusual interior dome and all-wood construction, the intimate performance space has wonderful acoustics, with a lovely warm sound. The center offers an active program of concerts, recitals, plays, readings, and other cultural events, but if you have the choice, go to a classical music performance—your ears will thank you. Every year the Howland Chamber Music Circle, a separate organization (845-297-9243 or www.howlandmusic.org), presents a series of eight chamber music concerts and three piano recitals at the center. Prices for performances at the center vary from free to no more than $30 for the chamber music series. Phone reservations are suggested for all performances.

TRUENORTH THEATRE PROJECT
Box 228
www.truenorththeatre.org
A collective of professional actors, writers, directors, and designers, TrueNorth Theatre Project is dedicated to bringing innovative theater to the Hudson Valley. The company performs both new plays and existing works. Performances are generally at the Beacon Institute for Rivers and Estuaries, although other venues in the Beacon area are also used. Admission is by donation. No reservations.

Poughkeepsie

BARDAVON OPERA HOUSE
35 Market Street
(845) 473-5288
www.bardavon.org
Founded in 1869, the Bardavon Opera House is the oldest continuously operating theater in New York State (take that, Broadway!) and is among the oldest in the country. Sarah Bernhardt, the Barrymores, Dizzy Gillespie, Frank Sinatra, Bob Dylan, and Al Pacino have all performed here. The magnificent building came perilously close to demolition in 1976, but was saved by becoming a nonprofit community arts organization.

Today the 944-seat Bardavon 1869 Opera House is a leading regional performance venue presenting the finest touring artists in theater, dance, music, opera, and other live arts. (See the Kidstuff chapter for information on children's programs.) Starting in 1999, the Bardavon has managed and presented the Hudson Valley Philharmonic, and in 2006 Bardavon took over the management of the Ulster Performing Arts Center (UPAC) in Kingston. The beautifully restored building is on the National Register of Historic Places. One of the glories of the Bardavon is its Mighty Wurlitzer Theatre Pipe Organ. Installed in 1928 to accompany silent films, the organ was sold to a private individual in the 1960s. After many vicissitudes, in 1993 it was returned to the Bardavon and restored by volunteers. The organ today is one of the few surviving Wurlitzers still playing in its original location (the organ in Radio City Music Hall is another). Ticket prices at the Bardavon vary with the event but generally range from $25 to $45. Tickets can be purchased through the box office or through Ticketmaster. Parking for events is in inexpensive nearby municipal lots.

POWERHOUSE SUMMER THEATER
Vassar College
124 Raymond Avenue
(845) 437-5902
www.powerhouse.vassar.edu
Every year since 1985, the Powerhouse Summer Theater at Vassar has brought together more than 200 theater professionals, along with 40 to 50 apprentices, to produce new plays. More than 50 plays that premiered at Powerhouse went on to major New York City productions, including works by such well-known playwrights as John Patrick Shanley, Eve Ensler, Eric Bogosian, and Beth Henley. The season generally includes two main stage productions along with a number of second stage and workshop productions and readings. The performances are sometimes experimental but always interesting and very professional. The schedule runs from the beginning of June to the end of July. Tickets are in the $25 to $35 range.

Rhinebeck
THE CENTER FOR PERFORMING ARTS AT RHINEBECK
661 Route 308
(845) 876-3080
www.centerforperformingarts.org
The huge red barn-shaped building that houses the Center for Performing Arts at Rhinebeck opened in 1998. It's an important regional community arts center and education facility. A lot of high-end community theater is put on here by groups such as the Gilbert & Sullivan Musical Theater Company, Up in One Productions, the Rhinebeck Theatre Society, and CENTERstage Productions. The center gets in a lot of great performances for kids (see the Kidstuff chapter for more on this). The space is also a performance venue for a wide variety of well-known national and international artists. Tickets are relatively inexpensive here—depending on the performance, seats range from around $14 to $22.

COCOON THEATRE
6384 Mill Street (Route 9)
(845) 876-6470
www.cocoontheatre.org
Cocoon Theatre is a nonprofit arts organization that brings theater and dance to the public, especially kids. A strong program of classes, workshops, and performances brings performing opportunities to the general public. Events at Cocoon include wonderful puppet shows and storytelling for kids, along with dance performances and plays for adults, such as Anton Chekhov's *The Cherry Orchard* and Thornton Wilder's *The Skin of Our Teeth*. Tickets are in the $12 to $20 range. The theater is intimate (small), and can sell out quickly. Performances are mostly on weekends year-round. Reserve tickets in advance if possible.

Orange County
West Point
EISENHOWER HALL THEATRE
United States Military Academy
(845) 938-4159
www.ikehall.com

Ike Hall, as this theater right on the USMA campus is affectionately known, presents an amazingly wide variety of performances. Everything from opera to dance to symphony orchestras to Broadway musicals to country and rock concerts happens here—and it all sounds great. Eisenhower Hall is an outstanding performance venue, with excellent sight lines, superb acoustics, and unusually comfortable seats. It's also one of the largest auditoriums in the country, second only to Radio City Music Hall. The theater complex also houses Ike's Riverside Café, a good spot for a meal before the show. The schedule follows the academic schedule for the cadets, so performances take place from September through May. Ticket prices are in the $25 to $50 range. Tickets can be purchased from the box office or from Telecharge. Parking at Ike Hall is free, but the lots can get congested. Also, because the theater is on the West Point campus, all visitors over the age of 16 must show photo ID to get on base. Between security and crowded parking, plan to arrive at least one hour before curtain.

Putnam County

Garrison

DEPOT THEATRE
Route 9D
(845) 424-3900
www.philipstowndepottheatre.org
As the name suggests, this venue is a former train station on the Hudson River. Today it's a community performing arts center for theater, children's programs, readings, chamber music, and film. The annual One-Act Play Festival in August draws a lot of critical attention. Tickets are generally under $15.

HUDSON VALLEY SHAKESPEARE FESTIVAL
Boscobel Restoration
Route 9D
(845) 265-9575
www.hvshakespeare.org
The region's only resident professional Shakespeare company performs in a state-of-the-art,

8,500-square-foot theater tent on the beautiful grounds of Boscobel Restoration (see the Mansions and Historic Sites: East chapter for more on Boscobel). This is very professional Shakespeare, presented against a backdrop of the magnificent Hudson Highlands. Two plays are presented in rotation every season. Festival performances usually play to sold-out crowds and critical acclaim—order your tickets early. The season runs from early June to the end of August; performances take place most evenings. Ticket prices range from $30 to $44. The grounds of Boscobel are opened to ticket holders for picnicking two hours before curtain—bring your own basket, order a gourmet picnic two days in advance through the box office, or purchase sandwiches, salads, and beverages at the concessions tent.

Ulster County

Kingston

ULSTER PERFORMING ARTS CENTER (UPAC)
601 Broadway
(845) 331-6088
www.upac.org
Built in 1927, UPAC was originally a movie palace and vaudeville house. It became a Walter Reade movie theater in 1947, but by 1977, Kingston's downtown had become shabby and the theater was closed. It was scheduled to be demolished to become a parking lot, but a group of concerned citizens raised the money to rescue the building and reopen it as the Broadway Theater of the nonprofit Ulster Performing Arts Center. The restored building is now listed on the National Register of Historic Places as one of the last great show palaces in New York State. With 1,500 seats, UPAC is the largest proscenium theater between Manhattan and Albany. In 2006, UPAC and Bardavon Opera House in Poughkeepsie agreed to merge, combining their strengths and finances to make their offerings in the region even better. As part of the merger, UPAC is now providing more school programming along with its ongoing presentations of outstanding headliners such as Kenny Loggins, Wynton Marsalis, Queen Latifah,

and Garrison Keillor. Tickets for these performances are on the pricey side, ranging from $45 to $80. Tickets can be purchased through the box office or through TicketMaster. Parking is in inexpensive nearby municipal lots or at meters on the street.

UNISON ARTS & LEARNING CENTER GALLERY
68 Mountain Rest Road
(845) 255-1559
www.unisonarts.org

A nonprofit community arts organization, Unison presents a wide variety of performing arts in an intimate, informal theater that seats only 90 people. Performances here are fun—the audience and the artists genuinely interact. The shows are mostly musicians of all sorts, from classical to world to jazz. Tickets are inexpensive at $16 for almost all performances.

Woodstock

WOODSTOCK FRINGE FESTIVAL
Byrdcliffe Theatre
Upper Byrdcliffe Road
(845) 810-0123
www.woodstockfringe.org

A month-long festival featuring experimental music and theater, the Woodstock Fringe happens every August. The works presented include plays, performance art, and music, including opera. While the works are often challenging, the performance level is always high and the shows are interesting if nothing else. Performances happen almost every evening during the festival. Tickets are in the $20 range. The $50 Fringe Pass is a real bargain if you can attend at least three events during the month.

WOODSTOCK PLAYHOUSE
103 Mill Hill Road
(845) 679-4101
www.woodstockplayhouse.org

The open-air Woodstock Playhouse offers performances throughout the summer months. Programs include family shows, musical events,

and two plays each season presented by the Playhouse's resident Bird-on-a-Cliff Theatre Company. The Woodstock Playhouse has a roof but no walls; seating is bleacher-style. Bring a jacket or sweater—the evenings in the Catskills are cool—and a cushion to sit on. Tickets are in the $10 to $20 range.

i The famed 1969 Woodstock festival didn't happen in the town of Woodstock—it was 50 miles to the southwest in Bethel, in Sullivan County. In 2006 the Max Yasgur farm, site of the festival, became the home of the Bethel Woods Center for the Arts, an outdoor performing arts venue that's beyond the region of this book. The excellent summer concert program features mostly rock and country musicians such as Cyndi Lauper, Ringo Starr, Lynyrd Skynyrd, and Willie Nelson (866-781-2922 or www.bethelwoodscenter.org).

DANCE

Dutchess County

KAATSBAAN INTERNATIONAL DANCE CENTER
120 Broadway
Tivoli
(845) 757-5106
www.kaatsbaan.org

A permanent nonprofit dance center dedicated to the growth, advancement, and preservation of professional dance, Kaatsbaan provides a creative home for national and international dance companies and choreographers. Dancers and dance artists stay at the center, which provides rehearsal studios, dorms, dining facilities, and performance space. While in residence, the artists can focus on creating new dances, rehearsing, and performing. Kaatsbaan is located on the site of the former Tivoli Farms, a 153-acre site that was once the home of Eleanor Roosevelt's grandparents. Today the site has three dance studios, including an intimate 160-seat performance theater, and residential space for 36 dancers. Unfortunately, in 2008 Kaatsbaan ran into serious financial difficulties. The property was put on the market and the future of the center is very much in doubt.

Ulster County

CATSKILL BALLET THEATRE
795 Broadway
Kingston
(845) 339-1629
www.catskillballet.org
Founded in 1981, Catskill Ballet Theatre is a regional ballet company based in Ulster County. The company is dedicated to preserving the legacy of classical ballet and bringing it to the community. Another major goal is giving young dancers in the region an opportunity to participate in full-scale ballet productions alongside working professional dancers. CBT performs all through the Hudson Valley in a number of venues—check the Web site for updates on performances.

MUSIC

Columbia County

CLARION CONCERTS
Box 43
Copake
(518) 325-3805
www.artscolumbia.org/clarionconcerts.html
The oldest classical music organization in Columbia County, Clarion Concerts presents three Leaf Peeper chamber music concerts every year in September and October. Every year the program includes a new work commissioned for the series. The concerts are fun—they're informal and a great mixture of old and new music played by top-level musicians. The venues are usually local churches in the area, including Chatham. Tickets are $20—students free—and can be purchased at the door. Check the Web site for the schedule.

Dutchess County

ASTON MAGNA SUMMER FESTIVAL
Bard College
Annandale-on-Hudson
(845) 758-7425
www.astonmagna.org
World famous for presentations of early music, Aston Magna is a chamber group performing on period instruments. The group tours internationally, but every summer it comes home to the Berkshires and presents a series of concerts in Great Barrington and Williamstown—and also at Bard College. There are 15 concerts in all: five programs, each performed at each venue. The series begins at the end of June and runs into early August. At Bard, the performances are on Friday evenings in Olin Hall, an ideal setting for chamber music. They start at 8:00 p.m.; there's a free pre-concert lecture starting at 7:00 p.m. Tickets are $30. Order tickets by phone by calling the Bard box office.

HOWLAND CHAMBER MUSIC CIRCLE
477 Main Street
Beacon
(845) 297-9243
www.howlandmusic.org
The Howland Chamber Music Circle presents two concert series every year at the Howland Cultural Center (previously listed). The Chamber Music Series spreads eight concerts across the fall and spring. The Piano Festival presents three piano recitals in the winter. The excellent musicians, amazing acoustics, and intimate setting make these concerts chamber music as it was meant to be. The concerts are on Sundays at 4:00 p.m. Tickets are $25 and sell out quickly—order in advance.

HUDSON VALLEY CHAMBER MUSIC CIRCLE
Bard College
Annandale-on-Hudson
(845) 339-7907
www.music.bard.edu
Founded as a summer concert series in 1950, the

Hudson Valley Chamber Music Circle has been associated with Bard College since 1979. Performances are in the acoustically excellent Olin Hall on the Bard campus, an intimate space ideal for chamber music. Performances are by some of the finest chamber groups around, including the Tokyo String Quartet and the Kalichstein-Laredo-Robinson Trio. The series is three Saturday night concerts in June; tickets are $28. Order well in advance if possible.

HUDSON VALLEY PHILHARMONIC
Bardavon Opera House
35 Market Street
Poughkeepsie
(845) 473-2072
www.bardavon.org/hvp.htm
The Hudson Valley's very own symphony orchestra lives at the Bardavon Opera House (previously listed). The orchestra has deep roots in the area—it gave its first public concerts in 1934. In the 1950s, a performance of Sergei Prokofiev's *Peter and the Wolf* had local resident Eleanor Roosevelt as the narrator. Today the HVP, under the baton of maestro Randall Craig Fleischer, presents five full-length symphonic concerts every year, along with a number of excellent programs that bring the orchestra to local schools and introduce kids to classical music (see the Kidstuff chapter for more on the children's programs). The concerts happen at the Bardavon and at UPAC, the sister theater in Kingston (previously listed). Ticket prices range from $25 to $36. Order through the box office or through TicketMaster.

RHINEBECK CHAMBER MUSIC SOCIETY
Box 465
Rhinebeck
(845) 876-2870
www.rhinebeckmusic.org
The Rhinebeck Chamber Music Society has been bringing world-class chamber ensembles to the Hudson Valley since 1981. The annual eight-concert series runs from September through March and brings in a number of highly regarded groups, such as the Cassatt String Quartet and Rebel, an ensemble specializing in Baroque music.

The concerts take place at the Church of the Messiah in Rhinebeck, which is noted for its excellent acoustics. The concerts alternate between Saturday evenings at 8:00 p.m. and Sunday afternoons at 4:00 p.m. Check the Web site for details. An informal talk is presented half an hour before the concert, and there's a reception with the artists afterward in the parish hall. Tickets are $25; students just $5; free for kids under 13. Tickets for these concerts are in demand, so order early.

Orange County

HUDSON VALLEY SOCIETY FOR MUSIC
26 Tamara Lane
Cornwall
(845) 534-8368
www.hudsonvalleysocietyformusic.org
Dedicated to the promotion of music at the community level, the Hudson Valley Society for Music supports two very different programs. The Potluck concert series is a very informal chamber music concert series presented at the Cornwall Presbyterian Church on occasional Friday evenings. The series is designed for those who aren't usually concert goers; coloring books and crayons are provided for kids (and adults), and dessert is on the menu. The performers are local professional musicians. The Hudson Valley BachFest is an annual event that takes place over three days early in September. Works by Johann Sebastian Bach are presented at the Cornwall Presbyterian Church, at Christ Episcopal Church in Poughkeepsie, and at various churches throughout the mid-Hudson region. Admission to Hudson Valley Society for Music performances is by donation.

NEWBURGH CHAMBER MUSIC
59 Coach Lane
Newburgh
(845) 534-3499
www.newburghchambermusic.org
Founded in 2000 with the goal of promoting music in the Newburgh area, Newburgh Chamber Music presents three chamber music concerts a year, along with sponsoring a music scholarship for local students and supporting

music education programs in the area. Performers include renowned ensembles such as the American String Quartet, the Chiara String Quartet, and guitarist Jorge Caballero. All concerts are at the beautiful St. George's Church on Grand Street in Newburgh. Tickets are $20; only $5 for students.

Ulster County

CHAMBER ARTS FESTIVAL OF MARBLETOWN
Box 663
Stone Ridge
(845) 687-2687
www.chamberartsfestival.org
A short, eclectic program of chamber music that runs for just nine days at the end of May, the Chamber Arts Festival is becoming one of the most respected local musical events in the region. The performers range from classical ensembles to jazz musicians to Celtic trios featuring the Irish harp. What ties them all together is a very high professional standard and appreciative audiences. The performances take place at the newly renovated Quimby Theater on the SUNY Ulster campus in Stone Ridge. Tickets are $25; $10 for students.

MAVERICK CONCERTS
Box 9
Woodstock
(845) 679-8217
www.maverickconcerts.org
The Maverick Concerts is America's oldest continuous summer chamber music series—it's been going on since 1916. The concerts take place in a rustic concert hall with near-perfect acoustics, set in the woods outside Woodstock. The name Maverick comes from the series founder, Hervey White, who used it for the collaborative colony of artists he established on the outskirts of Woodstock early in the 1900s; it refers to a wild white stallion that once roamed the mountains in Colorado. In 1924 sculptor John Flanagan carved the iconic horse that now graces the stage. Maverick has many claims to fame, but perhaps none is greater than the 1952 premiere of John Cage's *4'33"*. In this famous and controversial work, the pianist never actually plays a note. Maverick continues the tradition of supporting contemporary American composers such as David del Tredici and John Corigliano, whose works are often performed. Tickets to Maverick concerts are $25; $5 for students; kids under 12 are free. If you're willing to bring your own seating, admission is by donation. The box office accepts cash and personal checks only. There are no reserved seats at Maverick—all seating is first come, first served. For the best seats, aim to arrive an hour before the performance time. The excellent Young People's Concerts on Saturday mornings are free for kids and students and only $5 for adults. The evenings in the Catskills can be cool; bring a jacket or sweater.

PIANOSUMMER AT NEW PALTZ
SUNY New Paltz
1 Hawk Drive
New Paltz
(845) 257-3880
www.newpaltz.edu/piano
PianoSummer is an international summer institute and festival completely devoted to piano music. Under the artistic direction of famed pianist Vladimir Feltsman, students spend two or three intensive weeks taking lessons and attending master classes, lectures, student recitals, and festival concerts. The program runs from mid-July to early August. All events are open to the public. Ticket prices vary but range from $10 to $30. Check the Web site for the schedule.

WOODSTOCK CHAMBER ORCHESTRA
Box 711
Woodstock
www.wco-online.com
An ensemble drawn from the many talented local musicians in the region, the Woodstock Chamber Orchestra presents four full symphonic concerts every year. The repertoire is varied and always interesting, ranging from Bach concertos to concert performances of operas such as Mozart's *Don Giovanni* to world premieres of contemporary

music by modern composers such as Brian Fennelly. Each program is presented several times at various venues in the area, including Olin Hall at Bard College, Pointe of Praise Family Life Center in Kingston, and the Bearsville Theater in Woodstock. Tickets are $17; $5 for students.

MOVIE HOUSES

Columbia County

Chatham

CRANDELL THEATRE
46 Main Street
(518) 392-3331
www.crandelltheatre.com
Seeing a movie at the Crandell Theatre is like taking a step back into time. The theater is the oldest and largest in Columbia County. Built in 1926 as a vaudeville house, the Spanish-style brick-and-stucco building is basically unchanged since then. It's huge—there are 534 seats, 112 of them in the balcony. The theater's slogan is "The finest films at the lowest price," and they mean it. Admission is just $5 for adults and $4 for children under 12.

Hudson

TIME & SPACE LIMITED
434 Columbia Street
(518) 822-8100
www.timeandspace.org
TSL is a performing arts center with a strong social change mission. The center presents art exhibits and original theater, but it's best known in the region as a place to see really interesting independent films in a great space. The movie theater at TSL is small, but what makes it stand out are that all 84 seats are classic 1940s theater chairs. The filmmakers often present the showings and engage in discussions with the audience afterward. TSL is also a venue for the magnificent HD live broadcasts from the Metropolitan Opera. Movie prices are $5 and $7. Check the Web site for the film schedule.

i **FilmColumbia** is a county-wide film festival that takes place over four days every October. Indie films are shown at the famed Crandell Theatre in Chatham. Don't be fooled by the relaxed atmosphere of this low-key event—the films are top level. Some of the earliest showings of films such as *Sideways* and *Brokeback Mountain* were at this festival. Details are at (518) 392-1162 or www.filmcolumbia.com.

Dutchess County

Rhinebeck

UPSTATE FILMS
6415 Montgomery Street
(866) 345-6688
www.upstatefilms.org
Nonprofit and member-supported, Upstate Films has been showing the best of independent and foreign movies for more than 35 years. That Upstate Films can screen movies seven days a week year-round—more than 700 shows a year—is an indication of how much support there is for independent film in the culturally sophisticated Hudson Valley. The two screens here are the place to see films that don't make it to the local multiplex. There's also a strong program of guest speakers—often a film's director—who screen the movie and then discuss it with the audience. Upstate Films members get a discount on admission, with tickets only $4.50; the regular adult admission is $7.50. Check the Web site for the schedule. *Note:* Upstate Films uses real butter on its popcorn.

Greene County

Catskill

Community Theatre
373 Main Street
(518) 943-2410
www.thecommunitytheatre.com
OK, this isn't an art house—the movies are all first-run Hollywood productions. The setting, however, is historic enough to make seeing a movie here a little more interesting than seeing

the same movie in a boring multiplex. The Community Theatre dates back to 1920, when it was primarily a successful vaudeville theater. It eventually became strictly a movie theater. The outside marquee was redone in 1955, and after a fire in 1976 the lobby was "modernized" into a soulless box. The balcony was converted into a second theater, but the interior design of the main theater was never changed—it remains very much as it was in 1920, carpeted aisles, velvet draperies, and all. Admission is $7 for adults.

Orange County
Newburgh
DOWNING FILM CENTER
19 Front Street
(845) 561-3686
www.downingfilmcenter.com
The newest addition to the Hudson Valley art house scene, the Downing Film Center opened in 2007. The Downing offers an excellent selection of independent, classic, and foreign films. They're shown in an intimate, 55-seat theater in the renovated Yellow Bird Building on the Newburgh waterfront. Because the theater is so small, ticket reservations are a must—call in advance. The box office takes only cash. Seats are $8.

Ulster County
Rosendale
ROSENDALE THEATRE
408 Main Street
(845) 658-8989
The Rosendale Theatre is a classic turn-of-the-century red brick and wood structure that was once the local firehouse—once a week, the firemen would move the pumper outside so the townspeople could watch a movie. In 1949 the building officially became a movie theater and it's been one, pretty much unchanged, including the antique vending machines, ever since. The films shown here are an eclectic mix. There's the usual feature films, shown a few weeks later than the multi-screens, and an always-interesting selection of independent films and festival award winners.

Evening showings are at 7:20 p.m. only; if enough people show up, there's a Sunday matinee at 4:00 p.m. Closed Tuesdays. Admission is $4.

Saugerties
ORPHEUM MOVIE THEATER
198 Main Street
(845) 246-6561
An old-fashioned neighborhood theater with a classic 1930s marquee, the Orpheum dates back to the 1890s, when it was built as a vaudeville house. Today the theater is a triplex showing first-run movies, but most of the period details have been retained.

Woodstock
TINKER STREET CINEMA
132 Tinker Street
(845) 679-6608
www.tinkerstreetcinema.com
Located in the heart of Woodstock, the Tinker Street Cinema is a small, single-screen theater housed in a converted church. It's an art house, showing primarily independent and foreign films. It's also a major venue for the films shown at the annual Woodstock Film Festival (see the Annual Events chapter for details).

i Not too many drive-in movies are still in operation anywhere, which makes the three in the mid–Hudson Valley that much more remarkable. You can enjoy cinema under the stars (in season) at the Hi-Way Drive-In on Route 9W between Catskill and Coxsackie (518-731-8672; www.hiwaydrivein.com), the Hyde Park Drive-In in Hyde Park on Route 9 (845-229-4738; www.hydeparkdrivein.com), and the Overlook Drive-In at Degarmo and Overlook Roads (between Routes 44 and 55) in Poughkeepsie (845-452-3445; www.overlookdrivein.com).

MULTIPLEX MOVIE THEATERS

Dutchess County

LYCEUM SIX
Route 9
Red Hook
(845) 758-3311
www.greatmovieslowerprices.com

REGAL CINEMAS
Hudson Valley Outlet Center
Route 9
Fishkill
(845) 896-1090
www.regmovies.com

REGAL CINEMAS
Galleria Mall
2001 South Road
Poughkeepsie
(845) 297-0785
www.regmovies.com

ROOSEVELT CINEMAS
Route 9
Hyde Park
(845) 229-2000
www.greatmovieslowerprices.com

SILVER CINEMAS
South Hills Mall
836 South Road
Poughkeepsie
(845) 297-5993

Orange County

DESTINTA 12
215 Quassaick Avenue
New Windsor
(845) 569-8181
www.destinta.com

SHOWTIME CINEMAS
1124 Union Avenue
Newburgh
(845) 566-8800
www.showtimecinemas.net

Ulster County

NEW PALTZ CINEMA
2 New Paltz Plaza
New Paltz
(845) 255-0420
www.greatmovieslowerprices.com

REGAL CINEMAS
Hudson Valley Mall
1300 Ulster Avenue
Kingston
(800) 326-3264
www.regmovies.com

ART IN THE VALLEY

The Hudson Valley has hosted a lively art scene ever since Thomas Cole, the artist who is considered the founder of what came to be called the Hudson River School, began painting the area's magnificent scenery in the 1820s. He was soon joined by other notable artists, including Asher Durand, Jasper Cropsey, and Frederic Church. The area got another major boost as an art center in 1903, when the Byrdcliffe arts and crafts colony was founded in Woodstock by a wealthy Englishman named Ralph Radcliffe Whitehead. Byrdcliffe created an exciting artistic tradition in the area that continues to this day—it is quite possibly the oldest continuously operating arts and crafts colony in the country. For more than a century, the colony has attracted artists and craftspeople to the surrounding Woodstock area. In 2003, the region got another huge boost when Dia:Beacon, the museum of the Dia Art Foundation, opened. Located on the Beacon waterfront in southern Dutchess County in a massive converted factory that once printed boxes for Nabisco, Dia:Beacon presents a world-class collection of contemporary art, most of it on a very large scale. With the opening of this astonishing showplace, an already strong art community has really taken off. The mid-Hudson area today is home to an exciting and growing array of artists, galleries, museums, sculpture parks, and art events. In fact, there are so many places to see great art, and the scene is so dynamic, that some hard choices had to be made for this chapter. The galleries listed here were selected on the basis of being well established and oriented primarily toward the display of art by more than one artist—there simply isn't space to list all the studios of individual artists and all the smaller venues, such as local coffee shops, that also display art. Also listed in this chapter are local and regional arts organizations that sponsor shows, art walks, gallery tours, and other events.

Price Code

$	under $10
$$	$10 to $15
$$$	over $15

MUSEUMS AND ART PARKS

Columbia County

Ghent

THE FIELDS SCULPTURE PARK AT OMI INTERNATIONAL ARTS CENTER
59 Letter S Road
(518) 392-2181
www.artomi.org
The Fields Sculpture Park, founded in 1998, is located on the beautiful 300-acre campus of the Omi International Arts Center, a residency program for international visual artists, writers, musicians, and dancers. The rolling and varied terrain of the sculpture park is dotted with nearly 100 outstanding works by internationally recognized contemporary artists, including Steve Siegel, Donald Lipski, Grace Knowlton, Bernar Venet, and Peter Stempel. Approximately 10 new works are added to the park every year, including a number of site-specific works. In addition, the park has temporary exhibits and the occasional one-person show. The works cover about 90 acres in six areas. That sounds like too much to see comfortably in one visit, but most of the sculptures are arranged in six areas along a circular path that takes you through the park around the edge of a large natural pond; the open fields

and wooded areas form a backdrop for the art. At a moderate walking pace you can see pretty much all of them in a couple of hours. To make viewing easier (and more fun), the park provides free bikes; picnic tables and seating areas are scattered throughout. One of the most enjoyable aspects of the park is the way the art and the landscape blend together so naturally. The Fields is open every day from dawn to dusk at no charge. Concerts, exhibitions, public readings, and other special events are held throughout the year; call or check the Web site for information. Free guided tours are available with reservations for groups of six or more.

Hudson

OLANA STATE HISTORIC SITE $
Route 9G, 1 mile south of the
Rip Van Winkle Bridge
(518) 828-0135
www.olana.org
Olana is the spectacular Moorish-style home of the renowned artist Frederic Church. One of the most prominent members of the Hudson River School and a student of Thomas Cole, Church was famous for his very large canvases of panoramic landscapes such as his famed 1867 painting of Niagara Falls. Although he traveled the world to find subjects for his art, Church's heart was always at Olana, the 126-acre farm he purchased in 1860. Over the following four decades the house he built and the grounds he landscaped here became works of art in themselves. Church died in 1900; the property remained in family hands until 1966, when it was purchased by Olana Preservation and then turned over to the State of New York. Today Olana has been restored to very much how it looked during Church's lifetime. Though only a few of Church's paintings are on view (most are now in private collections and museums), a visit here gives a vivid glimpse into the life and works of one of America's greatest artists. The beautifully landscaped grounds at Olana are open daily from 8:00 a.m. to sunset at no charge. The house is open by guided tour only; hours are Tuesday through Sunday

from 10:00 a.m. to 5:00 p.m. from the end of March through the week of Thanksgiving. From Thanksgiving week to the end of March, tours are offered only Friday to Sunday from 11:00 a.m. to 4:00 p.m. Although reservations aren't required, the number of daily tickets is limited. To avoid disappointment, especially on weekends and holidays, make a phone reservation up to two weeks in advance of your visit. Admission is $7 for adults; $5 for seniors and students; free for children 12 and under. Parking is free.

Spencertown

TACONIC SCULPTURE PARK AND GALLERY
Stever Hill Road off Route 203
(518) 392-5757
www.taconic.net/kanwit/park.htm
This entry is an exception to the single artist rule of this chapter. Why? Because anyone driving north on the Taconic Parkway in Columbia County near Spencertown gets such an intriguing glimpse of Roy Kanwit's massive sculptures from the road that he has to be included here. Many more of Kanwit's marble, steel, and cement sculptures can be seen in the spacious and very quiet park and in his studio. The park is open seasonally on weekends only, from 9:00 a.m. to 5:00 p.m. To be on the safe side, call ahead.

Dutchess County
Annandale-on-Hudson

HESSEL MUSEUM OF ART,
CENTER FOR CURATORIAL STUDIES (CCS)
AT BARD COLLEGE
33 Garden Road
(845) 758-7598
www.bard.edu/ccs
The Center for Curatorial Studies (CCS) at Bard is an exhibition and research center focused on art and exhibition practices from the 1960s to the present day. To that end, the center offers both exhibitions of contemporary art and a prestigious graduate program in curatorial studies. The original 9,500-square-foot exhibition and research center at CCS was completed in 1991. In 2006 the center was expanded and renovated and the

Hessel Museum of Art, a separate 17,000-square-foot building, opened. The Hessel Museum is dedicated to the Marieluise Hessel Collection of more than 1,700 contemporary paintings, sculptures, photographs, works on paper, artists' books, videos, and video installations. (Hessel was one of the co-founders of the CSS.) More than 900 contemporary international artists are represented. The new museum complements the regular exhibits held at the CSS Galleries. The Hessel Museum and the CSS Galleries are open to the public Wednesday through Sunday, 1:00 to 6:00 p.m. Admission is free.

Beacon

DIA:BEACON $$
Riggio Galleries
3 Beekman Street
(845) 440-0100
www.diaart.org

When the astonishing Dia:Beacon museum opened in May 2003, it was the catalyst that set an already active arts scene alight in the Hudson Valley. The museum houses the famed permanent collection of the Dia Art Foundation, consisting of major works of art from the 1960s through the present day. Because the museum is housed in a historic 300,000-square-foot former printing factory, it can display large-scale installations by artists such as Richard Serra, Robert Smithson, Agnes Martin, Andy Warhol, Sol LeWitt, and many others—works that can't easily be accommodated by more conventional museums. Perhaps the most amazing sculpture at Dia is Michael Heizer's massive *North, South, East, West*. Originally created in 1967 in California, the whole gigantic sculpture was re-created at Dia as a permanent installation. *North, South, East, West* consists of four very large and diverse sculptural elements, one for each direction in the title. All together, the elements form a series of negative spaces that are more than 125 feet long and sink from the floor of the gallery to a depth of 20 feet. The piece is so large that you can take a free guided tour of it at 10:30 every morning the museum is open. In addition to the

important permanent collection, the museum sponsors year long, in-depth exhibitions by individual artists. The museum is just a short walk from the Beacon train station on MetroNorth, making this one of the few sites in this book that is easily accessible by public transportation. On weekends from late April to the end of October, the city of Beacon operates a free trolley that runs from the train station to the museum and then on to the shops, galleries, and restaurants on East Main Street. Dia:Beacon's summer hours (mid-April to mid-October) are Thursday through Monday, 11:00 a.m. to 6:00 p.m. Winter hours are 11:00 a.m. to 4:00 p.m., Friday through Monday. The museum bookshop and very pleasant cafe open at 10:30 a.m. year-round. The museum is closed on Thanksgiving Day, Christmas Eve Day, Christmas Day, and New Year's Day. Admission is $10 for adults, $7 for students and seniors, free for children under 12, and free for members. Parking is free. Gallery talks by curators, art historians, and writers are offered at 1:00 p.m. on the last Saturday of each month. The talks are free with admission—call or check the Web site for the schedule.

Poughkeepsie

FRANCIS LEHMAN LOEB ART CENTER
Vassar College
124 Raymond Avenue
(845) 437-7745
www.fllac.vassar.edu

When Vassar was founded in 1864, it became the first college in the nation to open with its own permanent art collection and gallery. In 1993 the expansive collection moved into a beautiful new building designed by renowned architect Cesar Pelli and named in honor of Francis Lehman Loeb, a graduate of the class of 1928 and a trustee of the college. The Art Center contains 20,000 square feet of exhibit space, including an 8,600-square-foot sculpture garden. The art collection is encyclopedic—its 15,000 works range from antiquity to the present. Of particular note are the Warburg Collection of Old Master prints, a significant group of Hudson River School paintings, and a major collection of 20th-century paintings. The permanent collection galleries feature antiquities, Medieval, Baroque, and Renaissance art, 19th-century European and American art, 20th-century art, photographs, prints and drawings, and Asian art. Special exhibitions at the Art Center draw primarily on the permanent collection. The Art Center is open to the public at no charge Tuesday through Saturday, 10:00 a.m. to 5:00 p.m. (9:00 p.m. on Thursdays) and on Sunday from 1:00 to 5:00 p.m.; closed Monday. Tours, led by student docents, are available on weekends— check the Web site or call to find out what special tours are scheduled.

Greene County
Catskill
CEDAR GROVE, THE THOMAS COLE NATIONAL HISTORICAL SITE $
218 Spring Street
(518) 943-7465
www.thomascole.org

The founder of the Hudson River School of Art, Thomas Cole was one of America's foremost landscape painters. From 1836 until his death in 1848, Cole and his family lived at Cedar Grove, a modest Federal-style brick home with beautiful views of the Catskill Mountains. The house remained in the Cole family until 1979. In 1998 the property was purchased by the Greene County Historical Society; it was declared a National Historic Site in 1999. After restoration, Cedar Grove was opened to the public in 2001, two centuries after Thomas Cole's birth. The "Old Studio," where Cole painted some of his best-known works, such as the "Voyage of Life" series, has also been restored. Four original paintings by Thomas Cole are on exhibit at Cedar Grove. In addition, the gallery rooms in the main house have changing exhibitions of works from the Hudson River School and by other artists as well. The Main House and Old Studio are open by guided tour from 10:00 a.m. to 4:00 p.m. Friday, Saturday, and Sunday from the first Saturday in May through the last Sunday in October. The house is also open on Memorial Day, Labor Day, Columbus Day, and Independence Day

from 1:00 to 4:00 p.m. Tours begin approximately every hour on a first come, first-served basis. Each tour lasts about 40 minutes and is limited to 12 people. Admission is $7 per person, $5 for students and seniors. The beautifully landscaped grounds, including the historic perennial gardens, are open at no charge.

i The Hudson River School Art Trail brings you to eight sites that inspired America's first great landscape painters, all within 15 miles of Olana and Cedar Grove. Many of the views, such as Catskill Creek, are remarkably unchanged from the 1800s. To walk in the footsteps of the Hudson River School artists, pick up a free trail brochure at Cedar Grove or Olana, download it from www.thomascole.org, or call (800) 355-2287, ext. 5. Most stops are easily reached by car followed by a short walk, but be prepared for a fairly strenuous hike to reach Kaaterskill Falls and North-South Lake.

Orange County
Mountainville
STORM KING ART CENTER $$
Old Pleasant Hill Road
(845) 534-3115
www.stormking.org

Five hundred acres of beautifully landscaped lawns, rolling fields, woods, and the Hudson Highlands are the backdrop for the Storm King Art Center's permanent collection of sculpture dating from 1945 to the present. The collection includes works by many of the 20th century's most influential artists, including Henry Moore, Isamu Noguchi, Louise Bourgeois, Alexander Calder, and Louise Nevelson. A number of the permanent pieces were designed specifically for the site. Andy Goldsworthy's amazing *Storm King Wall*, for instance, is a 2,278-foot-long sculpture made using stones gathered from the Art Center property. The permanent collection is complemented by both temporary installations outdoors and exhibitions in the museum building. The center is very visitor-friendly. A free tram runs through the grounds every half hour beginning at noon; you can get on or off at designated points all afternoon. The center is open from early April to mid-November, Wednesday through Sunday, 11:00 a.m. to 5:30 p.m. (5:00 p.m. in November). From the end of May to the end of August, the grounds are open until 8:00 p.m. on Saturdays. Admission is $10 for adults, $9 for seniors and college students, $7 for students K–12; and free for kids under 5. A lovely picnic area (no cooking) is located near the north parking area. Parking is free.

Putnam County
Garrison

BOSCOBEL RESTORATION $$
1601 Route 9D
(845) 265-3638
www.boscobel.org

One of the finest examples of Federal architecture in the country, Boscobel was the home of the States Dyckman family. A Loyalist who became a prominent merchant after the Revolution, Dyckman modeled Boscobel after a British-style country estate. The house, completed in 1808, is located on a bluff overlooking the Hudson River; the United States Military Academy at West Point is opposite it across the river and Storm King Mountain is to the north. (The dramatic story of how this stunning house was rescued from demolition in the 1950s is in the Mansions and Historic Sites: East chapter.) Today Boscobel has been meticulously restored and contains one of the nation's finest collections of furniture and decorative arts from the Federal period. Outstanding works by New York cabinetmakers such as Duncan Phyfe and Michael Allison are on display in beautiful period interiors. The grounds at Boscobel are as beautiful as the interiors. The magnificent rose garden, with more than 600 plants representing more than 150 varieties, is not to be missed, especially in June. The great lawn in front of the mansion offers dramatic views of the Hudson Highlands; the Constitution Marsh Sanctuary is directly below. Be sure to stroll

down to the belvedere overlook for a sweeping view up and down the river. The 1.25-mile Woodland Trail winds through 29 acres of woodland and features spectacular river vistas. Boscobel is open every day except Tuesdays, Thanksgiving, and Christmas; the museum and grounds are closed to the public in January, February, and March. From April through October, hours are 9:30 a.m. to 5:00 p.m.; in November and December hours are 9:30 a.m. to 4:00 p.m. The mansion can be seen only by guided tour. The last tour of the day begins at 4:15 p.m. April through October and 3:15 p.m. in November and December; the tour takes about 45 minutes. Admission is $10 for adults, $9 for seniors, $7 for children ages 6 to 14, and free for children under 6. Friday through Sunday, a trolley service connects Boscobel with the Cold Spring and Garrison stations of MetroNorth. The ride costs just a dime (a nickel for seniors). Call Boscobel for the schedule

Ulster County
Kingston

FRED J. JOHNSTON MUSEUM AND FRIENDS OF HISTORIC KINGSTON MUSEUM $
63 Main Street
(845) 339-0720
www.fohk.org

Fred Johnston was both a nationally known antiques dealer and a passionate preservationist for the historic city of Kingston. On his death in 1993, he left his home and personal treasury of 18th- and 19th-century furnishings to the Friends of Historic Kingston (FOHK). Today, his collection is beautifully displayed in eight showcase room settings in his carefully restored 1812 Federal-style residence. The house is now a centerpiece of Kingston's historic Stockade District. In fact, it's the starting point for the Stockade tours offered by FOHK (there's more about this in the Mansions and Historic Sites: West chapter). The classic lines of the house were nearly lost in 1938, when it was scheduled to be demolished to make way for a gas station. Fred Johnston rescued the building and restored it to its original severe beauty. The collection contains outstanding examples of

American furniture, American glassware and pottery, Staffordshire porcelain, pictorial needlework, and other decorative arts. The Friends of Historic Kingston Museum is adjacent to the Johnston House and offers changing exhibitions on the history and heritage of the city. Both museums are open from 1:00 to 4:00 p.m. Saturday and Sunday from May through October and by appointment year-round. The Johnston House can be seen only by guided tour; the fee is $5 for adults, $2 for children under 16. The FOHK Museum is free. Parking is available behind the Ulster County Courthouse at 285 Wall Street, just north of the museums.

New Paltz

SAMUEL DORSKY MUSEUM OF ART
State University of New York at New Paltz
One Hawk Drive
(845) 257-3844
www.newpaltz.edu/museum

In 2001 the former College Art Gallery at SUNY New Paltz was transformed into a modern, 9,000-square-foot museum, thanks to a generous donation from philanthropist, businessman, and gallery owner Samuel Dorsky. The Samuel Dorsky Museum of Art now houses a permanent collection of some 3,500 pieces spanning 4,000 years, with special emphasis on 20th-century prints and paintings, decorative art, photographs, Asian art, and pre-Columbian artifacts. The museum has a special commitment to collecting important works by artists whose careers are linked to the Hudson Valley and the Catskill region. This collection is on display in the Morgan Anderson Gallery and contains works by George Inness, Milton Avery, George Bellows, and a number of artists linked to the historic Woodstock Art Colony. The museum is open Tuesday through Friday from 11:00 a.m. to 5:00 p.m. and Saturday and Sunday from 1:00 to 5:00 p.m. It's closed on some school breaks, so call ahead to be sure. Admission is free; voluntary contributions are encouraged. Parking is in lot #28, located directly across from the Hopfer Admissions and Alumni Center (use the designated visitor parking spots). On weekends and after 5:00 p.m., visitors may park in any campus lot.

Saugerties

OPUS 40 AND THE QUARRYMAN'S MUSEUM $$
50 Fite Road
(845) 246-3400
www.opus40.org

Opus 40 is definitely one of the more extraordinary places to visit in the Hudson Valley. The saga began in 1938, when sculptor Harvey Fite discovered an abandoned bluestone quarry in the tiny hamlet of High Woods. Fite bought the land and began to clear away the rubble, unknowingly beginning an artistic project that would last the rest of his life. Over the years, Fite single-handedly transformed the quarry into a massive environmental sculpture covering 6.5 acres, while also teaching art at nearby Bard College. Opus 40 consists of platforms, spiral ramps, paths, terraces, pools, bridges, sculptural pieces, and a massive central monolith, all cut and set by Fite alone. (The hand tools he used to create Opus 40 are on display in the Quarryman's Museum on the second floor of the visitor center.) Fite named his work Opus 40, thinking it would take him 40 years to complete. He was just three years short of that number when he was killed in 1976, at the age of 72, in an accident at the quarry. Today Opus 40 is open to visitors from noon to 5:00 p.m. Friday to Sunday from late May to early October. The Opus 40 Art Gallery on the site shows works by local artists. The site is sometimes closed for special events such as weddings, so call ahead; also call to find out about special arts programs. Admission is $10 for adults, $7 for students and seniors, and $3 for school-age children; free for children under 6. Picnicking on the grounds is welcome. The bluestone walkways are rough—no baby strollers are allowed, and the site is not accessible to wheelchairs. Individuals with mobility issues may have difficulty here.

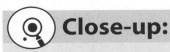 # Close-up:

Art Along the Hudson

Art Along the Hudson brings together four riverfront cities—Kingston, Beacon, Poughkeepsie, and Newburgh—to celebrate all the arts on rotating Saturdays throughout the year. First Saturday belongs to Kingston; Second to Beacon; Third to Poughkeepsie; and Last to Newburgh. On each Saturday, the relevant city offers art shows, gallery openings, artist receptions, live music and theatrical performances, restaurant and culinary events, and special activities at cultural venues. In addition to serious art, there's plenty of fun stuff. The annual Beacon Hat Parade and Music Fest, for instance, takes place on the second Saturday in May. It's a day long festival of wearable art and family fun. Anyone wearing any sort of hat—the more outlandish the better—can march in the parade. On Last Saturday in Newburgh, the River Art Walk brings local artists out to an open-air gallery along the city's beautiful waterfront promenade. In Kingston, First Saturday is a chance for more than 30 galleries and arts venues to hold receptions and exhibits. Visitors can get to them easily by hopping the free Arts Trolley. Four times a year, Poughkeepsie extends the Third Saturday to the whole weekend. To celebrate creativity and culture in the city, Weekend on Main offers art exhibitions, musical performances, a farmer's market, craft artists, and children's activities.

Art Along the Hudson is a collaborative effort of local arts organizations, with generous county, city, and corporate sponsorship. For general information about upcoming events, contact www.artalongthehudson.com or call (845) 454-3222. For information about First Saturday in Kingston, contact the Arts Society of Kingston (ASK) at www.askforarts.org or call (845) 338-0331. For information about Second Saturday in Beacon, contact Beacon Arts Community Association (BACA) at www.beaconarts.org or call (845) 546-6222. For information about Third Saturday in Poughkeepsie, contact www.arthoptours.com or call (845) 454-2263; for information about Weekend on Main contact www.weekendonmain.org or call (845) 471-2550. For information about Last Saturday and River Art Walk in Newburgh, contact www.newburgharts .com or call (845) 564-4184.

If you're further north on a nice Saturday afternoon, check out the Woodstock Second Saturdays. Sponsored by the Woodstock Arts Consortium (WAC), a group of 11 local nonprofit arts organization, Second Saturdays run June through December. Events include gallery openings, art exhibits, children's art activities, poetry readings, and music and theater performances. Admission to most events is free or for a small donation. WAC also sponsors Woodstock Arts Day, which celebrates the town's long heritage in all the arts, on the last Saturday in May. For more information, contact WAC at www.woodstockartsconsortium.org or call (845) 679-2079. On the east side of the river, the Columbia County Council on the Arts (CCCA) sponsors ArtsWalk in Hudson for 10 days, starting the last week of September. The event includes works by more than 250 artists (including famed local residents Ellsworth Kelly, Richard Artschwager, and Mihail Chemiakin) in curated exhibits, along with outdoor sculptures, concerts, and dance performances. This event gets bigger and better every year—for details, contact CCCA at www .artscolumbia.org or call (518) 671-6213.

GALLERIES

Columbia County

Chatham

JOYCE GOLDSTEIN GALLERY
16 Main Street
(518) 392-2250
www.joycegoldsteingallery.com

The shows at this excellent gallery focus on contemporary art, both of the recent past and the present. The gallery has featured artists such as Fred Mitchell, an important abstract painter active more than 50 years ago, and modern-day artists such as Holly Sears and Michael Tong. Always worth a visit. Gallery hours are Thursday through Sunday, noon to 5:00 p.m., and by appointment.

Hudson

ADD GALLERY LTD.
22 Park Place
(518) 822-9763
www.addgallery.net
Art Design Digression (A.D.D.) Gallery exhibits the work of mature artists—no emerging artists here. The works are abstract, minimal, and nonobjective. They're also vibrant, serious, and really, really nice to look at. Artists connected with the gallery include Jan Cunningham, Roger Shepherd, and Peter Acheson. Open Saturday and Sunday, noon to 5:00 p.m., and by appointment.

ALBERT SHAHINIAN FINE ART
415 Warren Street
(518) 828-4346
www.shahinianfineart.com
Albert Shahinian Fine Art is a full-service gallery specializing in established original contemporary and 20th-century artists, regional artists, and Hudson River art. The gallery moved its main operations to Hudson in 2008, although the gallery in Poughkeepsie (198 Main Street, 845-454-0522) remains open. Hours are Friday, Saturday, and Sunday, noon to 6:00 p.m., and by appointment.

ART IN A LANDSCAPE $$$
For one weekend a year in late May, many contemporary artists in Columbia County open their studios to visitors. The Arts in a Landscape tour is organized by the Columbia County Council on the Arts. Tickets for the weekend are pricey at $25 a person or $75 a vehicle, but how often do you get a chance to see art where it's made? For more information and to order tickets, contact CCCA at www.artscolumbia.org or call (518) 671-6213.

BCB ART
116 Warren Street
(518) 828-4539
www.bcbart.com
A long list of well-regarded contemporary artists, ranging from local to international, have been shown at BCB Art. Gallery artists include Mark Briscoe, Scott Reynolds, Eric Rhein, Lucio Pozzi, Alice Aycock, Rodney Alan Greenblatt, and many others. BCB Art offers both group exhibits and solo or small group shows. Hours are Saturday and Sunday from noon to 6:00 p.m. and Friday by appointment.

CARRIE HADDAD GALLERY
622 Warren Street
(518) 828-1915
www.carriehaddadgallery.com
For a city to go from being in decline to being revitalized, someone has to be first. For the city of Hudson, that someone was Carrie Haddad, who opened the first gallery there in 1991. It quickly became, and has remained, one of the premiere galleries in the Hudson Valley. Presenting eight major exhibitions a year, Carrie Haddad shows the works of both established and newly discovered artists of the Hudson Valley. Works on display range over just about every media, including works on paper and photography (the upstairs room at the gallery always has an interesting photo show). To get a good grasp on who the finest artists in the area are, this is the gallery to visit. Open daily except Wednesday, 11:00 a.m. to 5:00 p.m.

CCCA GALLERY
209 Warren Street
(518) 671-6213
www.artscolumbia.org
This gallery is sponsored by the Columbia County Council on the Arts (CCCA), a volunteer group of local artists and performers. The exhibits draw from the works of member artists and are curated by a rotating gallery committee. With several hundred member artists to choose from, the shows tend to be on the eclectic side—but always interesting and well presented. The CCCA also sponsors the annual Art in a Landscape tour, the annual ArtsWalk, and several juried shows each year. Gallery hours are 11:00 a.m. to 5:00 p.m. Monday through Saturday.

DEBORAH DAVIS FINE ART
510 Warren Street
(518) 822-1890
www.ddfagallery.com

When Deborah Davis moved to her new space on Warren Street a few blocks away from her old establishment, she set the space up in a more informal way, more like a living room than a gallery. The art is still a good mix of works by local and regional artists in a wide range of styles; an interesting selection of folk art from the South is also offered. Hours are Thursday through Monday, 11:00 a.m. to 5:00 p.m., and by appointment.

HUDSON OPERA HOUSE
327 Warren Street
(518) 822-1438
www.hudsonoperahouse.org

One of the cultural jewels of Columbia County, the Hudson Opera House is a multi-arts center that offers an art gallery and a year-round schedule of free or low-cost arts and cultural programming. It all takes place in a renovated historic building that began life in 1855 as City Hall. Frederic Church and other artists exhibited their work on the first floor. Around 1880, the building started to be called Hudson Opera House. Operas and other performances and events (even poultry shows) were put on in the upstairs auditorium, but the first floor continued to be used for various municipal purposes. When a new city hall was built in 1962, the building was abandoned and sat vacant for nearly 30 years, until a group of local citizens banded together to save it and restore it as a cultural and civic center. The first renovated room opened in 1997; other spaces, including two gallery rooms, have opened since then. In recent years HOH has presented exhibitions in all genres by dozens of artists, curators, and community organizations. The works are quite varied and change fairly often. They're always worth a visit—and take a tour of the building while you're there. Gallery hours are Monday through Saturday, noon to 5:00 p.m. If you're inspired by the art you see, you can look into taking some of the inexpensive art classes and workshops. Hudson Opera House also sponsors the very enjoyable Winter Walk on the first Saturday of December—there's more about it in the Annual Events chapter.

JOHN DAVIS GALLERY
362½ Warren Street
(518) 828-5907
www.johndavisgallery.com

Far from the standard white-walled cube, the John Davis Gallery is more of a whole two-story house and then some, including a sculpture garden and four-story carriage house (the former elevator shaft is now one of the exhibit spaces). The sheer size and unusual architectural aspects of this gallery allow for larger works, including installations, although the emphasis is mainly on abstract paintings and sculpture. The roster of artists here is quite lengthy and includes John Van Alstine, Jon Isherwood, Sara Jane Roszak, and John Ruppert. Leaving aside the outstanding contemporary artists, this gallery is worth seeing just for the exhibit space alone. Open Thursday through Monday, 10:00 a.m. to 5:30 p.m.

LIMNER GALLERY
123 Warren Street
(518) 828-2343
www.slowart.com

The travels of this artist-owned gallery are a microcosm of the New York City art scene. The gallery began in the East Village in 1987, at the center of the alternative art scene. Chased by rising rents, it moved to Lower Broadway in Soho, then to the fringes of Soho, then to Chelsea, and then, in the wake of 9/11, out of the city altogether to Phoenicia in Ulster County. In 2006 the gallery moved to Hudson. Despite all the moves, gallery manager Tim Slowinski has remained committed to his art and that of the outsider artists who exhibit at the gallery—works that are controversial and often provocative. This isn't art for the faint-hearted, but it is art worth seeing. The gallery is open Wednesday from noon to 5:00 p.m., Thursday from 11:00 a.m. to 4:00 p.m., Friday from noon to 5:00 p.m., Saturday from noon to 6:00 p.m., and by appointment.

NICOLE FIACCO GALLERY
506 Warren Street
(518) 828-5090
www.modogallery.com

When Nicole Fiacco began her gallery back in 1999, it was called Modo and featured mostly the work of contemporary Native American artists, with a heavy emphasis on ceramics. Over the years, her interests expanded, and in 2005 the gallery transitioned into exhibiting the creations of many other contemporary artists from around the country and the world, working in all media. As the roster became more diverse, the name changed to the Nicole Fiacco Gallery. Today the gallery presents approximately eight major exhibitions annually. Ceramics are still important, but the works shown cover a broad and interesting range. Open Thursday through Monday from noon to 6:00 p.m.; closed Tuesday and Wednesday.

PETER JUNG FINE ART
512 Warren Street
(518) 828-2698
www.peterjungfineart.com

Specializing in 19th- and 20th-century American and European paintings, particularly those from 1850 to 1950, Peter Jung is a serious dealer in serious art. His lovely gallery, located in a historic building, is open by appointment during regular weekday business hours. The general public is invited to visit most weekends, but call ahead to be sure the gallery will be open.

ROSE GALLERY FINE ART
444 Warren Street
(518) 671-6128
www.rosegalleryfineart.com

One of the older galleries in the Hudson area (it dates back to 1989), Rose Gallery Fine Art shows the work of a small but outstanding group of respected contemporary artists, including Maria Dioguardi, Caitlin Legere, and Maggie Siner. Look for the distinctive purple entrance to the gallery. Hours are Thursday through Monday, noon to 5:00 p.m., and by appointment.

Spencertown
SPENCERTOWN ACADEMY
790 Route 203
(518) 392-3693
www.spencertownacademy.org

Housed in a historic 1847 Greek Revival schoolhouse, Spencertown Academy is a nonprofit community arts organization. The academy is well known in the area for its musical performances (see the Performing Arts and Film chapter for more). The academy also offers The Gallery, made up of two exhibition spaces. The Gallery puts on eight shows—solo, group, and thematic—a year, each lasting about six weeks. Gallery I shows the work of regional visual artists; Gallery II typically shows crafts. The galleries are worth visiting if you're in the area or arriving early for a performance. Hours are Thursday through Sunday, 1:00 to 5:00 p.m.

Dutchess County
Beacon
bau
161 Main Street
(845) 440-7584
www.beaconartistsunion.com

The collective gallery of the Beacon Artists Union, bau primarily shows the work of the eight or so member artists. Founded in 2004 by six local artists with the goal of helping member artists grow, present, and market their work, bau has quickly grown to become an important focal point for the Beacon arts community. Member exhibits and events are held year-round. In June 2007, for example, member Elizabeth Winchester began a printmaking project that converted the gallery into a working studio, complete with a group of artists and a print press, for a month. This sort of imaginative collaborative work is the bau hallmark. The gallery is open Saturday and Sunday, noon to 6:00 p.m., and by appointment.

FRESHMAN FINE ARTS GALLERY
4 South Chestnut Street
(914) 440-8988
www.freshmanfineartsgallery.com
Freshman Fine Arts (open since 2006) offers contemporary art featuring both abstract and realistic works, photography, and documentary art. Hours are Monday through Saturday, 10:00 a.m. to 5:00 p.m., and Sunday, noon to 5:00 p.m.

GO NORTH—A SPACE FOR CONTEMPORARY ART
469 Main Street
(845) 242-1951
www.gonorthgallery.blogspot.com
Go North aims to present challenging new works by many different artists working in a wide range of media. In addition to the usual paintings, drawings, and sculptures, the gallery features photography, video art, installations, and performance and sound-based works. Hours are Friday through Sunday, noon to 6:00 p.m., and by appointment.

VAN BRUNT GALLERY
460 Main Street
(845) 838-2995
www.vanbruntgallery.com
Main Street in Beacon is home to a lot of contemporary art, but for the edgiest and most contemporary work of all, the Van Brunt Gallery is the place. The works here, by a long and very diverse roster of artists working in a wide range of media, are thought-provoking if nothing else. If you can't get to the gallery, check out the online gallery at the Web site. It's extremely well done. Gallery hours are every day, 11:00 a.m. to 6:00 p.m., and by appointment.

WILD WOOD GALLERY
442 Main Street
(845) 831-0333
www.wildwoodgallery.org
Wild Wood Gallery is one of the few in the Hudson Valley devoted solely to the photographic arts. The gallery presents ongoing shows by a number of outstanding photographers; they work in traditional photo media and also create digital fine art of archival quality. The shows here, such as Bill Jagde's landscapes of the Southwest, are often documentary and exquisitely beautiful. Open Friday through Sunday, noon to 6:00 p.m.

Millbrook

MABBETTSVILLE GALLERY
3788 Route 44
(845) 677-0035
www.mabbettsvillegallery.com
Mabbettsville opened with a splash in 2004 with an exhibition of landscape paintings by local artists. Since then the gallery has concentrated on two areas: established and new painters from the Hudson Valley region, and selections from owner Jack Banning's outstanding collection of 20th-century modernist photography and graphic design. This is an excellent place to see representational work by some of the finest local artists, including John A. Parks, Adrianne Lobel, and Emily Fuller. The gallery is open May through December only. Hours are Thursday through Saturday from 10:00 a.m. to 5:00 p.m., and Sunday from noon to 5:00 p.m.

MERRITT BOOKSTORE
57 Front Street
(845) 677-5857
www.merrittbooks.com
The Upstairs Gallery at the Millbrook branch of the Merritt Bookstore hosts rotating exhibits of individual local artists and group shows. What sets this friendly space apart is the way owner Scott Meyer invites well-known artist-authors to exhibit original artwork in conjunction with a book signing. Artists who have participated in these enjoyable events include Will Moses, Enid Futterman, Vincent DiFate, and James Gurney of Dinotopia fame. Author-artist events take place about once a month on Saturday mornings; check the events calendar on the Web site or call the store to find out who's appearing next.

MILLBROOK GALLERY & ANTIQUES
3297 Franklin Avenue
(845) 677-6699
www.millbrookgalleryandantiques.com
Established as a way to bring together artists and collectors, this gallery specializes in the work of living artists from the tri-state area. The works shown are, for the most part, representational. The gallery is also affiliated with the Cary Collection, presenting vintage equestrian and sporting art. In addition, owners Jeff and Thelma Zwirn represent a number of skilled portraitists available to portray animals of all sorts—human, canine, feline, or equine. Hours are Friday through Monday, noon to 5:30, and by appointment.

Poughkeepsie
BARRETT ART CENTER
55 Noxon Street
(845) 471-2550
www.barrettartcenter.org
Twice a year, the Barrett Art Center, a community organization that offers a wide range of classes in the visual arts, puts on an outstanding juried exhibit of work by local and regional artists. The exhibit attracts a lot of regional and national attention and is worth visiting. The center opened in 1934 and gets its name from its founder, Thomas Weeks Barrett Jr., a well-known American regionalist painter. Today 485 member organizations support the center. Gallery hours are Thursday and Friday from 11:00 a.m. to 5:00 p.m., Saturday from 11:00 a.m. to 3:00 p.m., and Tuesday and Wednesday by appointment.

CUNNEEN–HACKETT ARTS CENTER
9 and 12 Vassar Street
(845) 486-4571
www.cunneenhackett.org
The Cunneen-Hackett Arts Center is located in not one but two landmark Victorian buildings in the heart of Poughkeepsie (and within easy walking distance of the MetroNorth train station). The buildings were originally underwritten by the famed Vassar Brothers, nephews of Matthew Vassar, the founder of Vassar College. The large Italianate building at 9 Vassar Street was designed as a home for the aged. Today it houses a number of local nonprofit organizations—and an art gallery. The building at 12 Vassar Street has been an arts center since its construction in 1883. It now houses a renovated 200-seat theater, a large dance studio, a music instruction studio—and an art gallery. Both galleries regularly show the work of local and regional artists; exhibits are generally sale/showings and run for six weeks. The Reception Room Gallery at 12 Vassar is open weekends only from 9:00 a.m. to 5:00 p.m. The Hallway Gallery at 9 Vassar is open Monday through Friday from 9:00 a.m. to 5:00 p.m.

GALLERY AND STUDIO (G.A.S.)
196 Main Street
(845) 486-4592
www.galleryandstudio.org
Opened in spring 2007, this gallery of contemporary art is a cooperative effort of seven local artists, including Michael Asbill, Patrick Wing, and Joanne Klein. With 1,400 square feet of gallery space and an 800-square-foot courtyard behind the building, G.A.S. functions as both an innovative multimedia gallery for the visual arts and a performance space. The art exhibits include the usual visual arts along with computer and video art, mixed media works, and installations. Exhibits rotate on a monthly basis; other events such as poetry readings and film screenings happen regularly. Gallery hours are Friday through Sunday, noon to 6:00 p.m., and by appointment.

Rhinebeck
GALLERY LODOE
6400 Montgomery Street
(845) 876-6331
www.gallerylodoe.com
Specializing in contemporary arts and artifacts from Asia, Gallery Lodoe opened in 2008 with an exhibit of works by two Burmese artists. Some of the works here are continuations of centuries-old artistic traditions, while other artists build on those traditions to create work that is very much in line with contemporary influences. Open daily, 11:00 a.m. to 6:00 p.m.; closed Tuesday.

JO AARONS GALLERY
22 East Market Street, 2nd floor
(845) 876-6248
www.joaaronsgallery.com

Established in 1984, this gallery specializes in fine art prints from a wide range of well-established modern artists, including Joseph Stella, Milton Avery, Philip Pearlstein, Alice Neel, and many others. This gallery is oriented more toward serious collectors than casual browsers. Hours are weekends and by appointment; it's best to call first.

Tivoli

TIVOLI ARTISTS' CO-OP
60 Broadway
(845) 757-2667
www.tivoliartistsco-op.com

A friendly gallery in a charming little village, the Tivoli Artists' Co-Op is owned and operated by its members, 40 local artists and artisans; it was founded in 1993 and has been extremely active ever since. The annual landscape show, held in the late spring, focuses on art inspired by the beauty of the Hudson Valley. A dozen or more exhibits over the rest of the year typically feature group shows by member artists. The gallery is open Friday from 5:00 to 9:00 p.m., Saturday from 1:00 to 9:00 p.m., and Sunday from noon to 5:00 p.m.

Greene County

Catskill

BEGINNER'S MIND GALLERY
401 Main Street
(518) 943-9100
www.beginnersmindgallery.com

Beginner's Mind is a cross between a gallery and an open working studio. Artist/owner Lee Anne Morgan creates her vivid encaustic works in her studio here and exhibits them in the gallery. The name comes from the Zen Buddhist concept of being able to see things as if for the first time—a useful attribute not just in meditation but in art. Also shown in revolving exhibits are the works of a handful of nationally recognized guest artists, including contemporary fine art, photography, sculpture, ceramics, and jewelry. Hours are Friday through Sunday, noon to 5:00 p.m., and by appointment.

BRIK
473 Main Street
(518) 943-0145
www.brikgallery.com

The town of Catskill is noted for its well-preserved historic architecture. BRIK brings contemporary art to an elegant and spacious gallery in a historic 1805 building. It's an unexpected juxtaposition, but it works extremely well. The gallery has three separate areas, including one designed for performance art. Exhibits at BRIK (the name is a nod to Catskill's history as a brick-making center and to the brick architecture on Main Street) have included figurative works, abstracts, and landscapes. In 2006 owner Frank Cuthbert produced an outdoor exhibit of photographer Uwe Ommer's massive *1000 Families,* based on his photos of families around the world. BRIK is open Saturday and Sunday, noon to 5:00 p.m., and by appointment.

GALLERY 384
384 Main Street
(518) 947-6732
www.gallery384.com

Located in a historic building that dates back to the 1880s, Gallery 384 is devoted to emerging artists who are inspired by the Hudson River School or who identify themselves as Hudson Valley artists. Landscapes are not the sole focus or even the main focus—most of the work shown is very contemporary—and the Hudson Valley connection isn't always there. But rules, especially when they apply to art, are made to be broken, and the work on display here is always extremely interesting. The gallery is open Saturday, 2:00 to 6:00 p.m., and by appointment Thursday and Friday; closed Monday through Wednesday.

GCCA CATSKILL GALLERY
398 Main Street
(518) 943-3400
www.greenearts.org

In addition to its important work as a catalyst for all the arts in the area, the Greene County Council on the Arts (GCCA) sponsors two galleries—one upstairs, one downstairs—at its headquarters on Catskill's lively Main Street. (Another site is the Mountaintop Gallery on Main Street in the ski-resort town of Windham, outside the scope of this book.) The galleries showcase the work of local and regional artists. Hours are Monday through Friday, 10:00 a.m. to 5:00 p.m., and Saturday, 10:00 a.m. to 4:00 p.m. GCCA is also a sponsor of the Second Saturday Strolls in Catskill, when local shops and galleries stay open late.

M GALLERY
350 Main Street
(518) 943-0380
www.mgallery-online.com
The primary focus at M Gallery is the landscape and portrait work of owner Patrick Milbourn. As is fitting for an artist living in the hometown of Thomas Cole, the landscapes are strongly influenced by the beauty and variety of the Catskills region. The gallery also shows paintings by other contemporary artists as well as drawings and paintings of the 19th and 20th centuries. M Gallery is open only on weekends from noon to 5:00 p.m. and by appointment.

OPEN STUDIO
402 Main Street
(518) 943-9531
When Dina Bursztyn and Julie Chase moved to Catskill in 2005, they started Open Studio primarily as a place to show their own found objects sculptures and collages. They soon realized that they had enough space to show the work of other artists as well, and have since offered group shows on a regular basis. The art here often features works by women artists living in the area. Gallery hours are Friday through Sunday, noon to 6:00 p.m., and by appointment.

WILDER GALLERY
375 Main Street
(518) 697-9086
Owner Hilary Wilder brings an edgy modern sensibility to the works shown here. Most are by local artists with a political bent—the art here isn't always easy to like, but it is heartfelt and powerful. The gallery is in a loft space on the third floor. There's no elevator, so it may not be accessible for those with mobility issues. Open weekends, noon to 6:00 p.m., and by appointment.

Orange County
Newburgh
ANN STREET GALLERY
140 Ann Street
(845) 562-6940
www.annstreetgallery.org
A nonprofit undertaking, Ann Street Gallery specializes in contemporary emerging and established artists. The opening exhibit in 2007 featured Orange County and Hudson Valley artists; rotating exhibits represent a variety of artists and styles. Open Thursday through Saturday, 11:00 a.m. to 5:00 p.m.

Putnam County
Garrison
GARRISON ART CENTER GALLERY
23 Garrison's Landing
(845) 424-3960
www.garrisonartcenter.org
Founded in 1966, the Garrison Art Center is a nonprofit arts organization offering a range of art classes—including a fully equipped ceramics studio. In addition, the Gilette and Anita Hart Balter Galleries exhibit the work of GAC members and local artists. The center is worth visiting not only for the art but for its setting on a lovely little riverside park with spectacular views of West Point across the Hudson. Gallery hours are every day, noon to 5:00 p.m.

Ulster County

High Falls

BEGALLERY
11 Mohonk Road (off Route 213)
(845) 687-0660
www.begallery.com
Owner Barbara Esmark (the "BE" of the name) opened this two-story gallery in a restored old Victorian residence in the summer of 2006. It's a nice addition to the scenic town of High Falls, which already attracts visitors to its restaurants and the remnants of the historic Delaware & Hudson Canal. The gallery displays the work of local fine artists, including Barbara herself along with Sara Harris, Judith Hoyt, and Paul Rowntree, and also has a wider focus on more nationally and internationally known artists. Special exhibitions of other work, such as contemporary Mexican art and folk art, are regular occurrences here. Gallery hours are Friday through Monday, 11:00 a.m. to 6:00 p.m.

Kingston

ARTS SOCIETY OF KINGSTON (ASK)
ASK Arts Center
97 Broadway
(845) 338-0331
www.askforarts.org
Founded in 1995 as an informal gathering of local artists, the nonprofit Arts Society of Kingston has grown into an important force in the Valley art scene. Each year, ASK hosts upwards of 10 shows of members' work at the main gallery in the organization's headquarters in the historic Rondout section, along with shows of featured artists. Exhibits are also sponsored at other venues in the Kingston area. Gallery hours are Thursday through Saturday from noon to 5:00 p.m. or by appointment. In odd-numbered years ASK also sponsors the Kingston Sculpture Biennial Outdoor Exhibition, running from mid-July to mid-October. During the Biennial, more than 60 sculptures in just about every imaginable style and material are placed throughout the city. When the show is on, the sculptures add a very enjoyable aspect to an afternoon of Kingston gallery-hopping; a free map is available at ASK headquarters.

DONSKOJ & COMPANY
93 Broadway
(845) 338-8473
www.donskoj.com
Photographer Nancy Donskoj and stained-glass artist and restorer Yourij Donskoj are the guiding lights behind this gallery of contemporary art. The gallery is open Thursday through Saturday, 1:00 to 6:00 p.m., and by appointment. Donskoj & Company has a well-deserved reputation for worthwhile exhibits, particularly of contemporary photography, but the gallery is probably better known in the area for its sponsorship of the annual Artists' Soapbox Derby every August. (See the Annual Events chapter for more information.)

THE FIREHOUSE STUDIO
3 Dunn Street
(845) 331 6469
www.thefirehousestudio.com
Six artists form the Firehouse Studio collective and work out of a historic two-story Twaalfskill firehouse, originally built in 1853. The Firehouse Studio is a Kingston landmark now equipped with glass, woodworking, and metal studios where the artists work. Firehouse is worth visiting just to see the building, but be sure to time your visit for the first Saturday of every month, when the artists host open studio and workshop exhibitions. At other times, visits are by appointment.

THE GALLERY AT R&F
Millard Building, 2nd floor
84 Ten Broeck Avenue
(800) 206-8088 or (845) 331-3112
www.rfpaints.com
R&F Handmade Paints produces high-quality encaustic paints and oil-based pigment sticks. The company really means the *handmade* part—the factory employs local artists for the complex, slow process of making its outstanding products in small batches. Encaustic is a type of paint made with pigments combined with beeswax and resin. It has to be applied while it's melted; it then dries quickly and becomes very durable. Painting in encaustic is an ancient technique that can be

traced back to the fifth century B.C. (Encaustic is what gives tomb paintings from Roman Egypt, which are more than 2,000 years old, their vividly preserved colors and detail.) Today it's very popular with contemporary artists such as Jasper Johns and Richard Serra, who appreciate the rich colors, the flexibility, and the durability these paints provide. The pigment sticks, available in more than 80 colors, are also popular—they have the same consistency as traditional oil paints but are easier and cleaner to use. R&F has sponsored a gallery at the factory, showing only works done in encaustic and pigment sticks, since 1995. Shows at the gallery are both solo and group; each exhibit runs for about two months. Since 1997, R&F has also sponsored a juried biennial. Gallery hours are Monday through Saturday, 10:00 a.m. to 5:00 p.m.

KINGSTON MUSEUM OF CONTEMPORARY ARTS (KMOCA)
105 Abeel Street
www.kmoca.org

One of the newest additions to the Rondout-area galleries, KMOCA plans to be more than just a place to exhibit art. The owners hope to make the gallery into a space where art can mingle with film, music, and readings. They're off to a good start. A recent show by photojournalist Chad Hunt, who was embedded with the U.S. military in Afghanistan in 2006, was filled with evocative shots of the people—civilian and military—and breathtaking scenery he encountered. The gallery is open Saturday only from noon to 4:00 p.m.

THE *LIVING*ROOM
45 North Front Street
(845) 338-8353

Dedicated to contemporary art by local artists, The *Living*room was founded in the mid-1990s, making it one of the older galleries on the Kingston scene and something of a pioneer in the historic Stockade area. The gallery offers mostly group shows in a range of styles and techniques. It is open Friday and Saturday, noon to 9:00 p.m., and by appointment.

SILENT SPACE GALLERY
596 Broadway (opposite UPAC Theater)
(845) 331-7432
www.silentspacegallery.com

The art at Silent Space Gallery can be a bit challenging to look at. An exhibit in 2006 by Woodstock artist Tom Zatar Kay, for instance, used black light and spinning Day-Glo paintings to transform the gallery into a psychedelic experience that was definitely interesting, if nothing else. The gallery is open only on Saturday from 1:00 to 4:00 p.m.

WATERMARK/CARGO GALLERY
111-113 Abeel Street
(866) 405-8076 or (845) 338-8623
www.watermarkcargogallery.com

Located along the historic Rondout Creek, Watermark/Cargo specializes in two areas: art and artifacts from Africa and contemporary works in all media by American artists. In the African art realm, the gallery offers a range of works from the Baule, Yoruba, Kuba, Dan, and Dogon cultures. The knowledgeable staff members are happy to explain the features of the African art. On the contemporary art side, the gallery carries works by a number of well-known artists, including Robert Bero, Mel Edwards, Benny Andres, and Bruce Bleach. Hours are Thursday and Friday 3:00 to 9:00 p.m., Saturday 1:00 to 9:00 p.m., Sunday 1:00 to 5:00 p.m., and by appointment.

New Paltz

MARK GRUBER GALLERY
New Paltz Plaza
(Main Street west of Route 17)
(845) 255-1241

The artists on exhibit at the Mark Gruber Gallery bring a contemporary vision to the traditional themes of the Hudson River School. The gallery presents eight exhibits a year of new work by Hudson Valley artists, including original oils, watercolors, pastels, drawings, and large-format photography. This is one of the oldest and best-established galleries in the region—it dates back to 1976. Hours are Monday from 11:00 a.m. to

5:30 p.m., Tuesday through Friday from 10:00 a.m. to 5:30 p.m., Saturday from 10:00 a.m. to 5:00 p.m., and Sunday from noon to 4:00 p.m.

UNISON ARTS & LEARNING CENTER GALLERY
68 Mountain Rest Road
(845) 255-1559
www.unisonarts.org

Unison is a nonprofit arts center offering performance and visual arts programming and arts activities for children and families. Every year eight individual and group shows by local artists are on exhibit, but the real fun comes from the annual outdoor sculpture exhibition, featuring the work of both established and emerging artists. The sculptures can be seen daily in the center's woodland garden from dawn to dusk, starting in the beginning of June and running through the end of October. Gallery hours are Monday, Wednesday, and Thursday, 10:00 a.m. to 3:00 p.m., or by appointment. Unison also recently opened a gallery in the Water Street Market shopping village in New Paltz. Shows here focus on smaller pieces and change monthly.

Saugerties
CATSKILLS GALLERY
106 Partition Street
(845) 246-5552
www.thecatskillsgallery.com

This small, elegant gallery presents the works of established contemporary artists in group and solo shows. Works shown include paintings, sculptures, prints, and photos. The gallery is open Monday through Friday from 9:00 a.m. to 5:00 p.m and on weekends from noon to 5:00 p.m.

Stone Ridge
MUROFF KOTLER VISUAL ARTS GALLERY
SUNY Ulster
Vanderlyn Hall, Room 260
(845) 687-5113
www.sunyulster.edu

Located on the campus of SUNY Ulster, the Muroff Kotler Visual Arts Gallery is a center for artistic activity for both the university and the surrounding community. On exhibit are selections from the university's permanent art collection (which includes the important permanent print collection of the Woodstock Center for Photography) as well as rotating exhibits of works by students and faculty. In addition, shows by outside artists are presented on a regular basis. Some originate with the gallery; others are shown as part of national tours. Gallery hours are Monday through Friday, 11:00 a.m. to 3:00 p.m., and by appointment. The gallery is closed when the university is (for holidays, intersession, and days when there are no classes for some reason).

Woodstock
CENTER FOR PHOTOGRAPHY AT WOODSTOCK
59 Tinker Street
(845) 679-9957
www.cpw.org

The Center for Photography at Woodstock has a long and distinguished history of supporting emulsion-based art. The center's permanent print collection of more than 1,000 contemporary photographs has been transferred on extended loan to the Samuel Dorsky Museum of Art at SUNY New Paltz (previously listed). On exhibit at the Woodstock space are rotating group and individual shows of contemporary creative photography. CPW also sponsors photography workshops open to the public. Gallery hours are Wednesday through Sunday, noon to 5:00 p.m.

EAST VILLAGE COLLECTIVE
8 Old Forge Road
(845) 657-6204
www.eastvillagecollective.com

East Village Collective is a storefront space run by husband-and-wife team Bahram Foroughi and Serena Van Rensselaer. The gallery is eclectic, offering exhibits of contemporary photography, painting, sculpture, jewelry, glass, and other media. Open daily except Tuesday, noon to 6:00 p.m., and by appointment.

ELENA ZANG GALLERY
3671 Route 212
(845) 679-5432
Located in the hamlet of Shady just west of Woodstock, the Elena Zang Gallery shows the work of some of today's finest talents, including painters Melinda Stickney-Gibson, Mary Frank, Joan Snyder, and Robert Baribeau, sculptor Peter Reginato, and ceramist Paul Chaleff. This gallery is a bit off the beaten Woodstock path but worth a visit—be sure to check out the small but delightful sculpture garden. Open every day from 11:00 a.m. to 5:00 p.m.

FLETCHER GALLERY
40 Mill Hill Road
(845) 679-4411
www.fletchergallery.com
Founded in 1992, Fletcher Gallery represents contemporary artists such as realist painter HongNian Zhang and sculptor Anthony Krauss as well as works by early and mid-20th-century artists such as Josef Presser and abstract artist Rolh Scarlett, who was a longtime Woodstock resident. Gallery hours are Thursday through Sunday, noon to 5:00 p.m.

GALERIE BMG
12 Tannery Brook Road
(845) 679-0027
www.galeriebmg.com
An elegant, two-story space, Galerie BMG is devoted to contemporary fine art photography. Owner Bernard Gerson, a photographer himself, showcases the work of both established and emerging artists from around the country and around the world. This is a gallery that takes photography very seriously and exhibits it beautifully. Hours are Friday through Monday, 11:00 a.m. to 6:00 p.m., and by appointment.

JAMES COX GALLERY
4666 Route 212 (in Willow)
(845) 679-7608
www.jamescoxgallery.com
One of the most enjoyable things about this gallery is that it's not the standard-issue white cube.

Instead, it's a converted old barn, comfortably furnished with sofas, and with the art arranged as if in a living room. The works on display are regional and historic—this is one of the finest galleries in the area for important work by serious artists. The extensive inventory covers most of the 20th century, but James Cox also displays the work of contemporary artists. James Cox Gallery is a full-service gallery, which is something of a rarity. Services include appraisal, restoration, estate management, auctions, and research and consulting in American art. Gallery hours are Tuesday through Friday, 10:00 a.m. to 5:00 p.m. For other services, it's best to call first and arrange an appointment.

VARGA GALLERY & STUDIO
130 Tinker Street
(845) 679-4005
www.vargagallery.com
Christina Varga has exhibited her own work and that of other artists at her small studio/gallery since 2003. This gallery is a bit controversial, because Varga features outsider, naïve, and self-taught artists. The works shown can sometimes be uncomfortably uninhibited and flamboyant—prepare to have your ideas about art challenged. Open Thursday through Sunday, noon to 5:00 p.m., and by appointment.

WOODSTOCK ARTISTS ASSOCIATION AND MUSEUM
28 Tinker Street
(845) 679-2940
www.woodstockart.org
The oldest artists' organization of its kind in the United States, WAAM traces its roots back to the 1920s. The museum, located in the center of Woodstock, is devoted to exhibiting and collecting work in all media by area artists—the collection here is deep in regional works. The Main Gallery hosts monthly group exhibitions; the Downstairs Gallery hosts solo shows. The Phoebe and Belmont Towbin Wing exhibits art from the important permanent collection of more than 1,500 paintings, prints, sculptures, photos, and crafts. Featured artists include luminaries such

as Milton Avery, George Bellows, Philip Guston, and George Ault. Works related to Woodstock's artistic heritage from other institutions are also shown. If you can see only one gallery in Woodstock, this is the one to visit to get a real sense of why this community has such an important place in American art. Hours are Friday and Saturday from noon to 6:00 p.m., and Monday, Thursday, and Sunday from noon to 5:00 p.m.; closed Tuesday and Wednesday.

ANTIQUING THE VALLEY

The Hudson Valley is an antique lover's paradise. In addition to all the antiques on display at the great estates and historic sites up and down the valley, there's hardly a town without at least one antiques shop. Indeed, there are places, such as the famed five-block stretch along Warren Street in the city of Hudson in Columbia County, that are pretty much nothing but antiques shops.

All that wonderful antiquing across six counties causes a real problem for writers of guidebooks—there's simply not enough space to be comprehensive and discuss each shop in detail. Instead, this chapter includes short listings for a number of multi-dealer galleries, larger shops, and some specialist dealers. It also includes a section listing local auction houses, information on local antiques dealers associations, and a close-up look at the famous antiques fairs held in Rhinebeck three times a year.

Most antique dealers have shop hours when the public is welcome to browse, but hours and open days can vary quite a bit. Many shops are open only part of the week (often Thursday through Monday), and some may have shorter hours, irregular hours, or be closed for more days (or be closed altogether) in the colder weather. Because of that variability, the days and hours given here are only approximate and in some cases aren't given at all. As many dealers add when giving their usual hours, "and by chance," check ahead. Most dealers are happy to accommodate visitors by appointment.

COLUMBIA COUNTY

Chatham

CLAUDIA KINGSLEY ANTIQUES
12 Main Street
(518) 392-8871
Americana, decorative objects, antique quilts. Open by appointment.

MARK FEDER & SONS
161 Hudson Avenue (Route 66)
(518) 392-3738
Specialist in antique sterling silver flatware, including discontinued and obsolete patterns. Hours by appointment.

PITKIN CO. REFINISHERS AND ANTIQUES
14 River Street
(518) 392-3162
Antique furniture—all types and periods. Open

Monday through Friday, 8:00 a.m. to 5:00 p.m., and Saturday, 8:00 a.m. to noon.

ROUTE 66 ANTIQUES
14 Main Street
(518) 392-6878
Vintage fine Bakelite, designer costume, designer silver, and designer copper jewelry, along with vintage purses and accessories. Hours are Wednesday through Sunday, 11:00 a.m. to 5:00 p.m.

WELCOME HOME ANTIQUE CENTER
34 Main Street
(518) 392-5848
www.welcomehomeantiques.com
Five dealers under one roof; broad, eclectic mix of merchandise, including china, pottery, folk art, vintage jewelry, lamps and lighting, and furniture. Open every day except Tuesday from 10:00 a.m. to 5:00 p.m.

Claverack

SIGNED CORRECTLY ANTIQUES & COLLECTIBLES
19 Route 23
(518) 851-7257
Furniture, glass, and collectibles.

East Chatham

ANTIQUES AT PEACEABLE FARMS
983 Route 295
(518) 392-5157
Country furniture, antiques, and collectibles, including antique dolls. Antique chair repair, including cane, splint, rush, and Shaker tape.

Hillsdale

HILLSDALE BARN ANTIQUES
10394 State Route 22
(518) 325-1357
www.hillsdalebarnantiques.com
Two thousand square feet of American country furniture, folk art, hooked rugs, quilts, baskets, stoneware, and accessories in a wonderful 19th-century barn. Shop hours are 11:00 a.m. to 5:00 p.m.; days vary seasonally, so check ahead, but the barn is open on Friday, Saturday, and Sunday most of the year. Open by appointment in November and closed from December to March.

RODGERS BOOK BARN
467 Rodman Road
(518) 325-3610
www.rodgersbookbarn.com
A wealth of wonderful books—more than 50,000 titles on a wide variety of subjects, plus records. Hours are seasonal. November through March, Saturday and Sunday from 10:00 a.m. to 5:00 p.m., Monday and Friday from noon to 5:00 p.m. April through October, Saturday from 10:00 a.m. to 5:00 p.m., Sunday from 11:00 a.m. to 5:00 p.m., and Monday, Thursday, and Friday from noon to 5:00 p.m. *Note:* Even for rural Columbia County, this store is hard to find. Call ahead or check the Web site for directions.

Hudson

AD LIB ANTIQUES & INTERIORS
522 Warren Street
(518) 822-6522
www.adlibantiques.com
Formal and informal rustic French furniture along with chandeliers, sconces, and other lighting.

ALAIN PIOTON/THE HUDSON ANTIQUES CENTER
536 Warren Street
(518) 828-9920
www.alainpiotonantiques.com
The oldest antiques shop in Hudson, Alain Pioton specializes in French antiques of the 18th to the 20th centuries. The Hudson Antiques Center represents 10 dealers specializing in a wide variety of antiques covering all periods. Open every day except Wednesday, 11:00 a.m. to 5:00 p.m.

ANGELIKA WESTERHOFF ANTIQUES
606 Warren Street
(518) 828-3606
www.angelikawesterhoffantiques.com
High-end fine antique furniture, rare books, lighting, mirrors and wall decorations, jewelry, watches, and decorative objects.

i The Hudson Antique Dealers Association (HADA) represents more than 65 shops in the city. HADA provides a detailed map showing the location of all the dealers, along with contact information. For details, call (518) 828-1999 or visit www.hudsonantiques.net.

THE ARMORY ART & ANTIQUE GALLERY
State and North Fifth Streets
(518) 822-1477
More than 60 antiques dealers display their wares in this restored historic armory. Hours are Thursday through Monday, 11:00 a.m. to 5:00 p.m.

THE ART OF THE GRAPE
515 Columbia Street
(518) 822-0770
www.artofthegrape.com
High-end wine cabinets, tables, and accessories for the discerning wine enthusiast. Open Thursday through Monday, 11:00 a.m. to 4:00 p.m.

BOTANICUS
446 Warren Street
(518) 828-0250
Eighteenth- and early 19th-century furniture.

BOULAY ANTIQUES
530 Warren Street
(518) 929-6979
www.boulayantiques.com
Twentieth-century furniture, fine art, textiles, and decorative art objects.

CAROUSEL ANTIQUE CENTER
611 Warren Street
(518) 828-9127
A large multi-dealer shop with a wide range of styles and prices. Open every day from 11:00 a.m. to 5:00 p.m.

CUMMINGS ANTIQUES
306 Warren Street
(518) 822-1432
www.cummingsantiques.com
High-end Continental furniture, Asian and Western porcelain, and decorative arts.

EUSTACE AND ZAMUS ANTIQUES
513 Warren Street
(518) 822-9200
www.ezantiques.com
Three floors of period American antiques, decorative accessories, and furniture, specializing in Hepplewhite, Federal, Sheraton, Empire, and Chippendale. Shop hours are Thursday through Monday, noon to 5:00 p.m.

FOXFIRE ANTIQUES
538 Warren Street
(518) 828-6281

Antique Asian porcelains, Staffordshire porcelain, Sheffield silver, fine lighting, and American, English, Continental, and Asian antique furniture. Open from noon to 5:00 p.m. every day except Wednesday.

FRANK SWIM ANTIQUES
430 Warren Street
(518) 822-0411
www.frankswim.com
Antiques and decorative objects, with emphasis on furniture, Blenko glass, and lighting.

> **i** Warren Street is the antiques district in Hudson. The core of the district is the 400 block between Fourth Street and Fifth Street, but the shops stretch along Warren Street from Third Street on the west to past Seventh Street to the east. The shops are in lovely 19th-century buildings amid a neighborhood of restored Victorian homes.

GOTTLIEB GALLERY
524 Warren Street
(518) 822-1761
www.gottliebgallery.1stdibs.com
Continental and Neoclassical antiques, decorative objects, and garden appointments.

HUDSON ANTIQUES ASSOCIATES
428 Warren Street
(518) 828-6982
American period furnishings, paintings and prints, folk art, decorative accessories. Specializing in antiques from the 17th to 19th centuries. Open Thursday through Monday, 11:00 a.m. to 5:00 p.m.

HUDSON CITY BOOKS
553 Warren Street
(518) 671-6020
Rare books, first editions, and good used books.

HUDSON HOUSE ANTIQUES
738 Warren Street
(518) 822-1226
www.hudsonhouseantiques.com
Specialists in furniture from the American Empire,

Gothic, Neoclassical, Renaissance Revival, and Eastlake Aesthetic periods. Open Thursday through Monday, noon to 6:00 p.m.

HUDSON SUPERMARKET ANTIQUES
310–312 Warren Street
(518) 822-0028
www.hudsonsupermarket.com
Located in—you guessed it—a former supermarket, this is a 7,000-square-foot multi-dealer space featuring five dealers. The collections span a wide range of styles and eras. Open Thursday through Monday from noon to 6:00 p.m.

HUDSON TRADING COMPANY
516 Warren Street
(518) 828-2084
www.hudsontradingcompany.com
Featuring American and Continental furniture, decorative arts, and collectibles from the 17th, 18th, and 19th centuries. Hours are Thursday through Monday, noon to 5:00 p.m.

KENDON ANTIQUES
508 Warren Street
(518) 822-8627
www.kendonantiques.com
In business since 1996 and specializing in quality 18th- and 19th-century American formal and country furniture, folk art, Americana, vintage toys, and 19th-century paintings, drawings, and prints.

KEYSTONE ANTIQUES
746 Warren Street
(518) 822-1019
www.godmanskeystone.com
Architectural elements, religious statuary, garden furniture, and ceramics. Open Thursday through Monday, 10:00 a.m. to 5:30 p.m.

MARK MCDONALD LTD.
555 Warren Street
(518) 828-6320
www.markmcdonald.biz
Mid-20th-century modern design in furniture, glass, ceramics, lighting, jewelry, and decorative

objects. Open Thursday through Monday, 11:00 a.m. to 5:00 or 6:00 p.m.

NOONAN ANTIQUES
551 Warren Street
(518) 828-5779
www.noonanantiques.com
Specialist in fine American and Continental furniture from the 18th through the 20th centuries. Closed Tuesday and Wednesday.

PETER JUNG FINE ARTS
512 Warren Street
(518) 828-2698
www.peterjungfineart.com
Specialist in 19th- and 20th-century American and European paintings. Gallery open most weekends.

RELICS ANTIQUES
550 Warren Street, 2nd floor
(518) 755-2753
www.relicsantiques.com
Decorative furniture, porcelain, and objects

SKALAR ANTIQUES
438½ Warren Street
(518) 828-1170
www.skalarantiques.com
Featuring Art Deco and mid-20th-century modern furniture, lighting, and decorative accessories by European designers. Open Thursday through Monday, 11:00 a.m. to 5:00 p.m.

SUTTER ANTIQUES
556 Warren Street
(518) 822-0729
www.sutterantiques.com
On Warren Street since 1991; specialist in Biedermeir, Empire, and Art Deco furniture, lighting, and decorative objects.

20TH CENTURY GALLERY
605 Warren Street
(518) 822-8907
www.20thcenturygallery.net
Mid-century furniture and objects, especially

seating, tables, mirrors, case pieces, lighting, and garden elements.

VINCENT R. MULFORD ANTIQUES
419 Warren Street
(518) 828-5489
www.vmulford.com
An antiques dealer since 1980, Vince Mulford opened his shop in Hudson in 1990. He specializes in high-end antique furniture, lighting, and decorative objects.

Kinderhook

KINDERHOOK ANTIQUES CENTER
Route 9H
(518) 758-7939
Early glass, china, kitchen collectibles, textiles, furniture, ironware, and tools. Known for reasonable prices. Open Friday through Sunday, 10:00 a.m. to 5:00 p.m.

THE PAVILION ART AND ANTIQUES
17 Broad Street
(518) 758-1788
Fine American period furniture, art, folk art, and decorative arts. Open most Saturdays from 10:00 a.m. to 6:00 p.m. and Sundays from noon to 6:00 p.m.

Valatie

JGA ANTIQUE AND COLLECTIBLES
3025 Main Street
(518) 758-6393
Generalist antiques dealer offering furniture, estate jewelry, costume jewelry, glassware, and decorative arts. Open Wednesday through Monday, 10:30 a.m. to 5:30 p.m.

DUTCHESS COUNTY

Beacon

EARLY EVERYTHING
468–470 Main Street
(845) 838-3014
Large selection of antiques and collectibles, along with beeswax candles. Closed Tuesday.

THE MILL ANTIQUES
474 Main Street
(845) 231-3566
Nineteenth-century folk art, Americana, and quality New England country antiques in a gallery setting. Open Thursday through Monday, 11:00 a.m. to 6:00 p.m.

STUDIO ANTIQUES
458 Main Street
(845) 765-0484
Fine arts and antiques from a variety of periods and styles. Open Thursday through Monday, 11:00 a.m. to 5:00 p.m.

Hopewell Junction

HOPEWELL ANTIQUE CENTER
Route 82 and Route 376
(845) 221-3055
Twenty-five dealers spread across 12,000 square feet and four floors. Antiques, home furnishings, and decorative accessories. Open daily from 11:00 a.m. to 5:00 p.m.

Hyde Park

HYDE PARK ANTIQUES CENTER
544 Albany Post Road (Route 9)
(845) 229-8200
www.hydeparkantiques.net
Large, 10,000-square-foot multi-dealer center, with more than 70 vendors in 14 rooms. Open every day from 10:00 a.m. to 5:00 p.m.

KINGS HIGHWAY ANTIQUES
4312 Albany Post Road (Route 9)
(845) 229-1669
Authentic European and American items from the late 18th century to the early 20th, including furnishings, cupboards, marble-topped furniture, pottery, porcelain, glass, lighting, and vintage jewelry. Open Thursday through Monday, noon to 5:00 p.m.

VILLAGE ANTIQUES CENTER
Route 9
(845) 229-6600
More than 30 dealers offering fine antiques, collectibles, selected classic reproductions, furniture, glassware, silver, china, vintage jewelry, postcards, bronzes, Hummels, toys, and dolls. Open daily from 10:00 a.m. to 5:00 p.m.

Milan
WILTSIE BRIDGE
Route 199 and Route 308
(845) 758-4001
www.wiltsiebridge.com
Rustic equestrian decor, antiques, and artisan handcrafted gifts.

Millbrook
MILLBROOK ANTIQUE CENTER
3283 Franklin Avenue
(845) 677-3921
A 40-dealer group space with 6,000 square feet on two floors. Specialties here include sterling silver, Persian rugs, dolls, coins, maps, china, and period furniture. Look for the yellow building with the green awning. Open Monday through Saturday from 11:00 a.m. to 5:00 p.m., Sunday 11:30 a.m. to 5:30 p.m.

MILLBROOK ANTIQUES MALL
3301 Franklin Avenue
(845) 677-9311
www.millbrookantiquesmall.com
More than 40 shops under one roof. Specialists in 18th- and 19th-century European and American furniture, collectibles, and decorating accessories. Open Monday through Saturday, 11:00 a.m. to 5:00 p.m., and Sunday noon to 5:00 p.m.

MILLBROOK GALLERY & ANTIQUES
3297 Franklin Avenue
(845) 677-6699
www.millbrookgalleryandantiques.com
Fine arts, rare books, collectibles, sporting art, equestrian art and antiques, and antique

furniture. Hours are Friday through Monday, noon to 5:30 p.m.

RED SCHOOL HOUSE ANTIQUES
3300 Franklin Avenue
(845) 677-9786
Quality fine English and American furniture and decorative objects. Open Thursday through Sunday, 11:00 a.m. to 5:00 p.m.

VILLAGE ANTIQUE CENTER
Franklin Avenue
(845) 677-5160
More than 40 dealers offering country furniture, American and European silver, fine china, estate jewelry, pottery, quilts, and watches. Open Monday through Friday from 11:00 a.m. to 5:00 p.m., Saturday from 11:00 a.m. to 5:30 p.m., and Sunday from noon to 5:30 p.m.

YELLOW CHURCH ANTIQUES
2545 Route 44
(845) 677-6779
www.yellowchurch.com
Located in a beautifully restored old church, the collection specializes in fine 18th- and early 19th-century English and Continental furniture. Open Friday through Sunday, 11:00 a.m. to 5:00 p.m.

Red Hook
ANNEX ANTIQUES CENTER
23 East Market Street
(845) 758-2843
More than 25 dealers in an old Deco-era movie theater. Vendors offer fine furniture, Depression glass, postcards, toys, vintage costume jewelry, '50s kitsch, and more. Open daily, 11:00 a.m. to 5:00 p.m.

CIDER MILL ANTIQUES
5 Cherry Street
(845) 758-2599
www.cidermillantiques.com
Specialist in yellow ware, a type of American pottery popular from about 1850 to 1930. Other specialties include textiles and quilts, baskets,

country decorative objects, and primitive country furniture. Open Thursday through Monday, 11:30 a.m. to 5:00 p.m.

HOFFMAN'S BARN SALE
19 Old Farm Road
(845) 758-5668
An eclectic jumble of antiques and used items—the huge stock holds treasures for those willing to look. Open Friday, Saturday, and Sunday, 10:00 a.m. to 5:30 p.m.

RED HOOK ANTIQUE CENTER
7531 North Broadway
(845) 758-2223
Quality antiques and collectibles ranging from primitive to Deco. Open Wednesday through Monday, 11:00 a.m. to 5:00 p.m.

Rhinebeck

ASHER HOUSE ANTIQUES
6380 Mill Street
(845) 876-1794
www.asherhouse.com
Set in a beautifully restored 1796 Dutch Colonial house, Asher House Antiques offers 4,000 square feet of imported antique furniture and accessories, including pottery and French enamel. Asher House specializes in tables, chairs, ladders, buffets, and bookcases. The lovely back garden offers garden furnishings. Open daily from 10:00 a.m. to 5:30 p.m.

BEEKMAN ARMS ANTIQUE MARKET
24 West Market Street
(845) 876-3477
With more than 30 dealers in a two-story red barn behind the Beekman Arms hotel, this is one of the best antiques stores in the region. Vendors specialize in Americana, country and primitive furniture, jewelry, books, decorative accessories, and more. Open every day from 11:00 a.m. to 5:00 p.m.

GATEHOUSE AT OLD MILL
7085 Route 9
(845) 876-0685

The Rhinebeck Antiques Fair

One of the best antiques fairs in the country and unquestionably the best show in the Hudson Valley, the Rhinebeck Antiques Fair passed its 30th anniversary in 2006. Nearly 200 top-level dealers participate every year, coming from all over the Northeast and as from far away as Ohio and North Carolina. The shows are held three times a year at the Dutchess County Fairgrounds on Route 9 in Rhinebeck. The spring show is the third weekend in May; the Summer Magic show is the last Saturday in July; and the fall show is the second weekend in October (Columbus Day weekend). Hours are 10:00 a.m. to 5:00 p.m. Saturday and 11:00 a.m. to 4:00 p.m. Sunday. All the exhibitors are entirely indoors, so the show goes on rain or shine. An extensive food court offers really good food, not just the usual hot dogs, and there's an on-site delivery service. For details and dates of upcoming shows, check the Web site at www.rhinebeck antiquesfair.com. Admission is $9 per person. Look for discount cards at local merchants and for newspaper ads offering discounts. Free parking. No pets allowed. The Dutchess County Fairgrounds are completely wheelchair accessible.

Formerly known as Old Mill House Antiques, this shop specializes in Americana, country, and primitive. Open 11:00 a.m. to 5:00 p.m. Thursday through Monday.

LUISA CAVANAUGH ANTIQUES
37 West Market Street
(845) 876-3876
Antiques, furniture, jewelry, and home accessories. Open Thursday through Monday, 10:00 a.m. to 5:00 p.m.

PORTLY PUG ANTIQUES
11 West Market Street
(845) 876-6896
www.portlypug.com
Eclectic collection of antiques decorative accessories, Black Forest carvings, inkwell, tea caddies, Georgian and Victorian jewelry, early kitchenware, and fine art. A fun part of this store is the large collection of animal-related items.

RHINEBECK ANTIQUES & ARTISANS
7 West Market Street
(845) 876-5555
A multi-dealer shop with some interesting specialties, including American Belleek and other pottery and porcelain, jewelry, silver, art glass, and lace. Hours are Thursday through Monday, 10:30 a.m. to 5:30 p.m.

RHINEBECK STONE CHAPEL ANTIQUES
5768 Albany Post Road (Route 9)
(845) 876-0373
Stylish antique objects from the 18th, 19th, and 20th centuries, primitive furniture, folk art, and fine art, all in a historic old stone chapel on the southern outskirts of Rhinebeck. Open Friday through Monday, 11:00 a.m. to 5:00 p.m.

Stanfordville

B & D JOHNSON ANTIQUES
5979 Route 82 (Market Square Plaza)
(845) 868-7464
www.bdjohnsonantiques.com
Specializing in fine 18th- and 19th-century American, English, and Continental furniture and fine arts. Open Thursday and Friday afternoons and all day Saturday and Sunday.

OLD CAROUSEL ANTIQUES CENTRE
Route 82 North
(845) 868-1586
Large multi-dealer shop covering 8,500 square feet. Vendors specialize in furniture, vintage jewelry, glassware, pottery, linens, vintage clothing, antique tools, vintage Christmas decorations, and more. Open from 10:00 a.m. to 6:00 p.m. every day except Tuesday.

GREENE COUNTY

Catskill

PHILIP AND KATHLEEN SEIBEL ANTIQUES
40 North Jefferson Avenue
(518) 943-2256
Specializing in early American and primitive cupboards; also offering fine American textiles and 18th- and 19th-century furnishings in a restored Dutch brick farmhouse. Hours by appointment.

TOWN HOUSE ANTIQUES
375 Main Street
(518) 943-7400
Furniture, 19th- and 20th-century decorative objects, art pottery, fine vintage toys.

Coxsackie

COXSACKIE ANTIQUE CENTER
12400 Route 9W
(518) 731-8888
www.coxsackie.com
One of the largest multi-dealer shops in the region, the Coxsackie Antique Center brings together 100 vendors in a 15,000-square-foot sales area. The center bills itself as a repro-free zone—no fakes are allowed. The center also has an extensive reference library. Open daily, 10:00 a.m. to 8:00 p.m.

ORANGE COUNTY

Newburgh

BRIDGES OVER TIME
97 Liberty Street
(845) 569-8191
www.bridgesovertime.com
Specialists in 19th- and 20th-century antiques, fine art, and garden items. Hours by appointment.

> **i** It's a little out of the region, but the large Orange County Flea Market, held every weekend from 8:00 a.m. to 5:00 p.m. at the Orange County Fairgrounds (100 Carpenter Avenue, Middletown; 845-227-1154), is a fun place to visit.

PUTNAM COUNTY

Cold Spring

ART & ANTIQUES/DOWNTOWN GALLERY
40 Main Street
(845) 265-2334
www.artantiquegallery.com
A large multi-dealer shop with more than 30 vendors in over 5,000 square feet, this gallery offers a very wide variety of antiques and collectibles. It's the largest antiques center in Putnam County. Hours are Thursday through Monday, 11:00 a.m. to 5:00 p.m.

BIJOU GALLERIES, LTD.
50 Main Street
(845) 265-4337
www.bijougalleries.com
Thirty dealers offer a large selection of antiques, collectibles, art, and decorative objects in a space that is unusually well-lighted and spacious. Look for the famous hockey stick chair—it's interesting if nothing else. Open every day, 11:00 a.m. to 5:00 p.m.

> **i** The Cold Spring Antiques Dealers Association (97 Main Street; 845-265-6366) is a good source of up-to-date information about antiques in the area.

COLD SPRING ANTIQUES CENTER
77 Main Street
(845) 265-5050
www.coldspringantiquescenter.com
More than 25 dealers offering a wide range of antiques and collectibles. The vendors are located in a restored Victorian bank building, complete with the original bank vault. Open every day but Tuesday, 11:00 a.m. to 5:00 p.m.

DECADES ANTIQUES
131 Main Street
(845) 265-9515
Antiques and collectibles, including Depression glass, pottery, vintage textiles, and furniture.

FOUNTAIN SQUARE ANTIQUES
104 Main Street
(845) 265-0400
Wide range of styles and periods, including Depression glass, pottery, postcards, and old tools.

HEAVENLY TREASURES
93 Main Street
(845) 265-5532
www.heavenlytreasuresny.com
Specializing in sterling silver, porcelain, art glass, and Art Deco through 1960s period furniture and objets d'art. Special collection of signed vintage costume jewelry. Open Thursday through Sunday, noon to 6:00 p.m.

JANE KRENACH ANTIQUES
114 Main Street
(845) 265-5002
www.janekrenachantiques.com
Specializing in fine 18th- and 19th-century American, English, and Continental furniture.

NELSONVILLE ANTIQUES
93 Main Street
(845) 265-2373
Quality vintage and antique furniture, fine art, silver, and decorative objects.

i The annual Cold Spring Antiques Show happens on the second Sunday in June at Mayor's Park overlooking the Hudson. More than 60 dealers from the region and beyond participate. There's a free shuttle bus from the MetroNorth train station. For information call (845) 265-4414 or check www.coldspringantiqueshow.com.

ONCE UPON A TIME ANTIQUES
101 Main Street
(845) 265-4339
Vintage dolls and toys.

OTHERS' OLDIES
171 Main Street
(845) 265-2323
Coins and currency. Hours by appointment.

SERIOUS TOYZ
82 Main Street
(845) 265-6543
www.serioustoyz.com
Fine vintage toys and collectibles for kids of all ages. Huge collection of tin, pressed steel, die-cast, plastic, and character toys. Open Thursday through Monday, noon to 6:00 p.m.

SPOOKY RIVER ANTIQUES AND COLLECTIBLES
135 Main Street
(845) 265-2978
www.spookyriverantiques.com
Fine pottery, Currier & Ives lithographs and original 19th-century prints, Stickley and Arts and Crafts furniture.

STARK FINE ART & ANTIQUES
144 Main Street
(845) 809-5275
www.starkfineartandantiques.com

Fine American and French furniture of the 18th century, along with American and French decorative arts of the early 20th century. Open Wednesday and Friday from noon to 5:00 p.m. and Saturday from 1:00 to 6:00 p.m.

TACA-TIQUES ANTIQUES
109 Main Street
(845) 265-2655
www.taca-tiques.com
Specialist in American, Victorian, and estate sterling silver, beveled glass mirrors, and jewelry. Open Wednesday through Friday from noon to 4:00 p.m., Saturday and Sunday from noon to 5:00 p.m.

ULSTER COUNTY

Gardiner
GRANDPA'S ANTIQUES
Route 208 and Route 44/55
(845) 255-6217
Wide variety of classic furniture, vintage clothing, jewelry, and collectibles. Open Thursday through Monday, 11:00 a.m. to 5:00 p.m.

i For up-to-date information on antiques in Ulster County, contact the Antiques Dealers Association of Ulster County at Box 246, Hurley, NY 12443, or www.ulsterantiques.com. Ask for the annual pamphlet "A Treasure Hunter's Guide."

HIHO HOME MARKET AND ANTIQUE CENTER
132 Main Street
(845) 255-1123
Seven antiques dealers in 15 rooms of home decor and antiques. The permanent Christmas room, with vintage ornaments and running toy train, is a lot of fun. Open every day except Tuesday.

TUTHILLTOWN ANTIQUES
1021 Albany Post Road
(845) 255-9404
www.tuthilltownantiques.com

Antiques and collectibles in a renovated barn near the historic Tuthilltown gristmill in this hamlet near Gardiner. Specialties include country-style items, furniture, vintage linens, and postcards. Open Thursday through Sunday and most holidays, 10:00 a.m. to 5:00 p.m.

High Falls

THE BARKING DOG
7 Second Avenue at Route 213
(845) 687-4834
Two full floors of assorted antiques, plus the garden and barn. Open every day from 11:00 a.m. to 5:00 p.m.

CAT HOUSE ANTIQUES
136 Bruceville Road
(845) 687-0790
www.cathouseantiques.com
Vintage kitchens are the specialty here. Painted furniture from the 1930s and 1940s, enamel and Formica tables, Hoosier-style cabinets, vintage tablecloths, glassware and dinnerware, and kitchen implements. Open Friday through Monday.

The D&H Canal Sunday Market, held at the Canal Park on Route 213 in High Falls, is a great place to buy antiques, collectibles, crafts, and products from local artisans. Open Sunday, weather permitting, from May through October. For more information, call the D&H Canal Museum at (845) 687-9311.

Highland

ANTIQUE CENTER AT VINTAGE VILLAGE
134 Route 44/55
(845) 691-6000
www.vintagevillage.com
Vintage Village is a complex of five buildings that used to be part of a historic sawmill and lumberyard. Today the three-acre site has been restored as a commercial and historical center. The Antique Center part is a multi-dealer shop in the old 4,800-square-foot sawmill—the only

antiques shop you're likely to visit that has a stream running through it. No reproductions are allowed. The Furniture Barn is a bargain-hunter's delight. It contains a large collection of antiques that may need some restoration. Open daily from 11:00 a.m. to 5:00 p.m.; closed Tuesday and Wednesday from January through May. *Note:* No admission fee for the antiquing, but there is a small fee to visit the exhibits.

Hurley

FROM THE GRAPEVINE ANTIQUES
60 Main Street
(845) 331-4852
Reasonably priced antiques and vintage furnishings in an old barn in Hurley's historic district. Open most days—call ahead.

VAN DEUSEN HOUSE ANTIQUES
59 Main Street
(845) 331-8852
Located in the historic district, Van Deusen has a large stock of country furnishings, early porcelain, antique tools, paper ephemera, and more. Open every day.

Kingston

CATSKILL MOUNTAIN ANTIQUE CENTER
462 Route 28
(845) 331-0880
More than 20 dealers selling vintage furniture, porcelain, glass, and Native American objects. Open every day but Tuesday, 10:00 a.m. to 5:00 p.m.

MEZZANINE ANTIQUE CENTER AND CAFÉ
79 Broadway
(845) 339-6925
www.mezzanineantiquecenter.com
Located in the historic Rondout waterfront district, Mezzanine is a multi-dealer shop in a restored 1820s Federal-style building. Vendors here specialize in vintage costume jewelry, art, ceramics, folk art, ephemera, glassware, and furniture. Take a break from antiquing with an espresso in the cafe. Open Friday through Monday, 11:00 a.m. to 5:00 p.m.

OUTBACK ANTIQUES
72 Hurley Avenue
(845) 31-4481
"Shabby chic" antiques and collectibles in a 125-year-old barn. Specializing in vintage clothing, linens, and lace. Open daily, 10:00 a.m. to 5:00 p.m.; closed Sunday and Tuesday. By appointment only from January through March.

SKILLYPOT ANTIQUES CENTER
41 Broadway
(845) 338-6779
A multi-dealer shop in the waterfront Rondout district, featuring furniture, Depression glass, nautical items, postcards, toy trains, jewelry, and gifts. The unusual name comes from an old chain ferry boat called the *Riverside* that ran from Kingston across the Rondout Creek to Port Ewen. Because the boat was not only slow but also ran only sporadically, it was nicknamed the *Skillypot*, from an old Dutch word for tortoise. Open daily, 11:00 a.m. to 5:00 p.m.; closed Tuesday through Thursday, January through March.

VELSANI ARTS AND ANTIQUES
334 Wall Street
(845) 340-8400
www.velsani.com
Well regarded as a specialist in Murano glass, the gallery also offers a collection of other exceptional objects, including pre-Columbian antiquities and Spanish Colonial art from Latin America and international Art Deco furnishings. Open daily from 11:00 a.m. to 5:00 p.m.

ZABORSKI EMPORIUM
27 Hoffman Street
(845) 338-6465
Specializing in architectural elements, hardware, plumbing, fixtures, lighting, and doors. If you need a claw-foot bathtub, this is the place to find it.

New Paltz

EMERSON ANTIQUE BARN
680 Albany Post Road
(845) 255-0793
www.emersonantiquebarn.com
A huge barn filled with a wide range of antiques and collectibles. The turnover is high here, so the selection changes rapidly. Open most afternoons until 5:00 p.m.

JENKINSTOWN ANTIQUES
13 Old Route 299
(845) 255-4876
www.jenkinstownantiques.com
Antique and collectible items from the Hudson Valley, along with country and formal furniture. Expert appraisals. Open Thursday through Monday, 11:00 a.m. to 5:00 p.m.

MEDUSA EMPORIUM AND GALLERY
215 Main Street
(845) 255-6000
www.medusaantiques.com
Outstanding collection of furniture, cabinets, tables and desks, seating, outdoor and garden elements, and lighting. Much of the stock comes from the Mediterranean and Asia, including imports from Japan, but there's also fine American antique furniture. Refuel for more antiquing at the Japanese fusion cafe within the building. Open every day from 10:00 a.m. to 5:00 p.m.

NUTTING HOUSE ANTIQUES
191 Plains Road
(845) 255-2050
Folk art, country furniture, and textiles, especially hooked rugs. Textile mounting and restoration. Open by appointment.

VINTAGE STUDIO
11 Church Street
(845) 255-3022
Eclectic is the word here: antiques, vintage clothing, vintage and new home furnishings, garden urns, old pottery, and jewelry. Open every day from 11:00 a.m. to 5:00 p.m.

WATER STREET MARKET
10 Main Street
(845) 255-1403
www.waterstreetmarket.com
Two separate multi-dealer shops are within the Water Street complex: the Antiques Barn and the Antiques Center. More than 40 vendors offer a very broad mix of antiques. Prices tend toward the affordable. Take a break from antiquing by visiting the cafes, restaurants, and other shops in the market. Open every day from 10:00 a.m. to 5:00 p.m.

Saugerties

FED-ON LIGHTS ANTIQUES
34 Market Street at Livingston
(845) 246-8444
www.fedonlights.com
Antique and vintage lighting—including antique chandeliers and sconces and classic period light fixtures—are the specialties here. Architectural elements are also sold, as are claw-foot bathtubs, antique marble-top sinks, and antique glassware and furniture. The store is in a restored 1820s building that is crammed with merchandise literally from floor to ceiling. The display of tubs is impressive, and every inch of ceiling space is taken up with antique lighting. Open Friday through Monday, noon to 5:30 p.m.

FROM EUROPE TO YOU, INC.
2910 Route 9W
(845) 246-7274
www.fromeuropetoyou.com
Probably the largest inventory of antique and architectural items in the region. Huge selection of European furniture and architectural objects, with specialties in marble mantles, gazebos, and fountains. Excellent selection of garden ornaments. Open every day from 9:00 a.m. to 6:00 p.m.

RED HORSE ANTIQUES
171 Ulster Avenue
(845) 246-5852
www.red-horse-antiques.com

High-quality estate items, including fine antiques, rare books, estate heirlooms, fine estate jewelry, and assorted collectibles. Open every day from 10:00 a.m. to 5:00 p.m.

SAUGERTIES ANTIQUE CENTER
220 Main Street
(845) 246-8234
Multi-dealer store offering furniture, jewelry, pottery, china, glass, and more at affordable prices. Open daily from 10:00 a.m. to 5:00 p.m.; noon to 5:00 p.m. on Sunday.

SAUGERTIES ANTIQUES GALLERY
104 Partition Street
(845) 246-2323
High-quality European and American antiques from the 18th and 19th centuries, specializing in bronzes, clocks, furniture, lamps, and porcelain. Open every day from 10:00 a.m. to 5:00 p.m.; noon to 5:00 p.m. on Sunday.

Stone Ridge

OLD FARM ANTIQUES
710 Peak Road
(845) 687-7568
Vintage glass, china, toys, furniture, kitchen utensils, and Christmas items. Open Saturday and Sunday from noon to 6:00 p.m. Closed from mid-December through April.

STONE RIDGE ANTIQUES
3659 Main Street
(845) 687-0257
Multi-dealer shop in an old house, showcasing a wide range of periods and styles. Open daily from 11:00 a.m. to 5:00 p.m.; closed Tuesday.

THUMBPRINT ANTIQUES
209 Tongore Road
(845) 687-9318
Quality antiques in a rustic barn, including furniture, china, glass, silver, and lampshades. Open Saturday and Sunday from noon to 5:00 p.m.

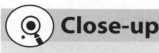 **Close-up**

Country Auctions

Going to a country auction in the Hudson Valley is a lot of fun even if you're not a big antiques fan. The lots that come up often are real antiques, but many fall more into the vintage or collectible categories, meaning that while bidding can get spirited, it rarely gets up into four figures. The area has a fair number of auctions year-round. Auction dates and what's available for sale are so variable that the list below gives only basic information. Check ahead for dates, preview and auction times, auction places, and a catalog if there is one. Today many auctioneers post preview pictures and details of upcoming auctions on their Web sites.

EAST SIDE

Absolute Auctions & Realty/United Country
45 South Avenue
Pleasant Valley
(800) 243-0061
www.absoluteauctionrealty.com

George Cole Autioneers
7578 North Broadway
Red Hook
(845) 758-9114
www.georgecoleauctions.com

Copake Auction
266 Route 7A
Copake
(518) 329-1142
www.copakeauction.com

Hyde Park Country Auctions
323 Hibernia Road
Salt Point
(845) 266-4198
www.hpcountryauctions.com

Hudson Valley Auctioneers
432 Main Street
Beacon
(845) 838-3049
www.hudsonvalleyauctioneers.com

Stair Galleries
549 Warren Street
Hudson
(518) 751-1000
www.stairgalleries.com

WEST SIDE

Deer Ridge Farm Antiques
2991 Route 9W
Saugerties
(845) 246-1572
www.deerridgefarm.net

JMW Auction Gallery
287 Pearl Street
Kingston
(845) 339-4133
www.jmwauction.com

Pine Bush Auction
157 Ward Street
Montgomery
(845) 457-4404
www.pinebushauction.com

Savoia's Auction
117 McClaren Road Extension
South Cairo
(518) 622-8000
www.savoias.com

Sterling Auction House
40 Railroad Avenue
Montgomery
(845) 457-7550
www.sterlingauctionhouse.com

Marc Stolfe Auction and Appraisal Services
41 Steve's Lane Industrial Park
Gardiner
(845) 255-7700
www.mstolfe.com

FARM MARKETS AND WINERIES

Farming has been a major part of the economy in the Hudson Valley for centuries. Dairy farms, apple orchards, and other farms covered many thousands of acres. Franklin D. Roosevelt used to list his occupation on his tax forms as tree farmer. Agriculture since FDR's day has become less important in the region, but it remains a significant part of the economy. In fact, despite the relentless development pressures on farmland in the region, agriculture here is now on the upswing, thanks in large part to increased demand for high-quality farm products grown using sustainable methods. The farmers' markets in the region are going strong and expanding; and community-supported agriculture (CSA) farms can barely keep up with the clamor for shares in their products. So strong is the demand from restaurants and consumers that today farmland that was long out of production is being brought back into use. It's an encouraging trend that looks likely to continue.

The wine industry in the Hudson Valley dates back about as far as agriculture does. The French Huguenots who settled the New Paltz area planted vines as early as 1677. Winemaking in the region was never a big part of the agricultural picture, however, until Prohibition came along. Wine for sacramental purposes was exempted, however. Because the loophole allowed for a broad interpretation of sacramental, there was enough of a market to keep winemaking barely alive in the region. For decades after Prohibition, heavy taxes and restrictive regulations kept winemaking in New York to a minimum. All that changed in 1976 with the passage of the Farm Winery Act, which reduced the taxes and eliminated the onerous regulations. Suddenly, winemakers in the Hudson Valley were able to do things like make their own wine and offer it to the public at the winery. Vineyards and winemaking took off. Today, there are some 30 wineries on both sides of the river. The vineyards have helped save a lot of agricultural land from development. They're pretty much all small, family-run operations. Visiting the wineries is a popular tourism activity in the region. It's fun—you get to tour the vineyards and meet the winemakers, sample the vintages, maybe picnic among the grapes, and buy a few bottles or cases to take home.

FARMS AND FARMERS' MARKETS

Although the dairy farms, fruit orchards, and vegetable farms that once covered the regional landscape are now far fewer in number, there are still a fair number of small working farms. Most have long histories, some going back into the 1700s; some are new ventures on old agricultural land.

Today consumers have a variety of ways to get farm-fresh produce easily. Many farms in the region operate seasonal farm stands where you can buy whatever happens to be fresh-picked that day. These farms also often have stands at one of the many wonderful local farmers' markets in the region. Some farms let you come right on the property and pick your own. It's a good way to remind yourself of where your food comes from—and have some fun at the same time. There are so many farm stands and u-pick operations in the region that not all of them can be listed here. This section focuses on some of the best-known operations and gives priority to farmers who use sustainable methods.

i Hudson Valley Fresh is a cooperative of local dairy farms offering premium- quality milk. No antibiotics, no hormones, just very fresh milk from happy cows grazing the rolling hills of Dutchess and Columbia Counties. It's available at many local stores and supermarkets in the mid-Hudson region. For more information: (845) 264-2372; www.hudsonvalleyfresh .com.

Many farms in the region now offer an innovative concept called community-supported agriculture (CSA). The concept behind CSA is simple: Support your local farmer. How? By purchasing a share of the crop in advance. Here's how it works: The farmer offers shares in the upcoming year's produce to the public for a price. In return, the shareholders receive generous weekly portions of the produce, fresh from the farm. Shareholders pick up their supply at the farm and sometimes also at designated sites elsewhere. The bounty usually includes seasonal vegetables and fruits and may also include other farm products, such as eggs, cheese, and meat. The farmer gets cash in advance and a guaranteed outlet for the produce, while consumers get absolutely fresh produce grown using sustainable methods. The annual cost of a share can usually be reduced somewhat if you're willing to volunteer for some farm labor—an approach that is strongly encouraged. And because the bounty each week is usually enough for a family of four hearty eaters, those who can't use that much can usually purchase half shares or arrange to split their share with others. CSA has gone from being a somewhat out-there idea to being almost the norm in the region. Most farms sell out their shares early in the year and even have waiting lists. Fortunately for those who can't participate in CSA, the farms sometimes sell their surplus at the farm stand or local farmers' market. Here too, there are now so many great CSA operations in the region that only the best-known can be listed here.

FARM STANDS AND U-PICKS

Fresh, locally grown produce, along with other goodies such as cider, baked goods, pickles, and preserves, are all available directly from local farm stands. Days and hours vary seasonally—check ahead if possible. And what could be better and fresher than fruit you pick yourself? A number of farms and orchards in the area allow visitors to pick their own. Kids love this, and it's fun for grown-ups, too. The farms usually also offer other fun attractions, such as hayrides and farm animals. These operations are seasonal, so call ahead to find out what's ripe and check on picking conditions.

Columbia County

Ancram

THOMPSON-FINCH FARM
750 Wiltsie Bridge Road
(518) 329-7578
www.thompsonfinch.com
A certified organic fruit farm now run by the fifth generation of the family, Thompson-Finch specializes in strawberries, raspberries, blueberries, and apples. Most people come and pick their own berries (not the apples), but there's also a farm stand offering fruit and vegetables. The fruit is also available at Hawthorne Valley Farm in Ghent (see later listing). Before planning a trip here, always call first to check on what's ripe and the picking conditions.

Claverack

PHILIP ORCHARD
270 Route 9H
(518) 851-6351
A historic farm that has been in the same family since 1732, Philips Orchard is nonetheless an innovator. The farm was one of the first to get into the u-pick business in the 1960s; today it is a leader in using integrated pest management for natural insect control. The seasonal offerings here include Bartlett, Anjou, and Harrow Sweet pears, more than a dozen apple varieties, and

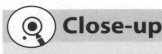 **Close-up**

Farmers' Markets

The growth of farmers' markets in the Hudson Valley region has made wonderful, farm-fresh products and other local foods (cheese, meat, honey, baked goods, and much more) easily available to anyone. The markets vary from place to place, but most happen once a week between late May and October or even November, rain or shine. The opening and closing times and dates may vary seasonally—if possible, call or check the Web site in advance. The weekly markets are more than just food that you can buy from the person who made it. They're community events, often with live music and seasonal celebrations. It's something of a tradition to bring your well-behaved dog (on a leash, please) to the farmers' market. They're very welcome, but be prepared to clean up after your pet.

COLUMBIA COUNTY

Chatham
15 Church Street
(518) 392-3353
Fridays, 4:00 to 7:00 p.m., June through October

Hudson
DMV parking lot, Sixth and Columbia Streets
(518) 828-7217
Saturdays, 9:00 a.m. to 1:00 p.m., May through November

Kinderhook
Village Square
(518) 758-1232
Saturdays, 8:00 a.m. to 12:30 p.m., July through October

Stuyvesant
Historic Stuyvesant Railroad Station
(518) 758-6474
Fridays, 4:00 to 8:00 p.m., June through October

DUTCHESS COUNTY

Arlington
Vassar College Alumni House, Raymond and Collegeview Avenues
(845) 471-2770
www.arlingtonbid.com
Thursdays, 3:00 to 7:00 p.m., June through October

Beacon
Ferry dock, Beacon train station in summer; Beacon Sloop Club in winter

(845) 562-0192
Sundays, 10:00 a.m. to 4:00 p.m., May through November; Saturdays 10:00 a.m. to 4:00 p.m., December through April

Fishkill
Old Grand Union parking lot, 1004 Main Street (Route 52)
(845) 897-4430
Thursdays, 10:00 a.m. to 2:00 p.m., July through October

Hyde Park
Hyde Park Drive-In, Route 9
(845) 229-9111
Saturdays, 9:00 a.m. to 2:00 p.m., July through October

LaGrange
120–130 Stringham Road (near Town garage)
(845) 635-9168
Saturdays, 9:00 a.m. to 2:00 p.m., June through November

Millbrook
Front Street and Franklin Avenue
(845) 677-3125
www.millbrookfarmersmarket.org
Saturdays, 9:00 a.m. to 1:00 p.m., May through October

Pleasant Valley
Town Hall, Route 44
(845) 635-3918
Fridays, 3:00 to 7:00 p.m., July through November

Poughkeepsie
253 Main Street
(845) 473-1415
www.farmproject.org
Fridays, noon to 6:00 p.m., June through
October

Poughkeepsie Plaza, 2600 Route 9
(845) 471-4265
Fridays, noon to 5:00 p.m., June through
October

Rhinebeck
Municipal parking lot, East Market Street
(845) 679-7618
www.rhinebeckfarmersmarket.com
Thursdays, 3.00 to 7.00 p.m., Sundays, 10.00
a.m. to 2:00 p.m., May through November

Village of Wappingers Falls
Mesier Park, East Market Street and Route
9D
(845) 297-2837
Fridays, 3:00 to 7:00 p.m., June through
October

GREENE COUNTY

Catskill
Catskill Point (Main Street at the Hudson
River)
(518) 622-9820
Saturdays, 9:30 a.m. to 2:30 p.m., July
through October

ORANGE COUNTY

Highlands Falls
Municipal parking lot, Main Street
(845) 446-2459
Sunday, 9:00 a.m. to 2:30 p.m., July
througsh October

Newburgh
Downing Park
(845) 565-5559
Fridays, 10:00 a.m. to 5:00 p.m., July
through October

PUTNAM COUNTY

Cold Spring
44 Chestnut Street (Route 9D)
(845) 809-5167
www.csfarmmarket.org
Saturdays, 8:30 a.m. to 1:30 p.m., May
through November

ULSTER COUNTY

Highland
Village Field next to business district
(845) 691-8112
Wednesdays, 3:00 to 7:00 p.m., July through
October

Kingston
Wall Street at Old Town Stockade
(845) 338-4629
Saturdays, 9:00 a.m. to 2:00 p.m., May
through November

New Paltz
Main Street (across from Wachovia Bank)
(845) 255-6093
Sundays, 10:00 a.m. to 3:00 p.m., June
through October

Rosendale
Rosendale Recreation Center, 1055 Route 32
(845) 658-3467
Sundays, 9:00 a.m. to 2:00 p.m., June
through October

Saugerties
Main and Market Streets
(845) 246-9371
www.saugertiesfarmersmarket.com
Saturdays, 9:00 a.m. to 2:00 p.m., July
through October

Woodstock
Woodstock Farm Festival
6 Maple Lane
www.woodstockfarmfestival.com
Wednesdays, 4:00 to 8:00 p.m., end of May
to late September

blackberries, raspberries, and plums. Open daily during the growing season; call ahead to find out what's ripe and check on picking conditions.

Ghent

HAWTHORNE VALLEY FARM
327 Route 21C
(518) 672-7500
www.hawthornevalleyfarm.org
A well-established organic farm that has been producing high-quality food for more than 35 years, the nonprofit Hawthorne Valley Farm has a large farm market offering produce, baked goods, dairy products (including raw milk), and homemade sauerkraut along with a deli menu. The market is open every day from 7:30 a.m. to 7:00 p.m.; 9:00 a.m. to 5:00 p.m. on Sunday; closed on major holidays. The farm also offers community-supported agriculture shares.

LOVEAPPLE FARM
1421 Route 9H
(518) 828-5048
www.loveapplefarm.com
LoveApple is popular for both its farm stand and its u-pick operation. As the farm name suggests, apples are the big attraction here: Visitors can pick 40 varieties. They can also pick many varieties of other fruits, including pears, peaches, nectarines, plums, and cherries. The farm stand offers fruits and vegetables, famous homemade pies and other baked goods, fresh cider, and homemade ice cream. There's also a petting zoo for the kids. Open seasonally every day from 8:00 a.m. to 6:00 p.m.—call ahead to check on what's ripe for picking.

i An excellent source of up-to-date information about farms and farm markets in the region is the Farmers' Market Federation of New York, 117 Highbridge Street, Suite U-3, Fayetteville, NY 13066; 315-637-4690; www.nyfarmersmarket.com.

Hudson

FIX BROTHERS FRUIT FARM
215 White Birch Road
(518) 828-7560
www.fixbrosfruitfarm.com
Just over a century old, this fruit farm is now run by the fourth generation of the Fix family. It's well known as a regional producer, including some hard-to-find varieties, such as morello cherries. Fix is mostly a wholesale operation, and it's not certified organic. The cherry, apple, and peach orchards and pumpkin fields are open to the public for u-picking seasonally. Call ahead to find out what's ripe and for picking conditions.

Kinderhook

SAMASCOTT ORCHARDS
5 Sunset Avenue
(518) 758-7224
www.samascott.com
At Samascott the focus is apples—you can pick more than 50 different varieties of them. Also available for picking are strawberries, blueberries, raspberries, cherries, pears, plums, asparagus, and corn. The fruits and veggies are also sold at the stand, along with peaches, peas, beans, tomatoes, and peppers. Check ahead to find out what's ripe and for picking conditions. The farm stand is open daily for most of the year, but call ahead in the colder weather.

Old Chatham

OLD CHATHAM SHEEPHERDING COMPANY
155 Shaker Museum Road
(518) 794-7733
www.blacksheepcheese.com
Artisanal sheep's milk cheeses and yogurt are the product here. Open every day. Milking happens daily at 6:30 a.m. and 3:30 p.m.; cheese is made every weekday.

Valatie

GOLDEN HARVEST
3074 Route 9
(518) 758-7683
www.goldenharvestfarms.com
It's hard to miss this well-established, year-round farm stand and u-pick apple orchard—in apple season there's a huge apple balloon flying above it. The farm stand offers apples, apple cider, peaches, cherries, pumpkins, squash, and strawberries in season along with seasonal vegetables, cider donuts, and fresh baked goods. Apple picking starts in early September and runs through October. The farm stand is open every day from 9:00 a.m. to 6:00 p.m.

Dutchess County

Annandale-on-Hudson

MONTGOMERY PLACE ORCHARDS FARM MARKET
Annandale Road and Route 9G
(845) 758-5461
www.hudsonvalley.org
Produce from the orchards at historic Montgomery Place (see the Mansions and Historic Sites: East chapter for more) and from local farms is sold at this attractive farm stand. Apples, berries, peaches, plums, pears, and apricots from the orchards are available seasonally. Honey from the hives in the orchard, homemade jams, and fresh eggs are also available. Open daily June through November.

Pleasant Valley

REMSBURGER MAPLE FARM AND APIARY
756 Traver Road
(845) 635-9168
www.remsburgermaple.com
A plantation of sugar maple trees counts as a farm, at least for this chapter. Remsburger Maple Farm and Apiary produces all its own maple syrup, maple products (the maple cream is unbelievably good), honey, and honey products. The products are available at the farm and are also sold through the Web site and at local farmers' markets. The annual Maple Weekend at the end of March, when the sap is running strong, is both fun and educational, plus there's a pancake breakfast every day and they make maple cotton candy on the spot. Check in advance for the dates and times.

WIGSTEN FARM
1096 Salt Point Turnpike
(845) 635-1570
Organically grown fruits and vegetables from a third-generation family farm. The farm stand is open seasonally Monday through Friday from 10:00 a.m. to 6:00 p.m., Saturday from 9:00 a.m. to 6:00 p.m., and Sunday from 9:00 a.m. to 5:00 p.m.

Poughkeepsie

SPROUT CREEK FARM
34 Lauer Road
(845) 485-9885
www.sproutcreekfarm.org
Artisanal farmstead cheeses made from the milk of the farm's herd of grass-fed cows. Also offers educational programs. Market and creamery open Wednesday to Saturday from 10:00 a.m. to 6:00 p.m. and Sunday from 10:00 a.m. to 4:00 p.m.

Red Hook

GIGI MARKET
227 Pitcher Lane
(845) 758-1999
www.gigimarket.com
A year-round farm market offering produce from local growers, Gigi Market also offers baked goods, local meats, poultry, cheese, and other artisanal food products. The market also offers prepared foods. Because Gigi Market has the same owner as Gigi Trattoria in Rhinebeck (see the Restaurants: East chapter), the prepared dishes are very good indeed. Open daily from 9:00 a.m. to 6:00 p.m.

GREIG FARM
223 Pitcher Lane
(845) 758-1234
www.greigfarm.com

Pick your own produce here, starting with peas in mid-June and moving on to blueberries, blackberries, apples, raspberries, and pumpkins. The Greigs have been farming in Red Hook for generations. Produce from the farm is also sold at Gigi Market next door.

Rhinebeck

MIGLIORELLI FARM
Route 199 and River Road
(845) 757-3276

The farm, family-owned since 1933, is actually in Tivoli, but the produce is sold at the farm stand here as well as at the Rhinebeck and Kingston farmers' markets. Seasonal fruits and vegetables. Open May through December.

Staatsburg

BREEZY HILL ORCHARD & CIDER MILL
828 Centre Road (Route 18)
(845) 266-3979
www.hudsonvalleycider.com

Apples, more apples, and cider are the main crops at this beautiful location. Pick your own, buy them on the spot, or buy them at the Breezy Hill stand at Manhattan's Union Square Greenmarket. Open seasonally—call ahead for days and hours and to learn about special events, such as concerts.

Tivoli

AWESOME FARM
433 West Kerley Corners Road
(845) 332-2927
www.awesomefarmny.com

A new venture that got under way in 2007, Awesome Farm raises pasture-based, free-range chicken, lamb, turkey, and eggs. Meat and poultry is available by advance order only. Eggs are sold at the nearby Montgomery Place Farm Stand in Annandale-on-Hudson. Awesome Farm is on land held by Hearty Roots Farm. Visitors and volunteer workers are welcome on the farm.

MEAD ORCHARDS
Scism Road
(845) 756-5641
www.meadorchards.com

Since 1916, the 180-acre Mead Orchards has been growing apples—the kind that once made the Hudson Valley famous for fruit. The beautiful property is still family-owned, and today the Meads raise nearly 40 apple varieties, along with peaches, pears, plums, cherries, strawberries, and other berries—and also summer vegetables, winter squashes, pumpkins, and decorative gourds. From late June through October—on weekends and Monday holidays *only*—the farm is open to the public from 10:00 a.m. to 5:30 p.m. You can buy fruits and vegetables at the farm stand, or you can pick fruit and pumpkins yourself. What produce is available when is subject to a lot of variables, including how soon it's all picked, so call ahead.

Ulster County
Highland
WILKLOW ORCHARDS
341 Pancake Hollow Road
(845) 691-2339
www.wilkloworchards.com

Family-owned since 1855, Wilklow Orchards raises apples and pumpkins. The family has been participating in the Greenmarket in Brooklyn since 1984, making them agricultural pioneers of a sort. The apples and other farm products (jam, cider, baked goods, and more) are sold at the farm stand, but the real fun here comes when the apples are ready to pick. In season (Labor Day weekend through Halloween), visitors are welcome to come pick their own every day from 9:00 a.m. to 5:00 p.m. While you're there, enjoy the farm animals, picnic in the orchard, and take a hayride (weekends and holidays only). In October, come and pick your own pumpkin. Call ahead for picking conditions.

New Paltz

APPLE HILL FARM
124 Route 32 South
(845) 255-1605
www.applehillfarm.com
The farm stand here is in a restored 1859 barn. It's open to the public from August 1 through the end of October, offering homegrown peaches, fresh corn, tomatoes, and apples. The public can also come pick half a dozen apple varieties from Labor Day weekend through the end of October. Enjoy a day at the farm with hayrides, fresh apple cider, and the farm's famous apple cider donuts.

MEADOW VIEW FARM
105 Phillies Bridge Road
(845) 255-6093
Organically grown strawberries and a wide variety of other produce is available daily at the farm stand from late spring into the fall. Fresh eggs are available year-round. Meadow View also sells at the New Paltz farmers' market.

Stone Ridge

DAVENPORT FARMS
3411 Route 209
(845) 687-0051
www.davenportfarms.com
The farm stand of this family-owned operation offers a large selection of homegrown produce, including fresh strawberries, plus fresh baked goods and local products. The greenhouse offers fresh-cut flowers, perennials, and herbs. The amazing pumpkin patch is open to the public the last two weekends of October—choose your own pumpkin and pick it yourself.

STONE RIDGE ORCHARD
Route 213
(845) 687-4379
www.stoneridgeorchard.com
A 200-year-old family-owned orchard, Stone Ridge sells apples and other fruits, along with berries, heirloom vegetables, cider, homemade pies, and fruit products. Farm stand and orchards open daily from 9:00 a.m. to 6:00 p.m. In season,

pick your own apples and raspberries; hayrides, picnics, and farm tours are also available. Call ahead for hours, events, and picking conditions.

COMMUNITY-SUPPORTED AGRICULTURE

Columbia County

Kinderhook

ROXBURY FARM
2501 Route 9H
(518) 758-8558
www.roxburyfarm.com
One of the largest community-supported farms in the country, Roxbury covers 225 acres and has more than 850 shareholders. The land has been placed into conservancy and is protected and preserved for farming forever. Roxbury grows vegetables, herbs, melons, and strawberries, using only organic methods. Because the farm has so many supporters, pickups are at six sites in the Capital Region, two in Columbia County, six in Westchester County, and four in Manhattan.

Community-Supported Agriculture

CSA farms are scattered throughout the region. Many but not all also operate farm stands where non-members can buy produce; many also operate stands at nearby farmers' markets. All welcome visitors, especially those willing to help out for even an hour or two. Check ahead whenever possible for dates and times. Kids are welcome on the farm, but parents need to keep them under supervision at all times—farm equipment can be dangerous. To avoid crop damage and problems with livestock, please leave the dog at home.

A typical share provides anywhere from 10 to 17 pounds of produce each week, usually including 7 to 12 different vegetable varieties.

Dutchess County
Fishkill
COMMON GROUND FARM
Stonykill Environmental Education Center
Route 9D
(845) 831-6070
www.commongroundfarm.org
The first season at this nonprofit farm on land leased from the state-owned Stonykill Environmental Education Center was in 2002, with 60 CSA families. Today the farm has more than 160 family participants. The extra produce is sold at the farmers' markets in nearby Beacon and Fishkill. Common Ground also offers farm visits, educational tours, events, and a lot of community outreach.

Poughkeepsie
POUGHKEEPSIE FARM PROJECT
Vassar College Farm, Raymond Avenue at Hooker Avenue
(845) 473-1415
www.farmproject.org
A nonprofit organization, PFP offers tours and internships and donates between 10 and 20 percent of the produce to area shelters and food pantries. The produce is sold at the Poughkeepsie farmers' market; no sales at the farm.

Stanfordville
SISTERS HILL FARM
127 Sisters Hill Road
(845) 868-7048
www.sistershillfarm.org
Back in 1917, the Sisters of Charity were willed Hill Crest Farm in Stanfordville. The Sisters continued to run the farm and improve it until the late 1940s. The farm was left fallow until 1999, when the growing interest in community-supported agriculture brought the land back into production as the nonprofit Sisters Hill Farm. Starting with just one acre feeding 40 members and

growing to five acres feeding more than 200 families, Sisters Hill today harvests around 60,000 pounds of high-quality, organically grown produce, which works out to about 4 to 15 pounds a week of about 30 different kinds of vegetables. Pickup is at the farm or at sites in the Bronx and Hastings-on-Hudson. No sales at the farm.

Tivoli
HEARTY ROOTS COMMUNITY FARM
433 West Kerley Corners Road
(845) 943-8699
www.heartyroots.com
Hearty Roots offers a very popular CSA program with pickup sites at the farm and also in Woodstock and Brooklyn. No sales at the farm, but produce is available at the Montgomery Place Farm Market in Annandale-on-Hudson and at Gigi Market in Red Hook.

Ulster County
New Paltz
BROOK FARM PROJECT
Butterville Road
(845) 255-1052
www.brookfarmproject.org
Brook Farm is an educational, nonprofit farm on 70 beautiful acres at the foot of the Shawangunk Ridge on Mohonk Mountain House property. The farm once provided vegetables to the resort. In 2005 it was brought back into production as a CSA operation. Brook Farm raises berries, vegetables, and free-range meats and eggs, using only sustainable practices. The farm is also connected to SUNY New Paltz and serves as a farming education center demonstrating small-scale, sustainable agriculture. Educational programs are open to the public.

HUGUENOT STREET FARM
205 Huguenot Street
(845) 810-0033
www.flyingbeet.com
Located on historic Huguenot Street in the heart of New Paltz, this CSA farm uses strictly organic

methods to grow more than 125 varieties of vegetables, fruits, and cut flowers on 77 acres. Two hundred families belong and pick up their produce at the farm. No retail sales.

PHILLIES BRIDGE FARM PROJECT
45 Phillies Bridge Road
(845) 256-9108
www.philliesbridge.org
The land of Phillies Bridge Farm has been in cultivation since 1742. In 1994, 65 acres were leased from the owners; in 2003, the land was donated to the farm project and placed under a conservation easement. Today, in addition to the CSA part of the farm, Phillies Bridge also provides produce to local restaurants in the New Paltz area. Just as important on the farm are the education programs (including the weeklong summer farm camps for kids), new farmer

---

The Christmas Spirit in the Hudson Valley

Nothing gets you in the Christmas spirit more than choosing your own Christmas tree and cutting it down yourself. A number of tree farms in the region let you do just that—they even provide the saw and bale the tree for you. While you're there, you can often also buy wreaths and other holiday decorations, go for a ride in a horse-drawn wagon, and maybe even spot Santa. Cutting farms are seasonal operations and hours and conditions vary, plus they close for the year as soon as they've sold out, which could be well before Christmas Day. It's always best to call ahead. There are too many tree farms in the region to list them all here—check with the tourism offices for each county for up-to-date listings.

---

training, and environmental research activities. Members pick up their produce at the farm; nonmembers can buy it at the Health & Nutrition Center in New Paltz.

TALIAFERRO FARMS
187 Plains Road
(845) 256-1592
www.taliaferrofarms.com
Taliaferro Farms has been owned and operated by the Taliaferro family since 1995. In addition to the large CSA part, the farm also wholesales its certified organic produce to many of the region's finest restaurants, including the Culinary Institute of America. Some 120 different items from the farm are sold at the farm stand in season on Thursday from 8:00 a.m. to 7:00 p.m. and on Saturday from 9:00 a.m. to 3:00 p.m. The farm also has a booth at the Rhinebeck farmers' market.

HUDSON VALLEY WINE

Some of the many vineyards and wineries in the mid–Hudson Valley fall within the region covered by this book. The listings below cover only regional operations that make their own wine from their own grapes.

Fine wines from all over New York State are available online and at three retail locations from Vintage New York. In Manhattan, visit Vintage New York at 482 Broome Street, (212) 226-9463, or at 2492 Broadway, (212) 721-9999. In the Hudson Valley, the wines can be purchased at Rivendell Winery, 714 Albany Post Road, New Paltz, (845) 255-2494. For more info, check the Vintage New York Web site at www.vintagenewyork.com.

Uncork New York, a marketing association, provides detailed information on wineries in the region and in all of New York State. Call (585) 394-3620 or check www.newyorkwines.org.

i **Winery hours vary and are often seasonal; some wineries ask for advance reservations and have tasting fees. When planning a visit, call ahead to check.**

Dutchess County

Clinton Corners

CLINTON VINEYARDS
450 Schultzville Road
(845) 266-5372
www.clintonvineyards.com
Clinton Vineyards, founded in 1977 by Ben and Phyllis Feder, is on 100 exquisitely beautiful acres dotted with gardens, a pond, and historic Dutch barns. The 15-acre vineyard is devoted to Seyval Blanc grapes. The Feders make white wine, sparkling wines using the classic *méthode champenoise,* and a late-harvest dessert wine. They also make pure fruit dessert wines using only locally grown fruits, including an award-winning cassis. The winery and tasting room are open year-round, Thursday through Monday, noon to 6:00 p.m.; winter hours are Friday through Sunday, noon to 4:30 p.m.

Millbrook

MILLBROOK VINEYARDS AND WINERY
26 Wing Road
(845) 667-8383
www.millbrookwine.com
John Dyson, the man who created the "I ♥ New York" campaign when he was Commissioner of the New York State Department of Commerce, was also largely responsible for the 1976 legislation that made wineries financially possible in the state. In 1982 he purchased a former dairy farm and turned it into vineyards and a winery. The first commercial vintage was in 1985, and Millbrook quickly became known as the Hudson Valley's flagship winery. Today about 30 of the estate's 130 magnificent acres are planted with vines, about half of them Chardonnay. The winery produces a number of wines, including Chardonnays, Cabernets, and their own Hunt Country red. Tours are complimentary; no reservations needed. The tasting room is open every day from noon to 5:00 p.m.; 11:00 a.m. to 6:00 p.m. in the summer. The standard tasting fee is $6 per person; the reserved tasting is $15 per person.

Red Hook

ALISON WINES AND VINEYARD
231 Pitcher Lane
(845) 758-6335
www.alisonwines.com
Alison Wines and Vineyard is set on rolling farmland and fruit orchards; the winery and tasting room are in a converted 19th-century dairy barn. The wines include Seyval Blanc, Merlots, and their own Red Barn Red. Alison Wines has also

branched out into dessert wines made with local fruit, including fraise (strawberry), apple, and cassis. Hours are seasonal; open Saturdays and Sundays, 11:30 a.m. to 5:00 p.m., closed in the winter.

Ulster County
Marlboro
BENMARL WINERY AT SLATEHILL VINEYARDS
156 Highland Avenue
(845) 236-4265
www.benmarl.com
Benmarl was founded in 1957 by artist Mark Miller. Because Miller was instrumental in bringing about the Farm Winery Act that revived viticulture in the Hudson Valley, Benmarl holds license #1. Benmarl is located on 37 acres overlooking the Hudson. The winery makes reds and whites; the estate wine, made using Baco Noir, has won a number of awards. Benmarl offers a tasting room and retail sales, along with gourmet food items; special events, such as spring barrel tastings, happen often here—check ahead for dates. Open in May, Friday through Sunday, 11:00 a.m. to 5:00 p.m.; June through October daily from 11:00 a.m. to 6:00 p.m.; November through December, Friday through Sunday from 11:00 a.m. to 5:00 p.m. Closed January through April.

GLORIE FARM WINERY
40 Mountain Road
(845) 236-3265
www.gloriewine.com
Although Doug Glorie had been growing grapes in his vineyards since 1983, he only started making and selling his own wine in 2004. The winery is housed in a 1913 barn near the top of Mt. Zion, amid 54 acres of vineyards and orchards and with amazing views of the Hudson Valley. The wines are whites, including Seyval Blanc, and reds, including Cabernet and several blends. This is still a small, very personal operation, producing only 900 cases a year. Open from Memorial Day weekend through December, Saturday and Sunday, noon to 5:00 p.m.

ℹ Chatham Brewing is a new beer brewery located in Columbia County. The brewery makes British-style beers that are lively and flavorful—and very fresh. Three beers are currently made: amber ale, India pale ale, and porter. Kegs and growlers are available at the brewery; the beer is also served at a number of local restaurants in the area. For more information: Chatham Brewing, LLC, 30 Main Street, Chatham, (518) 697-0202, www.chathambrewing.com.

STOUTRIDGE VINEYARD
10 Ann Kaley Lane
(845) 236-7620
www.stoutridge.com
Grapes and fruit trees have been grown on the slopes of Stoutridge Vineyard for more than 200 years. Wine was first made here in 1902, but production ceased with Prohibition; it began again (leaving aside some illegal brandy production in the 1950s) in 2001 when owners Stephen Osborn and Kimberly Wagner bought the property. Since then, they've restored the old farmhouse and vineyards and installed a state-of-the-art, gravity-flow, solar-powered winery on the foundation of the original winery. The wines here are Germanic-style whites and Northern Italian–style reds. Open year-round, Friday through Sunday, 11:00 a.m. to 6:00 p.m.

New Paltz
ADAIR VINEYARDS
52 Allhusen Road
(845) 255-1377
www.adairwine.com
Since 1987, Adair Vineyards has been growing Seyval Blanc, Vignoles, Foch, and Millot grapes on 10 acres overlooking the scenic Shawangunk Mountains. They currently produce more than 20,000 bottles of estate-grown red and white wine every year. Open in May, Friday through Sunday from 11:00 a.m. to 5:00 p.m.; June through October daily from 11:00 a.m. to 6:00 p.m.; November through mid-December,

ⓘ Back in 2002, a change in state law made it financially possible for small distillers to operate in New York. One result is Tuthilltown Spirits (14 Gristmill Lane, Gardiner, 845-633-8284, www.tuthilltown .com), which produces a line of Hudson Valley whiskies and vodkas using local ingredients. The distillery is in a converted granary next to the historic Tuthilltown 1788 gristmill (no longer in operation) in the Ulster County town of Gardiner. Visitors welcome, but call ahead. State law prohibits sale of the spirits at the distillery; there's a list of retail outlets on the Web site.

Friday through Sunday from 11:00 a.m. to 5:00 p.m. Closed January through April.

RIVENDELL WINERY
714 Albany Post Road
(845) 255-2494
www.rivendellwine.com

Fifteen varietal wines under the Rivendell and Soho Cellars label are grown here on 50 beautiful acres. The landscaped property has a glass-enclosed tasting room with spectacular views out over the Wallkill Valley. Tastings offer not just the award-winning Rivendell wines but also boutique wines from all over New York State through the Vintage New York program. In addition to tastings, Rivendell offers many events, such as its annual May Fruit Wine Faire. Check ahead for schedules. The winery is open every day year-round, 10:00 a.m. to 6:00 p.m.

SHOPPING: EAST SIDE OF THE HUDSON

For people who love to shop, the east side of the Hudson is a great place to find all sorts of interesting and unusual stores. What makes shopping here especially interesting is that the towns with plenty of fun retail stores also tend to be the towns with lots of other interesting establishments like antiques stores (covered in the Antiquing chapter) and galleries (covered in the Art in the Valley chapter). The stores in towns like Hudson, Rhinebeck, and Cold Spring are owned by local businesspeople—there are no chain stores or big boxes in these towns—and shoppers get a big welcome and personal attention. The Poughkeepsie area has several large malls anchored by major department stores, most notably The Galleria and the South Hills Mall, both located on South Road (Route 9).

Not every one of the great retailers in the region can be included in this book. To keep this section to a manageable length, the focus here is on well established stores that carry merchandise that's interesting and different—it's specialized, unusual, unique, locally made, or perhaps just hard to find. Some outstanding bakeries, chocolatiers, and even an Italian deli are included here, but see the Farm Markets and Wineries chapter for more on shopping for local produce and wine.

As a general rule, the shops listed here are open every day. Exceptions are noted. Hours can vary considerably, and days and hours may change with the seasons. Check ahead if possible.

COLUMBIA COUNTY

Chatham

AMERICAN PIE
41 Main Street
(518) 392-6632
You might not realize that you really need a kiwi slicer until you've been browsing the eclectic and entertaining aisles of American Pie for a while, but that's what makes this modern-day general store fun. The focus here is mostly on attractive, practical, and affordable kitchenware and tableware, including the full Le Creuset line, but there's also a great selection of unusual gifts and hard-to-find household items.

> **i** Clothing and shoe purchases of $110 and under are exempt from the 4 percent New York State sales tax; county taxes may still apply.

BERKSHIRE BOOKS
2 Park Row, 2nd floor
(518) 392-2052
www.berkshirebooks.com
Good stock of carefully selected used, rare, and out-of-print books and CDs. Categories include modern firsts, cooking, art, sports, gardening, and collectible children's books. Open Weekends from 11:00 a.m. to 5:00 p.m. Look for the green and white BOOKS flag.

CHATHAM BOOKSTORE, LTD.
27 Main Street
(518) 392-4098
A full-service independent bookstore with more than 8,000 titles in stock, including a very good children's section.

THE CHOCOLATE MOOSE
34 Main Street
(518) 392-8732
www.chocolatemoosetreats.com
Handcrafted candies ranging from classics such as almond bark, creams and caramels, and truffles to new inventions such as chocolate-covered Oreos. Ask about the store's line of adult-only chocolates! Sugar-free, vegan, and kosher chocolates, all made on the premises, are also available.

COW JONES INDUSTRIALS
5 Main Street
(518) 392-2139
www.cowjonesindustrials.com
At this vegan boutique, style and fashion are hip and animal- and earth-friendly. The store carries leather-free and cruelty-free handbags, shoes, belts, jewelry, cosmetics, and accessories (including guitar straps) for both men and women. Closed Tuesday.

MADO PATISSERIE
10 Main Street
(518) 683-1649
Madeline Delosh, who learned her craft under legendary chef Jean-Georges Vongerichten, opened her patisserie in 2008. Her assorted tarts, muffins, scones, and other pastries were an immediate hit with locals and visitors alike. Come early—the shop is open Thursday through Sunday from 10:00 a.m. and closes when the stock of the day sells out.

MULTI-KIDS
1 Main Street
(518) 392-4868
www.multikidstoys1.com
Located in the historic clock tower in the center of Chatham, Multi-Kids specializes in quality toys for girls and boys. This is local headquarters for Lego lovers. The store carries a number of well-known lines, including Corolle Dolls, Douglas Plush, Only Hearts Club Dolls, ThinkFun, Toysmith, and Wild Planet Spy Gear. Closed Tuesday.

Claverack
LOOMIS CREEK NURSERY
29 Van Deusen Road
(518) 851-9801
www.loomiscreek.com
More than 600 different garden plants are sold here, including perennials, shrubs and vines, ornamental grasses, ferns, and annuals. In addition to all the usual standards, this nursery offers many plants that are distinctive and contemporary—this is a nursery for adventurous gardeners. Closed Monday.

Ghent
RED MAPLE BOOKS
1198 Route 21C
(518) 672-4050
www.redmaplebooks.com
Set in a 150-year-old schoolhouse, Red Maple Books offers fine books for adults, teens, and kids. The store offers a full selection of Penguin Classics, along with a good selection of anthroposophical literature (the Hawthorne Valley Waldorf School is nearby), poetry, and art. Also for sale are fine chocolates, candles, and greeting cards. Closed Sunday and Monday.

Hudson
CASA URBANA BOUTIQUE AND SALON
11 South Sixth Street
(518) 828-2690
The boutique offers a comprehensive selection of bath and body products, including products from Caswell-Massey, Thymes, Claus Porto, Jack Black, and Lafco Home. Closed Wednesday.

CÔTÉ FAMILLE
621 Warren Street
(518) 828-1391
Fair trade clothes, accessories, and toys for kids. The store offers American and European clothing by John Bourget, Oeuf, Tea, Hatley, and others, along with Diaper Dude bags and eco-friendly gifts. Footwear here isn't just for kids—grown-ups will find fun shoes as well.

COUNTRYWOOL
59 Spring Road
(518) 828-4554
www.countrywool.com
Knitting and spinning supplies, including knitting patterns and kits, yarns and fibers, and needles and notions. Classes are also offered. This store is out in the country—call or check the Web site for directions. Closed Sunday through Wednesday.

DE MARCHIN MEN AND WOMEN'S WEAR
620 Warren Street
(518) 828-2657
European and American designer clothing and footwear, including Scotch & Soda, Velvet, IKKS, Gant, and American Apparel. Premium denim from Meltin Pot, AG, and 7 for All Mankind—plus Cosabella lingerie.

FACE STOCKHOLM
401 Warren Street
(518) 828-2657
www.facestockholm.com
The Hudson outpost of the famed Swedish cosmetics and skin-care company is located in a historic building that was once the site of Martin Van Buren's law office. The store is staffed with professional makeup artists and offers the full line of FACE products. There's another store in Rhinebeck.

HEDSTRÖM & JUDD
401 Warren Street
(518) 671-6131
www.hedstrom-judd.com
The light and elegant home furnishings sold here have a strong Scandinavian influence. The store features furniture, bedding, linens, Swedish throws and rugs, ceramics, new and old art prints, and wall fountains. Furniture lines sold here include Cote d'Ivoire, Swedish Blonde, and Allinwood. Closed Tuesday and Wednesday.

HUDSON CITY BOOKS
553 Warren Street
(518) 671-6020
Hudson City Books specializes in rare and collectible books and modern first editions, but this store also has a good general selection of gently used books.

HUDSON HOME
356 Warren Street
(518) 822-8120
www.hudson-home.com
Specializing in classic high-end home furnishings, Hudson Home offers a wide range of beautifully crafted furniture, lighting, linens, floor treatments, and more. The goal is contemporary furnishings suitable for comfortable country living.

KNOTTY WOODPECKER
318 Warren Street
(518) 828-2650
www.knottywoodpeckerinfo.com
The retail store for the Knotty Woodpecker line of men's and women's lounge wear, sleepwear, and underwear—fun, stylish, and somewhat eccentric apparel meant for keeping warm during country weekends.

LOUNGE
535 Warren Street
(518) 822-0113
The Hudson branch of this home furnishings store; see High Falls (page 205) for more information.

OLDE HUDSON
434 Warren Street
(518) 828-6923
www.oldehudson.com
Specialty foods, including an outstanding selection of cheeses both from local producers and from around the world. The store also carries an extensive selection of bath and body products.

ORNAMENTUM
306½ Warren Street
(518) 671-6770
www.ornamentumgallery.com
Ornamentum is an outstanding gallery of international contemporary art jewelry. The pieces here are unusual and unique—they're serious wearable art, sold at serious prices. The jewelry

comes from America and Europe, with a heavy representation of German artisans. The gallery is open Thursday through Monday; other days by appointment. The gallery is sometimes closed during out-of-town exhibitions—call in advance.

SPOTTY DOG BOOKS & ALE
440 Warren Street
(518) 671-6006
www.thespottydog.com

There are a surprising number of interesting independent bookstores in the mid–Hudson Valley, but there's none quite like this. It's definitely the only bookstore in the region (perhaps in the country) where you can drink a beer while you browse. You can also get wine, soda, juice, and, of course, coffee, but the beers here are from the outstanding Pump Station brewpub in Albany and from local brewers and are well worth sampling. The store is in a restored old firehouse and carries about 10,000 titles, including a good selection of local writers and books of local interest.

VASILOW'S CONFECTIONERY, INC.
741 Columbia Street
(518) 828-2717
www.vasilows.com

Vasilow's was a beloved local landmark from 1923 to 1969, when Louie and Jim, the brothers who founded the store, finally retired. The family confectionery tradition didn't die out, however, and in 2002 Louie's grandson reopened the store, bringing back many of the family's proprietary recipes. This is the place for old-fashioned favorites such as almond butter crunch, tangy fruit slices, peanut brittle, truffles, and marzipan. The store also offers a good selection of hard-to-find licorice candies from around the world.

VERDIGRIS ART & TEA
13 South Third Street
(518) 828-3139
www.verdigristea.com

More a gallery than a tea shop (though this is a great place for a tea break after a hard afternoon of antiquing), Verdigris features teas, herbs, and spices from around world, sold by the ounce. The gallery showcases handcrafted tea ware and a wide range of tea-related art, gifts, and books. Closed Tuesday.

WHITE RICE
531 Warren Street
(518) 697-3500
www.white-rice.com

White Rice features women's clothing made with gorgeous hand-dyed batik fabrics from Bali, along with clothing and accessories for men, women, and children. In addition to clothing, the store also offers Asian-themed home furnishings, antique Javanese furniture, and furnishings made from reclaimed teak.

DUTCHESS COUNTY

Beacon

ALPS SWEET SHOP
269 Main Street
(845) 831-8240
www.alpssweetshop.com

A third-generation chocolate shop, Alps Sweet Shop dates back to 1922. The handmade chocolates here come in a dizzying variety, including chocolate-dipped potato chips (surprisingly good, along the lines of chocolate-dipped pretzels) and many intriguing truffle flavors. The signature house confection is the fabulous Signal Fire Butter Crunch, made with butter, sugar, and almonds. The recipe supposedly dates back to Revolutionary War soldiers on Mt. Beacon guarding the Hudson Valley from the British. Second location: 1054 Main Street, Fishkill, (845) 896-8080.

BEACON ART SUPPLY
506 Main Street
(845) 440-7904
www.beaconartsupply.com

Providing supplies to the burgeoning community of artists in Beacon is a big job. Beacon Art Supply stocks a full range of high-quality artists' supplies in a wide variety of media. The store also carries a good line of art materials for kids. Closed Tuesday.

BEACON BARKERY
192 Main Street
(845) 440-7652
www.beaconbarkery.com
Beacon Barkery offers special treats for your furry best friends. The treats are healthy choices prepared with human-grade ingredients and no sugar, chocolate, or unsafe additives. Dogs love the Peanut Butter Puppies and Tail Bangers; cats enjoy Bonita Flakes and other seafood treats. The store also carries accessories and toys for pets. The owners are very active in community support for animal rescue and aid organizations. Closed Monday.

FIRE LOTUS
474 Main Street
(845) 235-0461
www.thefirelotus.com
Specializing in handmade crafts from northern Thailand, Fire Lotus offers fine jewelry, handbags, apparel, paper products, and folk art, all personally selected by the owners.

HUDSON BEACH GLASS
162 Main Street
(845) 440-0068
www.hudsonbeachglass.com
The work of four local glass artisans and also that of contemporary glass artists from around the world are featured at this gallery, located in an old firehouse. Functional glass objects such as bowls, serving platters, trays, jars, and soap dishes are for sale, usually in your choice of 14 colors. The glassblowing demonstration studio is well worth a visit to see the modern approach to the ancient craft of glassblowing.

HUDSON VALLEY PACK & PADDLE
45 Beekman Street
(845) 831-1300
www.hvpackandpaddle.com
Canoes, kayaks, and paddling equipment are the main theme here, but Hudson Valley Pack & Paddle also carries a good selection of gear for hiking, climbing, mountaineering, and camping. The store location is very close to Beacon's Riverfront Park, making it easy to take a test paddle.

MOUNTAIN TOPS OUTDOORS
144 Main Street
(845) 831-1997
www.mountaintopsonline.com
A hiker's paradise, Mountain Tops Outdoors offers a great selection of outdoor apparel and gear—you can even outfit your dog for the trail. The store carries all the top brands, with perhaps the best shoe and hiking boot selection in the region.

PEARL DADDY
183 Main Street
(845) 765-0169
www.pearldaddy.net
A boutique jeweler specializing in traditional and contemporary freshwater pearl jewelry, Pearl Daddy is also an art gallery exhibiting the work of regional artists. The jewelry end also offers custom design, pearl restringing, and repair. Closed Monday and Tuesday.

Fishkill
JOE'S ITALIAN MARKETPLACE
1083 Route 9
Lawrence Farms Plaza
(845) 297-1100
www.joesmarketplace.com
Joe's Italian Marketplace carries one of the broadest selections of imported and domestic Italian specialties in the region. Bread from the Arthur Avenue bakery in the Bronx is delivered daily—and the fresh mozzarella is homemade. The deli offers a wide variety of fresh sausages, stuffed breads, foccacia, and other home-style specialties. There's also an excellent selection of cheeses, including some hard-to-find Italian imports.

Hopewell Junction
SABELLICO GREENHOUSES AND FLORIST
33 Hillside Lake Road
(845) 226-5943
www.sabellico.com

A local fixture since 1950, Sabellico grows premium-quality plants and flowers in an extensive greenhouse complex. Vegetables, flowers, herbs, perennials, shrubs, roses, tropicals, house plants, and seasonal potted plants such as Easter lilies and poinsettias are all available. There's a good selection of aquatic plants, which are hard to find in the region. Sabellico also carries a full line of home, lawn, and garden supplies. Hours are seasonal; check ahead.

Hyde Park

THE KITCHEN DRAWER
4068 Albany Post Road
(845) 229-2300
As you might expect from a store located near the famed Culinary Institute of America, The Kitchen Drawer has an outstanding selection of kitchenware and one of the largest selections of top-quality knives in the region. Professional knife sharpening is available on the premises.

Millbrook

ARROWSMITH FOR THE HOME
3275 Franklin Avenue
(845) 677-5057
www.arrowsmithforge.com
Arrowsmith Forge is well known in the furniture world for steel manufacturing. Arrowsmith for the Home lets the general public share in what is usually available only to the design trade. The retail store showcases gifts for the home, Arrowsmith chandeliers and other steel products, and decorative accessories from the Hudson Valley and beyond.

KEEPER'S MARKET
3293 Franklin Avenue
(845) 677-0740
An unusual and whimsical shop, Keeper's Market specializes in gourmet foods, high-end coffees and teas, and old-fashioned candy. The store creates amazing custom gift baskets.

MERRITT BOOKSTORE
57 Front Street
(845) 677-5857
www.merrittbooks.com
Family owned and operated, Merritt Bookstore is a Millbrook institution and an outstanding example of what an independent bookstore should be. The store carries an excellent selection of current books and classics, along with a great kids' section and many titles of local interest. The Hudson Valley has a number of well-known writers, and it often seems as if every one of them has appeared at Merritt—there's a book signing here almost every week. The store sponsors and provides meeting space for a number of local book clubs. The helpful staff knows most customers by name, giving this store a great small-town feel. The staff will happily order any book not in stock—most orders arrive within a day or two. Second location: 7496 Broadway, Red Hook, (845) 758-BOOK.

MINNIE'S MEMORIES
59 Front Street
(845) 677-0700
www.minniesmemories.com
Minnie's Memories carries a full line of miniatures and dollhouse products, including dollhouse kits, furnishings, housewares, hardware, and, of course, dolls. The store even carries some products for boys. Classes and workshops are offered—you can even have a children's birthday party here. Call ahead for hours.

A NEW LEAF
2986 Church Street (Route 199)
(518) 398-6607
The name's a little misleading, because this bookstore has more than 10,000 used books under one historic roof. New books aren't anywhere in sight, although this is a good spot to pick up former best sellers cheap.

PINE PLAINS
Hammertown Barn
3201 Route 199
(518) 398-7075
www.hammertownbarn.com

An award-winning home and lifestyle store, Hammertown Barn features Lee Furniture and Mitchell Gold + Bob Williams furniture, lighting, kitchenware (including Fishs Eddy glassware and dishware), rugs, bedding, antiques, and an array of housewares. There's a second location in Rhinebeck (and also one in Great Barrington, Massachusetts).

Poughkeepsie

ADAMS FAIRACRE FARMS
765 Dutchess Turnpike (Route 44)
(845) 454-4330
www.adamsfarms.com
Adams Fairacre Farms began as a roadside farm stand in Poughkeepsie back in 1919. It's grown over the decades into a well-known upscale grocery, with high-quality meats, seafood, cheese, baked goods, gourmet products, and an excellent choice of local foods and locally grown produce. Still run by family members, Adams is also famed for its garden center, which features homegrown plants and nursery stock.

BARNES & NOBLE BOOKSELLERS
2518 South Road (Route 9)
(845) 485-2224
www.barnesandnoble.com
Located in the Post Road Plaza right across the road from IBM, this branch of Barnes & Noble is a stand-alone store on two floors. Story time for kids happens on Tuesday and Thursday mornings; a number of local groups and book clubs meet at the store in the evenings. Open every day, 9:00 a.m. to 11:00 p.m.

CATSKILL ART AND OFFICE SUPPLY
800 Main Street
(845) 452-1250
www.catskillart.com
The Poughkeepsie branch of Catskill Art is in a new 10,000-square-foot building near Vassar College. The store carries a wide selection of discount art and office supplies and offers complete copy services (including large-format scans) and custom picture framing. The original store is in

Woodstock; there's another branch in Kingston.

THE DREAMING GODDESS
9 Collegeview Avenue
(845) 473-2206
www.dreaminggoddess.com
Tools for spiritual awareness are for sale here, including hundreds of tarot decks and lots of candles, crystals, incense, silver jewelry, and ritual and shamanic items. This is also probably the only place in the region to carry a full line of belly dance garb.

HUDSON VALLEY GOURMET
2600 South Road (Poughkeepsie Plaza Mall)
(845) 485-3507
www.hvgourmet.com
Fine food products from artisans in the Hudson Valley are gathered here. Many of these producers don't have retail shops, so this is a great place to discover new tastes. The store carries baked goods, pickles, sauces, jams and jellies, nuts, candy, and many other locally made gourmet products. The staff will help assemble your choice of products into a gorgeous gift basket and ship it anywhere in the United States.

MERRIWEATHER'S
39 LaGrange Avenue
(845) 454-5566
www.merriweathers.com
Located near Vassar College, Merriweather's sells their own lines of fine handcrafted soaps and all-natural creams, oils, salts, bath products, and skin-care products. Choose your favorite scent or customize your own. There's a second store in Rhinebeck. Open Wednesday through Saturday.

THREE ARTS
3 Collegeview Avenue
(845) 471-3640
A small but excellent bookstore aimed primarily at the Vassar community, Three Arts carries a wide range of titles and has a surprisingly good kids' section. The helpful staff knows the stock well and will special order any title. The store

has been here since 1946 and is the only locally owned independent bookstore in and around Poughkeepsie.

ZIMMER BROTHERS
39 Raymond Avenue
(845) 454-6369
www.zimmerbrothers.com
Owned and operated by the same family since 1893, Zimmer Brothers is one of the region's most distinguished jewelers—the place to go for Rolex watches, among other things. Diamonds are a major specialty here, but there's also a very wide selection of other jewels. Closed Sunday and Monday.

Red Hook

BASIC FRENCH
5 East Market Street
(845) 758-0399
www.basicfrenchonline.com
Basic French, as the name suggests, is a boutique carrying simple, classic products from France. The products sold here are very French—they're functional yet beautiful. The stock varies, but this is a great place to find unique housewares, linens, toiletries, soaps, sleepwear, stationery, and clothes for kids.

BEAD SPRING
7 West Market Street
(845) 758-9037
www.beadspring.net
A full-service bead store, Bead Spring offers a wide and eclectic selection of collectible, unusual, ethnic, and ancient beads, as well as contemporary beads at very fair prices. The store also offers beginning and advanced bead classes and workshops.

CONSCIOUS LIVING
7490 South Broadway
(845) 758-4383
www.consciousliving-hudsonvalley.com
Conscious Living sells fair-trade and sweatshop-free clothing, housewares, and accessories. The store also carries organic mattresses and box springs, along with a full assortment of beautiful organic cotton and hemp bedding. Closed Sunday, Monday, and Tuesday.

GIGI MARKET
227 Pitcher Lane
(845) 758-1999
www.gigimarket.com
Gigi Market is a year-round indoor farmers' market carrying a wide selection of products from local farmers and artisans. (The products sold here are the same used for the fabulous dishes at Gigi Trattoria in Rhinebeck—see the Restaurants: East chapter for details.) Prepared foods and baked goods to go are also available. The cafe serves paninis, salads, and thin-crust pizza. It's a good lunch spot—you can enjoy views of the scenic 500-acre Greig Farm property while you eat.

GRANDIFLORA GARDEN CENTER
144 Pitcher Lane
(845) 758-2020
Well stocked with annuals, perennials, herbs, trees, and shrubs (many homegrown), Grandiflora also offers a good selection of garden tools and accessories in a spacious, rural setting.

HOOKED ON DOGS
The Chocolate Factory
54 Elizabeth Street
(845) 758-BARK
www.hookedondogs.net
Natural products for dogs, including organic foods, along with a comprehensive line of equipment for canine athletes, fun toys, and a unique collection of collars, leashes, and accessories. The store also offers the area's only self-service dog wash.

J.B. PEEL, INC.
7582 North Broadway
(800) 231-7372
www.jbpeelcoffee.com
J.B. Peel makes one of the best cups of coffee in the Hudson Valley, but this isn't really a

coffeehouse—it's a store selling wonderful small-batch, freshly roasted coffee beans, a variety of interesting teas (including homemade flavored teas), and accompaniments to caffeine, such as biscotti and chocolate-covered espresso beans. Closed Sunday.

MERRITT BOOKSTORE II
7496 South Broadway
(845) 758-BOOK
www.merrittbooks.com
The Red Hook outpost of the Merritt Bookstore in Millbrook. Same great selection, friendly staff, and excellent service.

Rhinebeck
BREAD ALONE
45 East Market Street
(845) 876-3108
www.breadalone.com
Bread Alone is a famed European-style bakery located in Boiceville in the Catskills, a bit out of the range of this book. The Rhinebeck branch sells the bakery's traditional handcrafted, hearth-baked breads made using organic grains. The cafe part offers sandwiches, soups, and pastries. There's another branch in Woodstock.

CABIN FEVER OUTFITTERS
6423 Montgomery Street
(845) 876-6005
Clothing and accessories for the active outdoor lifestyle. This is a good source for gear from well-known manufacturers such as Patagonia, North Face, Marmot, Keen, and Mountain Hard Wear.

CESARE AND LILLI
6384 Mill Street
(845) 876-4009
Designer boutique for women, carrying clothing from Velvet, Calypso, Trina Turk, and Norma Kamali, a great selection of jeans, and T-shirts from Zooey, Grassroots, and others.

CHANGES
6422 Montgomery Street
(845) 876-1345
www.changesformen.com
Relaxed clothing for men, ranging from sweat pants to suits. The second home of the original store in Woodstock.

DR. TOM'S TONICS
6384 Mill Street
(845) 876-2900
Dr. Tom Francescott is a Board-certified naturopathic doctor, trained at the world-famous Bastyr University. His store is a modern-day apothecary filled with high-end natural products, supplements, and remedies for achieving maximum wellness. Dr. Tom or one of his colleagues is there at the shop to answer questions.

FACE STOCKHOLM
47 East Market Street
(845) 876-2200
The Rhinebeck branch of FACE; see the Hudson store listing for details.

FOUR WINDS
6423 Montgomery Street
(845) 876-8711
www.fourwindsathome.com
Unique handcrafted furniture and decorative accessories for the home, mostly imported from Southeast Asia, along with rugs and decorative lighting. The original store is in Stone Ridge.

HALDORA
28 East Market Street
(845) 876-6250
Haldora's exclusive designs are hand sewn at the shop, with the focus on style, comfort, and quality. Complementary clothing lines sold at Haldora include Hanro, Gentle Souls, Arche, and Margaret O'Leary.

HAMMERTOWN BARN
6423 Montgomery Street
(845) 876-1450
www.hammertown.com
The Rhinebeck branch of the Pine Plains home furnishings store.

HUMMINGBIRD JEWELERS
20 West Market Street
(845) 876-4585
www.hummingbirdjewelers.com
Master goldsmith Bruce Anderson crafts fine gold and diamond jewelry here, creating custom designs and also doing antique restoration and remounting. The spacious, attractive store showcases a rotating collection of fine designer jewelry. Closed Tuesday.

IDENTITIES
24 East Market Street
(845) 876-6607
www.identitiesforwoman.com
Clothing, jewelry, and accessories for women, featuring attire by Cut Loose, Bryn Walker, Pacific Cotton, and Maya Papaya and bags from Ten Bags, Erda, and VHeart.

JOOVAY
6423 Montgomery Street, Suite 4
(845) 876-8707
www.joovay.com
Elegant daywear, lounge wear, and intimate wear for women. The brands carried here include Spanx, Bedhead, Betsey Johnson, Gemma, La Perla, Hanky Panky, Kiyomi, Joelle, and Underwriters. The staff here are very knowledgeable and helpful.

KIDDLYDIVY
4 Garden Street
(845) 876-7959
A children's boutique with a great selection—lots of well-made toys, treats, and gifts, plus clothing for special occasions. Good selection of clothing for newborns up to size 10, including Zutano and Sweet Potatoes.

LAND OF OZ
41 East Market Street
(845) 876-1918
Toys for people of all ages but mostly kids. Lots of inventive toys from top manufacturers, including figurines and kits from Playmobil and Haba games and toys. If your kid just has to have the latest Webkinz critter or trading cards, this is the place. Closed Tuesday and Wednesday.

MERRIWEATHER'S
6402 Montgomery Street
(845) 876-8222
www.merriweathers.com
Merriweather's own line of handcrafted natural soaps and skin-care products is sold here, along with accessories, gifts, and handmade jewelry. This the Rhinebeck branch; the original store is in Poughkeepsie.

NORTHERN DUTCHESS BOTANICAL GARDENS
389 Salisbury Turnpike
(845) 876-2953
www.ndbgonline.com
Located in the most rural and beautiful part of Rhinebeck, North Dutchess Botanical Gardens is worth a visit for the drive there alone. The plants here are outstanding—there's an excellent variety of annuals, vegetables, and herbs. The perennial selection is large and varied and includes many shade plants. Hours are seasonal—call ahead.

NO SUGAR
41 East Market Street
(845) 876-6040
Hip clothes and accessories for babies and kids. Lots of fun rock 'n' roll T-shirts to start your kid on the path to indie stardom.

NO SUGAR WOMAN
6423 Montgomery Row, Suite 9
(845) 876-6050
The sister (or is that parent?) store to No Sugar. Moms need hip clothes and accessories too.

OBLONG BOOKS AND MUSIC
6422 Montgomery Street
(845) 876-0500
www.oblongbooks.com
The well-established parent store for Oblong Books and Music is based in Millerton, outside the region covered by this book. In Rhinebeck the store carries a good selection of books and CDs, welcomes special orders, and has a wide selection of regional-interest titles. Local authors often give readings and sign books—check the Web site for the calendar.

OLIVER KITA FINE CONFECTIONS
Astor Square
6815 Route 9
(845) 876-2665
www.oliverkita.com
A boutique chocolatier, Oliver Kita Fine Confections provides a stunning selection of handmade confections. Each individual chocolate is visually beautiful, like a little work of art. The visual pleasure gives way to an amazingly sensual taste pleasure when the rich organic chocolates are eaten. The flavors are subtle and unusual—black currant, fig, essence of passionflower, blood orange, and even smoky lapsang souchong tea. Gorgeous gift boxes are available and can be shipped anywhere. Visitors to the store can watch the chocolates being made. Hours are usually Wednesday through Saturday, 11:00 a.m. to 6:00 p.m., but the store is open additional hours before major holidays—call in advance.

PAPER TRAIL
6423 Montgomery Street, Suite 6
(845) 876-8050
www.papertrailrhinebeck.com
Paper Trail is an emporium for fine paper, custom invitations, and personalized stationery, along with an eclectic assortment of gift items. The store also carries a good selection of unusual and one-of-a-kind jewelry.

PET COUNTRY
6830 Route 9
(845) 876-9000
An outstanding selection of foods, accessories, and equipment for pets of all sorts, including supplies for birds, small animals, and aquariums. Horse and farm feeds are also available.

THE PHANTOM GARDENER
6837 Route 9
(845) 876-8606
www.thephantomgardener.com
All you need for an organic, sustainable garden is here at The Phantom Gardener. Everything from seeds to annuals and perennials to trees is sold here, along with a great selection of gardening books, garden hand tools, pottery, statuary, furniture, and other great garden essentials, such as bird feeders and stone Buddhas. The store offers an extensive series of workshops by expert gardeners—check the Web site for the schedule.

PIQUE BOUTIQUE
43 East Market Street
(845) 876-7722
Where the local fashionistas go for hip designer clothing from Seven for All Mankind, Juicy Couture, Revolver Los Angeles, True Religion, Ella Moss, and others.

RHINEBECK ARTIST'S SHOP
56 East Market Street
(845) 876-4922
www.rhinebeckart.com
Four floors of reasonably priced fine art materials, plus a good selection of cards and gifts for the artists in your life. Professional framing is available on the premises.

RHINEBECK DEPARTMENT STORE
1 East Market Street
(845) 876-5500
www.rhinebeckstore.com
Located in the heart of the village, Rhinebeck Department Store carries a strong line of high-quality attire for men and women. The classics are always in style here. Brands carried include Pendleton, Woolrich, Fresh Produce, Levis, Sarah Arizona, Columbia Sportswear, and Rainforest. A good selection of sportswear, outerwear, and

accessories rounds out the stock. The store is locally famous for sales—check the Web site.

RHINEBECK HEALTH FOODS
24 Garden Street
(845) 876-2555

Locally owned and operated, Rhinebeck Health Foods offers fresh organic produce from nearby farms, domestic and imported cheeses, and a good selection of bulk foods and herbs. The store also carries a wide range of dietary supplements along with green household supplies and personal products. The Garden Street Café in the store serves homemade organic and vegan-friendly soups, salads, sandwiches, and hot dishes.

A.L. STICKLE VARIETY STORE
13 East Market Street
(845) 876-3206

An old-fashioned store in an old-fashioned village, the Stickle Store, as it's called by locals, carries everything you need and can't find anywhere else—toys, housewares, sewing and craft supplies, notions, yarns and patterns, tools, paper products, and much more. Family-owned for more than 50 years, the Stickle Store is pleasantly cluttered. If you don't have time to browse for what you need, ask the staff—they can put their hands on anything in the store instantly.

WARREN KITCHEN AND CUTLERY
6934 Route 9
(845) 876-6208
www.warrenkitchentools.com

The best selection in the Hudson Valley for fine cutlery, professional cookware, appliances, serving pieces, and kitchen tools. The store carries unusual and rare knives from around the world and offers professional sharpening on the premises. Also available are an extensive selection of Cuisinart products, the full Le Creuset cookware line, and a selection of fine teas, coffees, spices, chocolates, and related equipment. Cooking classes and demonstrations are offered regularly—call or check the Web site for the schedule.

WINTER SUN AND SUMMER MOON
10 and 14 East Market Street
(845) 876-3555

Two stores side by side, Winter Sun carries unusual gifts and clothing from around the world, while the sister store Summer Moon carries gifts, personal care items, jewelry, and lifestyle accessories. Both stores are great for browsing, with lots of interesting items and an international feel.

Tivoli

BEADZO
60 Broadway
(845) 757-5306

An eclectic collection of ethnic, vintage, and collectible beads drawn from around the word, including selections from Tibet, Africa, and Asia. Open Thursday, Friday, Saturday, and Sunday; other times by appointment.

VILLAGE BOOKS OF TIVOLI
48 Broadway
(845) 757-BOOK
www.village-books.com

A really enjoyable general bookstore with more than 30,000 new, used, and out-of-print titles. Specialties include art and architecture, the Roosevelts, labor studies and radicalia, and New York, especially the Hudson Valley. Hours are Wednesday through Sunday, 1:00 to 8:00 p.m.

Wappingers Falls

LAVENDAR'S BLUE
Summerlin West Plaza
946 Route 376
(845) 227-3329
www.lavendarsblue.com

At this children's boutique, the clothing is hip, fun, comfy, and eco-conscious—most of the clothing here is made following fair trade principles and using certified organic all-cotton fabrics. Brands carried here include Kate Quinn Organic, Kaos Recycled, Oeuf, Folkmania, and Ugly Dolls. Open every day; seasonal Sunday hours.

MADINA PARK BOUTIQUE
Summerlin West Plaza
946 Route 376
(845) 223-6103
www.madinapark.com
A premiere women's clothing boutique, Madina Park carries signature pieces from leading designers such as Ann Paul, Sweet Pea, Robert Rodriguez, and Rachel Pally. The store also carries many jeans lines, including True Religion, Blue Cult, and Citizens of Humanity. The service is personal and comfortable, which makes shopping here a relaxing experience.

PUTNAM COUNTY

Cold Spring

ARCHIPELAGO AT HOME
119 Main Street
(845) 265-3992
www.archipelagoathome.com
Home furnishings and unique gift items, including an outstanding selection of elegant glassware, from artisans around the world.

ART TO WEAR
75 Main Street
(845) 265-4469
www.staleygretzinger.com
Art to Wear is the retail outlet for the women's clothing line created in 1986 by designers Meg Staley and Jerry Gretzinger. All Art to Wear clothing is handcrafted in workshops in Brooklyn and nearby Wappingers Falls. The artisans use silkscreen, hand-painted block prints, hand-dyed fabrics, and fabric appliqué techniques. Art to Wear clothing lines are carried nationally by hundreds of retailers, but here in Cold Spring you can buy direct from the designers—and find many one-of-a-kind designer samples as well. Open every day but Tuesday in the summer, Thursday through Sunday the rest of the year.

BACK IN IRELAND
103 Main Street
(845) 265-4570
Everything Irish is the rule here—the shop carries a wide variety of Irish imports and Irish-themed products, including beautiful wedding and claddagh rings, Belleek pottery, and Irish Dresden, Galway, and Cavan crystal. Items for Irish weddings are a store specialty.

COLD SPRING TRAIN WORKS
165 Main Street
(845) 445-4011
www.coldspringtrainworks.net
A serious shop for serious hobbyists, Cold Spring Train Works carries an extensive selection of top-quality model trains, locomotives, and accessories. Most of the trains are for grown-ups, but the store also carries a full line of Thomas Wood trains for kids, along with wooden train toys. Open Friday through Sunday.

HUDSON VALLEY OUTFITTERS
63 Main Street
(845) 265-0221
www.hudsonvalleyoutfitters.com
Only a block from the Cold Spring rail station, and only 10 minutes from the nearest trailhead, Hudson Valley Outfitters carries an excellent selection of gear for hikers, bikers, and kayakers. The store also rents kayaks for paddling on the Hudson from nearby Foundry Cove and provides kayaking instruction and tours. The friendly staff members know the area well and are generous with good advice.

KNITTINGSMITH
35 Chestnut Street
(845) 265-6566
www.theknittingsmith.com
Yarn, needles, and notions for knitters and crocheters, plus a great selection of patterns, including many by in-house pattern designer (and store proprietor) Penelope Smith. The store also offers classes and private lessons, custom knitting and finishing, and knitting repairs. Closed Sunday and Monday.

MOMMINIA
113 Main Street
(845) 265-2260
www.momminia.com
Momminia is a designer-owned boutique featuring unusual, avant-garde, and one-of-a-kind jewelry. The specialty here is beads—beaded jewelry, ancient and antique beads, gemstone beads, modern and vintage ethnic and glass beads, and beading supplies.

WOMEN'S WORK
66 Main Street
(845) 809-5299
www.womensworkbw.com
One of the more interesting shops in the region, Women's Work sells crafts, such as ostrich shell jewelry, baskets, and fabrics crated by San Bushman women in Botswana. The shop also sells San Bushman artwork and one-of-a-kind crafts, furniture, and objects imported from Botswana, Namibia, Malawi, Zimbabwe, and elsewhere in Africa. Closed Tuesday and Wednesday.

SHOPPING: WEST SIDE OF THE HUDSON

It's shopper heaven on the west side of the Hudson. Take just the charming village of Wood-stock—there are about 70 stores in a four-block radius, and not one of them is a chain. You'll find treasures here you won't ever see anywhere else. Other towns on the west side, like High Falls and New Paltz, also offer great shopping at unique stores. One of the nicest things about shopping in the small towns of the area is the relaxed atmosphere in the stores—the owners are often on the premises and go out of their way to be welcoming. If you have to shop at a big-box store, there's a lengthy stretch of them along Route 9W in Kingston; the Newburgh Mall on Route 300 has more than 65 chain stores.

There are far too many wonderful retailers in the region to include every one. This section focuses on well-established stores that are interesting, specialized, unusual, unique, or carry locally made or hard-to-find products. This chapter doesn't cover antiques shops—see the Antiquing chapter instead. And although this chapter does include some extra-special bakeries and candy stores, see the Farm Markets and Wineries chapter for more on shopping for local produce and wine.

As a general rule, the shops listed here are open every day. Exceptions are noted. Hours can vary considerably, and days and hours may change with the seasons. Check ahead if possible.

GREENE COUNTY

Catskill

THE CANDYMAN CHOCOLATES AND ICE CREAM STORE
4 Bridge Street
(518) 943-2122
www.thecandymanchocolates.com
Founded in 1985, The Candyman is well known in the area as a source of great homemade chocolates, fudge, and ice cream. The store also carries a good selection of nostalgic candy favorites, such as Mary Janes and old-fashioned stick candy. Open until 9:00 p.m. daily.

CITY LIGHTS
365 Main Street
(518) 943-5673
www.citylights-ny.com
City Lights offers a broad selection of brand-name decorative lighting and accessories in a

In New York State, clothing and shoe purchases of $110 and under are exempt from the 4 percent state sales tax; county taxes may still apply.

wide range of styles, from traditional to contemporary. Design consultants are on hand to create lighting plans and to custom-order fixtures.

DREAM
388 Main Street
(518) 943-5495
Indonesian furniture and home furnishings, art carvings, crafts, and gifts from around the world. Open Friday and Saturday only.

HOOD & COMPANY
432 Main Street
(518) 943-1891
Fine home furnishings, linens, and accessories for the bath. Closed Tuesday.

32 WEST KIDZ FOOTWEAR
32 West Bridge Street
(518) 947-6715
Footwear, clothing, hats, T-shirts, and backpacks for kids, plus footwear for adults—and a skate shop for everyone.

VARIEGATED
377 Main Street
(518) 943-1313
www.variegatedinc.com
Variegated offers fine home furnishings in crisp modern designs. The firm specializes in custom-made linens, cotton bedding, handmade pieced and patterned pillows, and artisan-crafted accessories. Open Thursday through Sunday.

VERSO
386 Main Street
(518) 943-7499
www.versofinearts.com
Outstanding examples of 20th-century antiques, antique furniture, fine arts, decorative objects, art glass and pottery, and fine books on art, antiques, architecture, and related subjects.

ORANGE COUNTY

Cornwall

ANNA LIISA BOUTIQUE
281 Hudson Street
(845) 534-3777
Fine clothing and accessories for women in a personal setting. Among the brands sold here are Del Forte denim, Lynn Ritchie, Red Engine jeans, Luna Luze, Pure Color jeans, and Suzi Roher belts. Closed Sunday and Monday.

i Although it's outside the region of this book, Woodbury Common, the famed premium outlets shopping mall, is in Central Valley in Orange County. Serious bargain hunters come from around the world to shop here. For more information about the 220 outlet stores, call (845) 928-4000 or check www.premiumoutlets.com.

CORNWALL YARN SHOP
227 Main Street
(845) 534-0383
www.cornwallyarnshop.com
The broad selection of yarns and patterns makes this shop a local favorite among knitters, crocheters, and other fabric crafts hobbyists. Classes ranging from basic to advanced work are offered. The advanced classes often feature guest instructors and specialists in unusual techniques.

Newburgh

ADAMS FAIRACRE FARMS
1240 Route 300
(845) 569-0303
www.adamsfarms.com
The Newburgh branch of the local grocery, fine foods, and nursery center chain based in Poughkeepsie.

BARNES & NOBLE BOOKSELLERS
Newburgh Crossing
1245 Route 300 (Union Avenue)
(845) 567-0782
www.barnesandnoble.com
Located in Newburgh Crossing, an upscale shopping plaza on Union Avenue, this branch of Barnes & Noble is open from 9:00 a.m. to 11:00 p.m. Monday through Saturday and from 9:00 a.m. to 9:00 p.m. Sunday. Check the Web site for the schedule of store events such as the weekly story time for kids.

COMMODORE CHOCOLATIER
482 Broadway
(845) 561-3960
Founded in 1935, Commodore Chocolatier is a Newburgh landmark. It's especially popular in the weeks before Christmas, when the store runs demonstrations on making candy canes. Commodore is famed for chocolate-covered strawberries, amazing heart-shaped boxed selections for Valentine's Day, and excellent boxed selections the rest of the year. You don't have to buy a box, of course—they'll gladly sell chocolate, fudge, and candies by the ounce or pound.

NATURE'S PANTRY
142 Route 17K
(845) 567-3355
A large natural and organic foods store (more than 4,000 square feet) offering locally grown organic produce, refrigerated and frozen foods, many gluten-free products, bulk foods, spices, herbs, and four aisles of personal care products.

NEWBURGH ART SUPPLY
87 Liberty Street
(845) 561-5552
www.newburghartsupply.com
Recently opened to serve the growing artistic community in the area, Newburgh Art Supply carries a full range of materials for professional and advanced artists, along with affordable, high-quality, student-grade materials. Works by local artists are displayed on the walls.

THE PALATINE SHOP
87 Liberty Street
(845) 561-5552
http://thepalatineshop.blogspot.com/
Located within Newburgh Art Supply (previous listing), the Palatine Shop specializes in antique and modern souvenirs of historic Newburgh. Appropriately, the shop entrance is just across the street from Washington's Headquarters (see the Mansions and Historic Sites: West chapter for more on this), the most visited tourist site in Newburgh.

ULSTER COUNTY

Bearsville

LOOMINUS HANDWOVENS
3257 Route 212
(845) 679-6500
www.loominus.com
Located just outside Woodstock, Loominus offers lovely hand-woven chenille and silk scarves for men and women, along with hand-woven chenille jackets and chenille throws. The designs by Marsha Fleisher are woven in the area by local crafters. Closed Sunday.

High Falls

BLUE CASHEW KITCHEN PHARMACY
1209 Route 213
(845) 687-0294
www.bluecashewkitchen.com
Blue Cashew calls itself "Your kitchen antidote," and they mean it. This store carries a vast array of high-quality (and reasonably priced) kitchenware and housewares—everything you need to cure your kitchen of missing equipment, boring serving pieces, and other ailments. Closed Wednesday.

HIGH FALLS MERCANTILE
113 Main Street
(845) 687-4200
www.highfallsmercantile.com
Founded in 2004, High Falls Mercantile offers home furnishings, including linens and textiles, rugs, dinnerware and tabletop accessories, lamps, farm tables, and upholstered furniture. The store also carries the complete line of Santa Maria Novella fragrances, soaps, and beauty products, imported from Italy.

LOUNGE
8 Second Street
(845) 687-9463
www.loungefurniture.com
Nicely designed earth-friendly furniture made using soy-based cushions, recycled fibers, organic fabrics, water-based stains, and certified forest products. The designs are elegant and contemporary. Open Thursday through Sunday, 11:00 a.m. to 5:00 p.m.; by appointment the rest of the week. There's a second store in Hudson.

THE NEW YORK STORE
103 Main Street
(845) 687-7779
www.thenewyorkstore.net
Operated by famed chef John Novi of the DePuy Canal House restaurant (see the Restaurants: West Side chapter for more), the New York Store carries fine food items made exclusively in New York State. The variety of gourmet foods is

amazing—the offerings here range from candy and cookies to cheese to sauces to martini fixings—along with Chef Novi's patented kitchen utensils. This is a great place to assemble personalized gift baskets or find wedding favors.

SPRUCE DESIGN + DECOR
105½ Main Street
(845) 687-4481
www.sprucedesigndecor.com
An eclectic blend of classic American and European 20th-century furnishings, lighting, and decorative objects, Spruce Design + Decor helps customers design and furnish sophisticated home interiors.

URSO JEWELRY
1204 Route 213
(845) 687-0899
www.ursojewelry.com
David Urso makes beautifully designed and crafted resin and sterling silver jewelry. This is jewelry as art, with sensual organic shapes and imaginative use of materials. Urso's work is carried by many fine galleries nationwide, but this is the place to see it where it's made. Call ahead for hours.

Highland
THE KILTMAKER'S APPRENTICE
54 Vineyard Avenue
(845) 691-3888
www.highlandkiltshop.com
All your Highlander needs can be met at this unusual shop, where kilts, outfits, and accessories can be bought and rented. Rentals fit ages 2 and up. Custom kilts, kilt repairs, and kilt alterations are also provided here. Closed Sunday and Monday.

Hurley
HURLEY PATENTEE LIGHTING
464 Old Route 209
(845) 331-5414
www.hurleypatenteelighting.com
World-famous for their authentic colonial lighting reproductions, Hurley Patentee Lighting is located in a historic Georgian stone mansion dating back to 1745. The showroom is in the basement of the manor house and is open to the public. Call ahead for hours.

Kerhonksen
CATSKILL NATIVE NURSERY
607 Samsonville Road
(845) 626-2758
www.catskillnativenursery.com
Native plant species are attractive, easy to maintain, and naturally grow well in the right environment, while providing food and habitat for birds, butterflies, and wildlife. At Catskill Native Nursery the plants are all North American natives. There's a great selection of nursery-propagated perennials, fruits, shrubs, and trees. The beautiful display gardens are a good source of ideas. Open seasonally and closed Tuesday and Wednesday—call ahead.

Kingston
ALTERNATIVE BOOKS
35 North Front Street
(845) 331-5439
A fixture of uptown Kingston's Stockade District, Alternative Books carries new, used, and rare books (mostly used). It's a great place to search for treasures in the arts, literature, and humanities, plus the store is also well regarded for its support of the local writing community. Readings, music, and other events happen here regularly at The Uptown next door—call ahead for the schedule.

AMERIBAG ADVENTURES
1161 Ulster Avenue
(845) 339-8033
www.ameribag.com
This is the retail home of the original Healthy Back Bag®, an ergonomically designed shoulder bag. Available in a wide array of colors and styles, these bags are very versatile—they're great handbags but also work well as gym bags, carry-on luggage, baby bags, and other uses. The store

also carries a full line of Euro comfort shoes, including Birkenstock, Mephisto, Allrounder, and Taos Footwear.

BARNES & NOBLE BOOKSELLERS
1177 Ulster Avenue
(845) 336-0590
www.barnesandnoble.com

A big-box store on a road lined with big boxes, this B&N store is in the Ulster Plaza mall, along with a nice assortment of other stores such as Bed, Bath and Beyond. Story times for kids are in English and in Spanish—check with the store for times. Art by local artists is often on display, and there's a good selection of local titles. Open 9:00 a.m. to 11:00 p.m. daily.

CATSKILL ART AND OFFICE SUPPLY
328 Wall Street
(845) 331-7780
www.catskillart.com

Located in the historic Stockade District, the Kingston branch of Catskill Art offers a broad selection of art supplies and studio furnishings, along with custom picture framing and a full-service copy center. The original store is in Woodstock.

COLUMBIA
66 North Front Street
(845) 339-4996

When you need a wig, a costume, face-painting supplies, stick-on tattoos, or beauty supplies, this is the place to go. Columbia is by far the region's best and largest costume shop, with thousands of costumes, accessories, and props for rent or sale. The store is a lot of fun, especially around Halloween, but it has a serious side—this is also the place to go for theatrical supplies and dancewear.

FLEISHER'S GRASS-FED AND ORGANIC MEATS
307 Wall Street
(845) 338-MOOO
www.grassfedmeat.net

One of the only butcher shops in the nation to carry only pasture-raised organic meat, Fleisher's is a major regional destination for serious foodies.

The store sells beef, pork, lamb, veal, and poultry, all raised and pastured on local farms without antibiotics or hormones. The store also sells its homemade nitrate-free bacon, heritage hams, wonderful homemade sausages, free-range eggs, artisanal cheeses, and local organic produce. Open Thursday, Friday, and Saturday only. Fleisher's opened in historic uptown Kingston only in 2004; since then, demand for their meat has been so high that a second store opened in Rhinebeck in 2007.

HANSEN CAVIAR COMPANY
881 Route 28
(845) 331-5622
www.hansencaviar.com

Six generations of the Hansen family have been in the caviar business since 1869, making this the oldest caviar house in the world. Today Hansen Caviar Company sells domestic American, imported Russian, and international caviars, along with imported smoked salmon and gravlax, foie gras, pâtés, and other poultry specialties from France, and other gourmet items, such as truffles and French escargots.

KENCO WORK AND PLAY OUTFITTERS
1000 Hurley Mountain Road
(845) 340-0552
www.atkenco.com

This very large independent sporting goods store carries a huge selection of active and leisure clothing, footwear, accessories, and gear, including packs, tents, boats, snowshoes, sleds, and cross-country skis. The annual truckload sale in April offers excellent bargains.

MOTHER EARTH'S STOREHOUSE
300 Kings Mall Court (Route 9W)
(845) 336-5541
www.motherearthstorehouse.com

The main branch of this family-operated three-store chain is the size of a small supermarket and carries a huge selection of organic produce and dairy products, bulk and packaged organic foods, gluten-free and wheat-free foods, and discounted vitamins and supplements. The Kingston store and the Poughkeepsie branch (1955 South

Road, 845-296-1069) have organic deli sections. There's also a Saugerties branch (249 Main Street, 845-246-9614).

POTTER BROTHERS
57 City View Terrace
(845) 338-5119
www.potterbrothers.com
A skier's paradise, Potter Brothers offers a huge selection of gear for downhill and cross-country skiing, snowboarding, and all other winter sports. Expert boot fitters are on hand, and the skilled staff does gear tune-ups and repairs. Rentals are also available. Potter Brothers has a seasonal store in Poughkeepsie (19 Collegeview Avenue, 845-454-3880) and another branch in Fishkill (1083 Route 9 South, Lawrence Farms Plaza, 845-297-2941). In the summer, the Kingston and Fishkill stores switch over to selling patio furniture.

SCHNEIDER'S JEWELERS
290 Wall Street
(845) 331-1888
www.schneidersjewelers.com
Schneider's Jewelers is a Kingston institution dating back to 1928. The main store is located in the historic Stockade District; there's a second store at 1290 Ulster Avenue (845-336-8600). At both stores, shoppers can choose from a wide variety of diamond jewelry, watches, estate jewelry, and bridal gifts. The store also offers appraisals and expert repairs.

SOMETHING DIFFERENT BAKERY AND CAFÉ
331 Hasbrouck Avenue
(845) 338-2255
What's different about this bakery is that the products are gluten-free but taste great anyway. The bakery offers baked goods and desserts; the cafe offers soups, sandwiches, and meals to stay or to go. Special orders are taken for those with diabetes and hypoglycemia.

Lake Katrine
ADAMS FAIRACRE FARMS
1560 Ulster Avenue (Route 9W)
(845) 336-6300
www.adamsfarms.com
Located just north of the main shopping strip in Kingston and technically out of the city, this is the Ulster branch of the local grocery, fine foods, and nursery chain based in Poughkeepsie.

AMAZING THREADS
2010 Ulster Avenue (Route 9W)
(845) 336-5322
www.amazingthreads.com
A paradise for knitters, spinners, and weavers, Amazing Threads offers all the supplies and products they need. In addition, the store has an active schedule of classes, special events, and in-store promotions—check the Web site for updates. Closed Sunday and Monday.

BOHEMIAN BOOK BIN
85 Carle Terrace
(845) 336-6450
www.bohemianbookbin.com
In 2008 the Bohemian Book Bin moved from its longtime Kings Mall location in Kingston to the new store in Lake Katrine. The oldest used bookstore in Ulster County, Bohemian Book Bin offers an unusually large and varied selection. Check out the "Bag-a-Books" deal—24 books for just $5.

Mount Tremper
EMERSON COUNTRY STORE
5340 Route 28
(845) 688-5800
www.emersoncountrystore.com
The merchandise carried at this very upscale store connected to the posh Emerson Resort and Spa (see the Accommodations: West chapter for details) is focused on comfort, style, and fun. The store carries organic chocolates, Mario Batali cookware, furniture, kites, and Dr. Hauschka skin-care products, among other items. The highlight

is the amazing kaleidoscope collection. While you're shopping, you can visit the world's largest kaleidoscope, housed in a 56-foot silo, and watch the multimedia kaleidoscope show ($5 a head, free for kids under 12). The show varies seasonally but is always mind-blowing.

New Paltz

BARNER BOOKS
3 Church Street
(845) 255-2635
Rooms full of used, rare, and out-of-print books—a New Paltz institution. The broad stock is excellent for browsing.

THE CHEESE PLATE
10 Main Street (Water Street Market)
(845) 255-2444
Despite all the artisanal producers, good specialty cheese shops are scarce in the Hudson Valley. The Cheese Plate offers a choice of about 50 different cheeses at any given time. Many are European imports, but the majority are domestic and local. Among other cheeses, this is the place to get semi-soft Ouray from Sprout Creek Farm in Dutchess County and cheese from Ronnybrook Farm in Columbia County. The store also carries cheese accessories and kitchenware. Closed Tuesday.

HANDMADE AND MORE
6 North Front Street
(845) 255-6277
www.handmadeandmore.com
Handcrafted, unique gifts, jewelry (great earrings), toys, clothing for women and children, and accessories have been sold here since 1974. Among other fun items, the store carries kaleidoscopes and musical instruments for nonmusicians. Free gift wrapping.

INQUIRING MINDS BOOKSTORE
6 Church Street
(845) 255-8300
www.newpaltzbooks.com
Independent and proud of it, Inquiring Minds Bookstore has an excellent and varied stock. The store carries textbooks and titles for SUNY New Paltz students and staff, but this is a full community bookstore. General fiction and nonfiction is available, along with a wide selection of books with local interest, books about hiking and climbing in the area, and a great kids' section. A second store is in Saugerties.

KNIT AND BE HAPPY
8 North Front Street
(845) 255-5333
www.knitandbehappy.com
Opened in 2007, this shop carries an extensive selection of yarns, patterns, and supplies for knitters and crocheters at all skill levels. Classes and workshops are offered—check the Web site for the schedule.

MAGLYN'S DREAM
10 Main Street (Water Street Market)
(845) 256-0522
www.maglynsdream.com
The specialty here is handcrafted art and handmade gifts created mostly by local artisans—no two pieces are the same. The store carries the work of more than 40 producers, including jewelry, glassware and dinnerware, paintings, sculptures, ceramic art and pottery, greeting cards, and hand-crocheted sweaters, hats, and shawls.

MANNY'S ART SUPPLIES
83 Main Street
(845) 255-9902
www.mannysart.com
Manny's Art Supplies has been offering one of the most complete selections of artists' materials in the region since 1963. The store also carries handmade art papers, greeting cards, crafts supplies, office supplies, and gifts.

MOHONK IMAGES GALLERY
10 Main Street (Water Street Market)
(845) 255-6800
www.gstevejordan.com
Featuring the stunning fine art photos of G. Steve Jordan, the pictures in this gallery capture the

natural beauty of the Mohonk Preserve, Shawangunk Mountains, and the Hudson Valley. Closed Tuesday and Wednesday in the winter.

PAWS OF DISTINCTION
10 Main Street (Water Street Market)
(845) 255-3991
www.pawsofdistinction.net
An upscale pet boutique located in the quaint Water Street Market complex, Paws of Distinction offers unique dog accessories, dog spa products, and delicious, healthy dog treats from the "pettiserie."

PEGASUS FOOTWEAR
27 North Chestnut Street
(845) 256-0788
www.pegasusshoes.com
The New Paltz branch of the well-known Woodstock store.

Rosendale

THE ALTERNATIVE BAKER
407 Main Street
(845) 658-3355
www.lemoncakes.com
This old-fashioned bakery, relocated from Kingston in 2008, is alternative in two senses. First, they make everything—from bread to wedding cakes—from scratch using only the finest organic ingredients. Second, they offer a special selection of delicious baked goods that are sugar-free, vegan, dairy-free, and gluten-free. On top of that, the bakery is famous for its amazing lemon cakes. Usually closed Tuesday, Wednesday, and Thursday, but call to check.

THE BIG CHEESE
402 Main Street
(845) 658-7175
A full line of cheeses from around the world, including many made by artisans from the Hudson Valley. The store also carries gourmet crackers, nuts, dates, and other items, and it's one of the few retail outlets for the locally made Jane's Ice Cream.

OUTDOOR DÉCOR
430 Main Street
(845) 658-8145
Stylish home furnishings for both indoors and outdoors, including a great selection of durable patio furniture.

THE SHOP AT VICTORIA GARDENS
Route 213 and 1 Cottekill Road
(845) 658-9007
www.victoriagardens.biz
Gifts, tools, supplies, and accessories for gardeners are all sold here, but the real focus is the plants. They're sourced from local growers and are selected because they're appropriate to the region and will do well here. Annuals, perennials, shrubs, and trees are all for sale, with special emphasis on deer-resistant choices. The store also offers an active schedule of workshops and speakers—check the Web site for updates.

Saugerties

FIRST STREET DANCEWEAR
10 First Street
(845) 247-4517
www.firststreetdancewear.com
The place for ballet, tap, and jazz dancewear, along with attire for yoga, gymnastics, and skating. Brands carried include Danskin, Capezio, Motionwear, Bunheads, and Dance Paws. Closed Sunday.

HOPE FARM PRESS AND BOOKSHOP
252 Main Street
(845) 246-3522
www.hopefarm.com
The bookshop part of Hope Farm carries a good general stock of books with a focus on books about New York State, local Hudson Valley history, and genealogy. The stock runs to thousands of new and used titles, many of them rare and unusual, but Hope Farm isn't a stuffy sort of place. The friendly and very helpful staff makes browsing fun. The press part is a small publishing company that produces books on regional history—the titles are available at the store.

HUDSON VALLEY DESSERT COMPANY
87 Partition Street
(800) 483-2669
www.hudsonvalleydesserts.com
The fabulous biscotti from Hudson Valley Dessert Company are served at fine restaurants up and down the valley. They're made right here in Saugerties (behind Café Tamayo), which means you can buy them for yourself fresh from the bakery. The biscotti sampler boxes make a great gift. You can also get the house special granola, chocolate espresso and other fancy cookies, and even order a birthday cake.

INQUIRING MINDS/MUDDY CUP
65 Partition Street
(845) 255-8300
www.newpaltzbooks.com
When a well-established independent bookstore combines forces with a popular local chain of independent coffeehouses, interesting things happen. This brand-new hookup is an integrated cultural experience—books, coffee and light snacks, readings, art on the walls, free Wi-Fi, and lots of interesting people. There's another Inquiring Minds Bookstore in New Paltz.

KRAUSE'S CHOCOLATES
41 South Partition Street
(845) 248-8377
www.krauseschocolates.com
A beloved regional favorite, Krause's Chocolates has been making hand-dipped confections and molded chocolates in Saugerties for more than 75 years. The store offers more than 50 varieties of hand-dipped chocolates, an assortment of fudges, and fabulous peanut brittle. The molded chocolates are also available at selected local stores.

LUCKY CHOCOLATE AND BISCUIT CO.
1534 Route 212
(845) 246-7337
www.luckychocolates.com
Handmade, small-batch chocolates made from organic and fair-trade chocolate are crafted here. The chocolates are imaginative and intensely flavored using concentrated fruit purees and other natural flavors. The store also makes chocolate-covered caramels, nut barks, and toffee, along with a line of homemade cookies. Closed Monday.

OUR BOOKSHOP
97 Partition Street
(845) 246-3106
OUR stands for old, used, and rare, but not just books. The store offers a wide collection of other printed material and ephemera, including old magazines, advertising materials, postcards, prints, catalogs, sheet music, maps, and photos. Dedicated browsers will find treasures here.

SIMPLY COUNTRY
135 Partition Street
(845) 246-0785
www.simplycountryny.com
Primitive home decor and gifts fill 16 rooms in this rambling shop. Everything for the home is here: kitchenware, bath accessories, prints and samplers, wreaths and garlands, tabletop items, and much more. There's also a huge collection of dolls and a special Christmas room. Closed Monday through Wednesday.

THE WILLOW TREE
243 Main Street
(845) 247-9046
This is a fun store, almost more a gallery than a retail shop. The focus is on country decor, including wooden signs, wreaths, dolls, prints, and primitive furniture and objects. There's also a great candle department. Closed Monday.

Stone Ridge
FOUR WINDS
3835 Route 209
(845) 687-9910
www.fourwindsathome.com
Handcrafted furniture made in Southeast Asia from teak and mahogany is the main focus here, along with handwoven wool rugs and kilims, decorative lighting, sterling silver jewelry, and an

extensive offering of tabletop items, textiles, and decorative accessories. There's another store in Rhinebeck.

West Hurley

CRAFTS PEOPLE
262 Spillway Road
(845) 331-3859
www.craftspeople.us
A vast gallery (6,000 square feet in four buildings) representing more than 500 regional and national craftspeople, this is the largest selection of crafts in the Hudson Valley. This is a wonderful place for browsing—bring a picnic lunch and enjoy it on spacious grounds. Closed Tuesday, Wednesday, and Thursday.

Woodstock

BREAD ALONE
22 Mill Hill Road
(845) 679-2108
www.breadalone.com
The main bakery for Bread Alone is in Boiceville in the Catskills, a bit out of the range of this book. The Woodstock branch sells the bakery's European-style hearth-baked breads, along with sandwiches, soups, and pastries in the cafe. There's another branch in Rhinebeck.

THE BYRDCLIFFE SHOP
34 Tinker Street
(845) 679-2079
Run by the Woodstock Byrdcliffe Guild (WBG), the nonprofit steward for Byrdcliffe, perhaps the oldest continually operating arts and crafts colony in the country (it dates back to 1903). The shop is dedicated to the heritage of the Arts and Crafts Movement; the retail space features work by artists in residence at Byrdcliffe. The store is nonprofit; all proceeds go back to furthering the mission of the WBG.

CANDLESTOCK
16 Mill Hill Road
(845) 679-8711
www.candlestock.com
Candlestock was founded in 1970 as a one-room store. A small drip candle burned in one corner. Today the store takes up the whole building, but the drip candle in the corner is still there—it's now nearly 8 feet tall. Candlestock carries a great collection of candles, including beeswax pillars, drip candles, and custom-crafted Glowing Words candles, hand-painted with famous sayings, poems, quotes, or your own words.

CATSKILL ART AND OFFICE SUPPLY
35 Mill Hill Road
(845) 679-2251
www.catskillart.com
The original Woodstock store for Catskill Art has been serving the creative community for more than 25 years. The store carries a wide selection of art supplies from the finest manufacturers for every medium; there's also a great selection of studio furnishings. The full-service copy center can arrange large-format scans through the Poughkeepsie store. Custom framing, stationery, and gifts round out the stock. There's also a store in Kingston.

CHANGES
19 Tinker Street
(845) 679-4750
www.changesformen.com
Relaxed, stylish clothing for men, ranging from sweatpants to suits. Brands carried include DKNY, Diesel, Penguin, and Jack Spade. This is the original store; there's a second store in Rhinebeck.

CHEZ GRAND'MERE
24 Tinker Street
(845) 679-8140
A longtime Woodstock fixture, Chez Grand'mere carries imported chocolates, L'Occitane fragrances and body-care products, and antique furniture.

CLOUDS GALLERY
1 Mill Hill Road
(845) 679-8155
www.cloudsofwoodstock.com
American contemporary crafts are the theme

here, with handcrafted glass, jewelry, pottery, and more by dozens of artisans.

DHARMAWARE
54 Tinker Street
(845) 679-4900
www.dharmaware.com
Dharma here refers to the various religions of India. The store provides the international Dharma community with puja supplies, including practice supplies, thangkas, prayer flags, statues, incense and herbs, and much more.

THE GOLDEN NOTEBOOK
29 Tinker Street
(845) 679-8000
www.goldennotebook.com
This wonderful shop calls itself "An independent bookstore for independent thinkers," a slogan particularly appropriate for Woodstock. The store carries a broad range of titles in a relaxed, country atmosphere and has a great children's section. The knowledgeable staff is very helpful. The Golden Notebook has a very active program of store readings, signings, and other events— check the Web site for updates.

MIRABAI
23 Mill Hill Road
(845) 679-2100
www.mirabai.com
A spiritual/holistic bookshop, Mirabai has been providing books, music, gifts, and enlightening workshops for a more conscious, healthy, and peaceful life since 1987. A mind-expanding place for browsing.

MODERN MYTHOLOGY
12 Tinker Street
(845) 679-8811
If you're a grown-up and like Harry Potter, this is the store for you. Basically a gift shop, the store carries merchandise relating to fairies, wizards, dragons, Tarot cards, crystals, candles and incense, and much more.

ONDINE
68 Tinker Street
(845) 679-5800
www.ondinebeauty.com
Organic beauty products, including makeup, skincare and body-care products, and bath accessories. Many products are locally made by hand.

PEGASUS FOOTWEAR
10 Mill Hill Road
(845) 679-2373
www.pegasusshoes.com
The best place in the region for aching or hard-to-fit feet. The expert staff will fit you with exactly the right shoes for comfort and style. The store carries more than 75 shoe brands, including Clarks, Ecco, Pratik, Dansko, Keen, Asics, and Merrell. There's a second store in New Paltz.

PONDICHERRY
12 Tinker Street
(845) 679-2926
www.pondi.biz
Everything you need for the serious practice of yoga, including videos, books, mats, and props. The store also carries traditional silver jewelry from India, a wide selection of world music, and an extensive collection of stone and bronze statuary from India. The shop is named for a seaport in south India that is home to Sri Aurobindo Ashram. The store carries many handicrafts from Auroville, an international community near Pondicherry, including beautiful jewelry, silk wall hangings, and hand-loomed yoga mats and cushions.

READER'S QUARRY
97 Tinker Street
(845) 679-5227
Housed in a charming country cottage just opposite the Woodstock public library, Reader's Quarry is basically a houseful of great used, rare, and out-of-print books. Serious antiquarian collectors will find a lot to like here—and so will rainy-day browsers. Closed Tuesday through Thursday in the summer; open only on weekends in the winter. Call ahead for days and hours.

SOARING EAGLE

62B Tinker Street

(877) 621-1908

www.soaringeaglestore.com

Soaring Eagle carries crafts, artifacts, jewelry, pottery, and leather goods handcrafted by Native American artists. Among the more interesting items are beautiful handmade Native American flutes by Odell Borg (Ojibwa) and Jonah Thompson (Navajo). The store offers flute lessons.

SWEETHEART GALLERY

8 Tannery Brook Road

(845) 679-2622

www.sweetheartgallery.com

Located near a dramatic waterfall, Sweetheart Gallery carries contemporary American art and fine handmade crafts, many from artisans in the Woodstock area. The gallery offers home furnishings, furniture, lighting, pottery, jewelry, glass, Judaica, fiber arts, paintings, photos, and prints.

TINKER TOYS TOO

5 Mill Hill Road

(845) 679-8870

www.tinkerstreettoys.com

Most of Woodstock is adult-oriented, making Tinker Toys Too a welcome oasis for visitors with kids. The store features educational toys, some of them hard to find, from a number of international manufacturers, including Brio, Beadshop, Lego, Ritterspielzug, Zolo, Treeblocks, Zinnfiguren, Design Science, and Rocket USA. Adults will enjoy the many retro toys, like the classic Mr. Machine robot.

VIDAKAFKA BOUTIQUE

43 Tinker Street

(845) 679-9139

This tiny, intimate shop—a longtime Woodstock institution—sells romantic lingerie and accessories. The experienced staff provides personal fitting and service.

WALKABOUT

68 Tinker Street

(845) 679-8288

www.walkaboutwoodstock.com

This amazing store carries exotic crafts and handiworks from around the world—from here, there, and everywhere. The international objects here include Day of the Dead skeletons from Mexico, retablos from Peru, soapstone figurines from Vietnam, puppets and dolls from everywhere, and an enlightening collection of carved deity figures. A varied collection of jewelry from all over the globe rounds out the collection.

WOODSTOCK BEAD EMPORIUM

54B Tinker Street

(845) 679-0066

www.beademporium.com

A complete bead store, with a complete line of seed beads and a good selection of beading supplies, including findings and books. The store features handmade, one-of-a-kind glass beads by owner Joseph Irvin. Closed Tuesday.

WOODSTOCK CANDY

60 Tinker Street

(845) 679-3750

www.woodstockcandy.com

Walking through the door of Woodstock Candy is certain to trigger nostalgia for the lost candies of your childhood. The store sells retro candies that are almost impossible to find today, such as Chuckles, Pixy Stix, Atomic Fireballs, Razzles—even candy cigarettes. Aside from all the candy you can buy by the piece, the store puts together wonderful candy gift baskets. Birthday baskets featuring candies popular in your birth year are especially popular.

ANNUAL EVENTS

Every year a huge variety of annual events takes place up and down the mid–Hudson Valley. Music festivals, food festivals, county fairs, outdoors celebrations, and much more happen every month. The listings here focus on larger events that generally draw visitors from around the region. There's simply not enough space to list all the smaller local street fairs and community celebrations. (Many annual dance, art, and classical music events in the region are listed in the Performing Arts and Film chapter or the Art in the Valley chapter.)

Many community events are free; other events have admission fees, usually well under $10 for adults. Kids usually get in for less, and younger children usually get in for free. The admission fee often goes to support the event and local community organizations.

The contact information given here is for the event sponsors, not for the event location. Venues such as the Dutchess County Fairgrounds and the Ulster County Fairgrounds host many different events throughout the year. While these sites usually provide some basic information, check with the event sponsor for details and updates.

Because many annual events are outdoor festivals, wheelchair accessibility can be a problem. Just about every event listed here will be at least partially accessible, but it's best to check ahead if possible.

JANUARY

FDR BIRTHDAY OBSERVANCE
Home of Franklin D. Roosevelt National
Historic Site
4097 Albany Post Road (Route 9)
Hyde Park
(845) 229-9115
www.nps.gov/hofr
Franklin and Eleanor Roosevelt are buried on the grounds of the FDR National Historic Site. Every year on January 30, a simple yet moving ceremony is held at the grave site to commemorate Franklin's birthday. Guest speakers memorialize the nation's 32nd president, cadets from the United States Military Academy at West Point provide an honor guard and a color guard, and local organizations lay wreaths. Similar ceremonies are held on Memorial Day and on Eleanor Roosevelt's birthday on October 11.

FEBRUARY

HUDSON VALLEY CHEESE FESTIVAL
Columbia County Bounty
507 Warren Street
Hudson
(518) 828-4417
www.hudsonvalleycheesefestival.com
A celebration of locally made artisan cheeses, the Hudson Valley Cheese Festival benefits Columbia County Bounty, an organization that supports local agriculture and communities. The events and tastings take place at various restaurants around the city of Hudson on the Sunday of Presidents' Day weekend. Tickets are $40; advance purchase is strongly recommended.

MARCH

HUDSON VALLEY RESTAURANT WEEKS
The Valley Table
152 Powelton Circle
Newburgh
(845) 561-2022
www.hudsonvalleyrestaurantweek.com
Presented by *The Valley Table* magazine, Hudson Valley Restaurant Weeks take place during the two middle weeks of March. More than 80 restaurants participate in the events, which include specially priced three-course lunches and dinners. The participant list grows every year—make your reservations early.

ST. PATRICK'S DAY PARADE
Kingston
(800) 331-1518
www.ci.kingston.ny.us
In Ulster County a major St. Patrick's Day parade is only to be expected, and this one is the biggest and best in the region. It steps off at 1:00 p.m. from the Kingston Plaza in the historic Stockade District in uptown Kingston and heads down Broadway to the Rondout area on the waterfront. The parade is co-sponsored by the City of Kingston and the Ulster Division of the Ancient Order of Hibernians. The date varies a bit, but it's *not* on the traditional March 17—usually it's the week before. Free.

TASTE OF RHINEBECK
NDH Foundation
99 Montgomery Street
Rhinebeck
(845) 871-3505
An annual event that benefits Northern Dutchess Hospital, the Taste of Rhinebeck sends participants on a delicious walking tour of Rhinebeck's many fine restaurants and food businesses. It's a sort of trick-or-treat for foodies as they stroll through the streets of this historic village. The date varies a bit, but it's usually the third Monday evening in March. Tickets are $75 and sell fast—order in advance to avoid being shut out.

APRIL

THE CHANCELLOR'S SHEEP AND WOOL SHOWCASE
Clermont State Historic Site
1 Clermont Avenue
Germantown
(518) 537-4240
www.friendsofclermont.org
The Chancellor was Robert J. Livingston Jr. (1746–1813), who was a member of the committee responsible for drafting the Declaration of Independence. As Chancellor of the State of New York, he administered the oath of office to George Washington as first President of the United States. When he wasn't busy with all that, Chancellor Livingston bred sheep here at his ancestral home of Clermont (see the Mansions and Historic Sites: East chapter for more). The sheep and wool show, held on a Saturday in mid-April from 11:00 a.m. to 5:00 p.m., honors him with lots of live animals, craft demonstrations, vendors of fine wool products, herding and shearing demonstrations, Celtic music, food vendors, and a silent auction. It's a really good and inexpensive family event. The entry fee is $7 per vehicle.

 Outdoor events generally take place rain or shine!

EARTH DAY FESTIVAL
Riverfront Park
Beacon
(845) 542-0721
www.beaconsloop.org
Sponsored by the Beacon Sloop Club, home of the Hudson River sloop *Woody Guthrie*, this annual Earth Day celebration is particularly meaningful because it's associated with the legendary folk musician Pete Seeger, a powerful voice for the environment. The event includes numerous exhibits focusing on solar and geothermal energy, wind technologies, composting, recycling, and other green activities. Hybrid and electric cars are on display. Live music, food and crafts, a children's area, display tanks of river life,

and tours of the sloop *Clearwater* are all on the schedule. The festival begins at noon and runs until 4:30 p.m. Free.

MAY

BEACON HAT PARADE
Main Street
Beacon
(845) 546-6222
www.beaconarts.org

Sponsored by the Beacon Arts Community Association, the Hat Parade is either a very enjoyable community-participation event or a very long collaborative sculpture, depending on your point of view (remember, this is the home of the Dia:Beacon art museum and a *lot* of artists). Marchers, if that's what they are, wear wildly decorated hats of all sorts—the wilder the better. So do a lot of the spectators, which just adds to the fun. Many prizes are awarded, including for Most Freaky, Most Fabulous, Most Fashionable, Best Kid Lid, and even Most Edible. The parade kicks off at 11:30 a.m. and winds down Main Street, accompanied by marching bands and floats. Food vendors and dance bands take over once the parade passes. This free event is very popular—arrive early to avoid parking frustration.

CELEBRATION OF CELTS
Columbia County Fairgrounds
Chatham
www.celebrationofcelts.com

An annual salute to the music, dance, and history of the Celtic nations of Scotland, Ireland, Wales, Cornwall, Isle of Man, Brittany in France, and Galicia and Austrias in Spain. Among other activities, enjoy music from pipe bands and popular Celtic fusion bands such as Enter the Haggis. The entrance fee is $15 for adults, $12 for seniors. Kids 12 and under are free.

HITS-ON-THE-HUDSON
454 Washington Avenue Extension
Saugerties
(845) 246-8833
www.hitsshows.com

The first of these equestrian events begins near the end of May. The program continues throughout the summer—see the Spectator Sports chapter for details.

i For some events, such as county fairs, advance tickets can be bought at a discount from local merchants or online. There's usually a separate gate for advance ticket-holders, which gets you into the event faster.

HUDSON RIVER VALLEY ANTIQUE AUTO ASSOCIATION CAR SHOW AND SWAP MEET
Dutchess County Fairgrounds
Route 9
Rhinebeck
(845) 876-3554
www.rhinebeckcarshow.com

Antique and custom car enthusiasts—and there are a surprising number of them—get together at this annual event in early May to exhibit their perfectly restored vehicles and swap parts and stories. The show is actually two shows: On Saturday, about 800 hot rods and customs are on display; on Sunday, it's about 1,200 antique and classic cars. Altogether, about 30,000 people will be there, along with hundreds of food and other vendors. The swap meet opens on Friday noon and runs until 5:00 p.m. that day and then runs concurrently with the rest of the show over the weekend from 8:00 a.m. to 5:00 p.m. on both days. A one-day ticket is $10; free for kids under 12. Three-day tickets are sold at a discount. Free parking. No pets. The entire fairground is wheelchair accessible.

HUDSON VALLEY MAYFAIRE
Ulster County Fairgrounds
Libertyville Road
New Paltz
(845) 594-1828
www.hvmayfaire.com

A weekend of family fun and Renaissance merriment, the Hudson Valley Mayfaire is a literally fantastic event featuring Henry VIII and a large cast of characters, including, of course, armored knights on horseback. Creatures from myth and legend, minstrels, storytellers, Shakespearean actors, jugglers, magicians, and comedians perform all day long. There's also the Kids' Kingdom, live steel combat, weapons demonstrations, and lots of great food. The event benefits The Queens Galley, a Kingston-area nonprofit organization that provides food and a soup kitchen to those in need (learn more at www.thequeensgalley.org). It takes place at the Ulster County Fairgrounds, which is transformed into a Renaissance kingdom for the weekend. Tickets are $10 for adults, $8 for children and seniors; a weekend pass is $15 for adults. Free parking. No pets. The Ulster County Fairgrounds are mostly but not completely wheelchair accessible.

RHINEBECK ANTIQUES FAIR
Dutchess County Fairgrounds
Route 9
Rhinebeck
(845) 876-1989
www.rhinebeckantiquesfair.com
The first of three outstanding antiques shows, the spring Rhinebeck Antiques Fair is held on the third weekend in May—see the Antiquing chapter for details. Admission is $9 per person. Free parking. No pets allowed.

RIVERKEEPER SHAD FEST
Boscobel Restoration
1601 Route 9D
Garrison
(800) 21-RIVER
www.riverkeeper.org
The Shad Fest happens during the late spring run of the American shad, a fish that spends most of its life in the Atlantic Ocean but returns to the brackish water of the Hudson River to breed. This event is sponsored by Riverkeeper, the environmental watchdog organization that has done a lot to clean up the Hudson and keep it that way. The festival happens on the stunning grounds of the Boscobel Restoration (for more on this mansion, see the chapter on Hudson Valley Mansions

and Historic Sites: East Side) around the third week of May on a Saturday from noon to 5:00 p.m. Participants enjoy a gourmet picnic featuring shad, along with live music, boat building, fly fishing, children's activities (including a puppet show and storytelling), a falconry show, and a variety of environmentally themed arts and crafts. At $100 per adult and $25 for kids 9 through 20 (free for kids 8 and under), this is a pricey event, but the cost is all-inclusive and the money goes to a very good cause. The festival can be reached by public transportation by taking MetroNorth to Garrison and then taking the free shuttle transportation to Boscobel.

RONDOUT WATERFRONT FESTIVAL
Cornell Park between Wurts Street and Post Street
Kingston
(800) 331-1518
www.krbaonline.org
Art in the street, music on the waterfront park, shad around the corner—it's the spring Rondout Waterfront Festival. Sponsored by the Rondout Business Association in conjunction with the Hudson River Maritime Museum's annual Shad Fest, this event happens on a Saturday around the second week in May. It starts with the 5K Trolley Run at 8:30 a.m. At noon the museum's Shad Fest begins, with Native American storytelling, puppet shows, live music, food, and a boat-building challenge. Visiting historic ships such as the schooner *Mystic Whaler* tie up at the museum dock and are open to visitors. At 1:00 p.m. the great live music festival begins in Cornell Park and runs all afternoon until 7:00 p.m. Local artists and craftspeople exhibit their work in the park at the same time. The festivities spill out all along the East Strand waterfront area with lighthouse tours, steamboat rides, trolley rides, face painting, and food vendors. The Rondout restaurants host the annual Taste of the Rondout at the same time. Most events, including the music festival, are free.

WOODSTOCK/NEW PALTZ ART AND CRAFTS FAIR

Ulster County Fairgrounds
Libertyville Road
New Paltz
(845) 679-8087
www.quailhollow.com

A well-regarded juried crafts show featuring over 300 artists and craftspeople from across the country. Exhibits, demonstrations, children's center, food vendors, craft supplies, live entertainment, and much more. The three-day fair takes place twice a year: Memorial Day weekend and again on Labor Day weekend. On Saturday and Sunday, the show is open 10:00 a.m. to 6:00 p.m. and on Monday from 10:00 a.m. to 4:00 p.m. Admission is $8 for adults; $7 for seniors; kids 6 to 16 $4.50; free for kids under 6. Parking is free. The Ulster County Fairgrounds are mostly but not completely wheelchair accessible.

JUNE

CLEARWATER FESTIVAL—THE GREAT HUDSON RIVER REVIVAL

Croton Point Park
Croton-on-Hudson
(845) 454-7673
www.clearwater.org

Sponsored by the Hudson River Sloop Clearwater, Inc., this festival was begun in the '70s by legendary folk singer and environmental activist Pete Seeger. The festival happens at beautiful Croton Point Park in Westchester County, which is south of the region covered in this book. It's included here not just because it's extremely popular with people in the Hudson Valley but also because it's extremely important. The festival promotes the beauty and environmental necessity of the Hudson River. It is the oldest and largest annual festival of its kind, and it has deep roots in the historic environmental movement to save the river that began in the 1960s and inspired environmentalists around the country. This celebration of the Hudson River is a weekend crammed with five stages full of wonderful music (including Pete himself and his many famous musician friends), dancing, theater, and storytelling—plus the chance to cruise the river aboard sloop *Clearwater* or schooner *Pioneer* (book in advance!). The Green Living Expo features environmental exhibits, displays, and grassroots activists booths. Proceeds are used to restore the Hudson River and support environmental education and research. The festival takes place on the Summer Solstice—the weekend after Father's Day, starting at 10:00 a.m. each day and ending at dusk. This is an unusually accessible event: American Sign Language interpreters are provided on the main stages and are available for other venues; large-print and Braille versions of the event schedule are available; and numerous volunteers are on hand to assist the mobility impaired. General day tickets are $45; weekend tickets are $60 (free for kids under 12). Order in advance on the Web site for substantial ticket discounts. No pets. Camping is available at the park—check the festival Web site for details.

CRAFTS AT RHINEBECK

Dutchess County Fairgrounds
Route 9
Rhinebeck
(845) 876-4001
www.craftsatrhinebeck.com

A very prestigious juried show, Crafts at Rhinebeck attracts more than 200 top-notch craftspeople—it's one of the premiere crafts events in the Northeast. The show is indoors. In addition to the crafts booths, there are food vendors, live music, and children's activities. The spring show is the third weekend in June; a fall show takes place at the very beginning of October. Hours are Saturday 10:00 a.m. to 6:00 p.m. and Sunday 10:00 a.m. to 5:00 p.m. Admission is $7; free for kids under 12. Free parking. No pets. Dutchess County Fairgrounds are fully accessible for people with mobility impairments.

GREEK FESTIVAL

Kimisis Greek Orthodox Church
140 South Grand Avenue
Poughkeepsie
(845) 452-0772

This large ethnic festival on the lovely church grounds features traditional Greek food and pastries, Greek folk dancers, live music, and vendors. The festival happens in mid-June and runs from Thursday through Saturday, 11:00 a.m. to 11:00 p.m., and Sunday from noon to 8:00 p.m. Entrance is free.

STRAWBERRY FESTIVAL
Riverfront Park
Beacon
(845) 542-0721
www.beaconsloop.org
Sponsored by the Beacon Sloop Club, proud owners of the *Woody Guthrie*, a gaff-rigged Hudson River sloop that is the companion vessel to the *Clearwater*, the Strawberry Festival takes place around the second weekend in June at Beacon Riverfront Park. Enjoy strawberries in lots of ways, including strawberry shortcake and chocolate-dipped strawberries, while listening to live music, enjoying fun events for kids and families, and taking a free ride on the *Woody*. Local vendors will also be on hand. The event begins at noon and ends at 5:00 p.m. Admission and parking are free.

JULY

GREAT HUDSON RIVER PADDLE
Hudson River Greenway Water Trail
(518) 473-3835
www.hudsongreenway.state.ny.us
The 156-mile Hudson River Greenway Water Trail (HRGWT) runs from Albany to New York City. In 2002 71 sites along the river were designated as part of the HRGWT. They provide access to the river, overnight accommodations, and access to attractions such as wildlife sanctuaries, historic sites, and downtown areas. The Great Hudson River Paddle is a 10-day event that starts at the beginning of July. Skilled paddlers can paddle the full length of the trail; less committed paddlers or those new to the sport have the chance to participate in local events that get people out on the water, usually at no charge.

HUDSON HARBOR FEST
Water Street
Hudson
(518) 822-8448
www.timeandspace.org
Sponsored by the City of Hudson and Time & Space Limited (see the Performing Arts and Film chapter for more on this arts organization), the Hudson Harbor Fest brings this city's lovely waterfront area alive with an outdoor performance program. The event kicks off with a three-day music festival over the Fourth of July weekend and continues every Saturday night for the rest of July. The music features local artists and many different genres, including hip-hop, folk, country, rock, blues, jazz, world, reggae, indie, and punk. Other events include dance, spoken word, and circus acts. Food vendors offer unusually good and interesting choices. Admission is free.

KINGSTON BIENNIAL SCULPTURE SHOW
Arts Society of Kingston
97 Broadway
Kingston
(845) 338-0331
www.askforarts.org
Outdoor and interior sculpture installations throughout the city of Kingston. The show happens in odd-numbered years and runs from July through October. A free map of the locations is available from ASK.

MID-HUDSON BALLOON FESTIVAL
Waryas Park and various other locations
Poughkeepsie
(845) 454-1700
www.pokchamb.org
One of the most photogenic events in the region, the Mid-Hudson Balloon Festival takes place the third weekend in June. It starts on Friday at 5:00 p.m. with a free carnival in Waryas Park. The live music and festivities continue until 11:00 p.m. Weather permitting, a mass balloon launch takes place at 6:00 p.m. from a number of spots around Poughkeepsie (the Hudson Valley Rowing Association boathouse on Water Street, for instance). Saturday features 6:00 a.m. balloon launches, a

bike race through Poughkeepsie in the morning, more carnival events and music at Waryas Park from noon to 11:00 p.m., another mass balloon launch at 6:00 p.m., and fireworks at Waryas Park at 9:00 p.m. On Sunday it's more carnival and balloon launches at 6:00 a.m. and again at 6:00 p.m. Each launch usually has at least 10 balloons, and they're visible all day long as they drift up, down, and around the Poughkeepsie area. Area businesses get into the spirit with special events as well. The festival is free.

NEWBURGH JAZZ FESTIVAL
Newburgh Waterfront (Front Street)
Newburgh
(845) 568-0198
www.newburghjazzseries.com
The Newburgh Jazz Festival is a long-running event that brings quality jazz and big-band swing to the region in a series of 18 free concerts every Wednesday and Thursday from 6:30 to 8:30 p.m. The concerts begin in early July and run through the end of August. Performers here include the Chiku Awali African Dance & Drum Company, the Gene Krupa II Orchestra, the Betty MacDonald Quartet, and the U.S. Military Academy Band's Jazz Knights. The concerts are outdoor events; bring your own blankets, chairs, and picnic supper. In case of rain, the concerts move indoors to the nearby Ritz Theater at 111 Broadway. A wheelchair-accessible parking lot is near the concert area.

RHINEBECK ANTIQUES FAIR
Dutchess County Fairgrounds
Route 9
Rhinebeck
(845) 876-1989
www.rhinebeckantiquesfair.com
The Summer Magic show of this famed antiques fair is the last Saturday in July. For more details, see the Antiquing chapter. Admission is $9 per person. Free parking. No pets allowed. The Dutchess County Fairgrounds are completely accessible to people with mobility impairments.

ROSENDALE STREET FESTIVAL
Main Street
Rosendale
(845) 943-6497
www.rosendalestreetfestival.com
The annual Rosendale Street Festival, held every year on a Saturday and Sunday in mid-July, offers five stages featuring dozens of bands—74 performed at the 2008 festival. This is a great way to scope out the local music scene for free, while enjoying all the usual street fair fun and food, provided by more then 100 vendors. This event is very popular, with attendance usually topping 20,000 for the weekend.

STONE HOUSE DAY
Hurley
(845) 331-4121
www.stonehouseday.org
Held the second Saturday of July, from 10:00 a.m. to 4:00 p.m. rain or shine, Stone House Day is a rare opportunity to see the interiors of some of Hurley's historic stone houses. Costumed guides, a militia encampment, period music performances, and other events bring history alive. Free buses take visitors to the houses not directly on Main Street. Stone House Day is arranged and sponsored by the Hurley Reformed Church. Tickets are $12.

TASTE OF COLUMBIA COUNTY BOUNTY
Columbia County Fairgrounds
Route 66
Chatham
(518) 828-4417
www.columbiachamber-ny.com
Some of the best chefs in the area cook the freshest produce from local farmers at this great event for foodies. It takes place at the Columbia County Fairgrounds in Chatham. Not only do you get to eat the food, you get to meet the people who grew it. This is a newish event and the date and costs aren't the same from year to year—check the Web site for updates.

ULSTER COUNTY FAIR
Ulster County Fairgrounds
Libertyville Road
New Paltz
(845) 255-1380
www.ulstercountyfair.com
The Ulster County Fair starts on the last Tuesday of July and runs for six days. It's a major regional event that celebrates the county's agricultural heritage. In addition to the farm animals on display, there's plenty of entertainment, including live music throughout the day and a headliner series of concerts each evening. The midway offers more than 20 rides, and there's a big food court with standard fair fare. Tractor pulls, antique farm machinery, a working blacksmith, and other exhibits add to the fun—and there are fireworks on opening night. The fair opens at 4:00 p.m. on Tuesday and stays open until 10:00 p.m. It opens at 8:00 a.m. the rest of the week and closes at 10:00 p.m. on Wednesday and Thursday, midnight on Friday and Saturday, and 8:00 p.m. on Sunday. Unusually for this sort of event, the price of $12 a head (free for kids under 4) is all-inclusive: parking, admission, and all the rides. Tuesday night is carload night—$30 per car with three or more people. No pets. The Ulster County Fairgrounds are mostly but not entirely accessible for those with mobility impairments.

AUGUST

ARTISTS' SOAPBOX DERBY
93 Broadway
Kingston
(845) 331-7517
www.artistsoapboxderby.com
One of the most enjoyable events in the area, this is a race where finishing first—in fact, finishing at all—is far down on the list of priorities. Prizes are awarded on a combined score of creativity and engineering. The first derby in 1995 had 8 entries and more than 500 spectators; in 2007, there were 42 entries and more than 8,000 spectators. In addition to the "race" itself, there's music and other performances all afternoon, along with plenty of food and merchandise vendors. The

free event starts at 1:00 p.m. at the corner of Spring Street and Broadway in the Rondout section of Kingston and ends two city blocks later at the corner of West Union Street and Broadway.

BETWEEN THE TIDES FESTIVAL
Saugerties Lighthouse
Saugerties
(845) 246-1844
www.saugertieslighthouse.com
Live music, dancing, local food, lighthouse tours, and swimming in the Hudson. Timing is important here: The festival is held on the third Sunday in August between 2:00 and 7:00 p.m., when low tide on the Hudson makes it possible to walk out on the half-mile trail to the lighthouse. Tickets are $20 per person, $35 for couples, $15 for seniors; free for children under 12.

COLUMBIA COUNTY FAIR
Columbia County Fairgrounds
Route 66
Chatham
(518) 392-2121
www.columbiafair.com
This small but very enjoyable six-day fair tends to get overlooked because it happens at the end of August through Labor Day weekend, just after the much larger Dutchess County Fair to the south. Columbia County has a lot of working farms, and the agricultural end of the fair is serious business. The exhibitions and competitions are traditional, as befits a fair that has been going on since 1840. Enjoy the domestic arts and crafts exhibits, the wool booth, the famed quilt show, and live farm animals. An exhibit that gets bigger every year is The New Face of Farming, featuring organic, community-supported, and niche farms. The competitions include more than 100 classes for fruits and vegetables, a hat-making contest, a pie-eating contest, and a hot dog–eating contest. A charmingly old-fashioned event is the School Girl Queen contest. Young women from the six school districts in the county vie for prizes based on personality, poise, and appearance. School spirit rules! The midway offers a good range of rides at reasonable prices, and the entertainment

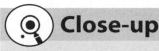

Close-up

Dutchess County Fair

The oldest, biggest, and best county fair in the region takes place for six days in late August at the Dutchess County Fairgrounds on Route 9 in Rhinebeck. The fairgrounds cover 160 beautifully landscaped acres—enough space to accommodate the half-million visitors every year.

This is still largely an agricultural show, with barns full of thousands of cows, pigs, sheep, and other farm critters. They're on display, but they're really there to be judged and win ribbons, not for their entertainment value. (Go fairly early during the weekday part of the fair to catch the judging.) Other agricultural exhibits include the Salute to Agriculture Tent, the excellent horticultural building, and the wonderful Dairy Birthing Center, where visitors can see calves being born and then experiencing their first days of life. There are horse shows, horse races, 4-H animal exhibits, pig racing, working antique farm machinery, craft demonstrations, flower and vegetable contests, and much more—from the agricultural perspective, the fair isn't all that different from when it began back in 1847.

Someone from back then would have a hard time recognizing the midway, food vendors, and merchandise vendors, however. The 100 or so rides are a good mix, including gentler rides for kids and scarier rides for grown-ups, and the midway games are varied and fun. More than 100 food booths offer mostly the usual high-calorie sugary or fried fare. Some local vendors and organizations provide a little variety—check out the amazing milk shakes made by the kids at the 4-H area. Building D features From Field to Table: A Celebration of the Foods We Eat. This is the place for the interesting and specialty foods, much of it from local providers. The merchandise from more than 300 individual vendors is mostly generic—hats, T-shirts, and a variety of other stuff—but some local businesses are also present. Musicians and entertainers of various sorts stroll the grounds during the day, in addition to daily performances in the talent tent. National headliners perform live every night on the large outdoor grandstand. The fair is open every day for six days from 10:00 a.m. to 10:00 p.m. Admission is $12; free for kids under 11. Parking is free. No pets. The entire fairground is wheelchair accessible. For more information: (845) 876-4001 or www.dutchessfair.com.

every night brings in headliner music acts. The fair runs from 5:00 to 11:00 p.m. on Wednesday, and from 10:00 a.m. to 11:00 p.m. the rest of the week. Admission is $10; $12 on Sunday. Kids under 12 are free. Thursday is Youth Day, when anyone under 18 gets in free before 4:00 p.m. The admission fee includes parking and all evening entertainment. No pets. The Columbia County Fairgrounds are mostly but not fully accessible for people with mobility handicaps.

CORN FESTIVAL
Riverfront Park
Beacon
(845) 542-0721
www.beaconsloop.org
Sponsored by the Beacon Sloop Club, the Corn

Festival takes place around the second weekend in August. Thousands of ears of corn are shucked and cooked by volunteers and sold for just $1 an ear. Live music (including an appearance by Pete Seeger), local vendors, activities for kids, and free rides on the Hudson River sloop *Woody Guthrie* round out the day. The event kicks off at noon and ends at 5:00 p.m. Admission and parking are free.

GREAT HUDSON VALLEY PEDAL
Albany to New York City
Parks and Trails New York
(518) 434-1583
www.ptny.org
A six-day, 200-mile bicycle tour from Albany to New York City, the Great Hudson Valley Pedal (GHVP) winds through the many scenic roads of

the region in mid-August. Many local bike races and rides are scheduled for the day the through-riders pass through the communities along the route—it's the closest the region comes to the excitement around the Tour de France. The GHVP is sponsored by Parks and Trails New York, a nonprofit organization devoted to expanding, protecting, and promoting a network of parks, trails, and open spaces throughout the state for the use and enjoyment of all. Check the Web site for schedule details.

HOOLEY ON THE HUDSON
T.R. Gallo Memorial Park
Kingston
(845) 338-6622
www.ulsteraoh.com

Celebrate America's Irish heritage on the last day of August from 11:30 a.m. to 9:00 p.m. on the historic Rondout waterfront. The event is sponsored by the Ulster County division of the Ancient Order of Hibernians and features live entertainment on two music stages along with a storytelling tent, many craft and food vendors, cultural exhibits, and lots of kids' activities. Free admission. Bring your own lawn chairs and picnic blankets.

HUDSON VALLEY RIBFEST
Ulster County Fairgrounds
Libertyville Road
New Paltz
(845) 306-4381
www.hudsonvalleyribfest.org

No matter what style of barbecue you prefer, you're likely to find it at this major three-day cook-off. Sponsored by the Highland Rotary and taking place the second weekend of August, the Hudson Valley Ribfest attracts more than 40 cooking teams every year, to say nothing of a wide range of other food vendors serving regional specialties. Other vendors sell barbecue-related items, and there are live music, cooking demonstrations, and activities for the kids. Admission is $5 a person; free for kids under 12. Parking is free. No pets. The Ulster County Fairgrounds are mostly but not completely accessible for people with mobility impairments.

WOODSTOCK GUITAR FESTIVAL
Various venues
Woodstock
(845) 247-0449
www.woodstockguitarfestival.com

Held over four days in mid-August, the Woodstock Guitar Festival happens at various venues throughout the Woodstock area. It features dozens of scheduled performances and plenty of informal guitar jams, along with opening and closing night parties that draw a celebrity crowd. Check the Web site for details about the schedule and tickets.

SEPTEMBER

CELTIC DAY IN THE PARK
Staatsburgh State Historic Site
Old Post Road
Staatsburgh
(845) 889-8851
www.staatsburgh.org

The spacious grounds behind Mills Mansion (see Hudson Valley Mansions and Historic Sites: East for details) are the longtime home to the annual Celtic Day in the Park, held in mid-September. Traditional Celtic music, dance, crafts, and other activities are highlighted—don't miss the pipe bands and the sheepdog herding demonstrations, to say nothing of the caber toss. The day culminates in a spectacular parade of pipe bands, clan associations, and flags of the Celtic nations. Admission is $10 for adults and $2 for children 12 and under.

GOOD GUYS HOT ROD AND CUSTOM CAR NATIONALS
Dutchess County Fairgrounds
Route 9
Rhinebeck
(925) 838-9876
www.good-guys.com

For hot rod fans, this huge three-day weekend event in mid-September is a regional must. It features more than 1,500 hot rods, custom cars, classic cars, muscle cars, and trick trucks—all dating from before 1972. Hundreds of vendors and exhibitors, live music, food vendors, a swap meet, and a kids' play area make this a family outing. Hours are Friday from 8:00 a.m. to 5:00 p.m., Saturday from 8:00 a.m. to 5:00 p.m., and Sunday from 8:00 a.m. to 3:00 p.m. Admission is $17 for adults; $6 for kids 7 to 12; free for kids 6 and under. Parking is free. No pets. The Dutchess County Fairgrounds are fully accessible for those with mobility handicaps.

HUDSON RIVER ARTS FESTIVAL
Waryas Park
Main Street at the Hudson River
Poughkeepsie
(845) 473-5288
www.bardavon.org
Nonstop live music, featuring reggae, bluegrass bands, and more, plus crafts, ethnic food, art exhibits, family activities, and fireworks over the Hudson that night. The festival takes place on a Saturday in mid-September from 2:00 to 10:00 p.m. Admission is free.

HUDSON RIVER VALLEY RAMBLE
Locations throughout the Hudson
River Valley
(518) 473-3835
www.hudsonrivervalley.com
The Hudson River Valley Ramble celebrates the history, culture, and natural resources of the Hudson River National Heritage Area. It's held over two weekends in mid-September and features everything from rugged hikes in wilderness areas to pleasant strolls through the grounds of historic sites. The area covered includes 10 counties— and 6 of them are in the mid-Hudson region. The event is sponsored by the Hudson River National Heritage Area and the Hudson River Valley Greenway. For details of events, check the Web site or call (800) 453-6665 for a free brochure.

HUDSON VALLEY GARLIC FESTIVAL
Cantine Field
Saugerties
(845) 246-3090
www.hvgf.org
The most pungent festival in the region takes place the last full weekend in September. It's

sponsored by the Kiwanis Club of Saugerties; the organizers are all volunteers and the profits go back into scholarships and community donations. The celebration of garlic includes garlic bulbs and braids, garlic-themed arts and crafts, live music, and lots and lots of garlicky food, including garlic ice cream (it's surprisingly good). Numerous vendors offer amazingly varied garlic-based products, as well as cooking demonstrations, garlic-braiding demonstrations, and expert advice on growing your own garlic. This is an extremely popular event, with more than 60,000 attendees. If you go on Sunday, get there early—many vendors sell out and go home by midafternoon. To find Cantine Field, just look for the huge garlic-shaped balloon floating above it. Hours are Saturday from 10:00 a.m. to 6:00 p.m. and Sunday from 10:00 a.m. to 5:00 p.m. Admission is $7 per person, free for kids under 12. Parking is free. No pets!

HUDSON VALLEY WINE AND FOOD FEST
Dutchess County Fairgrounds
Route 9
Rhinebeck
www.hudsonvalleywinefest.com
More than 40 wineries from all over New York State, along with wines from around the world, are featured at this weekend event in early September. Gourmet food, cooking demonstrations, fine art and crafts vendors, and live music round out the event. There's even kids' activities, but this really is an event for grown-ups, complete with designated drivers. The festivities run from 11:00 a.m. to 7:00 p.m. Saturday and from 11:00 a.m. to 5:00 p.m. Sunday. Tasting tickets are $30; designated driver tickets (you can still eat) are $15. No pets. Free parking. The Dutchess County Fairgrounds are fully accessible for people with mobility impairments.

OLD NEW PALTZ DAY
Huguenot Historical Society
18 Broadhead Avenue
New Paltz
(845) 255-1600
www.huguenotstreet.org

This festival focuses on the French Huguenot and Dutch roots of the Historic Huguenot Street district. Events include tours of the stone houses, interpreters in period dress, demonstrations, period performances, food vendors, and children's activities. The festival is held the second Saturday of September from 11:00 a.m. to 5:00 p.m. Events are free or have only nominal charges. *Note:* In previous years this event was known as Stone House Day or Colonial Street Festival.

TASTE OF NEW PALTZ
Ulster County Fairgrounds
Libertyville Road
New Paltz
(845) 255-0243
www.newpaltzchamber.org
A Hudson Valley festival of food and fun featuring great food from area restaurants, wineries, and breweries, plus crafts, kids' activities, a wellness and recreation expo, and live music all day. The event happens under tents on a Saturday in mid-September, from 11:00 a.m. to 5:00 p.m. Admission is $3 for adults, free for kids under 12. No pets. Free parking. The Ulster County Fairgrounds are mostly but not completely accessible for people with mobility impairments.

WOODSTOCK/NEW PALTZ ART AND CRAFTS FAIR
Ulster County Fairgrounds
Libertyville Road
New Paltz
(845) 679-8087
www.quailhollow.com
The Labor Day weekend edition of this well-regarded craft show—see the listing under May for details.

OCTOBER

CIVIL WAR WEEKEND
Huguenot Historical Society
18 Broadhead Avenue
New Paltz
(845) 255-1600
www.huguenotstreet.org

Hosted by the 120th New York State Volunteers, a reenactment group based on this historic regiment, the Civil War Weekend events take place at Locust Lawn and Terwilliger House, stone homes on historic Huguenot Street. The festivities include period displays of camp life and drills and demonstrations of battle tactics. The event is free.

COLUMBIA–GREENE RIVERFRONT FAIR AND CROSS-COUNTY CHILI COOKOFF CONTEST
Columbia County Chamber of Commerce
507 Warren Street
Hudson
(518) 828-4417
www.columbiachamber-ny.com
The annual one-day Columbia–Greene Riverfront Fair is held at Hudson Waterfront Park in Hudson (Columbia County on the east bank) and at Catskill Point in Catskill (Greene County on the west bank). The Cross-County Chili Cookoff Contest is just one of the events, but it draws the biggest crowd. Proceeds from the contest benefit Columbia County Bounty, an organization promoting local foods and agriculture. The fair usually happens the first Saturday in October, but it's sometimes moved to the end of September—check the Web site for details. It's free.

CRAFTS AT RHINEBECK
Dutchess County Fairgrounds
Route 9
Rhinebeck
(845) 876-4001
www.craftsatrhinebeck.com
The fall show for this very prestigious juried event takes place the beginning of October—see the listing under June for details.

IROQUOIS ART AND CULTURAL FESTIVAL
Dutchess County Fairgrounds
Route 9
Rhinebeck
(845) 876-4001
www.iroquoisfestival.com
Celebrate the Native American heritage of the Hudson Valley at this popular weekend event in early October. The culture of the Iroquois,

Mohawk, and other New York region tribes is featured. The festival showcases Iroquois social dancing and other Native American dance styles. Enjoy live music on Native American instruments, storytelling, and crafts demonstrations, including making cornhusk dolls, feathersmithing, and lacrosse stick making. The children's craft area is a real draw at this festival—kids get to try their hand at traditional crafts and take their masterpiece home. Food vendors are on-site. The festival runs from 11:00 a.m. to 6:00 p.m. both days. Admission is $7 for adults and $5 for kids 6 to 12; free for kids under 6. Free parking. No pets. The entire fairground is wheelchair accessible.

NEW YORK STATE SHEEP AND WOOL FAMILY FESTIVAL/GEM AND MINERAL SHOW
Dutchess County Fairgrounds
Route 9
Rhinebeck
(845) 756-2323
www.sheepandwool.com
If you're into wool this is the place for you, with more than 200 wool artists and all sorts of exhibits, to say nothing of the sheep themselves (a different breed is featured every year). Even if wool gives you a rash, this is a really enjoyable event, especially if you bring along some kids. You will find lots of animals (sheep, llamas, alpacas, goats, sheep dogs, and a petting zoo) and lots of other kid stuff as well. There are sheep dog trials, dog Frisbee, and the not-to-be-missed Hula Hoop sheep toss (the Hula Hoops, not the sheep, are tossed). The show is sponsored by the Dutchess County Wool and Sheep Growers and happens in mid-October. It's open Saturday from 9:00 a.m. to 6:00 p.m. and Sunday from 10:00 a.m. to 5:00 p.m. Admission is $10; free for kids under 12. The fee includes admission to the Mid–Hudson Valley Gem & Mineral Society show, which always runs concurrently. The fee also includes the annual Dutchess Community College Punkin' Chunkin', where teams of the school's engineering and science students compete to launch pumpkins at targets, using a variety of ingenious devices. The flinging begins at noon on Sunday.

Free parking. No pets. The entire fairground is wheelchair accessible.

NORTHEAST SMALL FARM AND RURAL LIVING EXPO
Ulster County Fairgrounds
Libertyville Road
New Paltz
(845) 677-8223
www.smallfarmexpo.org
The Northeast Expo brings together state agencies, organizations, and companies associated with farming and rural living from three states—New York, New Jersey, and Pennsylvania. More than 50 educational workshops, many including hands-on demonstrations, are offered, and a large exhibit hall showcases regional businesses and agencies who work with farms and rural communities. In addition to specific workshops, experts are on hand to answer questions related to small farms and rural living. A lot of serious stuff goes on here, but it's also a casual and enjoyable family event, with lots of animals to see and a variety of children's learning activities. The expo is on a weekend in mid-October. It runs from 9:00 a.m. to 4:00 p.m. each day. Admission is $5 per adult; $2 for children 5 to 14; free for children under 5. Free parking. No pets. The Ulster County Fairgrounds are mostly but not completely wheelchair accessible.

PUMPKIN FESTIVAL
Riverfront Park
Beacon
(845) 542-0721
www.beaconsloop.org
The Beacon Sloop Club sponsors this event on a Sunday in mid-October, just in time for Halloween. The festival includes crafts demonstrations, live music, pumpkin pie, and, of course, pumpkins and all sorts of pumpkin products for sale from local farmers. Free rides aboard the *Woody Guthrie,* a gaff-rigged Hudson River sloop, are offered. Dress for the weather—it can get cold on the waterfront. The festival begins at noon and ends at 5:00 p.m. Admission and parking are free.

REENACTMENT OF THE BURNING OF KINGSTON
Stockade District Visitors Center
308 Clinton Avenue
Kingston
(845) 331-9506
www.ci.kingston.ny.us
Kingston was declared the first capital of New York State in 1777. On October 16, 1777, the town was burned by British troops. The event is reenacted biennially in even-numbered years over a weekend in mid-October. Living history demonstrations, military reenacters, a ship battle on the Rondout Creek, and lots of other activities make this a great educational event. Free admission.

RHINEBECK ANTIQUES FAIR
Dutchess County Fairgrounds
Route 9
Rhinebeck
(845) 876-1989
www.rhinebeckantiquesfair.com
The fall show of this very popular antiques fair is the second weekend in October (Columbus Day weekend). For more details, see the Antiquing chapter. Admission is $9 a person. Free parking. No pets allowed. The Dutchess County Fairgrounds are completely wheelchair accessible.

WOODSTOCK FILM FESTIVAL
Various venues
Woodstock
(845) 679-4265
www.woodstockfilmfestival.com
A showcase for indie films, the Woodstock Film Festival the first week in October draws top talent and premieres outstanding new productions. In addition to the films, there are panel discussions and an extensive schedule of concerts. Despite the name, the actual screenings take place at several venues in the region, including the Tinker Street Cinema in Woodstock, Upstate Films in Rhinebeck, and the Rosendale Theater in Rosendale. Ticket prices are $8 to $20 for films and $15 to $20 for panel discussions. Concert prices vary. Order tickets in advance if possible; this event gets more popular by the year and tickets tend to sell out early.

NOVEMBER

ROSENDALE INTERNATIONAL PICKLE FESTIVAL
Community Center
Route 32
Rosendale
(845) 658-9649
www.picklefest.com
Held the Sunday before Thanksgiving, the International Pickle Festival is a quirky but very popular event. In addition to all the delicious pickles and pickle-related products available from the exhibitors, there's a pickle-judging contest, a pickle toss, a pickle-eating contest, and a pickle juice–drinking contest. Those who don't like to pucker up can enjoy lots of other food. In keeping with the international theme, the festival offers live entertainment with an ethnic slant, including Irish dancers, a Japanese tea ceremony, African drummers, and folk music. The event goes from 10:00 a.m. to 5:00 p.m. Admission is $5 per family; $3 for individuals. Free parking. Proceeds benefit the local youth center and local charities.

DECEMBER

COLD SPRING BY CANDLELIGHT
Main Street
Cold Spring
(845) 278-PARC
www.putnamarc.org
Cold Spring's many historic homes and sites are open to the public the first Saturday in December. There's also holiday caroling, discounts at local shops and restaurants, visits with Old St. Nick, and more. The Cold Spring trolley takes visitors around town. House tours are from noon to 6:00 p.m. Advance tickets are $20 for adults, $18 for seniors, and $12 for children under 12. Tickets are more expensive on the day of the event—order in advance if you can, because this event always sells out. The money benefits a local organization for children with developmental disabilities.

WINTER WALK
Warren Street
Hudson
(518) 822-1438
www.hudsonoperahouse.org

A mile-long outdoor party, the Winter Walk along Warren Street on the first Saturday in December is the kickoff to the holiday season in the historic city of Hudson. The street is closed to traffic from 5:00 to 8:00 p.m., and horse-drawn carriages and a trolley are available for those who need a lift. Warren Street is transformed for Winter Walk. Clowns, Victorian carolers, stilt-walkers, bagpipers, strolling musicians, and costumed characters join the throng. The shop windows contain amazing window installations featuring dancers posing as mannequins that come to life. Dance performances and a wide range of musicians perform on the street and in shops and restaurants. Mr. and Mrs. Santa Claus welcome the kids at City Hall. To top it all off, there are fireworks at Promenade Hill at the western end of Warren Street. More than 15,000 people attend this popular free event; parking can be a bit of a problem, so arrive early to get a spot.

PARKS AND THE OUTDOORS

The Hudson Valley is blessed with many wonderful parks, preserves, and hiking trails. In addition to the extensive system of New York State parks, the region has many outstanding county and town parks and a number of preserves managed by nonprofit organizations such as Scenic Hudson. Many of the Hudson River mansions and historic sites have extensive grounds with hiking trails—see the chapters on Hudson Valley Mansions and Historic Sites for details. In addition, the area has three wonderful rail trails—old railroad tracks that have been converted into linear trails—and access to the Appalachian Trail (AT). And, of course, there's all those miles of Hudson River waterfront with plenty of opportunities for boating and fishing. The possibilities for picnicking, hiking, swimming, biking, boating, fishing, nature-watching, winter sports, camping, and just having fun in nature are wide in the region.

PARKS AND PRESERVES

The parks and preserves described here are easily accessible, are free or have nominal entry fees, and often, though not always, offer facilities such as visitor centers, bathrooms, and water. Many are at least partially accessible to those with handicaps. Dogs are allowed in most of the places listed here, but they must be on leashes; be prepared to clean up after your pet. Most parks and preserves are open from dawn to dusk year-round, but be aware that access may be difficult in the winter.

Education is a big part of the mission for the area's parks and preserves. Many of the places listed here offer free or very inexpensive environmental education programs, such as ranger-led nature walks. Many also offer excellent activities and summer programs for kids. Check ahead if you're planning a visit. The management information given for each site is the best starting point for learning more.

In this section, the descriptions list the location of the main access point or parking area for each site. Some sites, especially the larger ones, have additional parking areas or access points. Information about them is usually available at the main entrance. Park only in designated areas—parking on the shoulders of narrow country roads isn't safe, plus it could get you a ticket.

New York State has an extensive network of wildlife management areas (WMAs) and state multiple-use areas (MUAs). These sites preserve many thousands of acres of open space and often have trail networks, but for the most part they're undeveloped and fairly rugged. These sites aren't covered here. For more information about WMAs and MUAs, check with the New York State Department of Environmental Conservation at www.dec.ny.gov or (518) 402-8013.

Columbia County
Ancram
LAKE TAGHKANIC STATE PARK
Access/parking: From the Taconic State Parkway 1 mile south of Route 82
Management:
1528 Route 82
(518) 851-3631
www.nysparks.state.ny.us
Lake Taghkanic State Park is the ideal recreation park—it has everything within its 1,569 acres. Beautiful Lake Taghkanic is the centerpiece here, covering 172 acres. Two swimming beaches are on the lake; visitors can change in the bathhouse built by the CCC in 1933. Other water sports

include rowboating and paddling (you can rent a rowboat at the park or bring your own canoe or kayak) and fishing (ice fishing in the winter). The park has pleasant picnic areas, a playground, a baseball field, and a number of hiking and biking trails. There is a nice camping area and some rental cottages. In the winter, ice-skating on the lake, cross-country skiing, snowmobiling, sledding, and snowshoeing are popular. No pets allowed. The vehicle entry fee is $7.

i During peak usage seasons, New York State parks charge a small vehicle entry fee, usually less than $5. Those fees can still add up. Heavy park users can purchase Empire Passports. The annual fee of $59 allows unlimited day-use vehicle entry. For more information, check with New York State Parks at www.nysparks.state.ny.us or (518) 474-0456.

Greenport

GREENPORT CONSERVATION AREA

Access/parking: Daisy Hill Road
Management:
Columbia Land Conservancy
49 Main Street
Chatham, NY 12037
(518) 392-5252
www.clctrust.org

The 714 acres of the Greenport Conservation Area contain meadows, forests, and wetlands along the Hudson River. The area has 4 miles of easy trails that meander in and out of the woods and through the fields. The "Access for All" trail, the first of its kind in the Hudson Valley, is a 1-mile trail with a firm surface suitable for wheelchairs. The trail leads to a beautiful overlook on the bluffs above the river. The trailhead, gazebo, and picnic shelter are paved with natural stone, making them accessible as well. Broader access to the other trails in the area will be available through the purchase of three all-terrain wheelchairs. The area is very popular with cross-country skiers in the winter. Deer hunting is allowed on the land; use caution if visiting the area in November and December.

Philmont

HIGH FALLS CONSERVATION AREA

Access/parking: Roxbury Road in the town of Claverack
Management:
Columbia Land Conservancy
49 Main Street
Chatham, NY 12037
(518) 392-5252
www.clctrust.org

Columbia County's highest waterfall is on view at this 47-acre preserve—the Agawamtuck Creek cascades 150 feet into a large pool. The water eventually finds its way to the Hudson River. The round-trip to an overlook with spectacular views of the falls is only about 1 mile of easy walking.

Stuyvesant

Lewis A. Swyer Preserve at Mill Creek Marsh
Access/parking: Route 9J
Management:
The Nature Conservancy
Eastern New York Chapter
265 Chestnut Ridge Road
Mt. Kisco, NY 10549
(914) 244-3271
www.nature.org

Freshwater tidal swamps are relatively rare—there has to be a riverbed that runs close to sea level for a long distance from its mouth. That describes the Hudson River exactly. At Swyer Preserve, 120 miles from the mouth of the Hudson, the impact of tides can be easily seen. The tides here can change the freshwater level of Mill Creek by 4 feet. The adjacent flat land is frequently flooded by the tides, creating one of only five freshwater tidal swamps in New York State. The site is rich in birdlife and unusual plants. The area is so environmentally significant that it was acquired by the Nature Conservancy in 1989. Even though the site is a swamp, visitors can explore it with dry feet. A half-mile boardwalk starts near the parking area. It runs through the swamp along Mill Creek and ends in a viewing platform overlooking the Hudson and the Amtrak rail tracks. Trains go past here fairly often—if you wave to the engineer, he'll wave back.

Dutchess County

Beacon

HUDSON HIGHLANDS STATE PARK

Route 9D

(845) 225-7207

www.nysparks.state.ny.us

Hudson Highlands State Park is largely undeveloped, but it is the site of Breakneck Ridge, one of the area's most challenging and worthwhile hikes (included in this chapter) and many other great trails. The park covers nearly 6,000 acres in several parcels stretching from the Peekskill area all the way to Dennings Point in Beacon. The extensive trail network makes it popular with hikers and mountain bikers. Most of the trails are fairly rugged, however, and this is not really a place for kids, dogs, or inexperienced hikers. The best map of the area is the New York–New Jersey Trail Conference's "East Hudson Trails. "

Millbrook

INSTITUTE OF ECOSYSTEM STUDIES

65 Sharon Turnpike

(845) 677-5343

www.ecostudies.org

Founded in 1983 by the eminent ecologist Dr. Gene Likens, the Institute of Ecosystem Studies is one of the largest ecological programs in the world. The main purpose here is scientific research, but IES is also open to the public. The grounds cover 1,924 acres and are laced with hiking trails. Trails and boardwalks wind through the habitats—the best part of the grounds for kids. As part of its educational mission, IES offers a wide range of free or inexpensive public programs for all ages and levels of interest. Call or check the online schedule for details. The grounds are open April 1 to October 31, Monday through Saturday from 9:00 a.m. to 6:00 p.m., and Sunday from 11:00 a.m. to 6:00 p.m. Hiking trails and roadways are closed for safety reasons from November 1 to March 31.

Pine Plains

THOMPSON POND/STISSING MOUNTAIN

Access/parking: Lake Road

Management:

The Nature Conservancy

Eastern New York Chapter

265 Chestnut Ridge Road

Mt. Kisco, NY 10549

(914) 244-3271

www.nature.org

Thompson Pond is an ancient kettle pond, formed nearly 15,000 years ago when a massive chunk of melting glacial ice formed a water-filled depression. The kettle gradually filled in, forming three interconnected water bodies, including Thompson Pond, which is the headwaters for the Wappinger Creek, a major tributary of the Hudson River. The pond and the surrounding 507 acres became a Nature Conservancy preserve in 1973. The preserve is an outstanding example of a calcareous (limey) wetland—more than 245 species of land plants and 142 wetlands species are found here, along with 162 bird species and 27 mammal species. Several easy trails lead around the pond. A steep trail from the parking area leads up to the top of Stissing Mountain, an unusual outcropping of gneiss that is more than one billion years old. The mountain rises to 1,403 feet above sea level. The historic fire tower, built by the WPA in 1939, adds another 80 feet. Even if you don't climb the tower, the views from here are spectacular. Two other trailheads lead to the top of Stissing Mountain: off Mountain Road in the town of Stanford, and from Hicks Hill Road in the town of Pine Plains.

Pleasant Valley

JAMES BAIRD STATE PARK

Access/parking: Off Freedom Plains Road on the west side, off the Taconic State Parkway on the east side

Management:

14 Maintenance Lane

(845) 452-1489

www.nysparks.state.ny.us

Recreation is the main idea at 600-acre James Baird State Park. The park offers spacious picnic areas, a sports complex with basketball, softball, tennis, and volleyball, and a playground. Seven miles of hiking/biking trails crisscross the park; in the winter they become cross-country skiing and snowshoeing trails. There's also a golf course and driving range—see the Golf chapter for details.

Red Hook

POET'S WALK ROMANTIC LANDSCAPE PARK
Access/parking: River Road (Route 103)
Management:
Scenic Hudson
1 Civic Center Plaza, Suite 200
Poughkeepsie, NY 12601
(845) 473-4440
www.scenichudson.org

Poet's Walk was once part of the vast Livingston family estates in the region. The 120-acre site was heavily modified in the mid-1800s by land-scape architect Hans Jacob Ehler to open up the river views and create walking paths designed to inspire beautiful thoughts—hence the name Poet's Walk. He did a good job. Poet's Walk today offers wonderful views of the Hudson, the Kingston-Rhinecliff Bridge, and the Catskills. Two miles of easy paths meander through woods and fields. A rustic cedar pavilion is a good spot for a picnic.

Rhinebeck

FERNCLIFF FOREST GAME REFUGE AND FOREST PRESERVE
Access/parking: Mount Rutsen Road
Management:
Ferncliff Forest Inc.
Box 1
Rhinebeck, NY 12572

A 200-acre preserve that has some of the finest old-growth forest in the Hudson Valley, Ferncliff Forest has 4 miles of uncrowded trails available for hiking, camping, mountain biking, cross-country skiing, fishing (on South Pond), and picnics. The land was once the property of the Astor family; it was donated to the Rhinebeck

Rotary by Brooke Astor in 1964. The viewing tower at Ferncliff Forest is its high point, both literally and figuratively. The current tower replaces the old military watch tower built during World War II to provide early warning of possible air attacks on President Roosevelt's house in nearby Hyde Park and on New York City. The World War II tower fell into disrepair and had to be closed in 2005. A new tower was constructed in 2007. It rises 75 feet from the top of Mt. Rutsen (350 feet above sea level) and offers wonderful views of the surrounding area.

Staatsburg

MARGARET LEWIS NORRIE STATE PARK AND OGDEN MILLS AND RUTH LIVINGSTON MILLS STATE PARK
Old Post Road
(845) 889-4646
www.nysparks.state.ny.us

Technically speaking, these are two separate parks, but for all intents and purposes they're one unit covering more than 1,000 acres along the Hudson River. The Mills part of the park includes Dinsmore Golf Club (see the Golf chapter for details) and Staatsburgh State Historic Site (see the Mansions and Historic Sites: East chapter). A good trail network for hiking, biking, cross-country skiing, and snowshoeing runs through both parks. A marina with 145 slips and a boat launch ramp makes this a popular stop for sailors and paddlers on the river. Fishing is allowed from the shore. The park also has picnic areas and a beautiful campground with cabin rentals. The Norrie Point Environmental Center has exhibits about the Hudson River and offers a number of excellent free environmental education programs for adults and kids—check ahead for the schedule.

Standfordville

WILCOX MEMORIAL PARK
Route 199
(845) 758-6100

Operated by Dutchess County, Wilcox Memorial Park covers 615 acres in the rolling hills of northern Dutchess County. The park has two small lakes with lifeguarded swimming beaches, a bathhouse, and rowboat and paddleboat rentals. Fishing is allowed from the shore and from rowboats. The park has picnic areas and pavilions that are very popular with groups. Kids enjoy the playground and the miniature golf course. Five miles of trails with a number of scenic overlooks loop through the park. The family campground has 27 sites. Wilcox Park is well known to amateur astronomers in the region for being very dark at night. The friendly folks at the Mid-Hudson Astonomical Association stargaze here (845) 255-4719; www.midhudsonastro.org). Dutchess County residents can use the park for free. Nonresidents pay a $5 vehicle entry fee ($10 on Memorial Day, July 4, and Labor Day).

Tivoli

TIVOLI BAYS WILDLIFE MANAGEMENT AREA

Access/parking: Kidd Lane
Management:
Hudson River National Estuarine Research Reserve
Bard College Field Station
Annadale-on-Hudson, NY 12504
(845) 758-7010

Covering 1, 722 acres, Tivoli Bays contains two large river coves and intertidal marshes and extensive woodlands. The area is environmentally significant as a breeding ground for Hudson River fish. It was designated as a New York State Important Bird Area in 1997. The area has 4 miles of trails for hiking and biking and is well known among local birders as the place to be during the spring and fall migrations. A canoe launch with parking is in the North Bay section. The Tivoli Bays Visitor Center is located in the village of Tivoli at the Watts dePeyster Fireman's Hall (1 Tivoli Commons, 845-889-4745, ext. 105). A foot trail to North Bay starts behind the center.

Wappingers Falls

BOWDOIN PARK

85 Sheafe Road
(845) 298-4600
www.co.dutchess.ny.us/CountyGov/
Departments/DPW-Parks/PPbowdoin.htm

A Dutchess County park located on the banks of the Hudson, Bowdoin Park covers 301 acres. It's a recreational park, with plenty of sports fields for baseball, softball, soccer, and lacrosse, along with a cross-country race course. The award-winning wheelchair-accessible playground is great for kids—they adore climbing on the water-spraying turtles. Four miles of well-maintained trails go through the park, including a wetlands area with boardwalks. The park has four pavilions (three of them wheelchair accessible) and lots of picnic tables scattered throughout the open areas. The lovely Ellessdie Chapel is a popular spot for weddings, and the Mapleknoll Lodge is available for receptions, parties, and other events. The band shell on a hillside offers outstanding free summer concerts, with programs ranging from the Hudson Valley Philharmonic to Kenny Loggins. The Community Center building has a well-equipped auditorium and meeting spaces. The park holds family-friendly community events year-round. Call the park office for updates. Entrance to the park is free. Fees are charged to use the pavilions, community center, chapel, ball fields, and Mapleknoll Lodge. All the facilities are very popular—make reservations well in advance, especially in the summer.

Greene County

Athens

COHOTATE PRESERVE AND GREENE COUNTY ENVIRONMENTAL EDUCATION CENTER

Access/parking: Route 385
Management:
Greene County Soil and Water Conservation District
907 Greene County Office Building
Cairo, NY 12413
(518) 622-3620
www.gcswcd.com/education/cohotate.html

A small but very interesting site, Cohotate Preserve is only 52 acres—but it has more than 3,500 feet of Hudson River shoreline. Kids like this spot because they can get right down to the water and look for driftwood, rocks, and other treasures. The preserve takes its name from the Iroquois word for the Hudson, meaning "water that flows two ways." The terrain is surprisingly varied, with several distinct forest types, ridges and rolling hills, and tidal wetlands. The paths are clearly marked and very easy. The remains of an old icehouse are on the Icehouse Path by the river. Interpretive signs here discuss the history of the ice industry on the Hudson decades ago. Picnic tables make this a good spot for lunch. The Environmental Field Station, used for classes, is nearby. The Riverside Trail meanders along the shoreline and leads to an observation deck overlooking the tidal wetland.

Catskill

RAMSHORN-LIVINGSTON SANCTUARY
Access/parking: Grandview Avenue
Management:
Scenic Hudson
1 Civic Center Plaza, Suite 200
Poughkeepsie, NY 12601
(845) 473-4440
www.scenichudson.org
This Scenic Hudson preserve protects 480 acres of the Hudson River's largest tidal swamp forest. It's an important breeding ground for American shad and bass. A 28-foot wildlife observation tower overlooking the river makes this a great place for bird-watching, especially during the spring migration. More than 3 miles of easy trails lace the preserve. If you don't mind carrying your canoe or kayak for about half a mile, you can paddle out through the swamp into the Hudson.

Orange County
Cornwall
BLACK ROCK FOREST
Parking/access: Reservoir Road
Management:
Black Rock Forest Consortium
129 Continental Road
Cornwall, NY 12518
(845) 534-4517
www.blackrockforest.org
A living laboratory for field-based scientific research, the Black Rock Forest covers nearly 4,000 acres of the central and highest portion of the rugged Hudson Highlands. The preserve is dedicated to scientific research, environmental education, and conservation of the natural ecosystem. It's managed by the Black Rock Consortium, a group of private and public educational and research institutions. The forest is open to the public as well, and an extensive trail system winds through it. Some of the trails are on the rugged side, but it's easy to put together trail loops for any level of hiking ability. As you hike, you may see some of the research areas in the forest. Look for trees with various kinds of markings painted on them, painted stakes, and monitoring equipment. The award-winning Black Rock Center for Science and Education is worth visiting. The building was constructed on green principles—it was built largely from wood taken from the forest, and it has a geothermal heating and cooling system. It also has composting toilets, which are always a big hit with kids. Education is the primary mission here; school groups often spend a day or an overnight. A lot of good programs for the public are offered on weekends. The consortium depends on voluntary contributions to cover some of the cost of maintaining the forest. The suggested donation is $2 for adults and $1 for children. No bikes allowed.

Putnam County

Cold Spring

CLARENCE FAHNESTOCK MEMORIAL STATE PARK

75 Mountain Laurel Lane
(Route 301)
(845) 225-7207
www.nysparks.state.ny.us

Fahnestock Park started out in 1929 as a large park of about 2,400 acres in the Hudson Highlands; over the years it has grown to become a huge park. Since the early 1990s, land donations have enlarged the park from some 6,000 acres to more than 16,000 acres of pristine woodlands, meadows, wetlands, lakes, and streams. The original part of the park is centered around beautiful Canopus Lake, which offers a large beach, swimming, rowboating, fishing, and picnic areas. The park has a scenic campground, an excellent nature center, and many good hiking and biking trails, including a section of the Appalachian Trail. A favorite hike is the Three Lakes Trail, which follows the AT for part of the way. Within the larger park is Fahnestock Winter Park, which offers 10 miles of machine-groomed trails for cross-country skiing and snowshoeing, plus a great sledding hill, a warming lodge, equipment rental, food and drink, and restrooms. (For weather updates, call the Ski Center at 845-225-3998.) The Winter Park is based at the Taconic Outdoor Education Center, but the center is active year-round and offers a wide range of educational programs and events. The vehicle entry fee is $7.

Garrison

CONSTITUTION MARSH AUDUBON CENTER AND SANCTUARY

127 Warren Landing Road
(845) 265-2601
www.constitutionmarsh.org

The 270 acres of Constitution Marsh include an extensive freshwater tidal marsh, one of only five along the entire length of the Hudson River. The marsh is a crucial breeding ground for fish and is highly attractive to birds—more than 100 species have been seen here. The highlight of a visit is the 1,000-foot boardwalk that leads through the marsh and opens out to some stunning vistas over the river and across it to West Point. The excellent visitor center is open Tuesday through Sunday, 9:00 a.m. to 5:00 p.m. Check with the visitor center for the schedule of free guided canoe tours and other activities. Paddlers can enter the marsh from the Hudson, but there's no launch point in the preserve (use Foundry Dock Park in Cold Spring). No dogs allowed.

MANITOGA/THE RUSSEL WRIGHT DESIGN CENTER

Parking and management:
584 Route 9D
(845) 424-3812
www.russelwrightcenter.org

The 75 acres of Manitoga, home of famed designer Russel Wright, contain more than 4 miles of hiking trails. (See the Hudson Valley Mansions and Historic Sites: East Side chapter for more on visiting the home.) The trails are part of a carefully designed landscape. It begins at the edge of Mary's Meadow (named for Wright's wife) with a set of stone steps. The paths then follow the land's natural contours. They go past dramatic rock formations and open out onto a variety of scenic vistas and lovely meadows. The paths are designed to go in one direction as a series of connected loops. Color-coded markers make them easy to follow. Paths at Manitoga connect to the Osborn Loop trail, which in turn connects to the Appalachian Trail in the southern portion of Hudson Highlands State Park. The suggested paths maintenance contribution is $5 for adults and $3 for kids.

Ulster County

Cragsmoor

SAM'S POINT PRESERVE
Access/parking: Sam's Point Road
(845) 647-7989
Management:
The Nature Conservancy
Eastern New York Chapter
265 Chestnut Ridge Road
Mt. Kisco, NY 10549
(914) 244-3271
www.nature.org

Ridgetop dwarf pine barrens are one of the rarest ecosystems in the world—and Sam's Point Preserve was created to protect one of the world's finest examples. The 5,400-acre preserve is perched on the highest point of the Shawangunk Ridge. In 1996, after nearly 25 years of negotiation, Sam's Point was finally protected for the public by a consortium of nonprofit groups led by the Open Space Institute (OSI). Today OSI owns the preserve, but it is managed by the Nature Conservancy. Sam's Point is a wonderful place for hiking, with fabulous views and the chance to see many rare plants. You can also visit the ice caves—fissures in the rock that are so deep and far from sunlight that they have ice in them even during the summer. (The ice caves may be seasonally closed—call ahead to be sure.) A visit here starts with Sam's Point Conservation Center, an energy-efficient building with restrooms, classrooms, and interactive exhibits, open Friday through Monday, 9:00 a.m. to 5:00 p.m. A short, easy trail (about half a mile) from the center leads to Sam's Point, an overlook that is 2,255 feet above sea level and one of the highest points in the 'Gunks. On a really clear day, you can see New York City from here. The trail to the ice caves is also short (less than half a mile) and easy; the circuit through the caves is short and goes along a boardwalk with artificial lighting—a major hit with kids. Longer trails also run through the preserve, including a section of the long-distance Long Path. A popular walk is the trail to Verkeerderkill Falls. It's nearly 6 miles to go and return, but the falls and the views are worth it.

Serious hikers should use the New York–New Jersey Trail Conference Shawangunk Trails map to put together loops within the preserve and hikes that connect to nearby Minnewaska State Park Preserve and the Mohonk Preserve (both sites are included in this chapter). The vehicle entry fee is $7.

Esopus

BLACK CREEK FOREST PRESERVE
Access/parking: Winding Brook Road just off
Route 9W
Management:
Scenic Hudson
1 Civic Center Plaza, Suite 200
Poughkeepsie, NY 12601
(845) 473-4440
www.scenichudson.org

A visit to 130-acre Black Creek Forest Preserve starts off with a bang: You walk into the preserve over a 120-foot suspension bridge that spans Black Creek. Kids love it. Black Creek takes its name from the dark color of the stream's bottom, caused by tannic acid from the hemlock trees that shade it. The water itself is filtered by wetlands and is crystal clear. Black Creek flows into the Hudson and is affected by the tides. It's a crucial spawning ground for Hudson River fish such as shad. Two miles of easy trails loop through the preserve and down to the shore. No bikes allowed.

SHAUPENEAK RIDGE
Access/parking: Lower parking area on
Old Post Road; upper parking area on
Poppletown Road
Management:
Scenic Hudson
1 Civic Center Plaza, Suite 200
Poughkeepsie, NY 12601
(845) 473-4440
www.scenichudson.org

With 570 acres basically taking up the side of a mountain, Shaupeneak Ridge offers outstanding hiking and mountain biking on 6 miles of trails. The ridge is a prominent geologic feature—it's what visitors to the Vanderbilt Mansion National Historic Park in Hyde Park see when they look across the Hudson (check the Hudson Valley Mansions and Historic Sites: East Side chapter for more on the Vanderbilt Mansion). Likewise, the views from the top of Shaupeneak Ridge look across to the east side of the Hudson and are terrific. The views to the west of the Catskills and Shawangunks are pretty good too. Louisa Pond at the top of the ridge is a very interesting glacially carved pond that also has a large boggy area with lots of unusual plants. The pond is good for canoeing—use the upper parking area for easy carry-in access. There's a gorgeous waterfall halfway up the ridge on the Yellow Trail from the lower parking area. Caution: The preserve has a lot of unmarked old woods roads, making it easy to get lost. Stick to the marked trails and you'll be fine.

Kerhonksen

MINNEWASKA STATE PARK PRESERVE
5281 Route 44/55
(845) 256-0579

Minnewaska State Park Preserve covers 13,000 acres on the rugged Shawangunk ridge (2,500 acres of the Awosting Reserve were added to the park in 2006). The park centers around two beautiful blue "sky lakes," Lake Minnewaska and Lake Awosting. Decades ago two resort hotels were in this area. The hotels are long gone (the original section of the park near Lake Awosting was acquired by New York State in 1971), but the 50 miles of carriage roads they built are still there. The old roads are wide and have gentle slopes—they're very easy walking. The roads lead around the lakes and into other areas of the park and link to the many foot trails that also lace the site. The park offers swimming and paddling on Lake Minnewaska, picnic areas, excellent hiking, cross-country skiing, horseback riding, and mountain biking. Technical rock climbing is permitted. Hikes in Minnewaska are just one scenic overlook after another—the park is spectacularly beautiful. For a short (under 1 mile) but very scenic hike, try the Beacon Hill Trail. The Castle Point Carriageway,

the highest trail in the park, starts near the Lake Minnewaska swim area and leads to an amazing lookout at Castle Point, at an elevation of 2,200 feet. The view is an unobstructed 360 degrees and well worth the 4-mile hike. Because the trails and carriage roads have a lot of intersections, it's fairly easy to put together some good loop walks here using the trail map available at the main entrance. Serious hikers should use the New York–New Jersey Trail Conference Shawangunk Trails map to put together longer hikes that connect to nearby Sam's Point Preserve and the Mohonk Preserve (both sites are described in this chapter). The vehicle entry fee is $7 between Memorial Day and Labor Day and $6 the rest of the year. *Note:* A serious forest fire in 2008 damaged more than 3,000 acres in the eastern section of the park; some parts of the park are temporarily closed to the public. For more information, call the preserve at (845) 255-0752.

New Paltz

MOHONK PRESERVE
Access/parking: Visitor Center, ½ mile west of the intersection of Route 44/55 and Route 299
Management:
Mohonk Preserve
Box 715
New Paltz, NY 12561
(845) 255-0919
www.mohonkpreserve.org

The Mohonk Preserve covers more than 6,500 acres in the Shawangunk Mountains. This magnificent site has a 65-mile network of old carriage roads and trails that are perfect for hiking, mountain biking, horseback riding, and cross-country skiing. The preserve also offers world-renowned rock climbing on more than 1,000 technical routes. The origins of the Mohonk Preserve date back to 1869, when the Smiley family purchased Mohonk Lake and built the famed Mohonk Mountain House resort (see the Accommodations: West chapter for more about the lodge). The preserve was established in 1963 by Smiley family members as a separate nonprofit organization to protect and manage the land for public use. Today some 10,000 individuals are members of the preserve, providing financial support for land stewardship, land protections, research, and education programs. Members of the public are welcome to enjoy the Mohonk Preserve year-round. Begin at the outstanding visitor center, where you can pick up trail maps, visit the butterfly garden and nature trail, and see exhibits on the ecology of the Shawangunks. The visitor center is open at no charge, but this is also where you buy your day pass: $9 for hikers, bikers, and riders; $15 for rock climbers; kids 12 and under are free with an adult. Great hikes are everywhere in the Mohonk Preserve. Some favorites are the easy 1.5-mile Trapps Mountain Hamlet Path, the moderate 3-mile Bonticou Crag Trail, and the more strenuous 7.5-mile High Peters Kill Trail. To watch technical rock climbers in action, follow the easy 5-mile Undercliff and Overcliff carriage roads. (Serious hikers should use the New York–New Jersey Trail Conference Shawangunk Trails map to put together loops within the preserve and hikes that connect to nearby Minnewaska State Park Preserve and Sam's Point Preserve—both sites are described in this chapter.) The staff and volunteers at the Mohonk Preserve offer an active schedule of programs, including hikes, historical walks, wildflower and bird walks, singles hikes, hikes for kids, and even hikes for dogs. Check the Web site or call for details. There's usually no fee beyond the general admission charge, but programs fill up fast—preregister as far in advance as possible. Wheelchair accessibility at Mohonk Preserve is limited. The visitor center is fully accessible, including the restrooms. The Shawangunk Sensory Trail there is a fairly level, self-guided loop that encourages visitors to use sight, sound, smell, and touch to enjoy the full experience. The carriage roads are mostly level, but they're not paved and they're not suitable for standard wheelchairs. Handicapped parking is available at most trailheads. Parking at the Mohonk Preserve can be a bit of a problem, particularly on summer and fall weekends. The lot at the visitor center trailhead fills very quickly—arrive early and carpool if possible. Alternative parking is at the Spring Farm trailhead off Mountain Rest Road. Also consider the long-term parking lots at the visitor center (half a mile from the intersection of Route 44/55 and Route 299) and at the West Trapps trailhead (1.5 miles from the intersection of Route 44/55 and Route 299). An even better solution is to visit during the week, when the preserve is less crowded.

Saugerties

ESOPUS BEND NATURE PRESERVE
Access/parking: Limited parking at Shady Lane entrance; additional parking on nearby Simmons Drive at Route 9W
Management:
Esopus Creek Conservancy
Box 589
Saugerties, NY 12477
(845) 247-0664
www.esopuscreekconservancy.org
One of the newest preserves in the region, Esopus Bend dates back only to 2004. The preserve is 161

Scenic Hudson

Scenic Hudson, Inc., has been a crusader for the Hudson Valley since 1963, when the organization was formed as part of the historic fight to save Storm King Mountain. Today Scenic Hudson remains deeply committed to environmental issues in the region and is a model for environmental organizations nationwide. It's also active in land preservation through its affiliated land trust—a number of Scenic Hudson preserves are discussed in this chapter. For more information about the organization: Scenic Hudson, 1 Civic Center Plaza, Suite 200, Poughkeepsie, NY 12601; (845) 473-4440 www.scenic hudson.org.

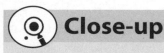 **Close-up**

Avoid Lyme Disease!

Lyme disease, a bacterial illness carried by the deer tick (also known as the black-legged tick), is a real problem in the Hudson Valley. Every year, several thousand cases in the region are reported. Deer ticks are active any time the temperature is above freezing, although they're most active from March to November. Prevention is the only way to avoid Lyme disease. The New York State Health Department recommends these precautions:

1. Avoid tick habitat (brushy and grassy areas) if possible.

2. Wear light-colored clothing so you can see ticks easily.

3. Tuck your pants into your socks and your shirt into your pants; wear a hat.

4. Check for ticks on your skin and clothing after every few hours of outdoor activity.

5. Check your body for ticks thoroughly—using a mirror—at the end of the day.

6. Consider using an insect repellent containing DEET. If you do, follow label instructions carefully.

Lyme disease symptoms include a bull's-eye or solid red rash around or near the site of the bite, chills and fever, headache, fatigue, stiff neck, muscle and joint pain, and swollen glands. Early symptoms usually appear within 3 to 30 days after the bite of an infected tick. If you suspect Lyme disease, see a doctor at once—the illness can be easily treated with antibiotics.

acres located on a dramatic bend in the Esopus Creek, less than a mile from the Hudson River. The property was a family farm for many years (locals still refer to it as the old Schroeder Farm), but farming ceased here in the 1960s and the land has largely returned to a natural habitat. The land here is a nice mix of forest, meadows, and flood plains. A number of easy trails run through the preserve, including the 1.2-mile Schroeder Trail, which follows an old farm road along the Esopus Creek to a nice overlook at Stony Point. Additional trails and improvements are planned. The Esopus Creek Conservancy is very enthusiastic about their preserve and run many fun nature programs—check the Web site for upcoming events. No bikes allowed.

Ulster

ULSTER LANDING COUNTY PARK
Ulster Landing Road
(845) 336-8484
www.co.ulster.ny.us
A county-owned recreational park, Ulster Landing

is one of the few places in the region where swimming in the Hudson is allowed. The park is designed for recreation. In addition to the lifeguarded beach, the park offers picnic areas, a playground, horseshoe pits, volleyball and basketball courts, and a boat launch. Some hiking (cross-country skiing in the winter) trails meander through the park; one is wheelchair accessible. Daily admission for Ulster County residents is $3 for adults and kids 13 and over; $1.50 for kids under 13. For nonresidents, the fee is $6 for adults and $3 for kids. No dogs allowed.

HIKING

Opportunities abound for hiking in the mid–Hudson Valley. Almost all parks and preserves have trails. Ditto for the many historic houses in the area, especially the Hudson River estates (see the chapters on Hudson Valley Mansions and Historic Sites for details). The discussion here can't be comprehensive—it focuses instead on rail trails and long-distance trails.

Rail Trails

The old rail beds of several defunct railroads in the region have been converted into popular community rail trails. Flat, 10 feet wide, and graded, rail trails are a lot of fun. They go through scenic areas but aren't far out of town, have lots of access points, and are very easy to walk or bike on. Some are even paved, which makes them good choices for in-line skating, families with kids in strollers, and people with mobility handicaps. (Motorized vehicles aren't allowed on rail trails, but motorized wheelchairs are acceptable.) Some trails allow horses; others don't. Dogs are allowed on leashes, but be prepared to clean up after your pet. The trails are open dawn to dusk year-round. All have free parking near the access points.

Columbia/Dutchess County

HARLEM VALLEY RAIL TRAIL
Management:
Harlem Valley Rail Trail Association
51 South Center Street
Millerton, NY 12546
(518) 789-9591
www.hrvt.org

The former Harlem Valley Railroad tracks that once ran from Wassaic in eastern Dutchess County to Chatham in central Columbia County is now the Harlem Valley Rail Trail. The first segment of this paved trail was opened in 1996. Today about 23 miles are open to the public, and another 23 miles are being acquired in Columbia County. The Dutchess County section of the trail begins at the MetroNorth station in Wassaic and runs 2.6 miles to the charming village of Amenia. From there the trail goes 4.5 miles to Coleman Station in the town of Northeast; it then goes about 3.6 miles to Main Street in Millerton. An 8-mile stretch from Millerton to Undermountain Road in the town of Ancram in Columbia County has just opened. From Ancram, the trail continues 4 miles to the entrance of Taconic State Park in Copake Falls. The portion of the trail in Dutchess County is a county park; the portion in Columbia County is part of Taconic State Park. Although the trail is maintained by the relevant county and state departments, the all-volunteer Harlem Valley Rail Trail Association assists with maintenance and is an excellent source of information about the trail.

Ulster County

HUDSON VALLEY RAIL TRAIL
Management:
Hudson Valley Rail Trail Association, Inc.
12 Church Street
Highland, NY 12528
(845) 691-8151
www.hudsonvalleyrailtrail.com

The Hudson Valley Rail Trail is a paved 2.3-mile trail in Highland on the rail bed of the former New York, New Haven & Hartford Railroad. The western end of the trail is on New Paltz Road (Route 12); the eastern end is in Tony Williams Park on Riverside Road. This pleasant trail will be extended westward toward New Paltz and eastward toward the Hudson to link up with the planned Walkway Over the Hudson. The trail is owned by the Town of Lloyd. The all-volunteer Hudson Valley Rail Trail Association helps with maintenance and is a good source of information.

WALLKILL VALLEY RAIL TRAIL
Management:
Wallkill Valley Rail Trail Association
Box 1048
New Paltz, NY 12561
www.gorailtrail.org

A peaceful and scenic trail that runs for 12.2 miles between New Paltz and Gardiner, the Wallkill Valley Rail Trail was opened in 1991. The views along the trail are fabulous: The Shawangunk Mountains flank it to the west, and the trail follows the Wallkill River. The northern end of the trail is on the Rosendale/New Paltz town line near Springtown Road (Route 7); the southern end is on the Gardiner/Shawangunk town line near Denniston Road. Huguenot Street in New Paltz is a good access point for the middle of the trail— head north on the trail about 2 miles to cross the Wallkill River on a restored railroad bridge. The trail is crossed by several local roads; watch

Walkway Over the Hudson

When the New York, New Haven & Hartford Railroad was in operation, it crossed the Hudson River over the Poughkeepsie Railroad-Highland Bridge. When the bridge was completed in 1888, it was the longest railroad bridge in the world, at 6,767 feet long and 212 feet above the river. This remarkable engineering feat was in service as the first and only rail crossing of the Hudson River south of Albany until a fire closed it down in 1975. In 2008, after years of discussion, work began on restoring the bridge as a 1.25-mile pedestrian walkway that will connect to the Hudson Valley Rail Trail on the west bank and to the Dutchess County Rail Trail (under construction) on the east. Walkway Over the Hudson, as the bridge is now called, will be 35 feet wide and will be fully accessible to individuals with disabilities (there will be an elevator on the Poughkeepsie side). The combination of railroad history and spectacular views makes this one of the more interesting walks in the region. The walkway will be managed as a New York State park. For more information on the bridge, contact Walkway Over the Hudson, Box 889, Poughkeepsie, NY 12602; (845) 454-9649; www.walkway.org.

Trust. The all-volunteer Wallkill Valley Rail Trail Association helps with trail maintenance and improvement.

Long-Distance Trails
The Appalachian Trail

The famed Appalachian Trail (AT) runs for more than 2,150 miles, from Georgia to Maine, and passes through 14 states—and it all began here in the Hudson Valley. The very first segment of the AT is in Bear Mountain State Park in Orange County. (This part of Orange County is out of the range of this book, but it's worth a visit for its historic significance.) The idea of the Appalachian Trail was first proposed in 1921 by Benton MacKaye in an article in the American Institute of Architects journal. Major William A. Welch, the general manager of Bear Mountain State Park, realized the idea meshed nicely with the trail system he was building in the park. The first section of the AT was a 16-mile path than ran from the foot of Bear Mountain to the top and then westward on through the park to Arden. It was officially opened on October 19, 1923.

In all, 88 miles of the AT run through New York State; 52 of those miles are in Putnam County and Dutchess County. In Putnam County, the AT begins at the eastern end of the Bear Mountain Bridge and runs through Hudson Highlands State Park and Fahnestock Park in Putnam County; the paths at Manitoga in Garrison link to trails that lead to the AT. Good access points with parking are:

- Anthony's Nose/Camp Smith Trail, Route 9D just north of the Bear Mountain Bridge.
- Route 9 and Route 403, just outside the southern portion of Hudson Highlands State Park. Good access to the Canada Hill portion of the trail.
- Fahnestock Park. Two good sections of the trail are the Old Mine Railroad Trail and the Canopus Lake Overlook.

All three areas are covered by the New York–New Jersey Trail Conference map "East Hudson Trails."

The trail enters Dutchess County in East

out for traffic at intersections. The surface here is packed cinders and gravel, good for walking and biking. Horses are permitted. In New Paltz, the trail is owned by the village or the town; in Gardiner it's owned by the Wallkill Valley Land

Outdoors with a Guide

Don't have a lot of time to research your own outdoors excursion? Don't have the equipment or experience to try kayaking or mountain biking? That's no excuse for staying indoors in the mid–Hudson Valley. The following companies offer a range of full-service outdoor activities, including equipment, training, and tours.

Hudson Valley Pack and Paddle
45 Beekman Street
Beacon, NY 12508
(845) 831-1300
www.hvpackandpaddle.com

The River Connection
9 West Market Street
Hyde Park, NY 12538
(845) 229-0595
www.the-river-connection.com

Storm King Adventure Tours
178 Hudson Street
Cornwall On Hudson, NY 12520
(845) 534-7800
www.stormkingadventuretours.com

Table Rock Tours and Bicycles
386 Main Street
Rosendale, NY 12471
(845) 658-7832
www.trtbicycles.com

Breakneck Ridge and Other Trails

A number of very popular trails lace the central Hudson Highlands area near Cold Spring in Putnam County and Beacon in Dutchess County. These trails are challenging and in many cases are definitely not for beginners. They follow a rugged escarpment that is generally 1,200 to 1,600 feet above sea level—there's a reason one well-known trail is called Breakneck Ridge. The trails run through Hudson Highlands State Park, head northeast along the Schofield Ridge into the city of Beacon, and from there into the 1,900-acre Fishkill Ridge Conservation Area. These areas are all undeveloped except for the trails. Use appropriate caution, don't hike alone or in questionable weather, and leave the dog and kids at home. Serious hikers can find more information about the trails in the area in the *New York Walk Book*, published by the New York–New Jersey Trail Conference; use the "East Hudson Trails" map—don't hike without it.

NYNJTC

The New York–New Jersey Trail Conference is a nonprofit federation of more than 100 regional hiking and environmental organizations and more than 10,000 individuals. NYNJTC is responsible for maintaining the Long Path and Appalachian Trail in New York State, along with many other regional trails. The federation publishes excellent trail maps (printed on waterproof and rip-proof paper), a guide with maps to the Appalachian Trail in New York, and the classic *New York Walk Book*. For more information and to order maps and publications, contact: New York–New Jersey Trail Conference, 156 Ramapo Valley Road, Mahwah, NJ 07430; (201) 512-9348; www .nynjtc.org.

Fishkill and heads northeast. A good access point for the Depot Hill section of the trail is in Stormville; look for the parking area on Route 52 near Stormville Mountain Road, south of Route 84. From here, the trail passes through the town of Beekman, out of the Hudson Valley, and on to the town of Pawling in southeast Dutchess County. The trail passes through the 1,071-acre Pawling Nature Preserve (outside the scope of this book but well worth a visit) and from there goes into Connecticut.

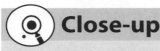 Close-up

Ski Areas

Cross-country skiing is available at many parks and preserves in the mid–Hudson Valley, but for downhill skiing and snowboarding, you'll have to leave the region. Thankfully, you won't have to go far. Several ski resorts with great facilities, including beautiful lodges, equipment rentals, snowmaking, terrain parks, and evening skiing, are within a two-hour drive or less from the region.

EAST SIDE OF THE HUDSON

Catamount
Route 23
Hillsdale, NY 12529
(518) 325-3200
www.catamountski.com
Ski in the Berkshires at a resort that straddles the New York–Massachusetts border. Vertical drop of 1,000 feet, 32 trails.

Thunder Ridge Ski Area
Route 22
Patterson, NY 12563
(845) 878-4100
www.thunderridgeski.com
Located in the hilly terrain of the northeastern corner of Putnam County. Thirty trails, three chair lifts.

WEST SIDE OF THE HUDSON

Belleayre Mountain
Route 28
Highmount
(845) 254-5600
www.belleayre.com

Owned and operated by the State of New York, Belleayre is only 35 miles west of Kingston in the Catskills. The resort has a vertical drop of 1,400 feet, 37 trails, and eight lifts.

Hunter Mountain
Route 22
Hunter, NY 12442
(800) HUNTERM
www.huntermtn.com
One of the best-known resorts in the Catskills, Hunter Mountain has a vertical drop of 1,600 feet, 54 trails, and 11 lifts.

Windham Mountain
Route 23
Windham, NY 12496
(518) 734-4300
www.windhammountain.com
Located in the Catskill Mountain High Peaks region on the northern edge of the Catsill Park, Windham has a vertical rise of 1,600 feet on two of the tallest peaks in the Catskills. The resort has 46 trails and nine lifts.

Hyde Park Trail System

Management: Town of Hyde Park Recreation Department
Town Hall
4383 Albany Post Road
Hyde Park, NY 12538
(845) 229-8086
www.hydeparkny.us/recreation

The town of Hyde Park has an extensive trail system that connects the three national park sites in town (the FDR home, Val-Kill, and the Vanderbilt Mansion—see the Hudson Valley Mansions and Historic Sites: East Side chapter for details) with town parks, nature preserves, and the Hyde Park central business corridor. The trail system now covers more than 14 miles and continues to expand. The trails are easy to moderate walking and are all well marked. Because the trails connect, it's easy to put together loops of varying distances. Trailheads are at Riverfront Park on West Market Street, the FDR home, Hackett Hill on East Market Street, Val-Kill, and Vanderbilt Mansion. Parking is free. Toilet facilities are available at the national park trailheads.

BIKING

The many quiet backcountry roads of the mid–Hudson Valley are great places for casual bike rides. It's easy to put together some good loops that take you through beautiful scenery and small towns. However, those country roads tend to be hilly, curvy, and narrow—bikers should exercise appropriate caution. All the Hudson River crossings in the region allow bikes. You can also take your bike on MetroNorth trains, with two caveats. First, you need to get a permit. It's $5 from any ticket agent and is good forever (unless you lose it, in which case you'll have to buy another). Second, you can't take your bike on a rush-hour train. For picking up good bike routes right from the train station, Cold Spring and Beacon are excellent choices. Cold Spring is so popular with bikers that the MetroNorth rail station has a special bike loading area.

i For a good brochure describing six scenic bike tour loops in Dutchess County, including maps and mile points, go to www.dutchesstourism.com/btours.asp or call Dutchess County Tourism at (845) 463-4000.

Many of the state highways in the region have been designated as part of the regional system of State Bike Routes. Some, but not all, of these roads have signs indicating bike lanes and shared roadways. The signs are no guarantee of safety or driver courtesy—stay alert and ride carefully. The list below gives the highway route numbers; an asterisk indicates the route is signed.

1. **Columbia County**
   Routes 9*, 9H, 22*, 23*
2. **Dutchess County**
   Routes 9*, 9D, 22*, 44*, 52, 55, 82, 199, 308
3. **Orange County**
   Routes 6, 9*, 9W, 17A, 17K, 22*, 32*, 42, 94, 97, 207, 208, 209*, 302
4. **Putnam County**
   Routes 6, 6N, 9*, 9D, 22*, 52, 311
5. **Ulster County**
   Routes 9W, 22*, 28*, 32*, 44, 55, 209*, 299

i Don't have a bike and want to ride the Wallkill Rail Trail and the surrounding New Paltz area? Rent a bike from Bicycle Depot, 15 Main Street, New Paltz, (845) 255-3859, www.bicycledepot.com. If you're in the Woodstock area, bike rentals are available from Overlook Mountain Bikes, 93 Tinker Street, (845) 679-2122, www.overlookmountainbikes.com.

The various signed State Bike Routes in New York State have been connected into a trail system. Many of the trails run through parts of the mid–Hudson Valley region; they're numbered according to the state highway route they follow (for the most part, anyway—the route often takes bikers off the main state highway). Here's the breakdown:

1. **State Bike Route 5**
   Beginning in Buffalo, this trail passes through Columbia County along Route 20; it intersects with State Bike Route 22 in New Lebanon.
2. **State Bike Route 9**
   Better known as the Hudson Valley Greenway Bike Route, this is a 340-mile bike route that starts in New York City and ends in Montreal, making it both an interstate (it passes briefly through New Jersey) and an international bike trail. It mostly follows Route 9, the major north-south road along the eastern Hudson. The trail passes through Orange County on Route 9W, then crosses the Hudson on the Bear Mountain Bridge and joins Route 9D and then Route 9 in Putnam County. The trail continues along Route 9 through Dutchess and Columbia Counties.
3. **State Bike Route 17**
   Beginning in Buffalo, this route goes across the southern tier of New York and passes through Orange County, then across the Beacon-Newburgh Bridge into Dutchess County. It ends where it intersects with State Bike Route 9 near Beacon.
4. **State Bike Route 22**
   The trail starts in Brewster in Putnam County

245

New York State Bike Law

According to New York State law, bicycle riders must:

- Wear helmets
- Obey all traffic signs and signals
- Ride with (never against) traffic
- Use hand signals
- Have only one person per bike (except for kids in approved carriers and tandem bikes)
- Use lights at night

FISHING AND BOATING

The Hudson River is a wonderful place for fishing—it's famous for its striped bass and shad runs. Trout streams (some stocked) and lakes full of fish are on both sides of the river. The Hudson is also a wonderful place to sail and paddle. Numerous boat-launching ramps are available on both sides of the river, and there are many coves and inlets just waiting to be explored by canoe or kayak.

A fishing license is required for anyone over 16 to fish in most New York State waters. There's one extremely large exception to this: No license is needed to fish the Hudson River south of the Troy Barrier Dam. Licenses are easily available from the town clerks of any municipality, at many sporting goods stores, and directly from the New York State Department of Environmental Conservation at www.dec.ny.gov or by calling (866) 933-2257. Fees for New York State residents are $19 for an annual license and $12 for a seven-day license. For out-of-state residents, the fee is $40 for an annual license and $25 for a seven-day license. The DEC also has a lot of good information on places to fish in the region. Also check with individual state and county parks for details on fishing.

i The Hudson River watershed is very large—and that means chemicals, pathogens, and heavy metals have found their way into the bodies of some fish species. The New York State Department of Health has issued fish consumption advisories for many Hudson River fish species. The list is updated annually and can be found by visiting the NYSDOH Web site at www.health.state.ny.us or calling (800) 458-1158.

and heads north along Route 22 through the rolling countryside of Putnam, Dutchess, and Columbia Counties. It ends in New Lebanon in northeastern Columbia County, where it intersects with State Bike Route 5. Perhaps the most beautiful and most traffic-free of all the regional state bike routes.

5. **State Bike Route 23**
    The eastern end of the Rip Van Winkle Bridge in Columbia County is the starting point for this east-west route, which follows Route 23 across the county to the Massachusetts border.

6. **State Bike Route 28**
    Not really in the region covered by this book, but included because the route starts at the roundabout outside the New York State Thruway tollbooths in Kingston. It heads northwest from there into the Catskills, ending at Belleayre Mountain in Highmount.

7. **State Bike Route 32**
    Starting at the west side of the Kingston-Rhinecliff Bridge, this route heads southwest through Ulster County to New Windsor in Orange County, where it intersects with State Bike Route 17.

Accessing the Hudson for shore fishing can be a bit of a problem, mostly because railroad tracks cut off the river on both sides. Do not attempt to cross railroad tracks where there is no signal gate or crossing point! The Department of Environmental Conservation is always looking for ways to improve public access to the Hudson. Today there are more than 90 boat launches and shore fishing locations on the river that are owned by municipalities, the DEC, other state agencies, or not-for-profit conservation groups. The fishing location list changes and expands every year. To see the latest maps showing fishing spots and boat launches (with details of hours, facilities, and accessibility), check with the DEC Hudson River Estuary Program at (845) 256-3016 or www.dec.ny.gov/lands/41728.html.

The Hudson River Greenway Water Trail stretches 156 miles from Battery Park in Manhattan all the way to the village of Waterford in Saratoga County. The Water Trail was started in 1992 to provide access points for boaters along both banks of the river, along with campgrounds and day-use sites. Today some 40 of the 81 designated Water Trail sites are in the mid-Hudson region, and the list gets longer all the time. For the most current information, check with the Hudson River Valley Greenway at Capitol Building, Room 254, Albany, NY 12224; (518) 473-3835; www.hudsongreenway.state.ny.us. The Greenway sponsors the annual Great Hudson River Paddle every July, a 144-mile kayaking and camping trip from Albany to New York City.

GOLF

The Hudson Valley abounds in excellent golf courses open to the public (private clubs also abound, but they aren't covered in this book). In fact, there are so many that they can't all be listed here—this section focuses on the most scenic and well maintained, and leaves out the many driving ranges in the region.

When planning a golf trip to one of these courses, bear in mind that golf in the Hudson Valley is a seasonal activity. Most courses are open every day from roughly mid-March through early December, but check with the individual courses for details. Spring conditions can be soggy. The yardages given here are from the back tees; the pars are for men.

Many clubs are accessible during the week—tee times may even be available the same day—but don't count on it. Reserve a tee time as far in advance as possible, and definitely make advance reservations for weekend and holiday play.

As a general rule, the courses listed here follow a country club dress code. Players are asked to wear proper attire, which means collared shirts, Bermuda-length shorts, and soft spikes. Tank tops, T-shirts, halter tops, running shorts, jeans, and other informal attire may not be permitted.

The fees listed here are the standard rates for weekdays and weekends and holidays. At some courses, golf cart rentals are included in the fee, but others charge separately. The fees are a baseline, but be sure to ask about discounts when booking your tee time. Most courses offer senior and junior rates, to say nothing of ladies days, off-season rates, early-bird and late-day discounts, and online specials.

COLUMBIA COUNTY

Valatie

WINDING BROOK COUNTRY CLUB
2839 Route 203
(518) 758-9117
Named for the lovely stream that meanders through the 265 acres of this championship course, Winding Brook is a serene and scenic place. A semiprivate club, Winding Brook is nestled between the mountains of the Berkshires and the Catskills, with lovely views in all directions. It's a par 72, 6,312-yard course that was designed by Paul J. Roth and dates back to 1963; the club has been owned and operated by members of the Roth family ever since. The holes here are fairly straightforward to play, making this a good course for inexperienced golfers. Watch

out for the many out-of-bounds stakes. Greens fees are $22 weekdays and $27 on weekends and holidays. Cart rental is $26; $20 for a single rider. The Club House bar and restaurant serves a casual menu every day but Monday.

DUTCHESS COUNTY

Fishkill

FISHKILL GOLF COURSE AND DRIVING RANGE
387 Route 9
(845) 896-5220
www.fishkillgolf.com
An excellent practice and instructional facility, the Fishkill Golf Course and Driving Range offers a 12-hole, par 41, 2,571-yard executive-length course. Practice areas include a grass tee range,

lighted, heated, and covered mat stalls on the driving range, practice chipping and putting greens, and a practice sand bunker. Just for fun, there's also an 18-hole miniature golf course. The four PGA and USGTF teaching professionals offer individual lessons, group instruction, and clinics for all ages and abilities. Greens fees are $18 for 12 holes, $30 for 24 holes. Cart rental is $15 for two players. At the driving range, a large bucket of balls is $10. Minigolf is $3. The 19th Hole Bar and Grill offers a full-service bar and pub fare.

i The Web site Hudson Valley Golf (www.hudsonvalleygolf.com) is a reliable source of information about golfing in the region. Purchasing the site's Hudson Valley Golf Pass for $50 a year gives you discount offers on greens fees, restaurant meals, pro shop merchandise, events, lodgings, and members-only specials.

Hopewell Junction
BEEKMAN COUNTRY CLUB
11 Country Club Road
(8450 226-7700
www.beekmangolf.com
Beekman Country Club is a public golf course with 27 championship holes in three regulation nine-hole sections. The sections play as three separate 18s. The Highland Nine starts at the clubhouse and climbs to an elevation of 510 feet, providing gorgeous views out over the Hudson Valley to Storm King across the river. Choose this par 36, 3,142-yard nine in the spring, when the dogwood trees that line the fairways are in bloom. The Valley Nine is par 35, 2,952 yards, goes through rolling terrain, and doesn't climb quite as high. Look for the massive oak tree by the sixth hole—it's one of the largest in the country—and for the breathtaking valley view from the seventh tee. The Taconic Nine is the most challenging set of holes. It's par 36, 3,125 yards, with fairways that are on the narrow side. The sixth hole has a water hazard in front of the green—precise shot-making is required.

Weekday greens fees are $56—the fee includes a cart and breakfast or lunch at the club restaurant. On weekends and holidays, greens fees vary with the time of day. Before 11:00 a.m., the fee is $77, with cart and breakfast or lunch. Between 11:00 a.m. and 1:00 p.m., the fee is $67, with cart and breakfast or lunch. After 1:00 p.m., it's $54, with cart and lunch or evening snack.

LaGrangeville
THE LINKS AT UNION VALE
153 North Parliman Road
(845) 223-1002
www.thelinksatunionvale.com
A links-style semiprivate course that could be somewhere in Ireland instead of southern Dutchess County, The Links at Union Vale was opened in 2000 and is perhaps the premier public course in the region. The course was designed by Stephen Kay and has plenty of links-style features, including lots of grassland, potbunkers, and natural water hazards. It's set on a lush, rolling landscape that offers wonderful views out over the Hudson Valley. This is a long, challenging course—from the championship tees it's par 72 and 6,839 yards. Because the property used to be a cattle farm, there aren't many trees, but there's plenty of waist-high grass if you miss the fairway. Accurate shot-making counts here. It's hard to pick a signature hole, but the deviously placed pot-bunker in front of the green on the par 4, 460-yard 15th hole is particularly challenging—it requires precise shot placement and a certain amount of nerve to get past it. Weekday greens fees are $62 with a cart before 2:00 p.m.; $47 with a cart after 2:00 p.m. On weekends and holidays, the greens fees are $89 with a cart from 7:00 a.m. to 2:00 p.m.; $58 after 2:00 p.m.. The Links offers championship practice facilities, including a 300-yard driving range with grass and mats, four target practice greens, two practice putting greens, and a practice sand bunker. The Links Bar & Grill offers a pub menu and daily lunch specials.

Pleasant Valley

JAMES BAIRD STATE PARK GOLF COURSE
James Baird State Park
280C Clubhouse Road
(845) 473-6200
www.nysparks.state.ny.us/golf

The regulation golf course at this large and popular state park (see the Parks and the Outdoors chapter for more) was designed by renowned golf architect Robert Trent Jones and was opened in 1948. The par 71, 6,616-yard course is set on former farmland and is relatively flat, with tree-lined fairways and small, fast greens. Six of the holes have water hazards. While some holes are fairly challenging (the 13th is par 5, 560 yards), overall this is a fairly forgiving course that's an excellent choice for new and intermediate players. Because the park offers lots of other recreation, it's a good choice for a family outing with nongolfers, who can find other things to do while you're on the course. Weekday greens fees are $23; weekends and holidays are $27. All week, cart fees are $27 before 2:00 p.m., $23 after 2:00 p.m., $19 for one rider. A driving range is available, and a full-service restaurant overlooks the golf course.

Poughkeepsie

CASPERKILL GOLF CLUB
2320 South Road
(845) 463-0900
www.casperkillgolf.com

Rated as the best golf value in the Hudson Valley by *Golf Digest*, Casperkill is a Robert Trent Jones design from 1944, originally built as a country club for executives from nearby IBM. It became a semiprivate club in 1995. The Casperkill creek winds through the grounds among huge old oaks and comes into play on seven holes. The regulation design is classic Jones—the natural rolling terrain has elevated tees, valley fairways, and terraced greens. At par 72 and 6,690 yards, this is a long and fairly challenging course. The second hole is one of the more difficult here. It's par 4, 416 yards, and runs steeply uphill. The most beautiful hole is the 10th—the view from the tee looks out onto the lower Hudson Valley. Greens

fees here are $40 on weekdays and $70 on weekends; riding carts are an additional $10 per golfer. The outdoor grill is open every day in season, offering sandwiches, burgers, salads, and beverages. A driving range, practice putting green, and practice chipping green are available.

MCCANN GOLF COURSE
155 Wilbur Boulevard
(845) 454-1968
www.mccanngolfcourse.com

A regulation municipal course operated by the city of Poughkeepsie, McCann Golf Course was originally designed by William Mitchell and built in 1972. In 2001 it was redesigned by Stephen Kay. The update was very successful. McCann is now rated four stars by *Golf Digest*; in 2007 it was named best golf course in the Hudson Valley by *Hudson Valley* magazine. It's a fairly standard course, par 72 and 6,524 yards—a good choice for advanced beginners and intermediate golfers. Weekday greens fees for nonresidents are $34; on weekends and holidays the fees are $39. At all times, greens fees are lower for residents of Poughkeepsie and Dutchess County. Golf cart rental is $28. The weekend reservation system here is primitive—start calling in at 6:00 p.m. on Thursday and keep dialing until you get through. There's a $4 fee for phone reservations. The course has a driving range. Christo's Restaurant serves casual Continental-style food.

VASSAR GOLF COURSE
124 Raymond Avenue
(845) 473-9838
www.vassargolfcourse.com

Located on the Vassar College campus, the Vassar Golf Course is a public, nine-hole course. It dates back to 1930 and is quite attractive, with lots of mature trees—there's a white oak in the woods to the left of the fourth green that's easily 150 years old. Even for a par 34, nine-hole course, Vassar is short, only 2,515 yards, and takes only a couple of hours to play. It's very walkable, although carts are available, and an excellent choice for beginning to intermediate players. There are no tee reservations here—all players are welcome on a first-come basis. Weekday greens fees are $19; $21 on weekends. Vassar students play for just $4 a round. Golf carts are $26.

Red Hook

RED HOOK GOLF CLUB
650 Route 199
(845) 758-8652
www.redhookgolfclub.com

Semiprivate Red Hook Golf Club started life as a nine-hole course amid an apple orchard back in 1932. It was expanded in 1995 by David Horn to an 18-hole, par 72, 6,519-yard course. Remnants of the old apple orchards are still scattered around the course. This is a fairly challenging course with some difficult holes. The par 5 13th, for instance, is a 480-yard beauty. The hole begins with a shot through a notch in the woods, aiming at a landing area that can't be seen from the tee but has a water hazard on the left and rough on the right. Greens fees here are $50 Monday through Thursday, Friday before noon, and Saturday, Sunday, and holidays after 2:00 p.m. (Weekends and holidays through 2:00 p.m. are reserved for members and guests only.) Cart rates are $18. The practice range includes a putting/chipping area and a second practice putting green. Cafe Lucchaela serves a full menu with a fully stocked bar year-round.

Staatsburg

DINSMORE GOLF COURSE
Old Post Road
(845) 889-4071
www.nysparks.state.ny.us/golf

Originally, Dinsmore was a private, nine-hole course built in the 1890s for the use of the many wealthy families who had nearby estates, including the Astor, Vanderbilt, Livingston, Dinsmore, Hoyt, and Mills families. In fact, this is the second-oldest public golf course in New York State. (The oldest is the Dutcher Golf Course in Pawling, founded in 1888 and out of the region covered by this book.) In 1959 the land was donated to the State of New York (as was Mills Mansion—see the Mansions and Historic Sites: East chapter for

more information). The course was expanded to 18 holes by Roland Stafford in 1962; the original course is now the south nine. The regulation course is a short layout, par 70 and only 5,719 yards. It's hilly, with great views of the Hudson. The original holes are on the short and easy side; the newer holes are more challenging. Greens fees are $20 on weekdays and $24 on weekends. Cart rates are $24. The Ironwood Grille restaurant offers casual dining year-round.

GREENE COUNTY

Catskill

CATSKILL GOLF CLUB
27 Brooks Lane
(518) 943-0302
www.catskillgolfclub.com

Play golf in scenic Rip Van Winkle territory on a championship course at this public club. The par 72, 6,480-yard course was opened in 1928 and features broad fairways lined with pine trees. This is a fairly standard course, with few surprises but with some challenging holes—a good choice for the intermediate golfer. It's also very scenic, with awesome views of the Catskills Mountains. Spring and fall greens fees are $30 on weekdays and $35 on weekends and holidays. In the summer (May 1 to October 31), the greens fees go up a bit to $39 on weekdays and $49 on weekends and holidays. Cart rental is included in the daily fee. The Fairways Restaurant is a full-service dining facility—a good spot for lunch before or after your game.

ORANGE COUNTY

West Point

WEST POINT GOLF COURSE
Route 218 and Route 9W
(845) 938-2435
www.westpointmwr.com

The golf course for the United States Military Academy at West Point is open to the public as well as to cadets and military personnel. It's a really beautiful course, with spectacular views of the Hudson River. The par 70, 6,007-yard course was designed by Robert Trent Jones and opened in 1948. Today it's managed by the Family and Morale, Welfare and Recreation Command. Although cadets and military personnel get a few extra days to reserve tee times, there are still plenty of slots for civilians. Many of the holes here are fairly challenging, if on the short side. The seventh hole stands out as the longest—it's a par 5, 509-yard big one, with a blind tee shot through woods on one side and woods and out of bounds on the other. Watch out for the very thick rough on this hole. The course is closed every Monday (except Monday holidays) for tournaments and outings. Greens fees for the general public are $41 on weekdays and $58 on weekends and holidays. Golf cart rental is an additional $12 per person. There's a driving range and a somewhat threadbare clubhouse.

PUTNAM COUNTY

Garrison

THE GARRISON
Route 9
(845) 424-4747
www.thegarrison.com

The sweeping views of the Hudson River from this 300-acre property perched 800 feet up in the Hudson Highlands are reason enough to play golf here. The par 72, 6,497-yard championship course was designed by Dick Wilson and built in 1961. The front nine is very hilly and heavily treed with old hemlocks and oaks; the back nine is a little easier, without quite so many trees. There are a lot of elevation changes and tee shots out over ravines—this is a course with some difficult holes, best suited for golfers who are intermediate or better players. Greens fees are $65 on weekdays and $90 on weekends; the fee includes a golf cart. The Terrace Grill behind the pro shop offers a casual all-day menu. The Garrison is also home to the Valley restaurant, one of the finest in the area (see the Restaurants: East Side chapter for details); overnight accommodations are available (see the Accommodations: East Side chapter for more).

HIGHLANDS COUNTRY CLUB
955 Route 9D
(845) 424-3727
www.highlandscountryclub.net

One of the oldest in the region, the nine-hole regulation course at Highlands Country Club dates back to 1898. At par 68 and 4,538 yards this course is relatively long, though not particularly challenging—it's a good choice for the casual golfer. Greens fees are $40 on weekdays and $47 on weekends; the fee includes a golf cart. The Tavern restaurant features fine dining—see the Restaurants: East chapter for more.

ULSTER COUNTY

Accord

RONDOUT GOLF CLUB
10 Bank Street
(845) 626-2513
www.rondoutgolfclub.com

The Rondout Golf Club layout was designed by Hal Purdy as a nine-hole course and opened to the public in 1969; the second nine was added in 1989. Today the course is a regulation par 72 and 6,468 yards. It's moderately challenging, with some elevation changes and a number of water hazards—tributaries of the Rondout Creek meander through the property. *Golf Digest* rates this club three stars. Greens fees on weekdays are $37, including cart; on weekends, the fee is $47, including cart. Ivan's Restaurant offers a good, casual menu; the restaurant has an outdoor deck with beautiful mountain views.

High Falls

STONE DOCK GOLF CLUB
12 Stone Dock Road
(845) 687-7107
www.stonedockgolfclub.com

A very relaxed place to golf, Stone Dock Golf Club is a nine-hole, par 36, 3,235-yard course. It's got a few challenging holes, making it a good course for new and intermediate golfers. The fourth hole is the signature hole here—it's par 4, 310 yards, with a tee shot across a ravine on a downhill slope against a background of the beautiful Rondout Creek. Tee time reservations are taken but aren't necessary here. Greens fees on weekdays are $35, cart included. On weekends the fees are $36, cart included. The Tap In Pub offers a casual menu for lunch or dinner.

Highland

APPLE GREENS GOLF COURSE
161 South Street
(845) 883-5500
www.applegreens.com

With 27 holes (15 of them with water hazards), Apple Greens offers championship golf on a public course. This is a relatively new course—it was created on the site of an old apple orchard (hence the name) and opened in 1995. Apple Greens One is par 36, 3,136 yards; Apple Greens Two is par 35, 2,944 yards; Apple Greens East is par 35, 3,052 yards. The holes here are interesting and fairly challenging, with large greens. The signature hole on Apple Greens One is number four. It's a par 5, 610-yard monster. Hole five is a different sort of challenge—it's par 3 and only 156 yards, but with an island green. Greens fees are $30 on weekdays and $46 on weekends; carts are an additional $13 per player. A 20-station driving range is also on the property. A cafe with a bar offers a casual menu for lunch and dinner.

New Paltz

MOHONK MOUNTAIN HOUSE
1000 Mountain Rest Road
(845) 256-2154
www.mohonk.com

The charming nine-hole golf course at this famed resort is more than 100 years old, making it one of the oldest courses in the country. It's got a real Scottish links feel, with four grass levels, some hidden tee shots, and hilly terrain with spectacular views. At par 35 and 2,630 yards, this is a short course with some challenging holes but also a forgiving nature—it's a good course for golfers of all levels. Greens fees are complimentary on weekdays for overnight guests (see the Accommodations: West chapter for more information). Day visitors pay greens fees of $16; weekend greens fees for guests and visitors are $24.

NEW PALTZ GOLF COURSE
215 Huguenot Street
(845) 255-8282
www.newpaltzgolf.com

A public course set against the background of the Shawangunk Mountains, the New Paltz Golf Course is par 36 and 3,450 yards. It's a nice length for nine holes, making this course a good choice for players of all levels. The course was designed by Hal Purdy and opened in 1972. The course is scenic and very well maintained; it also has two putting greens and a driving range with 15 tees. Weekday greens fees are $19; on weekends and holidays, the fees are $20. Cart rates are $18. The New Paltz Public House offers casual dining, and the Locust Tree restaurant offers some of the finest dining in the area (see the Restaurants: West chapter for more).

SPECTATOR SPORTS

The mid–Hudson Valley doesn't have any major-league professional sports teams. If you really want to attend a home game for one of the New York metro-area pro teams, or go to events such as the U.S. Tennis Open in Queens, you're only a few hours away by car or train (MetroNorth plans for trains to eventually stop right near the new Yankee Stadium). Local sports fans don't see much point in all that travel, though, because they can watch some exciting teams without leaving the region. Among other spectator sports, the area is home to great minor-league baseball and some of the best college sports in the country.

Price Code

$	under $10
$$	$10 to $15
$$$	over $15

AUTO RACING

ACCORD SPEEDWAY $$
299 Whitfield Road, Accord
(845) 626-3478
www.accordspeedway.com

All sorts of motor racing takes place here: modifieds, sportsman, pro stocks, pure stocks, and vintage modifieds, to say nothing of karts, quads, bikes, and lawnmowers. It's a fun if somewhat noisy night out. The season here runs from early April through mid-October; events are held on Wednesday and Friday nights. The spectator gate opens at 5:00 p.m., warm-ups start at 6:30 p.m., and racing begins at 7:00 p.m. Regular admission is $12 for adults, $10 for seniors, $8 for juniors (age 10 to 15); little kids (9 and under) get in for just a buck. Indoor seating is $18 for all adults and $12 for all kids. You might want to sit indoors if rain is threatening—in 2007 the announcer here was struck by lightning during a storm (he survived). Needless to say, bad weather can cancel racing, so call ahead or check the Web site if in doubt. Absolutely no pets are allowed on speedway property, not even in the parking lot.

LEBANON VALLEY SPEEDWAY AND DRAGWAY $$
1746 U.S. Route 20, West Lebanon
(518) 794-9606
www.lebanonvalley.com

Two tracks are at Lebanon Valley. The Speedway is a half-mile high-banked clay oval, while the Dragway is a quarter-mile NHRA-sanctioned drag strip. That makes for a lot of variety and a lot of races during the season, from early April through the middle of October. Drag races take place Saturday, Sunday, Wednesday, and Friday. Speed racing for big block modifieds, sportsman, prostocks, limited prostocks, and purestocks takes place on Saturdays and some weeknights. Gates open at 5:00 p.m., racing begins at 6:00 p.m. General admission is $10 for adults, $2 for kids under 11; all reserved seats are $12, and all tower and roof seats are $22. Some promotional events are slightly more or less expensive. Tickets cannot be purchased online. To charge tickets by phone, call Monday through Friday, 9:00 a.m. to 5:00 p.m.

BASEBALL

THE HUDSON VALLEY RENEGADES $
Dutchess Stadium
Route 9D, Fishkill
(845) 838-0094
www.hvrenegades.com

The Hudson Valley Renegades are a Class A minor-league team in the New York–Penn League, affiliated with the Tampa Bay Devil Rays organization. The team has been playing at Dutchess Stadium since 1994. A night out with the 'Gades is just plain fun—it's baseball as it's meant to be, especially if you're bringing kids along. A box seat ticket is just $9, general admission tickets are just $5, and parking is just $3 a car. (Two skyboxes are available for groups and private parties.) Games here are very family friendly. Alcohol sales are restricted to just two beers per ID and there's no smoking in the stadium. The players are delighted to sign autographs, and while the games are always well attended, tickets are never hard to get. It's still best to order ahead, however, especially if you want to attend a game with a promotional event like Fireworks Fridays. For an added touch of fun, you can arrange a short scoreboard message for just $10 (do it at least two days in advance). The team will even arrange picnics and birthday parties at the stadium. The season runs from mid-June through early September. Games start Monday through Saturday at 7:05 p.m. and at 5:05 p.m. on Sundays. The gates open an hour before game time.

COLLEGE SPORTS

MARIST COLLEGE $$$
North Road, Poughkeepsie
(845) 676-3000
www.marist.edu
In 2007 the Red Foxes women's basketball team came very close to an NCAA title, an event that led to sold-out flights to Dayton, Ohio, from airports in the region. That wasn't unusual—Marist College sports, and especially basketball, are a strong local tradition. The teams at Marist play in the Metro Atlantic Athletic Conference, a fairly competitive Division I league with 10 colleges. Ticket prices vary but are generally below $20. Availability varies as well. The McCann Center, where basketball games are played, can hold 4,000 people, but even so, order tickets well in advance. Ditto for football games at the new Tenney Stadium.

UNITED STATES MILITARY ACADEMY $$$
West Point
(845) 938-8146 (ticket office)
www.goarmysports.com
The storied Black Knights of the United States Military Academy play football at historic Michie Stadium. The school's admission standards and academic demands are too high to make the Army team competitive on a national level, but the game itself is almost beside the point. Football here is steeped in more than a century of athletic tradition—it's impossible to watch the entire Corps of Cadets parade in and not be moved. Other traditions here include a military flyover and the firing of a howitzer cannon after every Army touchdown. Tickets for home games aren't cheap. They start at $30 but still go very fast, so order well in advance. Free parking is available at several lots. Tailgating is allowed for small groups in the free lots, but larger groups of 50 or more need reservations—contact the ticket office for details. The famed Army-Navy football game, one of the most enduring rivalries in sports, is played in early December—but always on neutral territory, not at home. Other intercollegiate sports at West Point are also open to the public. The women's basketball team is pretty good and Army plays ice hockey at a highly competitive level. Call the ticket office or check the Web site for schedules.

HOCKEY

THE HUDSON VALLEY BEARS $
Ice Time Sports Complex
21 Lakeside Road, Newburgh

McCann Ice Arena
Mid-Hudson Civic Center
14 Civic Center Plaza, Poughkeepsie
www.hudsonvalleybears.com
A new addition to the local sporting scene, the Hudson Valley Bears play in the small Eastern Professional Hockey League. The first season for the Bears began in the fall of 2008. The young, enthusiastic players are fun to watch as they

take on league rivals such as the Danbury Mad Hatters and the New Hampshire Freeze. Home ice for the Bears alternates between the Ice Time Sports Complex in Newburgh and the McCann Ice Arena in Poughkeepsie—for schedules and tickets, check the Bears Web site (not the arenas). Bears hockey happens in a very relaxed, family-friendly atmosphere—it's an enjoyable night out with the kids.

HORSE SHOWS

HITS-ON-THE-HUDSON $
Washington Avenue Extension, Saugerties
(845) 246-8833
www.hitsshows.com

Horses in the Sun (HITS) hunter and jumper shows have been a big part of the national horse show circuit since 1982. You don't have to be a member of the horsey set to enjoy these shows—watching these beautiful animals and their riders compete in the ring is fun even if you have no idea what to look for. The 200-acre HITS equestrian facility is spectacular. Set against a backdrop of the Catskill Mountains, it has a Grand Prix amphitheater and a Grand Hunter amphitheater, 1,100 permanent horse stalls, and a separate complex of offices, shops, and restrooms. Two separate food service facilities offer a diverse menu prepared by local restaurants. The season runs from May through September. Seven show weeks are held over the course of the season,

with approximately 250 classes each week. Show days are Wednesday through Sunday, starting at 8:00 a.m. and running until about 5:00 p.m. The $25,000 Open Jumper Challenge is held on Thursdays and the Grand Prix class is on Sundays. Admission is free Wednesday through Friday. On Saturday and Sunday, admission is $5 per person; free for children 12 and under. The gate proceeds are donated to local charities. Parking is free. Call or check the Web site for show weeks, schedules, and special events.

ROLLER DERBY

HUDSON VALLEY HORRORS
ROLLER DERBY $
PO Box 2977
Kingston, NY 12402
www.myspace.com/hvrollerderby

Both a spectator sport and a spectacle, roller derby has made a comeback in recent years. The Hudson Valley now has its very own roller derby team, the all-girl Hudson Valley Horrors. They go by monikers such as Dawg Catcher and Lolita Lebruise, they skate around in punked-out costumes that include the obligatory fishnet stockings under their kneepads, and they're just plain fun to watch. The season usually includes half a dozen or so home bouts at various roller rinks in the region. Check the Web site for details and ticket information. Admission is usually $10 for adults and somewhat less for kids.

KIDSTUFF

The mid–Hudson Valley abounds with fun things for kids and families. The activities listed here were chosen for being accessible, reasonably priced, and appropriate for kids ranging from toddlers up to about 12. (For outdoor recreation, such as swimming beaches and fishing, see the Parks and the Outdoors chapter.)

In addition to the events and program described here, many of the places listed will also make arrangements for birthday parties and other private events. Check with the management as far in advance as possible. Some places also offer after-school and summer day camp programs. Availability, dates, and fees vary too much to discuss here. Again, check with management as far in advance as possible—many popular programs fill up very quickly.

The dates and times given below are accurate for most of the year. Many sites are seasonal, however, and some change their hours during school holidays and in the summer. Before piling everyone into the car, check ahead.

Price Code

The price range given here is based on the adult admission fee. In most cases, kids get in for less and little kids (usually under 5 or 3) get in for free. Many places also have money-saving family admission rates and some offer reduced rates on weekdays or during off-peak times. Some places are free. Check in advance.

$	$10 or less
$$	over $10 to $20
$$$	over $20

ANIMALS

CATSKILL ANIMAL SANCTUARY $
316 Old Stage Road, Saugerties
(845) 336-8447
www.casanctuary.org
Catskill Animal Sanctuary provides a safe haven on 100 acres for horses and other farm animals who have been rescued from abusive situations. Since its founding in 2001, CAS has provided refuge for more than 1,000 animals. One of the most famous is Buddy, the title animal in the wonderful book about the sanctuary, *Where the Blind Horse Sings*, by founder Kathy Stevens. The animals roam freely here—it's the people who have to go on a guided tour. Kids love it, but please leave the dog at home. The sanctuary is open to the public from April 1 through October 31, Saturday and Sunday only, from 11:00 a.m. to 4:00 p.m.

TREVOR ZOO $
Millbrook School
Millbrook School Road, Millbrook
(845) 677-3704
www.millbrook.org
The Trevor Zoo is the only zoo in the country located at a high school. It dates back to 1936, when it was founded by Frank Trevor, a biology teacher at this private prep school. Today the zoo is fully accredited and is home to more than 180 animals, including seven endangered species. The wallabies are particular favorites with visitors. There are also red wolves, lemurs, white-naped cranes, rheas, red pandas, and many more, for a total of some 80 species. The zoo is available for birthday parties—call in advance for information. Open every day from 8:30 a.m. to 5:00 p.m.

i The Catskill Game Farm, long a popular animal attraction in Greene County, is no more. It closed in 2006.

WOODSTOCK FARM ANIMAL SANCTUARY $

35 Van Wagner Road, Willow
(845) 679-5955
www.woodstocksanctuary.org

A nonprofit organization, Woodstock Farm Animal Sanctuary (WFAS) provides care, rehabilitation, and shelter to neglected, abused, and discarded farm animals. The chickens, cows, pigs, sheep, and other animals that have ended up here were mostly destined to be eaten but were rescued instead. The sanctuary encourages visitors and allows them to interact with the animals. It's fun and also educational, because another major purpose here is to learn more about the impact of factory farming and how to improve the welfare of farm animals. The sanctuary is open to visitors Saturday and Sunday from April 1 through October 31. Kids are welcome, but leave the dog at home or in the car. The suggested donation is $5 a person.

THE ARTS

THE BARDAVON 1869 OPERA HOUSE $

35 Market Street, Poughkeepsie
(845) 473-2072
www.bardavon.org

The historic Bardavon (see the Performing Arts and Film chapter for more on this venue) offers an extensive schedule of daytime performances for kids throughout the year. The programs vary but include ballets such as *The Nutcracker* and programs for little kids such as "The Very Hungry Caterpillar and Other Eric Carle Favorites." An annual highlight is the Young People's Concerts put on by the Hudson Valley Philharmonic. These outstanding daytime programs introduce kids in grades 3–6 to classical music.

THE CENTER FOR PERFORMING ARTS AT RHINEBECK $$

661 Route 308, Rhinebeck
(845) 876-3080
www.centerforperformingarts.org

Great shows for kids are produced regularly at this nonprofit arts organization. (They do great shows for grown-ups too—see the Performing Arts and Film chapter.) Magicians and puppeteers make regular appearances, as do programs such as Shakespeare for Kids by the Hampstead Stage Company. In addition to the shows, the center also offers a wide range of educational programs and summer camps for kids that teach them about theater arts and let them perform onstage.

MILL STREET LOFT $$$

455 Maple Street, Poughkeepsie
(845) 471-7477
www.millstreetloft.org

A nonprofit arts education center, Mill Street Loft offers year-round classes for kids ranging in age from preschoolers to teens. Arts programs here include the visual arts, sculpture, music, photography, drama, and dance. Mill Street also sponsors the Dutchess Arts Camp every summer in Millbrook and Poughkeepsie. Fees are very reasonable and classes fill up fast.

ULSTER PERFORMING ARTS CENTER (UPAC) $$

601 Broadway, Kingston
(845) 339-6088
www.upac.org

The Broadway Theater at UPAC hosts many performances throughout the year (see the Performing Arts and Film chapter), including some programs for kids—Young People's Concerts by the Hudson Valley Philharmonic, for instance. In 2007 UPAC merged with Bardavon, so more performances for kids may be happening here as the partnership moves forward.

UNISON ARTS & LEARNING CENTER $–$$$

68 Mountain Rest Road, New Paltz
(845) 255-1559
www.unisonarts.org

Kids can have a lot of fun at the varied programs offered at this nonprofit community arts organization. Performers such as storytellers and the popular Dog on Fleas trio make appearances here, and there are also hands-on activities such as craft and art classes, wildlife programs, and programs with names like "Fun with Energy." Unison sponsors multi-session programs such as a clay shop; there's also a summer arts program and a summer farm camp at nearby Phillies Bridge Farm. The offerings fill up quickly—call ahead as far as possible to reserve space.

ATTRACTIONS

BARTON ORCHARDS $$
Fishkill Farms: 9 Fishkill Farms Road,
Hopewell Junction
(845) 897-2266
Poughquag Farm: 63 Apple Tree Lane,
Poughquag
(845) 227-2306
www.bartonorchards.com
Barton Orchards provides family farm entertainment at two locations in southern Dutchess County. In addition to picking apples and other fruits and vegetables, the Barton family offers hayrides, petting zoos, craft demonstrations, live concerts and other entertainment, face painting, storytelling, a family fun park, even fireworks. On top of all that, they have fabulous themed corn mazes in both locations. There's enough to do that kids of all ages can enjoy a day here. The orchards open in June and stay open until mid-November; the corn mazes open in mid-August. Hours are generally 10:00 a.m. to 5:00 p.m. every day, but there are a lot of evening events, including flashlight nights in the corn mazes (bring your own light). Call ahead to check on hours, events, and picking conditions.

CATSKILL MOUNTAIN RAILROAD $$
Route 28, Mount Pleasant
(845) 688-7400
www.catskillmtrailroad.com
Take a ride on the Catskill Mountain Railroad Scenic Train as it travels a 12-mile round-trip between Phoenicia and Boiceville. The route goes along the scenic Esopus Creek. At Phoenicia, the train stops for a visit to the Empire State Railway Museum (listed next). The trip takes about 90 minutes and is a ton of fun, which is why it's included here even though it's a bit west of the region. The trains run on weekends and holidays from the end of May through the end of October; trains depart Mount Pleasant at 11:30 a.m., 1:30 p.m., and 3:30 p.m. Call ahead to confirm dates and times.

EMPIRE STATE RAILWAY MUSEUM
Phoenicia Station, Phoenicia
(845) 688-7501
www.esrm.com
Located in a historic 1899 station on the old Ulster & Delaware line, the Empire State Railway Museum preserves the history of the railroads that once operated rugged steam trains through the Catskill Mountains. The building houses exhibits of railroad photos, films, and artifacts and a gift shop. Volunteers at the museum are restoring some antique railway cars—visitors can watch them work and ask questions. Open from Memorial Day through Columbus Day, weekends and holidays only, 11:00 a.m. to 4:00 p.m. No admission charge, but donations are welcome.

HEADLESS HORSEMAN
HAUNTED HOUSE $$$
Route 9W, Ulster Park
(845) 339-2666
www.headlesshorseman.com
The Headless Horseman was created in 1820 by Washington Irving in his famous story "The Legend of Sleepy Hollow." In addition to Irving's work, the Hudson Valley has plenty of other ghost stories, and they all come to life (as it were) at this popular Halloween-season attraction. The property has 45 acres of suitably scary woods, along with three great haunted houses and a corn maze. A 1-mile horse-drawn horror hayride is part of the admission; three food cafes and five gift shops are on the site. Nightly entertainment features The John Shaw Pandemonium Midnight Sideshow. Great for teens and grown-ups, but not recommended for kids under 8; kids under 5 not admitted. The schedule varies from year to year, but it's generally the last three Saturday nights in September and Saturday and Sunday

nights in October, with some weeknights in October. *Note:* Reserve your tickets early, and be aware that there's a no-refund policy.

HURDS FAMILY FARM $
2187 Route 32, Modena
(845) 883-7825
www.hurdsfamilyfarm.com

A working family farm with a strong sideline in school groups and farm tourists, Hurds is a fun place to visit, with scenic orchards and great views. You can pick your own apples, pears, raspberries, pumpkins, and other produce, touch the farm animals in the petting zoo, enjoy fresh cider and baked goods, and take a hayride. The Hurds also host special events, such as Johnny Appleseed Day, on weekends during the apple season. They do a fabulous four-acre corn maze in October. Open daily from September 1 through October 31, 10:00 a.m. to 5:00 p.m. The admission fee covers all activities, including the hayride, corn maze, apple launchers, and cow train.

THE INNER WALL $$
234 Main Street, New Paltz
(845) 255-ROCK
www.theinnerwall.com

Indoor rock climbing is very popular with kids and their parents, and for good reason—it's a ton of fun, it's good exercise, it really builds confidence, and the whole family can enjoy it at a reasonable cost. The Inner Wall is a good place to get started or to improve your skills. This facility offers more than 4,000 square feet of climbing space designed for all levels of fitness and ability. The equipment you need—harnesses and climbing shoes—is available for nominal rental fees (or bring your own), and experienced instructors are on hand to teach safe climbing techniques and to supervise. Open every day but Monday. Weekday hours are seasonal, but the facility is usually open on weekends year-round from noon to 7:00 p.m. *Note:* This spot is a little hard to find—drive around behind the Eckerd's drugstore.

i The slogan at YMCAs nationwide is "We build healthy kids." The Ys in the region have excellent facilities, including pools, and offer a lot of great programs for kids (and adults). Dutchess County YMCA (35 Montgomery Street, Poughkeepsie, 845-471-9622, www.dutchesscountyymca.org); Newburgh Family YMCA (no pool) (10 Little Britain Road, Newburgh, 845-562-1088, www.newburghymca.org); YMCA of Kingston and Ulster County (507 Broadway, Kingston, 845-338-3810, www.ymcaulster .org).

KIDS EXPO $
Downtown Poughkeepsie
(845) 485-9803, ext. 500
www.kids-expo.org

A two-day festival held early every April in downtown Poughkeepsie, Kids Expo attracts some 25,000 people every year. It's a way for kids and their families to enjoy fun, safe, interactive learning experiences. Events include a parade, live music and other entertainment, a petting zoo, rock climbing, firehouse tours, health information, and more. The activities happen all around town, including at the YMCA, the Mid-Hudson Civic Center, and the Mid-Hudson Children's Museum. Events run from 10:00 a.m. to 4:00 p.m. on both days. Purchase tickets at the Y or the Civic Center—free for kids under 3.

OLD RHINEBECK AERODROME $$
Stone Church and Norton Roads, Rhinebeck
(845) 752-3200
www.oldrhinebeck.org

Amazing air shows using vintage aircraft, plus a museum of historic aircraft. This is often listed as a kids' attraction, and kids do love it, but it's really for everyone. Open seasonally, May through September. The museum is open every day in season, 10:00 a.m. to 5:00 p.m. Air shows are at 2:00 p.m. Saturday and Sunday, weather permitting.

SPLASHDOWN BEACH $$$
16 Old Route 9 West, Fishkill
(845) 897-9600
www.splashdownbeach.com

Lots of fun water attractions on 13 acres, including a giant halfpipe raft ride, three giant waterslides, the 400-foot Pirates Plunge ride, a wave pool, and a water playground for the toddler set. There's also a sand beach that can hold 400 people, plus snack bars, the Shipwreck Café, and picnic areas. For the Halloween season, the park is transformed on weekends into Skull Island Scream Park, featuring five water-themed scary attractions, including Pirate Town and Skull Island. SplashDown Beach is open weekends in June from 11:00 a.m. to 6:00 p.m., then every day in July and August from 10:00 a.m. to 6:00 or 7:00 p.m. Days and hours vary seasonally, so check in advance. Reduced-rate half-day admissions are available.

TROLLEY MUSEUM OF NEW YORK $
89 East Strand, Kingston
(845) 331-3399
www.tmny.org

This museum is discussed in Hudson Valley Mansions and Historic Sites: West Side chapter. It's listed again here because kids really enjoy it.

WING'S CASTLE $
717 Bangall Road, Millbrook
(845) 677-9085

This is a place that has to be seen to be believed— a true Gothic stone castle, complete with seven towers, gargoyles, and a moat. Kids will think they're in a real-life fairytale. The castle is a work in progress by craftsman/artist Peter Wing and his wife Toni, who have been building it since 1969, using mostly recycled and salvaged materials. The interior is furnished with architectural artifacts and antiques. The views from the castle are spectacular. Tours are available from June through December, Wednesday through Sunday, from 10:00 a.m. to 5:00 p.m. Hours are seasonal and vary, so call ahead. In the summer, the Annandale Troupe, a children's acting program, holds a summer program here and puts on performances of Shakespeare against this perfect backdrop. For details: (917) 881-6074 or www.annandaletroupe.org.

ZOOM FLUME WATER PARK $$$
Shady Glen Road, East Durham
(800) 888-3586
www.zoomflume.com

The largest water park in the Catskills, Zoom Flume is a little out of the region covered in this book—it's in western Greene County. The attractions here include giant waterslides, a 600-foot-long rapids chute, and the very scary Black Vortex—a waterslide that twists and turns in total darkness. There are also water attractions for small kids. Facilities include a restaurant with bar, snack bars, locker rooms, sun decks, and picnic tables. Open the last two weekends in June from 10:00 a.m. to 7:00 p.m., then every day from the end of June to the beginning of September from 10:00 a.m. to 6:00 or 7:00 p.m. The operating schedule is seasonal, so call ahead to check the hours.

ℹ️ Many historic sites in the region offer special programs for kids and families throughout the year. These popular programs can really bring history alive, and they tend to sell out quickly. Sign up in advance if possible.

MUSEUMS AND NATURE CENTERS

FASNY MUSEUM OF FIREFIGHTING $
117 Harry Howard Avenue, Hudson
(877) 347-3687
www.fasnyfiremuseum.com

Kids really enjoy this museum—they get to climb on some fire equipment—and it's educational as well. For more information, see the Mansions and Historic Sites: East chapter.

FORSYTH NATURE CENTER $
Kingston Point Park, Kingston
(845) 331-1682
www.forsythnaturecenter.org
Owned and operated by the City of Kingston Parks and Recreation Department, Forsyth Nature Center offers 15 animal exhibits (including a reptile house), five theme gardens, and more than 250 programs for kids and families every year. Programs include hikes with naturalists, kayak paddles on the Rondout Creek and Hudson River, special weekend afternoon programs, and weeklong Junior Naturalist summer programs. Most activities are free and open to all; fees are usually only a few dollars. Summer hours (from the end of May through Labor Day): Monday through Friday from 7:00 a.m. to 7:00 p.m., weekends and holidays from 9:00 a.m. to 5:00 p.m. Winter hours (October through May): Monday through Friday from 7:00 a.m. to 5:00 p.m., weekends and holidays from 9:00 a.m. to 1:00 p.m. Check ahead for program dates and times.

HUDSON HIGHLANDS NATURE MUSEUM $
Wildlife Education Center:
25 Boulevard, Cornwall
(845) 534-7781
Outdoor Discovery Center:
20 Kenridge Farm Drive, Route 9W, Cornwall
(845) 534-5506
www.museumhudsonhighlands.org
Founded in 1959, the Hudson Highlands Nature Museum has two facilities about 1.5 miles apart in Cornwall. The Outdoor Discovery Center, on 177 scenic acres, is a wildlife sanctuary and education center. In addition to the museum's headquarters, the site has classrooms, an art gallery, and restrooms. Several miles of hiking trails wind through the sanctuary. Fun activities for families include a family hiking club, a variety of weekend nature programs, and Discovery Quests, hikes that lead to different habitats on the site and teach about them. The Wildlife Education Center has exhibits, such as the Living Hudson exhibit, and offers a Meet the Animals program on weekend afternoons. The Outdoor Discovery

Center is open on weekends from May 1 through October 31. The Wildlife Education Center is open year-round, Friday through Sunday, from noon to 4:00 p.m. Most programs at both sites are in the afternoon. Check in advance to find out what's happening when and where.

MID-HUDSON VALLEY CHILDREN'S MUSEUM $
75 North Water Street, Poughkeepsie
(845) 471-0589
www.mhcm.org
The goal at this outstanding kids' museum is to enlighten minds through a fun and creative learning environment. That means lots of hands-on discovery activities through exhibits such as the giant bubble machine, the climb-through-the-heart play space, and the working Morse telegraph (Samuel Morse lived nearby, at Locust Grove—see the Hudson Valley Mansions and Historic Sites: East Side chapter.) A highlight is the full-size replica of a mastodon skeleton found in nearby Hyde Park in 1999. Numerous programs for kids through age 12 are also offered, including astronomy, Hudson River activities, history reenactments, and more. The play groups and summer day camp programs are very popular. The museum is open Tuesday through Sunday, 11:00 a.m. to 5:00 p.m. Check ahead for program times and more information on the play groups and day camps.

STONY KILL FARM ENVIRONMENTAL EDUCATION CENTER
79 Farmstead Lane, Fishkill
(845) 831-8780
www.dec.ny.gov/education
Stony Kill is operated by the New York State Department of Environmental Conservation as an educational center that's oriented mostly toward environmental activities for kids and families. The property includes more than 1,000 acres of woodlands, farmland, meadows, ponds, and fields. The working farmstead includes a 19th-century barn and farmhouse, an 18th-century Dutch stone house, a greenhouse, a pond, and community gardens. Cattle, pigs, sheep, and chickens live on the farm. In addition to visiting

the farm and walking on the easy, well-marked trails, families can participate in nature programs and hikes just about any Saturday afternoon. The grounds are open daily from sunrise to sunset. The Manor House Visitor Center has picnic tables and restrooms. Stony Kill is open weekdays from 8:45 a.m. to 4:30 p.m., Saturdays from 9:30 a.m. to 4:30 p.m., and Sundays in April, May, June, September, and October from 1:00 to 4:30 p.m. Entry and all programs are free.

TACONIC OUTDOOR EDUCATION CENTER $
75 Mountain Laurel Lane
Cold Spring
(845) 265-3773
http://www.nysparks.state.ny.us
The main focus at this center, located in Clarence Fahnestock Memorial State Park, is on outdoor education programs for school and community groups. The center also sponsors many public programs throughout the year, such as Winterfest in early February and a maple-sugaring celebration every March. Summer brings hikes and nature programs. The schedule varies—check ahead. Most programs are free. (For more information about this vast park, see the Parks and the Outdoors chapter.)

VOLUNTEER FIREMEN'S HALL AND MUSEUM
265 Fair Street, Kingston
(845) 338-1247
This small, very kid-friendly firehouse museum is in Kingston's historic Stockade District. For details, see the Mansions and Historic Sites: West chapter.

SPORTS

Bowling

As a rainy day activity or for a birthday party, bowling is a great choice. Bumpers and ramps make this sport fun even for little kids and beginners, and there's more fun to be had in the game rooms. The region has too many lanes to go into detail—there's only space for names and addresses. Check ahead for hours and prices.

BOWLERS CLUB
9 Simmons Plaza, Saugerties
(845) 246-4969

CATSKILL HOEBOWL
305 West Bridge Street, Catskill
(518) 943-4980

CHATHAM BOWL
248 East Chatham Road, Chatham
(518) 392-5050

FERRARO'S MID-CITY LANES
20 Cedar Street, Kingston
(845) 331-6161

FISHKILL BOWL
110 Route 82, Fishkill
(845) 896-7830
www.fishkillbowl.com

HOEBOWL COUNTRY LANES
425 Violet Avenue, Hyde Park
(845) 452-1645

HOEBOWL HOLIDAY LANES
1688 Route 9, Wappingers Falls
(845) 297-8110

HOEBOWL MARDI-BOB
45 Taft Avenue, Poughkeepsie
(845) 471-1820

HOEBOWL ON THE HILL
644 East Chester Street, Kingston
(845) 338-1414
www.hoebowlonthehill.com

RO-LIN LANES
Route 9G, Red Hook
(845) 876-6300

SOUTHERN DUTCHESS BOWL
629 Route 52, Beacon
(845) 831-3220

TARSIO LANES
173 South Plank Road, Newburgh
(845) 562-5250
Route 9W, New Windsor
(845) 562-2200
www.tarsiolanes.com

Ice-Skating

Ice-skating and junior ice hockey leagues are available at two places in the mid–Hudson Valley region. The **McCann Ice Arena at the Mid-Hudson Civic Center** in Poughkeepsie (14 Civic Center Plaza, 845-454-5800, www.midhudson civiccenter.com; $) offers public open skating on an NHL-sized rink along with instruction and leagues for recreational, hockey, and figure skating. Skate rentals are available. A lot of the ice time here is taken for organized programs, and public skating hours are limited to some weekdays. On weekends the hours are usually 2:00 to 4:00 p.m., but check ahead. In Newburgh, the **Ice Time Sports Complex** (21 Lakeside Road, 845-567-0005, www.icetimesports.com; $) offers lots of hockey instruction and leagues along with recreational and figure-skating instruction. Skate rentals are available. On Friday nights there's open skating with a DJ from 7:15 to 9:00 p.m. Open skating on other weeknights is limited; on weekends, open skating happens from 2:00 to 4:00 pm.

Roller Rinks

Roller-skating today is lot more than just circling round and round a rink to boring music. A roller rink is a pretty lively place, with lots of great music, DJs, special effects, dancing, and games. It's family fun at a reasonable price—nonskating parents and grandparents get in for free. At all the places listed here, bring your own skates or rent them for a nominal fee; bring your own skateboard. **Hyde Park Roller Magic** (4178 Albany Post Road, Hyde Park, 845-229-6666, www.hydeparkrollermagic. com; $) has a state-of-the-art lighting system and open skating with a live DJ on Friday and Saturday nights. Hours for open skating are Friday 7:30 to 10:30 p.m., Saturday 1:00 to 4:30 p.m. and 7:30 to 10:30 p.m., and Sunday 1:00 to 4:30 p.m. **The Skate Factory** in Ghent (1131 Route 9H, 518-822-8453, www.skatefactory.net; $) offers not only skating but also **SFX,** an indoor skateboard park. Public skating hours are family night (reduced admission) on Wednesday from 7:00 to 9:00 p.m.; Friday (funky family night with dancing), 6:30 to 10:00 p.m.; and Saturday and Sunday, 2:00 to 4:30 p.m. SFX is open Wednesday from 5:00 to 9:00 p.m., Friday from 5:00 to 10:00 p.m., and Saturday from 2:00 to 5:00 p.m.; closed Sunday. In Port Ewen, **Wood 'N Wheel** (Route 9, 845-331-9680, www.woodnwheel.com; $) has 10,000 square feet of maple skating surface, great lighting, and sound and special effects, and offers Laser Storm, an off-skates laser tag game. Open Friday from 7:00 to 10:00 p.m., Saturday from 1:00 to 3:00 p.m. and 7:00 to 10:00 p.m., and Sunday from 1:00 to 3:30 p.m. and 7:00 to 9:00 p.m. Closed Sundays in the summer. **Skate Time 209** in Accord (Route 209, 845-626-7971, www.skatetime209.com; $) is actually a bit out of the region, but it's a great facility offering both roller-skating and a 10,000-square-foot indoor skateboarding park. Open some weekdays; weekend hours are Friday from 2:30 to 6:00 p.m. and 7:00 to 10:00 p.m., Saturday from 1:00 to 5:00 p.m. and 7:00 to 10:00 p.m., and Sunday from 1:30 to 4:30 p.m. and 6:30 to 9:30 p.m.

HIGHER EDUCATION

Students from all over New York, all over the country, and all over the world converge on the Hudson Valley to attend the many outstanding colleges and universities here. In the mid–Hudson Valley region alone, students can attend one of 11 schools, ranging from some of the country's oldest and most distinguished colleges to some of the newest. Of those 11, 5 are independent private institutions. Five are divisions of the outstanding State University of New York (SUNY) system. And one, the United States Military Academy at West Point, is unique—the first and oldest service academy in the country.

With that many schools to choose from, students here can study just about anything—and they do. They bring diversity and a youthful vibe to the region. The education sector is also an important economic engine for the local economy. In 2007, for example, the State University of New York at New Paltz spent about $3.4 million on Ulster County businesses and $2.8 million on Dutchess County businesses, and the school employs 1,400 people in the area.

The campuses of the mid–Hudson Valley aren't just for young students, however. Most offer a wide range of nondegree courses for adults continuing their professional education or seeking training in a new field. All campuses are also active participants in their communities. Students from just about any college can be found volunteering in their neighboring towns, and local high school students get a taste of college life through programs that bring them on campus. Residents and tourists can be found on campus enjoying cultural activities, sports events, and even dinner at some of the finest restaurants in the region.

COLUMBIA COUNTY

Hudson

COLUMBIA-GREENE COMMUNITY COLLEGE
4400 Route 23
(518) 828-4181
www.mycommunitycollege.com
Columbia-Greene Community College celebrated its 40th anniversary in 2006–2007. Enrollment that year reached a historic high of more than 1,800 students; of those, just over 1,000 are attending full time. Students at C-GCC can choose from 33 different programs, all offering certificates or associate degrees. Popular degree programs include nursing studies, a variety of teacher education tracks, and automotive technology. A new program in massage therapy has been very successful. About 90 percent of C-GCC students go on to further education at a four-year college or into jobs directly related to their

program. Full-time students who are residents of New York State pay $1,536 per semester; part-time resident students pay $128 per credit. Tuition for nonresidents is double.

DUTCHESS COUNTY

Annandale-on-Hudson

BARD COLLEGE
30 Campus Road
(845) 758-6822
www.bard.edu
Founded in 1860, Bard is a four-year residential college of the liberal arts and sciences. The lovely 500-acre campus is located in the tiny hamlet of Annandale-on-Hudson, near the town of Red Hook in the northern part of the county. About 1,600 undergraduates study here; almost all live on campus. Entrance to Bard is highly

competitive. The curriculum is challenging and offers a bachelor of arts degree in a choice of more than 40 programs in four divisions: arts; languages and literature; science, mathematics, and computing; and social studies. Students are taught by a very distinguished faculty, including five MacArthur Fellows. The student/faculty ratio is 9:1. Since 1975, when Bard's dynamic president, Leon Botstein, took office, the college has expanded its undergraduate and graduate programs, added a number of institutes such as the Levy Economics Institute, and built some impressive new facilities, including the spectacular Fisher Center for the Performing Arts. (See Performing Arts and Film for more on this and on the annual Bard Music Festival.) In 2005, the Bard College Conservatory of Music opened. In this unique five-year program, students pursue a dual bachelor's degree in music and in a field other than music. Annual costs for tuition, room and board, and fees come to more than $47,000.

Hyde Park

CULINARY INSTITUTE OF AMERICA
1946 Campus Drive
(845) 452-9430
www.ciachef.edu

If you want to cook for a living, this is the place to learn how to do it. The Culinary Institute of America, better known in the area as the CIA, is widely considered the finest school in the country for professional culinary education. The facilities here are outstanding: a spectacularly beautiful 170-acre campus on the Hudson, 41 kitchens and bake shops, five famed public restaurants, an outstanding culinary library, and dorms for more than 1,000 students. The faculty consists of more than 125 instructors from 16 countries. About 2,800 students are enrolled in the degree programs; many more food-service professionals come to the school every year for continuing education courses. Learning to be a chef at the CIA is serious business—students graduate with more 1,300 kitchen hours in addition to classroom work. Annual tuition is just over $20,000—a bargain given the school's excellent record of job placement for graduates. Top employers in the food business come to Hyde Park every quarter to recruit students, and graduates consistently earn higher-than-average salaries. The CIA also offers a number of programs for culinary enthusiasts, including demonstration classes, hands-on daylong programs, and even cooking classes for kids. For information on dining at the CIA, see the Restaurants: East Side of the Hudson chapter.

Poughkeepsie

DUTCHESS COMMUNITY COLLEGE
53 Pendell Road
(845) 431-8000
www.sunydutchess.edu

Dutchess Community College provides open access to an affordable, quality post-secondary education. DCC was founded in 1957 as a comprehensive community college, which means it offers college transfer and occupational/technical degree programs, along with certificate programs and lifelong learning opportunities. About one-third of all Dutchess County high school graduates attend DCC—the highest percentage of any community college in the state—and 96 percent of the students who transfer to a SUNY college graduate with a four-year degree. DCC offers programs in a number of areas. The school is particularly noted for its programs in nursing and health care, education, and engineering. One reason nearly 8,000 students attend DCC every year is that the education is a genuine bargain. Dutchess Community College has the lowest tuition of any college or university in the state. A full year's tuition is just $2,700.

MARIST COLLEGE
3399 North Road
(845) 575-3174
www.marist.edu

Founded in 1905 as a training ground for future Marist Brothers, Marist College became a four-year liberal arts college in 1946. Since then, Marist has grown steadily in both size and prestige. Today it is an independent institution offering 32 undergraduate degree programs, 11 master's programs, and 20 certificate programs. Some

4,200 traditional undergraduates enjoy the lovely 180-acre campus stretching along the shore of the Hudson River; most live on campus in townhouse dorms. Marist is a leader in high-tech, with a completely wireless library, "smart" classrooms, 25 computer labs, and a working relationship with nearby IBM that has made the college one of the most technologically advanced in the country. Interested students can participate in the famed Marist Institute for Public Opinion, best known for the Marist Poll. Also on campus is The Hudson River Valley Institute, the academic arm of the Hudson River Valley National Heritage Area. Its mission is to study and to promote the Hudson River Valley and to provide educational resources (check www.hudsonrivervalley.net for more information). The college has excellent athletic facilities and boasts championship crew and basketball teams (see the Spectator Sports chapter for more on Red Fox teams). Undergraduate tuition and room and board at Marist work out to about $34,000 a year.

VASSAR COLLEGE
124 Raymond Avenue
(845) 437-7000
www.vassar.edu

Vassar College looks exactly like a movie version of an idealized college campus—except it's the real deal. The architecture ranges from collegiate Gothic to modernist, set among manicured lawns and formal gardens. Two campus buildings are National Historic Landmarks. Vassar was founded in 1861 as a women's college. In 1969 it became the first of the elite Seven Sisters schools to admit men, after turning down an offer to merge with Yale. The college is highly selective; it is consistently ranked among the top liberal arts colleges in the country. About 2,400 students are taught by more than 260 faculty members, giving a student/faculty ratio of 9:1; average class size is 17. Almost all students live on campus. Academics at Vassar are rigorous, but there is no core curriculum. Students may choose from a wide range of departmental majors, interdepartmental programs, and multidisciplinary programs. Campus life is very active—there are more than 100 student-run organizations

and clubs, as well as 23 NCAA Division III varsity teams, club sports, and intramural leagues. All that activity creates about 1,650 campuswide events annually, including guest lecturers, visiting artists, performers, workshops, athletic events, and concerts. Tuition, room and board, and fees add up to more than $44,000 a year.

ORANGE COUNTY

Middletown

SUNY ORANGE
115 South Street
(845) 344-6222
www.orange.cc.ny.us

SUNY Orange was founded in 1950 as the first county-sponsored community college in the state university system. Among other accomplishments, it was the first two-year college in the nation to offer the associate degree nursing program. The college now offers 44 academic programs in areas such as business, the health professions, liberal arts, and technology. Courses are taught both at the main campus in Middletown and at the Newburgh Extension Center. The college is strongly committed to helping adult students returning to school. The Center for Adult Life-Long Learning was developed several years ago to provide support for nontraditional students. An education at SUNY Orange is a great deal. The tuition is about $1,500 a semester for full-time students, among the lowest of the 30 community colleges in the state.

Newburgh

MOUNT SAINT MARY COLLEGE
330 Powell Avenue
(845) 561-0800
www.msmc.edu

Mount Saint Mary College dates back to 1883, when a small group of Dominican sisters arrived from New York City to start an elementary school in Newburgh. Soon there was an elementary school and a high school on the property. By 1959, the sisters had founded Mount Saint Mary as a four-year liberal arts college for women;

men were admitted in 1969. Today some 2,600 students study at the lovely 44-acre campus in historic Newburgh. The Mount offers more than 50 undergraduate programs; it has a superior reputation for undergraduate and graduate programs in education, nursing and health care, and business. Yearly costs for tuition, room and board, and fees come to about $30,000.

West Point

UNITED STATES MILITARY ACADEMY
2107 South Post Road
(845) 938-2638
www.usma.edu

West Point, as the United States Military Academy is familiarly known, was founded in 1802. Its core mission has remained unchanged: to prepare cadets for military service by developing their intellectual, physical, military, and moral-ethical abilities. Admission to West Point is by appointment from an approved source, such as a member of Congress. The process is highly competitive. Once admitted, cadets follow an academic program of 31 courses providing a balanced education in the arts and sciences, followed by electives toward an optional major. All cadets also take five engineering courses, and all graduating cadets receive a bachelor of science degree. Cadets learn basic military skills through the demanding military program, which begins as soon as they enter the academy and continues through summer programs. There are about 4,000 cadets at any given time; about 15 percent are women. West Point is a service academy, which means that tuition is free and cadets receive a salary as members of the Army; the current rate is approximately $600 a month.

ULSTER COUNTY

New Paltz

STATE UNIVERSITY OF NEW YORK AT NEW PALTZ
One Hawk Drive
(845) 257-7869
www.newpaltz.edu

New York's state university system is highly regarded nationwide, and the campus at New Paltz is one of the reasons why. It was recently ranked fifth in the nation among public universities by *U.S. News & World Report*. SUNY New Paltz is a highly selective college with some 8,000 undergraduate and graduate students. The 257-acre campus is located in the historic village of New Paltz, between the Shawangunk Mountains on the west and the Hudson River on the east. The college has five schools: Education, Fine and Performing Arts, Business, Science and Engineering, and the College of Liberal Arts and Sciences. More than 100 undergraduate and 50 graduate programs are offered. New Paltz is the only public four-year college in the Hudson Valley region. As is the case with State Colleges, the tuition here is an amazing bargain.

Stone Ridge

SUNY ULSTER
Cottekill Road
(845) 687-5000
www.sunyulster.edu

The motto at SUNY Ulster is: Start here. Go far. A two-year community college located near Kingston, SUNY Ulster has a good track record of transferring students into four-year programs. More than 70 percent of the students here go on to earn baccalaureate and graduate degrees elsewhere. SUNY Ulster offers degree and certificate programs in a number of areas, including business, communications, education, and nursing and public safety. The school has an excellent local reputation for courses in computers and technology, engineering, and industrial technology. A big part of the mission here is educating nontraditional students. About 30 percent of the students are returning adults, and the school accommodates them with accelerated learning options and a wide variety of noncredit courses. As with other community colleges in New York State, the costs are very reasonable.

HEALTH CARE

The mid–Hudson Valley region is fortunate indeed when it comes to health care. The region is located midway among three major hospital centers: all the many hospitals in New York City and the Westchester Medical Center complex to the south, and the hospitals of Albany, including Albany Medical Center and St. Peter's Hospital, to the north. High-level specialized care at a major hospital center is within relatively easy geographic access. Within the region, high-level hospital care, skilled physicians, and a broad range of health-care services are also within easy reach. In fact, there are so many great doctors and other providers in the region that they can't be listed here. This chapter focuses only on local hospitals. Fortunately, the hospitals and some county medical societies have referral services that can help you find physicians and other providers in local areas.

HOSPITALS

Columbia

COLUMBIA MEMORIAL HOSPITAL
71 Prospect Avenue, Hudson
(518) 828-7601
www.columbiamemorial.com
Columbia Memorial Hospital serves more than 100,000 residents in Columbia, Greene, and northern Dutchess Counties. The hospital has 192 beds and also operates Kaaterskill Care, a long-term care and rehab center. The hospital has an extensive network of primary care centers and outpatient specialty centers. Columbia Memorial has a state-of-the-art emergency room and surgical wing, an award-winning birthing center, and an innovative, multidisciplinary pain management center.

Dutchess

NORTHERN DUTCHESS HOSPITAL
6511 Springbrook Avenue, Rhinebeck
(845) 876-3001
www.northerndutchesshospital.com
Northern Dutchess Hospital serves northern Dutchess, southern Columbia, and parts of Ulster County. Although this is a small community hospital, the staff includes more than 200 practitioners offering services in more than 30 specialties. Among the special centers here are the Bone and Joint Center, a comprehensive orthopedic program offering an array of services, the Paul Rosenthal Rehabilitation Center, and the Neugarten Family Birth Center. Other facilities at Northern Dutchess include a sleep lab, a cardiac imaging lab, short-term residential rehab for orthopedic and neurological disorders and amputations at The Thompson House, and The Wellness Center, a community fitness center.

ST. FRANCIS HOSPITAL
241 North Road, Poughkeepsie
(845) 483-5000
www.sfhhc.org
St. Francis Hospital is a 300-bed acute-care facility serving patients in the entire mid–Hudson Valley. The facilities are extensive. A sleep disorders lab was opened in 1991. The hospital is also a leader in orthopedics and today offers the only fully dedicated joint replacement center in the region. In 1993 New York State designated the hospital as the area trauma center. Today it is the busiest Level II Trauma Center in the state and has recently been expanded to 16,000 square feet.

VASSAR BROTHERS MEDICAL CENTER
45 Reade Place, Poughkeepsie
(845) 454-8500
www.vassarbrothers.org

A 365-bed acute-care hospital, Vassar Brothers provides a full range of medical services to the mid-Hudson region. This historic hospital is now housed in modern buildings, but it dates back to 1887 and is named for the same Vassar brothers who gave their name to nearby Vassar College. There are four Centers of Clinical Excellence, including the Heart Institute, the Maternity Center, the Neonatal Intensive Care Unit (the only Level Three unit in the mid–Hudson Valley), and the Dyson Center for Cancer Care. The hospital also has a highly sophisticated, state-of-the-art suite for minimally invasive surgery.

Orange

ST. LUKE'S CORNWALL HOSPITAL
Newburgh Campus:
70 Dubois Street
(845) 561-4400
Cornwall Campus:
19 Laurel Avenue
(845) 534-7711
www.stlukescornwallhospital.org

Formed in 2002 by the merger of two hospitals, St. Luke's serves nearly 300,000 residents in Orange County and the surrounding region. It is one of the largest employers in Orange County The Newburgh campus has 242 beds and a number of specialized services, including a regional neonatology center and other pediatric subspecialties, a cardiac catheterization lab and cardiac rehab facilities, a pain management center, and a speech and swallowing center. The Cornwall campus has 125 beds, including 22 for mental health patients in need of acute care, and a new cancer treatment center. The Cornwall Medical Pavilion next door has physicians' offices, a wound care center, and a same-day surgery center. Both campuses offer recently upgraded emergency care centers.

Putnam

PUTNAM HOSPITAL CENTER
670 Stoneleigh Avenue, Carmel
(845) 279-5711
www.putnamhospital.org

Putnam Hospital Center is the only acute-care hospital in the county. An ongoing capital improvement program in recent years has given the hospital an up-to-date emergency care center, a birthing center, a new cancer center offering radiation therapy, and enhanced cardiology services. There's also a pain management program, a wound-healing center, and a sleep disorders clinic, plus the hospital has been designated as a stroke center by New York State.

Ulster

BENEDICTINE HOSPITAL
105 Mary's Avenue, Kingston
(845) 338-2500
www.benedictine.org

Benedictine Hospital began in 1901 as a seven-bed facility staffed by four Benedictine Sisters. By 1906 the hospital had grown to a 36-bed building on the site of the present hospital. Today Benedictine is a 222-bed acute-care facility serving the entire northern Hudson Valley region. A major cancer care center was opened in 2005, and the hospital is one of just a few in the entire Hudson Valley region to be designated a Community Cancer Hospital by the American College of Surgeons' Commission on Cancer. Benedictine offers a full range of other health services, including state-of-the-art imaging, a birth center, a stroke unit, and hospice care.

THE KINGSTON HOSPITAL
396 Broadway, Kingston
(845) 331-3131
www.kingstonregionalhealth.org

The Kingston Hospital has been providing outstanding health care to the region ever since it was founded in 1894. The hospital today is a 160-bed acute-care facility providing comprehensive medical services. Specialty areas include ambulatory surgery, diagnostic imaging, emergency medicine, obstetrics, inpatient and outpatient substance abuse detox and rehab, a dialysis center, and the Greenspan Center for Women's Health.

MEDIA

The mid-Hudson region falls in between two major media markets—New York City to the south and the Albany region to the north. That unfortunately means that the area doesn't get the coverage it should from the major media outlets in those markets. The *New York Times* occasionally ventures north, usually with articles that somehow relate to second homes in the country and hardly ever with any hard news. The *Albany Times-Union* focuses on the Capital District and rarely looks south at all. Many residents rely on weekly papers that report only local community news and events to find out what's happening nearby. Similarly, the area is a bit neglected by radio (with the exception of the outstanding public radio station WAMC) and television stations. Many radio stations in the New York metro area can be picked up in the southern portion of the region. In the northern portion of the region, many Albany-area stations come in well. Similarly, broadcast TV from the New York City and Albany areas reach much of the region, although reception is poor or nonexistent in the hillier rural areas. Cable television now covers a lot of the region, but some small, rural towns have yet to be wired—satellite TV is the only alternative.

Because the mid–Hudson Valley region has such a rich cultural life, a number of well-crafted magazines provide a good mix of articles, along with listings of events and activities.

DAILY NEWSPAPERS

DAILY FREEMAN
79 Hurley Avenue, Kingston
(845) 331-5000
www.dailyfreeman.com
The *Daily Freeman* is a daily morning newspaper in broadsheet format, with a weekday circulation of about 22,000. The paper is based in Kingston and covers the news in all of Ulster County and in the Hudson Valley portions of Columbia, Dutchess, and Greene Counties. A single issue is 75¢. Some but not all of the paper can be read on the Web site.

i Very few newsstands as such can be found in the region. Local papers can be purchased at freestanding kiosks and at local retail outlets such as supermarkets, gas stations, drugstores, and convenience stores. Free papers may have kiosks and are also given away at many local retail outlets.

THE POUGHKEEPSIE JOURNAL
85 Civic Center Plaza, Poughkeepsie
(845) 454-2000
www.poughkeepsiejournal.com
The PoJo, as it's affectionately known, was founded in 1785, which makes it the oldest newspaper in New York State and the third-oldest in the country. Today the PoJo is a Gannett Company newspaper with excellent coverage of Dutchess County and some coverage of points north, south, and across the river to the west. A daily morning broadsheet, it has a weekday circulation of approximately 40,000 and a Sunday circulation of about 50,000. The headquarters building in downtown Poughkeepsie is a lovely fieldstone Colonial Revival structure with wonderful murals in the lobby celebrating the freedom of the press. The building is listed on the National Register of Historic Places. Whenever President Franklin Delano Roosevelt stayed at his family home in nearby Hyde Park, the *Poughkeep-sie New Yorker,* as the paper was called in those

days, became the temporary media center for the nation. Single issues are $1.

REGISTER STAR
364 Warren Street, Hudson
(518) 828-1616
www.registerstar.com
Serving Columbia and northern Dutchess Counties since 1785, the *Register Star* is a tabloid morning daily with a circulation of about 8,000. It's the only daily paper in Columbia County. Single issues are $1. The paper has a good Web site that makes available almost all features of the print edition.

TIMES HERALD RECORD
126 Main Street, New Paltz
(845) 255-0600
www.recordonline.com
A daily paper published in Middletown, the *Record* is the only daily in Orange and Sullivan Counties. It also covers events in southern Ulster County. A morning tabloid, it has an average weekday circulation of 80,000. The *Record* was founded 1956. It was the first paper in the country to use cold type. The paper's other major claim to fame is that in 1959 it briefly employed the late Hunter S. Thompson, founder of gonzo journalism. Hunter was fired after vandalizing an office vending machine that had eaten his money. A single issue is 75¢; monthly home delivery is $10.99. The Web site, is attractive and easy to use.

WEEKLY AND BIWEEKLY NEWSPAPERS

DUTCHESS BEAT
82 Washington Street, Poughkeepsie
(845) 485-2711
www.weeklybeat.com
A weekly tabloid covering news and events primarily in Poughkeepsie and Hyde Park in Dutchess County, the *Dutchess Beat* has a circulation of about 3,000. It appears on Thursday and is given away free at many retailers.

GAZETTE ADVERTISER
7 Livingston Street
Rhinebeck
(845) 876-3033
www.gazetteadvertiser.com
Covering the Rhinebeck and Red Hook region of northern Dutchess County, this weekly local paper has a circulation of about 9,000. Single issues are 75. The paper is a broadside that appears on Thursday and is sold at local retail outlets.

HUDSON VALLEY BUSINESS JOURNAL
86 East Main Street, Wappingers Falls
(845) 298-6236
www.hvbj.com
A biweekly (Tuesday and Friday) tabloid covering news that's important to Hudson Valley businesses. The coverage area includes Columbia, Dutchess, Greene, Orange, and Ulster Counties.

HYDE PARK TOWNSMAN
3 Pine Woods Drive, Hyde Park
(845) 229-6610
www.hydeparktownsman.com
The weekly local paper for the Hyde Park region of Dutchess County has a circulation of only about 800. Single issues are 75¢. The paper appears on Thursday.

THE INDEPENDENT
Route 23, Hillsdale
(518) 325-4400
www.indenews.com
Published every Tuesday and Friday, *The Independent* serves all of Columbia County and southern Rensselaer County. A broadsheet with a circulation of 9,600, it's the official paper of Columbia County. Single issues are 75¢.

KINGSTON TIMES
322 Wall Street, Kingston
(845) 334-8205
www.ulsterpublishing.com
Covering events and news in the greater Kingston area of Ulster County, the *Kingston Times* is

a free tabloid paper with a circulation of about 1,600. It's given away at retail outlets in the area.

MID-HUDSON POST PIONEER
11 Church Street, New Paltz
(845) 255-7000
www.ulsterpublishing.com
This weekly tabloid paper covers events and news in the Highland area of mid–Ulster County. A free paper, it's found at retail outlets in the area.

MILLBROOK ROUND TABLE
Box 316, Millbrook
(845) 677-8241
www.millbrookroundtable.com
Covering news and events in Millbrook and the surrounding town of Washington, the *Round Table* is a weekly broadsheet with a circulation of under 1,000. Single issues are 75¢.

NEW PALTZ TIMES
259 Main Street, New Paltz
(845) 255-7000
www.ulsterpublishing.com
Covering events and news in the New Paltz area of southern Ulster County, this free tabloid has a circulation of about 4,500.

PUTNAM COUNTY COURIER
73 Gleneida Avenue, Carmel
(845) 225-3633
www.putnamcountycourier.com
Although this county-wide weekly broadside is headquartered in central Putnam County, the coverage of the Hudson Valley communities is reasonable. A single issue is 75¢.

REGISTER HERALD
Box 644, Pine Plains
(518) 398-7012
www.theregisterherald.com
This weekly broadside provides the news and events for Pine Plains, Milan, and towns in northeastern Dutchess County. That these are very small towns is shown by the paper's circulation, which is under 1,000. Single issues are 75¢.

SAUGERTIES TIMES
Box 3329, Kingston
(845) 334-8200
www.ulsterpublishing.com
The *Saugerties Times* covers this small town in northern Ulster County. It's a free tabloid with a circulation of about 2,000.

VOICE LEDGER
Box 316, Millbrook
(845) 677-8241
www.voiceledger.com
Covering news and activities in the Beekman/LaGrange area of central Dutchess County, this weekly broadside circulates to about 1,500 readers. Single issues are 75¢.

WOODSTOCK TIMES
Box 3329, Kingston
(845) 334-8200
www.ulsterpublishing.com
The Woodstock region is covered by this free tabloid with a circulation of about 5,000. Check at retail outlets in the area to pick up a copy.

MAGAZINES

ABOUT TOWN
Dutchess County edition:
The Chocolate Factory
54 Elizabeth Street, Suite 11, Red Hook
(845) 758-3616
Ulster County edition:
Box 474, New Paltz
(845) 691-2089
www.abouttown.us
There are two editions of this outstanding free quarterly community guide. The **Dutchess County edition** covers events and activities in northern Dutchess and into Columbia County, including Rhinebeck, Red Hook, Tivoli, Hudson, Annandale, Barrytown, Clinton, Milan, Germantown, Livingston, Rhinecliff, and more. The **Ulster County edition** covers Gardiner, Esopus, Rosendale, New Paltz, Stone Ridge, High Falls, the Highland/Route 9W corridor, and more. These

guides are much more than just calendar listings. Both offer excellent feature articles focusing on events, local history, local personalities, and local issues, along with restaurant reviews and a wide range of articles on other topics such as gardening and health. The guides are tabloids and are given away free at many retail locations in the towns they cover. The calendar and local business listings appear on the Web site as well; so do the current articles, along with a full archive of previous articles.

ALM@NAC
Ulster Publishing
322 Wall Street, Kingston
(845) 334-8205
www.ulsterpublishing.com
Ulster Publishing's weekly arts and entertainment, calendar, classifieds, and real estate supplement. It appears within the six Ulster Publishing papers: *Woodstock Times, New Paltz Times, Kingston Times, Saugerties Times, Mid-Hudson Post Pioneer,* and *Dutchess Beat.*

CHRONOGRAM
314 Wall Street, Kingston
(845) 334-8600
www.chronogram.com
A free monthly magazine, *Chronogram* focuses on the creative and cultural life of the Hudson Valley. The oversize format and glossy paper are ideal for the excellent articles on the arts and artists that appear every month. The calendar listings of event, exhibits, performances, readings, and other cultural activities are extensive. The magazine covers events in the entire mid–Hudson Valley region, including Ulster, Dutchess, Greene, Columbia, Orange, and Putnam Counties.

DUTCHESS
Box 316, Millbrook
(845) 677-8241
www.midhudsoncentral.com
Dutchess is a glossy bimonthly publication distributed mostly as a free insert in the local Journal Register weeklies such as the Rhinebeck *Gazette Advertiser.* The magazine covers activities in Dutchess County and has a good calendar. The feature articles usually focus on personalities such as local artists. The excellent reviews by Jack Kelly cover books of local interest. A subscription is $15.

HUDSON
Artform
19 Henry Avenue, Newburgh
(845) 562-2318
www.hudsonmagazine.com
A quarterly magazine targeted to wealthy home owners, *Hudson* covers the poshest and most upscale items in home design, gardens, and luxury. The magazine showcases elegant living throughout the Hudson Valley, ranging all the way to the Capital District and also incliudng the Litchfield Hills in Connecticut and the Berkshires. A subscription is $18.95.

THE HUDSON RIVER VALLEY REVIEW
Marist College
3399 North Road, Poughkeepsie
(845) 575-3052
www.hudsonrivervalley.org
Published by the nonprofit Hudson RIver Valley Institute at Marist College in Poughkeepsie, this semiannual journal of regional studies is accessible to the general reader. The journal takes an eclectic and interdisciplinary approach to the region. While it focuses mostly on every aspect of the history of the Hudson Valley, it also publishes articles about architecture, literature, the arts, along with poems, photos, and book and art reviews. The online archive goes back to the journal's founding in 1984. A subscription is $20 a year.

HUDSON VALLEY
22 IBM Road, Poughkeepsie
(845) 463-0542
www.hvmag.com
Hudson Valley has been covering the region in a glossy monthly magazine for more than 35 years. The features cover all lifestyle aspects of the area, with articles on individuals past and present, celebrities, dining out, destinations, real estate, interior design, and more. Since 1986, the magazine has sponsored the annual Best of the

Hudson Valley. The magazine is sold at retail outlets, but tends to sell out quickly. Subscriptions are $14.97 for 12 issues.

HUDSON VALLEY CONNOISSEUR
85 Civic Center Plaza, Poughkeepsie
(845) 451-4575
www.hvcmagazine.com

A nicely produced glossy bimonthly, *Hudson Valley Connoisseur* calls itself "The region's authority on refined living." Articles focus on the finer things in life as found in the Hudson Valley region, including food, wine, golf, interior design, gardening, and so on. The magazine is unabashedly targeted to the wealthy, but it makes good reading for anyone interested in the region. Copies are $5.

HUDSON VALLEY GREEN TIMES
Box 208, Red Hook
(845) 486-7070
greentimes@verizon.net

Published quarterly, *Hudson Valley Green Times* is a publication of the nonprofit Hudson Valley Grass Roots Energy and Environmental Network, better known as Hudson Valley GREEN, and a powerful force for environmental activism in the region. The *Green Times* is a newsprint tabloid. Articles focus on regional environmental issues such as invasive species, wetlands preservation, energy, organic farming, and sprawl and over-development. Every spring the journal includes a thorough guide to organic farm produce. Each issue also contains a green calendar of upcoming environmental events. The *Green Times* has some free distribution at retail outlets in the area, but the best way to get it is to subscribe by joining Hudson Valley GREEN for a minimum contribution of $20.

INSIDEOUT HUDSON VALLEY
Box 165, Athens
(518) 943-9200
www.insideouthv.com

A beautifully produced glossy, *InsideOut Hudson Valley* is a bimonthly for the LGBTQ and progressive community throughout the region. The articles are eclectic, featuring pieces on local celebrities, architecture, interior design, the arts, parenting, dining out, and much more. Outstanding photography accompanies many of the articles. The magazine is available free at some retail outlets, but the best way to be sure of getting each issue is to subscribe. Six issues a year are $19.95.

NEW YORK HOUSE
Schein Media
233 Fair Street, Kingston
(845) 340-9600
www.newyorkhousemagazine.com

A glossy oversize monthly magazine for prospective and current home owners throughout the entire Hudson Valley, from Manhattan to Albany. Every issue has a number of regular columns and features, including an area spotlight that focuses on a local community. Feature stories cover architecture, interior design, outdoor living, gardening, destinations, and other areas of interest. The magazine is distributed free at retail outlets throughout the Hudson Valley. Subscriptions to the digital edition are also free.

ROLL
Box 504, Rosendale
(845) 658-8153
www.rollmagazine.com

Roll magazine covers creative living in the Hudson Valley. Given the large cultural resources of the region, that means a monthly glossy with extensive music, art, theater, and film listings. Good feature articles focus mostly on the music scene but also cover the larger arts scene. *Roll* is distributed free at arts venues and retail outlets throughout the region. The articles and calendar listings are also fully available on the Web site.

THE VALLEY TABLE
152 Powelton Circle, Newburgh
(845) 561-2022
www.valleytable.com

The only publication in the region devoted exclusively to regional farms, food, and cuisine. It's a glossy published five times a year and distributed free through restaurants and retail outlets. Each issue has a calendar of upcoming events and directory listings for restaurants and local food producers. Regular columns cover new restaurants, seasonal food picks, and openings. Feature articles focus on the restaurant business, local foods, chefs, and other areas of interest to Hudson Valley foodies. A subscription is $20.

RADIO STATIONS

Adult Contemporary

WBWZ 93.3 FM (New Paltz)
WCTW 98.5 FM (Catskill)
WHUD 100.7 FM (Fishkill)
WKNY 1490 AM (Kingston)
WQQQ 103.3 FM (Sharon, Connecticut)
WRNQ 92.1 FM (Poughkeepsie)

Christian

WFGB 89.7 FM (Poughkeepsie)
WFRH 91.7 FM (Kingston)
WHVP 91.1 FM (Hudson)
WKHV 103.9 FM (Kingston)

Classical

WMHT 89.1 FM (Schenectady), 88.7 FM (Poughkeepsie)

College

WFNP 88.7 FM (SUNY New Paltz)
WMAR 88.1 FM, 1630 AM (Marist)
WVKR 91.3 FM (Vassar)

Country

WBPM 92.9 (Saugerties)
WKXP Kicks 94.3 FM (Kingston)
WRWD 107.3 FM and 99.3 FM, 1370 AM (Highland)
WTHN 99.3 FM (Ellenville)
WZAD 97.3 FM (Poughkeepsie)

Current Hits

K104.7 FM (Poughkeepsie)
MIX 97.7 FM (Hyde Park)

WPKF Kiss FM 96.1 FM (Poughkeepsie)
WSPK-FM 104.7 K-104 (Poughkeepsie)

Kids

Disney Radio, 1340 AM and 1390 AM

Light Rock

FOX 96.7 and 103.1 FM (Orange County)
Lite FM 92.1 FM Poughkeepsie)
WCTW 98.5 FM (Catskill)

News/Talk

WGNY 1220 AM (Newburgh)
WHUC 1230 AM (Hudson)
WKIP 1450 AM (Poughkeepsie)

Oldies

WBPM 92.9 FM (Saugerties)
WBNR 1260 AM (Beacon)
WCKL 560 AM (Catskill)
WCZX 97.7 FM (Poughkeepsie)
WGHQ 920 AM (Kingston)
WGNY 1220 AM (Newburgh)
WHUC 1230 AM (Hudson)
WHVW 950 AM (Hyde Park)
WKIP 1450 AM (Poughkeepsie)
WRNQ 92.1 FM (Poughkeepsie)
WZCR 93.5 FM (Hudson)

i RISE is a 24-hour radio information service for the blind and print-disabled of the Hudson Valley and Capital Region. RISE transmits on a subcarrier of WMHT-FM; participants hear it on specially tuned tabletop radio receivers. If you can receive the radio station in your area, you can probably also receive RISE. For more information, contact rise@wmht.org or call (518) 880-3406.

Public Radio

WAMC 90.3 FM (Albany)

One of the more interesting commercial stations in the region is WKZE, 98.1 FM, in Red Hook. Musical diversity is the rule here. The station slogan is "The antidote to boring radio!" Folk, blues, roots, rock, alt-country, reggae, world music, jazz, bluegrass, zydeco—it's all on the air here.

Rock/Classic Rock

WDST 100.1 FM (Hudson Valley), 102.3 FM (Newburgh),106.3 FM (Poughkeepsie)
WPDH 101.5 FM (Poughkeepsie)
WRRB 96.9 FM (Arlington)
WRRV 96.9 FM (Poughkeepsie)
WVKR 91.3 FM (Poughkeepsie)

Standards

WCKL 560 AM (Catskill)

TELEVISION

Albany-Area Network Affiliates

WEWB (The WB, channel 45)
WMHT (PBS, channel 17)
WNYA (UPN, channel 15)
WNYT (NBC, channel 13)
WRGB (CBS, channel 6)
WTEN (ABC, channel 10)
WXXA (Fox, channel 23)

Cable and Satellite Providers

CABLEVISION/OPTIMUM TV
(800) 577-2225
www.cablevision.com

TIME-WARNER CABLE OF NEW YORK AND NEW JERSEY
Kingston/Poughkeepsie area:
(845) 331-1711
Middletown area: (845) 692-6796
Newburgh area: (845) 567-0036
Other Hudson Valley areas:
(800) 431-8878
www.timewarnercable.com

DIRECTV SATELLITE NETWORK
(888) 777-2454
www.directv.com

DISH NETWORK
(888) 825-2557
www.dishnetwork.com

AMC is a member of National Public Radio and an affiliate of Public Radio International. The network also gets programming from the BBC and CBC and produces many local and national shows.

To listen in the region, tune to:
1. WAMC 90.3 FM (Albany)
2. WAMC 1400 AM (Albany)
3. WAMK 90.9 FM (Kingston)
4. WOSR 91.7 FM (Middletown)
5. WAMQ 105.1 FM (Great Barrington, Massachusetts)
6. W280DJ 103.9 FM (Beacon)
7. W271BF 102.1 FM (Highland)
8. W246BJ 97.1 FM (Hudson)
9. W299AG 107.7 FM (Newburgh)

No matter where you are, you can listen to the live stream and to the archives at www.wamc.org.

INDEX